Contents

List of Illustrations   vii

Prologue: 'To Her'   1

1   'The *enfant terrible* of Montmartre'   5

2   'A mere cook'   17

3   'The glory of the edifice'   31

4   'The messenger of death'   52

5   '*Chérie, Chérie, Cerrito!*'   69

6   'Cook and dress ten ears . . .'   88

7   'A broth of a boy'   108

8   'Our eyes sparkle and our palates yearn'   135

9   'Sir Oracle'   153

10   'The world his Club, his guests are universal'   176

11   'Its halls once more glitter'   200

12   'Vexation, disappointment and loss'   232

13   '*Pro bono publico*'   253

14   'Captain Cook'   282

15   'He has no successor'   310

Epilogue   323

Acknowledgements   326

Bibliography   329

Index   333

For Jeremy

'The most admirable and attractive of all chefs has been given an equally admirable and attractive biography' A A Gill

'Sparkling . . . If only all history were written like this'
Sunday Business Post

'The story of [Soyer's] vigorous life is a potent one, and Cowen's comprehensive, sensitive recording of it is long overdue'
Daily Telegraph

'Ruth Cowen's lively new biography . . . is a highly readable account of an important life' *Guardian*

'Cowen captures the curious combination of his astute commercial skills . . . and his selfless philanthropy' *Sunday Express*

'Engrossing biography . . . A sybarite and dandy with a social conscience and hustling entrepreneurial streak, Soyer was an intriguing, contradictory figure' *Financial Times*

'A serious and scholarly work' *New Statesman*

'I was riveted from start to finish. What a fascinating, endearing, complex, contradictory man Soyer was, and what a life!'
Deborah Moggach

'A masterly account not only of a Victorian chef but of a Victorian era'
Martin Gilbert

'A riveting book with all the elements of a Hollywood Oscar winner'
Clarissa Dickson Wright

'A truly stunning achievement' *Camden New Journal*

'Cowen gives us a fascinating insight into Victorian society, with all its flaws, energy and strengths along with a starring cast of spivs and saints who made the period their own' *Scottish Legion News*

'His colourful life story – he was a bigamist, bankrupt and alcoholic – is told brilliantly by Ruth Cowen' *Soldier*

'Very well-written and researched book'
Bulletin of the Military Historical Society

'Alexis Soyer deserves a biography of flair, passion and frivolity. Ruth Cowen has delivered just such a book' *Field*

Ruth Cowen is a journalist, writer and editor. She has written for all the major newspapers, including the *Daily Telegraph*, the *Daily Mail*, the *Financial Times*, the *Independent*, the *Guardian*, the *Daily* and *Sunday Express* and the *Evening Standard*. She has also written a number of award winning documentaries for BBC Radio 4. This is her first book. Ruth lives in North London with her husband and children.

Relish

The Extraordinary Life of Alexis Soyer, Victorian Celebrity Chef

Ruth Cowen

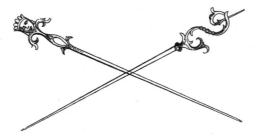

PHOENIX

A PHOENIX PAPERBACK

First published in Great Britain in 2006
by Weidenfeld & Nicolson
This paperback edition published in 2007
by Phoenix,
an imprint of Orion Books Ltd,
Orion House 5 Upper Saint Martin's Lane,
London, WC2H 9EA

1 3 5 7 9 10 8 6 4 2

A CIP catalogue record for this book
is available from the British Library.

ISBN 978-0-7538-2196-1

Typeset at The Spartan Press Ltd,
Lymington, Hants

Printed and bound in Great Britain by
Clays Ltd, St Ives plc

The Orion Publishing Group's policy is to use papers that
are natural, renewable and recyclable products and
made from wood grown in sustainable forests. The logging
and manufacturing processes are expected to conform to
the environmental regulations of the country of origin.

LIST OF ILLUSTRATIONS

Section One

Emma Soyer's monument
Marie Taglioni in *La Gitana*, painted by Emma Soyer (*Dansmuseet Stockholm*)
Meaux-en-Brie by J. P. F. Barrois (*Musée Bossuet*)
A self-portrait of Emma Soyer (*The Gastronomic Regenerator*)
Alexis Soyer painted by Emma Soyer (*Private Collection*)
M. Soyer, at Home (*Pictorial Times*)
The Reform Club (*Mary Evans Picture Library*)
The Reform Club Kitchen (*Mary Evans Picture Library*)
The banquet for Ibrahim Pasha (*Private Collection*)
M. Soyer's Model Soup Kitchen (*Illustrated London News*)
King Soyer resigning the Great Stewpan (*Private Collection*)
The banquet for Prince Albert in York (*Private Collection*)
Roasting a baron of beef, Exeter (*Illustrated London News*)
The Lady Blessington salon at Gore House (*Weidenfeld Archive*)
Crystal Palace crowds (*Mary Evans Picture Library*)
M. Soyer's Symposium (*Illustrated London News*)
The Metropolitan Sanitary Association Dinner at Soyer's Symposium, Gore
   House (*Illustrated London News*)
The Bower of Ariadne, or The Vintage Palazzo by G. A. Sala (*Private Collection*)
The Grotte des Neiges Éternelles, or The Aurora Borealis by G. A. Sala (*Private
   Collection*)
La Salle des Noces de Danae, or The Shower of Gems by G. A. Sala (*Private
   Collection*)
La Fôret Péruvienne, or The Night of Stars by G. A. Sala (*Private Collection*)

Section Two

Fanny Cerrito by François Simonau (*Private Collection*)
Louis Jullien at Covent Garden (*Mary Evans Picture Library*)
Fanny Cerrito dancing (*New York Public Library*)
Cerrito's Sultane Sylphe à la Fille de l'Orage (*The Gastronomic Regenerator*)

French Cookery in the person of M. Soyer, by G. A. Sala (*Private Collection*)
Cooking on the Magic Stove in the Acropolis at Athens (*A Culinary Campaign*)
Sebastopol Hospital (*Mary Evans Picture Library*)
M. Soyer's Kitchen at Scutari (*Illustrated London News*)
Mrs Seacole and Soyer in the 'British Hotel' (From *Wonderful Adventures of Mrs Seacole in Many Lands* by Mary Seacole) (*Private Collection*)
Soyer's Field Kitchen (*Mary Evans Picture Library*)
The Soyer Stove (*A Culinary Campaign*)
Painting the Grass (*A Culinary Campaign*)
Florence Nightingale (*The Illustrated London News*)
Florence Nightingale's carriage (*The Illustrated London News*)
Crimean soldiers, photographed by James Robertson, 1855 (*Mary Evans Picture Library*)
The Mission of Mercy: Florence Nightingale receiving the Wounded at Scutari by Jerry Barrett, 1857 (*National Portrait Gallery, London*)
Soyer at Wellington Barracks (*Illustrated London News*)
Soyer's Phidomageireion or Modern Gas Cooking Apparatus (*Bridgeman Art Library*)
The Scutari Teapot (*Private Collection*)
Soyer's Twelve-sided Kitchen Table (*The Gastronomic Regenerator*)
The Tendon Separators (*The Gastronomic Regenerator*)
The Magic Stove (*Science Museum Science and Society Picture Library*)

Prologue

'To Her'

TO HER. On the quiet eastern edge of Kensal Green cemetery the shortest possible inscription decorates the largest tomb in sight. It is an ostentatious stone column, a dozen feet high and topped by a gigantic statue of Faith, her right hand pointing heavenward, clouds and cherubim at her feet. On the front of the pillar is a worn marble cameo of a young woman's head, on the back an oval cavity that once housed her brushes and palette behind a glass cover.

It is shabby now, but you can still see remnants of the wooden pegs that held the glass in place, and at the top of the shaft a gas flue – half hidden behind the putti – which provided the fuel for an everlasting flame. But the gold cross that Faith clasped in her left hand has long gone, along with the famously expensive carved wooden railings, which now exist only on the paper plans housed in the Victoria and Albert Museum.

The tomb is that of twenty-eight-year-old Emma Jones, a successful portraitist who died in childbirth during the sweltering summer of 1842. It was erected by her husband, the Reform Club's celebrated *chef de cuisine* Alexis Soyer, and it was said that the six months of hard work it took him to design, plan, execute and pay for the lavish monument saved him from sinking into an irretrievable depression. The splendid statuary is typical of Soyer's extravagance, yet the most affecting part of the shrine is that simple inscription, TO HER. For once, the man known all over England for being garrulous to the point of exasperation was lost for words. Soyer is also buried there. Sixteen years after Emma's death and just fifteen months after his triumphant return from the Crimean campaign, he was interred beneath Faith and her marble embellishments on Wednesday, 11 August 1858, following a simple ceremony. He was forty-eight years old and virtually broke, and his name and dates were added to the monument in letters so small they are easy to miss.

The low-key service was held promptly at 11.30 on a warm and breezy morning, an unusually early hour for a funeral. A last-minute change in timing, coupled with the botched handling of the invitations and publicity, meant the crowd was smaller than it should have been. There were enough black-clad mourners to jostle for a spot by the graveside – friends and relatives, servants and fellow chefs, a cluster of journalists and a few allies from the Crimean war. But there was little sense of occasion, and no state recognition of the unique contribution to British life that had led Alexis Soyer into this early grave.

The liturgy was read by Reverend Mr Steward 'in a very feeling manner', reported the *Morning Chronicle*, before Soyer's body was lowered into the ground to the accompaniment of muffled sobs. As the congregation began to drift back towards the cemetery gates a short balding man of around fifty – Charles Pierce, maître d'hôtel of the Russian Embassy and one of Soyer's oldest friends – stepped back to the graveside. Embarrassed by the inadequacy of the proceedings, Pierce abandoned funeral etiquette to improvise a loud and sentimental eulogy. 'My long-loved friend, Soyer!' he shouted. 'Friend, companion – often tried and never found wanting. Great in heart, fresh in spirit, bright in genius, who can hope to repair thy loss? Farewell, dear friend! Kindest and dearest of men! Adieu, Alexis.' It was, said the papers, a heart-stopping moment.

People were shocked by the absence of any mark of respect from the government or the army, considering how both had benefited so hugely from Soyer's genius. 'None great and noble stood around his grave,' thundered the *Chronicle*, 'no soldier mourned, with grateful tear, one whose health had been shaken in continued efforts for the comfort of the British Army.' It was a sentiment echoed in all the dailies, and became much talked about in the following weeks. It had been widely expected that at the end of the Crimean campaign the government would give Soyer a decoration, or at the very least a pension for all he had accomplished, but he had got nothing, and to his supporters this final snub was a crushing insult. A month after his death two of his former secretaries, François Volant and James Warren, published a memoir in which they recorded their bitterness at how they felt he had been treated. 'We cannot withhold our assent to the prevailing opinion that the great Alexis Soyer was not buried with due honour,' they wrote. He should have had a military parade at the very least. 'If the preparations had been entrusted to parties who would have been proud to give *éclat* to his memory, his funeral might have been as memorable as that of many other public men.' So who was this public man, whose death, according to the usually dour and understated Florence Nightingale, was 'a great disaster' for the nation?

Alexis Soyer was a working-class Frenchman from an unremarkable town north-west of Paris. His exceptional cooking skills, ebullient personality and eye for the main chance had turned him into Britain's first true celebrity chef. He was the first to publish a succession of best-selling cook books – one selling more than a quarter of a million copies, an extraordinary figure for the mid-nineteenth century. He was also the first to produce branded merchandise, including a stove that fitted in the pocket and a succession of ingenious kitchen gadgets. He was the first to understand the importance of nurturing a public profile, which he did through a combination of brilliant self-publicity and shameless press manipulation. He cultivated an eccentrically dandyish – and therefore immediately recognisable – image, which was later used, complete with trademark red beret, to decorate the labels of a range of bottled sauces, which were manufactured and marketed by his friends Edmund Crosse and Thomas Blackwell.

From his lofty position at the Reform Club (where his Lamb Cutlets Reform are still on the menu) he cooked fabulously lavish, thirty-course banquets for leading politicians, visiting dignitaries and royalty. This was the world of aristocratic haute cuisine, in all its decadent excess. Pre-posterously decorated desserts ten feet high were not exceptional, he had a signature dish that cost a hundred guineas to create, and his cavernous underground kitchens – widely regarded as the best in Europe – incorporated many of his own inventions. An entrepreneur to his fingertips, one venture into the restaurant business led to the creation of an extravagant eating empire in Hyde Park, touted as a culinary rival to the neighbouring Crystal Palace.

But these were not the achievements that were to earn Soyer the public's respect or, latterly, its gratitude. His life's purpose both came into focus and found its dramatic climax at precisely the moment when he renounced this sybaritic life, and elected to travel, for no pay and in the face of real danger, across Europe first to Scutari and later to Balaclava, where thousands of British troops had died of disease and malnutrition during the first long, bitter winter of the Crimean war. One of the first to understand fully the rudiments of good nutrition and mass catering, Soyer had already introduced new principles of large-scale cookery to Ireland during the potato famine of 1847, and now he was to extend his expertise to the British army with spectacular results.

So why, following his early death, did this great philanthropist and reformer drop so completely from public view? Perhaps the truth is that Soyer was never regarded as truly respectable. For a start he was French and working-class – two unforgivable sins in early Victorian England. Then his buffoonish appearance and irrepressible exuberance had made him the butt of countless cartoons and satires. He was, recalled his friend George Augustus Sala, 'frequently disparaged as a charlatan', with the implication that the charge was not entirely unjust. Yet the crimes that kept him out of the high-minded Victorian history books are no more than the routine controversies we would expect from any self-respecting modern celebrity.

Soyer was able, through his considerable skills and driven personality, to carve out for himself a unique place in society – he was courted and applauded by royals, nobles and cabinet ministers, but his friends included cooks, tradesmen, showgirls and soldiers. He achieved great things, yet was always willing to cut corners – and shamelessly harness personal ambition to his charitable work. As Sala wrote, he was truly 'an original', a deeply flawed yet worthy man, and his story is a compelling one.

1

'The *enfant terrible* of Montmartre'

The heat was intolerable. Before a vast wood fire several hands cranked heavy iron spits strung with sirloins, game birds and fowl. A dozen *rôtis* chefs tended the massive charcoal ovens in which forty set-piece entrées were nearing completion. On open ranges along the far wall of the kitchen cauldrons of soups and ragoûts simmered, while in a steaming bain-marie rows of sauces were maintained at optimum temperature. Just to add to the stifling atmosphere, the windows had been sealed so no draughts could cool the hot dishes before they processed to the banqueting chamber on the shoulders of a small army of footmen.

In the cooler outrooms there was just as much activity as the rest of the brigade prepared *removes, flancs, entremets* and *relevés* – all essential elements of a classic dinner *à la français*, which over three formal courses would see several hundred dishes laid before the diners. They prepared platters of ornately stacked cold meats and poached fowl, while whole fish were suspended, mid-twist, in heavily decorated aspic glazes. There were game pies, veal and venison pâtés, lobster and crayfish salads and vegetable macédoines. The *pâtissiers* finished the blancmanges and fruit creams, the *gâteaux*, soufflés, layered jellies, iced bombes and charlottes. In the middle of the preparation tables stood ready their elegant *pièces montées* – elaborate carvings of ruined temples, windmills, bridges and pavilions, created entirely of almond paste and sugar. Meanwhile, supervising the main kitchen and quite unmoved by the furnace-like conditions, was senior cook and second-in-command, Alexis Soyer, the fast-talking, precocious young star of Parisian culinary circles. As carriages clogged the streets and ministers, dignitaries, nobility and the beau monde swept into the courtyard of the magnificent palace on the Quai d'Orsay, Soyer marshalled his troops for the dramatic performance ahead.

The evening was 26 July 1830, and this was possibly the grandest political dinner to be held in Paris for some years. Its host, France's unpopular first minister, Jules Armand, Prince de Polignac, certainly intended it to be. The banquet was Polignac's defiant gesture to all those reformers, socialists, Bonapartists, republicans and bourgeois upstarts who were intent on destroying his administration and shaking the king from his tottering throne. For that morning, Polignac had finally persuaded Charles X to implement a series of emergency decrees that would, he trusted, crush the loathsome democrats at last and unequivocally secure the king's power base. Chief among these measures, to become known as the July Ordinances, was the dissolution of the newly elected Chamber of Deputies before it had even had a chance to convene – in flagrant breach of the constitution. Further, the measures slashed the electorate by some seventy-five per cent and quashed the influence of the increasingly strident opposition newspapers by the imposition of draconian press controls.

It was the culmination of a hard-fought political battle. Stiff, patrician, deeply religious Polignac, former ambassador to the English court, was part of the die-hard royalist old guard, appointed by a king whose obsession with clawing back his dynastic powers and prerogatives was totally out of step with public sentiment. What Polignac and the king had failed to appreciate was that the people had been through far too much to hand political control back to any monarch. If the Revolution had destroyed the *ancien régime* and the Empire re-established order, the Restoration, if it was to flourish, had to be constructed on an entirely new basis – that of a constitutional monarchy. To survive it would have to be a modern institution, one based on democratic freedoms, not some antiquated notion of the Divine Right of Kings.

Louis XVIII, the first Bourbon to be returned to the throne after Napoleon limped into exile, had understood this need for compromise, but his brother Charles would accept no rival authority. In the six years since his accession his arrogant contempt for the French Assembly, coupled with a deepening recession, had plunged the country into yet another crisis. In desperation the king had appointed Polignac Foreign and First Minister the previous August, but by March the Chamber of Deputies, with its Liberal majority, was demanding his dismissal.

Charles's knee-jerk response was to dissolve the chamber and call an election, but when the opposition was returned with an even bigger majority, he panicked. Together, Charles and Polignac devised and published the July Ordinances, and to mark this historic triumph over the threatening forces of republicanism, Polignac was determined to celebrate in style.

Throughout that afternoon the Foreign Office was decorated with a profusion of flowers. By early evening, rows of widely spaced trestle tables had been laid with the very finest linen, plate, gilt and glassware. Several tons of silver had been polished – fluted candelabra, sparkling cruets and table ornaments, the heavy flatware and fashionable four-foot-high *épergnes*, their myriad branches holding up dazzling satellites of cut-glass fruit dishes. In the kitchen, Soyer was in his element. If not conventionally handsome, at the age of twenty he had a look and a presence that already grabbed the attention – tall and slim, with strong features, curling brown hair and an easy air of authority, he was also the veteran of many society banquets. Trained from childhood in the great Restaurant Rignon in the Rue Vivienne, at seventeen he had been appointed *Premier de l'Administration* at the ultra-fashionable Maison Douix of Montmartre, with a dozen chefs beneath him. Soyer combined his undisputed culinary brilliance with a genuine relish for ostentatious display and a genius for orchestrating complex culinary events, and in the past year he had honed these skills by working freelance for a variety of high-ranking Parisian families. He had reached the pinnacle of his trade by joining the household of France's first minister just a month earlier.

The first course went off smoothly, with the sophisticated flavours of the carefully blended soups complementing the light, elegantly sauced fish dishes – sole, perch, turbot and salmon. Then came the first *removes*, literally the dishes that 'removed' the fish and soup, which included mutton and turkey *en daube*, the smaller entrées of cutlets, cheek of veal and sweetbreads. Circling these symmetrically positioned platters were tiny dishes of *hors d'oeuvres* – miniature crab rissoles, bite-sized oyster vol-au-vents and lobster croquettes – small dishes of dainty *amuse-gueules* to titillate the most jaded of appetites. As the wine flowed the laughter levels rose sharply as the pages cleared away the dishes in readiness for the next service. The top tablecloth was peeled away to reveal a clean one underneath, a snow-white tabula rasa in preparation for the fresh assault on the senses. Then the show pieces were carried in: the kitchen's *pièce de résistance* – a whole baron of beef – plus haunches of lamb and other large roasts, accompanied by vegetables, salads and sweet entremets – jellies, creams and ices – the professional table-setters taking care to ensure the finished tableau was one of exquisite abundance.

By now it was getting dark. Downstairs, in the suffocating humidity of the basement, the clatter of speeding feet disguised the high level of concentration as the ritual formalities of the dinner unfolded. Soyer, having moved away from the *rôts* to supervise the savouries, pâtés, cheeses, sweets, fruit tarts and cakes that were being assembled for the third service, was oblivious to the increasingly angry crowds that had been gathering for some time outside the palace railings. In fact no one in the kitchen heard the commotion until it was too late. Suddenly, the gates gave way and the courtyard was flooded with insurgents. The censorship of the press imposed by the July Ordinances had been the last straw for the demoralised citizens. Led by the disaffected printers, they were finally taking the law back into their own hands. Somehow, between the roast partridges and the *pommes meringuées*, a riot had developed and the hastily armed strikers had the despised Polignac in their sights.

Several of Polignac's guards were killed as the shouting rioters rushed the palace. Soon they were spilling into the kitchen and began grabbing at the food, ripping birds from the spits, scooping pastry croustades from the returned dishes and handfuls of cake from the lines of *gâteaux* waiting to be taken above stairs. The chefs themselves were next in the line of fire – to be beaten as traitors working for the enemy. During the fighting two of them were shot. With every exit blocked there was no way out of the basement. Then, a lone voice rose above the racket, clear and strong. It was singing 'The Marseillaise'. *Allons, enfants de la Patrie, Le jour de gloire est arrivé!* As the deep voice grew louder it had a calming effect on the rest of the rabble, and was slowly picked up around the room – *Liberté, liberté chérie, Combats avec tes défenseurs!* The loyal revolutionary was hoisted onto the shoulders of his confrères and carried through the kitchen up into the great hall. At the end of the first anthem he confidently segued into a rousing version of '*La Parisienne*'.

Except that the musical hero wasn't a revolutionary at all. It was Alexis Soyer, who had kept his wits about him and, with a commendable sense of self-preservation, ripped off his splattered aprons to join the throng. Once carried upstairs, he kept on singing until he could locate an escape route, at which point he jumped to his feet and pushed through the crowds into the night.

Next day the riot fanned out across the capital. Three newspapers defied the ordinances and published as usual, with the result that the king ordered the immediate closure of the presses. In response, five thousand journalists, printers and sellers took to the streets, screaming for the dismissal of the government. Others quickly joined in. Road blocks were set up around the centre of the city, looting began in earnest and the three days' fighting that followed were to go down in Parisian legend as *les Trois Glorieuses*. Despite an initially strong military presence, before long former members of the National Guard, disbanded by the government three years earlier, could be found among those manning the barricades. Shortly afterwards, they were joined by entire army units stationed within the city.

With the troops turning tail and the Hôtel de Ville taken by the insurrectionists, the king saw that the game was up. Three days later he annulled the ordinances and dismissed Polignac. Under the auspices of a hastily constituted temporary government, Polignac was immediately arrested, tried and sentenced to life imprisonment. But even this sacrifice came too late for Charles, who was forced to flee – first to Versailles then to the ancient château of Rambouillet. It was there, on 2 August, that he finally abdicated in favour of his grandson, whom he officially proclaimed Henri V. But the people were having none of it – their choice was the egalitarian Louis-Philippe, Duke of Orléans, whom they trusted to climb off his prerogative and become a 'Citizen King' – less a King of France, more a King of the French. The Municipal Commission called him to the throne on 7 August, and two days later his accession was confirmed. The victorious newspapers, led by *Le Temps* and *Le National*, reported the collapse of the regime with predictable exultation. Yet even in this orgy of triumphalism they didn't forget or forgive those who had served the leaders of the old order. It wasn't only the politicians and royal toadies who came in for a drubbing. The finger was also pointed at a certain Alexis Soyer – singled out for special contempt as a star of the disgraced first minister's household.

Soyer's behaviour was not what had been expected from the man the newspapers had previously lauded as the skilled and exuberant *enfant terrible* of Montmartre. For Alexis's fame had rested as much on his reputation for high living as on his fabulous cooking. By the late twenties La Maison Douix was one of the most fashionable restaurants in Montmartre, patronised by actors, singers and dancers from the neighbouring opera house and music halls; the Opéra Comique, the Comédie Française and the Théâtre des Variétés. This starry clientele had been happy to make a pet of the precocious young chef, who had risen to the top of his profession while still in his teens. And Alexis had rewarded such patronage by being excellent company at whichever table he joined for a glass of wine – a devoted habitué of the Théâtre des Variétés, he was particularly skilled at mimicking the comic turns of whichever show was playing. He had a musical ear and sang, by all accounts, nearly as well as Levasseur, one of the most admired bass singers in France. A dandy with a penchant for outlandish costumes, a terrible flirt, a skilled storyteller and an impish practical joker, Alexis had even considered switching careers to try his luck on the stage.

Alexis Benoist Soyer was born at 10 p.m. on 4 February 1810 in Meaux-en-Brie, a small city twenty miles to the east of Paris and famous, then as now, for the hot, spicy mustard that has been blended in the town since the age of Charlemagne, and which prompted the great critic Brillat-Savarin to declare, 'If it isn't Meaux, it isn't mustard!' Gourmets also sought out the town's other speciality, the large wheels of butter-soft cheese in a downy white rind, the simply named *brie de Meaux*, which an assembly of straight-faced diplomats at the 1814 Congress of Vienna officially proclaimed *le Roi des Fromages*. An important trading centre since Roman times, Meaux was founded on the fertile plains between the Montceaux forest and the Morin valleys, and has since spread along the shores of the winding River Marne. By the time Soyer's family arrived, cereals, wool and dairy produce had been at the region's economic heart for centuries, with Meaux's mills supplying much of Paris with the flour for her daily baguettes and brioches. A bishopric was established in Meaux as early as the fifth century, and around the imposing Bishop's Palace a cloistered town-within-a-town was laid out, existing in the midst of the townspeople, but largely closed to them. In 1800 Meaux still retained its medieval outline, dominated by a massive castle and bisected by the river – with *la ville* firmly on the right bank and *le marché* on the left. These distinct residential and commercial districts were linked by an ancient stone bridge strung with dilapidated, six-storey mills which extended outwards on sturdy wooden stilts, and many of the town's seven thousand citizens would cross and recross it several times a day.

Importantly to our story, Meaux was also the crucible of French Protestantism – the first community was established in the fourteenth century and organised along the same lines as John Calvin's pioneering church in Strasbourg. The first Protestant priest in France was ordained in Meaux in 1521, and the Huguenot cause gained ground as other humanist intellectuals were drawn to the city. And despite occasional periods of persecution, Meaux remained a Protestant stronghold throughout the wars, massacres and exiles of the intervening centuries. At the turn of the nineteenth century it was a depleted community but still a functioning one, and with the new spirit of tolerance that had been ushered in with the First Republic, Meaux once again began to attract Protestants from other parts of the country. Among the first wave of settlers were two twenty-one-year-olds, Emery Roch Soyer and his wife, Marie Chamberlan, who arrived in 1799 on the advice of a relative employed as the town's notary. A son, Philippe, was born shortly after their arrival, swiftly followed by three more, Louis, Paul and René. René died within a fortnight of his arrival in June 1805, and Paul two years later, at the age of four. But Philippe and Louis thrived, and Alexis arrived to complete the family in February 1810.

At first, Emery and Marie prospered in Meaux. In 1800 they moved from their temporary lodgings in the central square after taking on a grocer's shop in the Rue du Tan. The smells from the ancient tannery at the end of the road became particularly noxious in the summer, but it seemed a good location, in the centre of the business district and close to the river. But somehow they could not make the shop pay, and over the next decade the family moved several times as Emery – always industrious if rarely successful – tried a series of other trades, including that of goldsmith and saddler. Eventually he was forced to take on work as a labourer on the Ourcq canal project – one of Napoleon's many expensive schemes to modernise Paris, but which was doomed to be overtaken by the railway within a generation. By the time Alexis was born, Emery was frequently unemployed and the family had been forced to move again, this time to the Rue Cornillon in the Faubourg de Cornillon, the cheapest part of town.

Which is why Emery found himself crossing the old stone bridge late in the afternoon of 6 February 1810, en route to the town hall, wrapped up against the bitter winds and accompanied by three of his friends – a bookseller, a tanner, and a retired Alsatian captain – who were due to act as witnesses for the registration of the birth of his youngest son two days earlier. Also with them was Louise Henries, a friend of Marie's and the child's godmother. The birth was registered by one of the town's deputy mayors, and on the certificate thirty-one-year-old Emery chose to style himself a 'former grocer'. It was a telling obfuscation – the Soyers felt demeaned by their economic slide into the labouring classes. Alexis would grow up living with that sense of humiliation, and perhaps it accounted, in part, for his twin obsessions in adulthood with respectability and social acceptance – qualities he would rate far above money or security. Like his English contemporary, Charles Dickens, whose family experienced a similar downward mobility, both men would spend their adult lives seeking to reverse that early degradation.

There is little concrete information about Alexis's life before he joined Georg Rignon's famous restaurant at the age of eleven. A friend, François Volant, who was to become Alexis's secretary, later described in his *Memoirs of Soyer* the beautiful singing voice that apparently gained Alexis, at the age of nine, a coveted place in a church choir and thereafter at the Protestant seminary, where he was fast-streamed for the clergy. There are no surviving records of his enrolment in any school. Although Volant was not always to prove the most reliable of biographers, what seems entirely plausible is the story of how much the energetic child – and individualist even then – hated the claustrophobic environment of the seminary, and how often he begged Emery and Marie to allow him to leave.

Failing to move his parents, Alexis claimed that he decided instead to engineer his own expulsion and, by enlisting the help of some classmates, succeeded in ringing the church bells at midnight. Although a classic childhood prank, this was a serious matter in Meaux, as the bells doubled as the town's fire and attack alarm. He therefore roused not just the townsfolk, but also the garrison. The Cuirassiers de la Garde Royale had been installed in the Quartier Luxembourg two years earlier, further down the Rue Cornillon where the Soyers lived, which no doubt gave him the idea. The panicking soldiers were soon 'under arms' according to Volant, and the ensuing uproar inevitably spelt the end of ten-year-old Alexis's educational career. But while he may have got what he wanted, the premature end to his school days was to have knock-on effects throughout his life. Always insecure about his poor spelling and hand-writing, he would go to great lengths to avoid having to put pen to paper, employing both English and French secretaries to handle his correspond-ence even when money was tight. Despite the string of books to his name, he preferred others to take down his words. Although his writing improved significantly over time, he rarely used a pen to do more than apply his signature.

Following this disgrace Alexis spent a few months at home, but Emery and Marie could not afford to support idle hands. As soon as he turned eleven, Alexis was sent to Paris to join Philippe and find a job. At twenty-two, the eldest Soyer boy was establishing himself as a talented chef, but Alexis continued to dither for some time, unsure whether or not to follow suit. Eventually Philippe arranged an apprenticeship for him at his friend Georg Rignon's top restaurant in the Rue Vivienne near the Passages des Panoramas. Later, Rignon was to move to the Boulevard des Italiens, beside that most sybaritic of Parisian eateries, the Café Anglais.

Life at Rignon immediately suited Alexis. There he revealed a capacity for hard work, a cheerful willingness that made him a good team player and a sensuous appreciation of excellent food. He found that he loved the theatricality of the trade – each service its own performance – and he quickly developed a practical perfectionism which thrived on the pressure to get it right every time. There is no doubt that working in a restaurant was about as modern and glamorous a job as a bright but semi-literate lad from Meaux could hope to find. For while the restaurant scene in Paris had been born before the Revolution – Antoine Beauvilliers had established the sumptuous Grande Taverne de Londres as early as 1782 – the new fashion for communal dining was undoubtedly boosted by the number of chefs who, having lost their noble patrons to the guillotine, decided to confer their talents on the nation's newly empowered bourgeoisie. By the time of Alexis's arrival in 1821, the city boasted more than five hundred restaurants, and was the undisputed culinary capital of the world.

However, these temples of gastronomy represented far more to their clientele than an opportunity to leave domestic cookery at home for once and sample the artistry of France's top chefs. Restaurants were important social arenas: places for the rich to display their wealth, social status and fashion sense. Just as one went to the theatre to ogle the audience as much as the play unfolding on stage, so a visit to a restaurant was invested with the same dramatic potential – only here the audience paid even more eagle-eyed attention to who-arrived-with-whom, and the quality and splendour of the silks and jewels around the neighbouring tables. The restaurants provided a perfect backdrop with their high-ceilinged, white-clothed luxuriousness, the obsequiousness of the *maître d'* and his black-coated waiters, and the ostentatiously long menus and wine lists. Brillat-Savarin defined a restaurant as having four essential ingredients: an elegant room, smart waiters, a choice wine cellar – and only then, finally, did he mention the superior cooking. For Alexis, who was busy discovering the pleasures of all the various forms of show business then available in Paris, it was his ideal milieu. By his mid-teens, with the stamina that stayed with him through life, Alexis had developed a taste for the city's nightlife, and after finishing a tough shift he would often be out until dawn, partying hard or spending his meagre earnings on trips to his beloved theatre. Volant's *Memoirs* relate how during this period Philippe 'had the greatest trouble imaginable to keep him from the stage', and Alexis was never to lose his love of performing in public – or writing songs, poems and even, on one occasion, a ballet.

In 1826 Alexis left Rignon to move further down the Boulevard des Italiens, then the most fashionable restaurant district in Paris, to join the enormous Maison Douix, where within a year he had been promoted to *chef de cuisine* with a team of twelve chefs beneath him. For a seventeen-year-old to make head chef was exceptional, and Alexis had to counter understandable hostility within the brigade from professionals twice his age. It was under such pressures that the teenager learned to drink heavily, a habit he never lost. In one favourite anecdote he described how, during his first winter at Douix, he was sent to organise the dessert at a lavish ball held at the home of a rich banker. Below stairs, the household staff, knowing what a good singer he was, begged him for a few songs, and as he obliged he gradually became riotously drunk on glass after glass of the banker's champagne. Reeling off at one in the morning, he was next seen staggering into the restaurant the following day, just as his colleagues were turning up for work. He'd lost his tray of china and cutlery, his memory of the night before and, most embarrassingly, his trousers. The china and trousers were later returned by the police, having been found on the building site where Alexis had passed out and identified by the name Douix on the wooden tray. But Alexis remained a laughing stock for weeks to come.

Alexis stayed at Douix for three years before following the career trajectory of any serious chef, gaining experience as a freelance caterer by running high-profile banquets in a variety of aristocratic households. Getting the Foreign Office job in June 1830 was a tremendous break: whatever the unpopularity of Polignac, at that moment it was the top job in Paris. So when the press had turned on him, Alexis was mortified. For it was not just that his personal popularity took a battering, it made him virtually unemployable. No one perceived as a lackey for the right-wing élite would be welcomed back into the bohemian restaurant scene, and neither would any sensible aristocratic family touch him during such politically tense times.

To make matters worse, within weeks of his joining the Foreign Office his lover, Adelaide Lamain, had given birth to a son, Jean Alexis, born on 2 June in a tiny apartment on the Quai de l'École, directly opposite the Louvre. A working-class girl, at twenty-five Adelaide was five years older than Alexis and the daughter of a butcher from Fontainebleau. Little else is known about her, so effectively have her details been effaced from the record. Certainly if she expected marriage and fidelity from her young lover, she was to be disappointed, and would remain in lowly paid, low-status jobs for the rest of her short life. As for Alexis, in little more than a year he had found himself transformed from single man-about-town, a darling of the theatrical set, to a father with new responsibilities but no work and no money. At first he put on a brave face. Although the Polignac affair had given him a terrible fright, he tried to laugh off his narrow escape, punning that the incident had landed him 'doubly in the soup' – *Lorsque toutes ces somptueuses préparations furent doublement consommées par eux!* He even wrote a comic song about the experience called '*Le Patriote Mécontent*' (producing feeble doggerel was to become a lifelong habit) but his financial crisis and poor prospects were extremely disturbing.

The escape route that eventually presented itself came from an unexpected quarter – London. Alexis's eldest brother, Philippe, who had organised Alexis's apprenticeship to Rignon at the tender age of eleven, had been working in England for some years, and by 1830 was well established as head chef to George III's seventh son, the amiably eccentric Duke of Cambridge, at his Palladian mansion in Piccadilly. By taking up such a post Philippe was following the well-trodden route of many skilled French chefs, who following the collapse of the *ancien régime* had found themselves with a dearth of aristocratic employers at home. With the restaurant industry in its infancy, although growing fast, the other favoured option was to seek work in private service abroad. England, which was stable, wealthy, civilised, and packed with noble families who appreciated their talents, was a popular destination.

What was more, these aristocratic households were prepared to pay handsomely for the services of the most fashionable chefs, with the very best able to dictate their terms. Carême had led the way as *chef de cuisine* for the Prince Regent, with Ude, Francatelli, Peron, and Crépin following him over the Channel. Anecdotes abounded of the extravagant contracts demanded by such culinary artists, and of their equally dramatic resignations when they found their employers unappreciative, demanding, too plebian in their tastes or of the wrong political persuasion. In Carême's case, not even a massive pay hike could compensate for the bad weather and unrefined royal palate, and in 1818 he fled the prince's household after barely two years' service. Yet for less temperamental chefs there were fortunes to be made in the land of simple roasts and pudding, and it was against this backdrop that Philippe, sympathetic to his brother's difficulties, offered to find him a job in the duke's kitchen.

It was hardly a difficult decision. For one thing, living abroad offered a way out of his responsibilities to Adelaide and Jean. While he may have been prepared to give them financial support, the fact that he wasn't named on the baby's birth certificate implies he had no intention of marrying the mother. England promised a fresh start and the chance to earn real money. It had a stable government, with no danger of more revolutionary trauma, and there was even a new king to consider. Since George IV had finally eaten himself to death at the end of June – his deathbed meal included two pigeons, three steaks, wine, champagne, port and brandy – his brother William had been assembling a new court in Windsor, and wherever there were changes in the royal pay roll, the job prospects for sophisticated French chefs were greatly improved. Alexis was too young to be a has-been and too ambitious to let such an opportunity go unexplored. And so it was that one early evening in 1831 he found himself standing on the deck of a gently rocking ship in the middle of the English Channel, en route to London and an unusually mild summer.

2

'A MERE COOK'

St George's Church, Hanover Square, had been London's most fashionable venue for society weddings since the 1730s. In the middle of Mayfair, north of Piccadilly and south of Oxford Street, it has no churchyard, being bound by streets and alleyways on all sides. But it compensates for this landlessness with a soaring bell tower and immense classical portico, which juts so far into Maddox Street as to make its vast Corinthian columns visible from the bottom of St George Street. At least two princes and any number of earls had married at St George's, which was doing such brisk matrimonial work by the 1810s that it became known as London's Temple of Hymen, its register 'an autograph-book of noble and illustrious signatures'. Any self-respecting couple with social aspirations would travel up from the shires to have the connubial knot tied at St George's, and hope to earn themselves a few paragraphs in the morning papers.

It was under St George's gilded chandeliers that the Duke of Sussex, sixth son of George III, plighted his troth to handsome Lady Augusta Murray – a marriage that had to be hastily annulled when the groom's father refused the royal consent. And it was in a pool of light refracted through St George's exquisite stained-glass windows that Percy Shelley solemnly renewed his marriage vows to his teenage wife, Harriet Westbrook, in March 1814. His desertion of the pregnant Harriet just weeks later would lead to her eventual suicide. In the 1830s the shoes of worshippers still clicked on the original stone floor as they filed into wooden box pews beneath the canopied pulpit. They heard music from the immense, 1,500-pipe organ approved by Handel, and gazed on William Kent's luxurious painting of the Last Supper above the altar;

17

the rich red robes of the reclining apostles adding a sensuous touch to an atmosphere of otherwise austere elegance.

There were two ceremonies scheduled for St George's, Hanover Square, on 12 April 1837. One was, indeed, a grand society wedding, with no less a personage than the elderly Duke of Wellington in attendance, and in preparation for this event work had started early that Wednesday morning. The floors had been swept and the pews cleaned, the precious beadle's staves, crowned with silver effigies of St George and the dragon, had been fixed to the churchwardens' pews, and the wide nave was filled with elaborate arrangements of spring flowers and silver twist.

However, just before the main event of the day a shorter, simpler service was performed. This was the marriage of Alexis Soyer, recently appointed *chef de cuisine* of the fashionable new Reform Club in Pall Mall, and a twenty-three-year-old artist called Emma Jones. A portrait of Emma at this period shows a sweet young woman with an ample bust and a direct gaze. She is wearing a fashionable pelerine collar, and her long brown curls are bisected by a neat central parting. On her wedding day, however, her pretty lace gown had to compete for attention with the gorgeously attired groom, as Soyer gave full rein to his penchant for outlandish outfits with a dandyish velvet waistcoat, watered silk trousers and highly polished boots. The marriage was solemnised by one William Dickinson, attended by the groom's elder brother, Philippe, the bride's mother and stepfather, Elizabeth and François Simonau, and witnessed by her friend Charlotte Walrow. Signing the register with a faltering hand, for the first time Alexis dropped the 's' from his middle name, Benoist, opting for the more sophisticated Alexis Benoit Soyer, while Emma inscribed her full name, Elizabeth Emma Jones.

The second witness to sign the register was Alexis's great friend and mentor, the plump, extravagant, irascible Louis Eustache Ude. As self-styled former chef to Louis XVI (a claim many disbelieved), Ude had been at the vanguard of the culinary artists who fled Paris after the Revolution. Once in London he had been snapped up by the hunch-backed Earl of Sefton, a voracious gourmet who gave him an annual salary of three hundred guineas and a pension of another hundred. Ude had also found fame as the author of a popular if splenetic cook book, *The French Cook*, which went into many editions. After twenty years he had left private service to launch a new career as a club chef, starting at the United Service Club and then moving to the splendid Crockford's in St James's Street, the grandest, snootiest and most fashionable gambling establishment in London. Now a key attraction to new members, Crockford's paid Ude the stupendous salary of £1,200 per annum for his culinary services. To twenty-seven-year-old Alexis, in the spring of his career and new to the club scene, the arrogant, witty, celebrated Ude was an impressive role model.

Shortly after the small party had stepped into the spring sunshine of Maddox Street and set off to the wedding breakfast, the second, much larger and smarter congregation began filing into St George's. The groom, Lord Marcus Hill, strolled across Hanover Square from the Georgian house in which he had been born, accompanied by his elder brother, Arthur, the second Baron Sandys, and the venerated Wellington, legendary military commander and former Tory prime minister, who was to act as one of the witnesses. Arthur had been Wellington's aide-de-camp at Waterloo twenty-two years earlier, and there remained a great affection between the two soldiers. Marcus, however, was a committed Liberal who had eschewed the military for a life in the diplomatic service. Educated at Eton and Edinburgh, he had spent fourteen years in postings from Lisbon to Rio de Janeiro before settling back in England to embark on a parliamentary career. Nearing forty, this was his first marriage. At the appointed hour his bride, seventeen-year-old Louisa Blake, arrived on the arm of her father, Joseph, the organ struck up, and the formalities began.

These two weddings, one modest and the other noble, celebrated in the dying days of King William's reign, were linked by more than date and venue. For Hill was a founder, leading light and chairman of the Reform Club, where, over more than a decade, Soyer would, with Hill's unwavering support, establish a name for himself that would eventually spread all over the world. Hill's affection was based on an admiration of Soyer's many extraordinary qualities, but no doubt Soyer also kept alive for both of them the sentimental association of their mutual wedding day.

In the six years since his arrival in England Alexis had moved among a number of aristocratic houses, rapidly increasing his experience and reputation in the process. After swiftly leaving behind the lowly job in the Duke of Cambridge's kitchens procured for him by Philippe, he went as sous chef to the household of the rich and spoiled young nobleman, Henry de la Poer Beresford, the 'Mad Marquess' of Waterford. Waterford's huge estates in Curraghmore on the southern Irish coast had been in the family since the twelfth century, and Henry had inherited the title and lands in 1826, at the disastrously young age of fifteen. By the time

Soyer joined his staff in 1832 the impressionable marquess was already a notorious drunk and brawler, with a partiality for puerile practical jokes and a habit of beating up night watchmen after heavy nights out with a gang of hangers-on. His frequent arrests were manna for the scandal sheets. One of Waterford's most infamous pranks concerned a letter sent to the London and Greenwich Railway Company, in which he offered to pay them £10,000 if they would arrange for him to witness a train crash – specifying that both engines must be driven towards each other at top speed. He had a penchant for spraying paint on public buildings and statues, and once daubed the noses of some granite lions in Regent Street sky blue for a bet. A few years later, in April 1837, while visiting Melton Mowbray for race week, Waterford and his cronies embarked on a particularly boisterous spree in which they painted houses, shops and even the pub bright crimson – giving rise to a popular new expression of 'painting the town red'.

It is unlikely that Waterford took much interest in his new chef, Alexis Soyer, but as the unrepentant marquess was increasingly ostracised by good society, his was not a household any ambitious cook would wish to be associated with for too long. Alexis prudently sought work elsewhere, and his next employer was seventy-four-year-old George Granville Leveson-Gower, the plump and extravagant Marquess of Stafford, whom the following year King William was to create the first Duke of Sutherland. The Sutherlands were one of the richest landowning families in Scotland – their possessions included the entire county of Sutherland – and in the early part of the century they had been responsible for the shameful Highland Clearances, when thousands of families were evicted, often violently, from their tiny crofts, as the land was emptied to make way for new industries and lucrative sheep farms.

The Sutherlands lived in unrivalled splendour on the fruits of these so-called land improvements, and Stafford House, their London home, was widely considered the grandest residence in the capital. Sandwiched between St James's Palace and the eastern boundary of Green Park, it had been commissioned by King William's recklessly extravagant brother Frederick, Duke of York, and its magnificence showed up neighbouring Buckingham Palace for the draughty old farmhouse that it was. Frederick had cared nothing for budgets, and Stafford House was a monument to excess, its immense interior a riotous mini-Versailles of intricate gold plasterwork, thirty-foot marble columns, and lavish velvet and silk furnishings, carpets and curtains. When Frederick died in 1827 his debts amounted to the equivalent of £36 million, and the government, forced to pay off his mortgage, sold Stafford House to the Sutherlands, who had been among his major creditors, at a discount. Although Soyer spent less than a year employed in Stafford House, his connection with the Sutherland family continued for the rest of his life. Just months after his arrival the old duke died, and the domestic reins were picked up by his glamorous daughter-in-law, twenty-seven-year-old Harriet, who would become an invaluable patron throughout Alexis's career. Harriet was a close friend of Queen Victoria, who often made the short journey from Buckingham Palace to visit her, joking that she had 'come from my house to your palace'. Over time Stafford House would become an increasingly important Liberal rallying point, and Harriet used her influence with the queen to promote many of her favourite political and charitable causes. It was in this way that she would become essential to the success of Soyer's work in both Ireland and the Crimea.

London in the early 1830s suited Alexis well. As a single, anonymous new arrival he relished all the experiences that the greatest metropolis in the world had to offer. The city itself was in the process of the biggest upheaval in centuries. The capital was effectively a building site. The effects of the Industrial Revolution were swelling the population of the city at an unprecedented rate, and since the end of the Napoleonic wars, a revived economy and renewed confidence meant people were able to build as they never had before. There were factories and docks developing along the Thames, as Britain's new steam-powered manufacturing plants conquered new markets around the world. There were new housing developments, gracious public buildings and modern leisure facilities springing up to accommodate and entertain this new mass of Londoners. The West End was blossoming, with areas around St James's, Mayfair and Marylebone being redeveloped along grand classical lines. The palatial clubs along Pall Mall went up, a potent symbol of this new era of big business and growing fortunes. The traffic-clogged streets were still full of clattering carts, cabs, coaches and carriages but at night the black roads were now lit up by gas, and the great railway enterprise was taking off which would soon see all the major termini in place – Euston, Waterloo, Victoria, Paddington, King's Cross and St Pancras. The stations, tracks, and carriages were being assembled that would make distant towns as accessible as the suburbs and bring the rest of the country into the lower-middle-class Londoner's orbit for the first time. Within a few years Charles Wheatstone would have perfected his electric telegraph and Henry Fox Talbot patented a new photographic system which could create multiple images from a single negative.

While these were days of invention and growing prosperity for many, abject, crushing poverty was the lot of many more, and the gulf between the rich and poor was as great as it had ever been. The great Reform Bill of 1832 may finally have extended the electorate, but it did nothing to provide jobs, improve the desperate working conditions or alleviate the widespread hunger of the poorest city-dwellers, who lived, by horrible contrast to the smart new terraces of the middle classes, in slums of almost unfathomable squalor. Alexis, despite his love of extravagant good living, was always acutely aware of the filth and misery that existed cheek-by-jowl with the wasteful world that his masters moved in, and that contrast was the chief motivation for his later charitable work. After all, he had grown up in a family that lived in the shadow of destitution, and he knew how tenuous prosperity could be.

For now though, Alexis's chief concern when off duty was to enjoy himself, and he particularly loved the theatres, which easily rivalled those he had left behind in Paris. The lengthy evening bills, which included melodramas and farces as well as the main attraction, would begin at six and continue well beyond midnight, which suited his long working hours. He could finish the dinner service at Stafford House, effect a quick change from his greasy clothes into one of his ever more raffish costumes, then dash through the old streets of St James's and reach Covent Garden just in time to qualify for the half-price 'pit and box' tickets available at the end of the first play. He became a regular at both the Theatre Royal in Haymarket and and the Theatre Royal in Drury Lane, which was enjoying a period of critical success under the guidance of the great tragic actor William Charles Macready. He became an habitué of the fashionable Royal Olympic after it was reopened by the sensational Madame Eliza Vestris, London's first female theatre manager, a talented comic singer and actress who was not averse to showing off her impressive curves in risqué boys' costumes. He also loved the Italian operas and French ballets that were the standard fare at Her Majesty's, and would hang out in 'Fops' Alley', the narrow passageway below the boxes and between the benches where the dandies congregated to laugh and ogle the women.

More accessible women could be chased at Vauxhall pleasure gardens, and elsewhere, in out-of-town Finsbury, the disreputable, ale-soaked Sadler's Wells occasionally provided an even rowdier night out. Because of arcane laws which forbade the presentation of spoken plays at the venue, the management often mounted 'aquatic spectacles', such as re-enactments of naval battles. However, they had to rely heavily on the alcoholic refreshment they supplied to attract patrons to these shows. So it is hardly surprising that a young Charles Dickens, writing his first journalistic sketches for *Bell's Life in London*, described Sadler's Wells audiences as 'the most ruffianly that London could shake together', with fights breaking out at almost every performance and 'resounding with foul language, oaths, catcall shrieks, yells, blasphemy, obscenity – a truly diabolical clamour'.

Along with a taste for rough and ready nights out, Alexis was developing a lifelong love of simple English cookery. With a few of his growing network of friends he would dine on chops, kidneys, rabbits or steak at one of his favourite taverns or dining rooms: the Albion in Little Russell Street – where he ordered scalloped oysters or Welsh rarebit made with a pint of port – Frost's in Bow Street, or the Provence in Leicester Square. These and many other venues would be packed with playgoers in the early hours of the morning, and the food would be served up, as Dickens also noted, 'amidst a noise and confusion of smoking, running, knife clattering, and waiter chattering, perfectly indescribable'. On other nights, Alexis was just as happy dining off the fast food available from the wealth of street-sellers: hot chestnuts, fruit, muffins, pork pies, penny pies, ham and cheese sandwiches, or salty baked potatoes from the Coventry Street end of the Haymarket. He bought whelks and oysters from the fish shop next door, where you stood at the counter and sprinkled pepper and vinegar on your supper from bottles with perforated corks and paid extra for crusty bread and pats of butter. He was particularly partial to the fried fish sold by Jewish vendors in the East End, and would later use adaptations of their recipes in his cook books.

Heavy drinking inevitably played a big part in Alexis's social life, as it did for most Londoners. For one thing alcohol was safer to drink than the cholera-infested water – these were the decades before the stench from the disease-ridden Thames finally forced Parliament to allow the engineer Joseph Bazalgette to create his eighty-two-mile underground network of sewage pipes, pumping stations and treatment works. The Temperance movement had yet to make its presence felt and in the meantime drink still operated as social lubricant: whether it was the champagne of upper-class soirées, the thick brown London porter of tavern habitués or the cheap, sorrow-drowning gin of the poor, the city was saturated with booze and Alexis needed no encouragement to join the drinkers. The best nights combined two of his favourite pastimes – drinking and singing – at one of the city's innumerable male glee clubs. These 'harmonic meetings' were generally held in upstairs tavern rooms, and would start with songs from a couple of professional singers as a warm-up, before the master of ceremonies asked for contributions from the floor. Alexis's superb voice and love of performance meant that his wide repertoire of romantic songs and comic ballads was always in demand, in spite of – or perhaps helped by – his strong French accent. The proceedings were eased along by the enthusiastic consumption of gin, brandy, stout and cigars, and the music-lovers would frequently reel out at three or four in the morning.

Alexis was now confident that his career setbacks in France were safely behind him. At twenty-three he was rapidly rising through the ranks in one of the grandest kitchens in Europe, and was confident that he would soon be running his own brigade. He may not yet have attained the fame he had once possessed in Paris, but his prodigious talent meant that his reputation was growing steadily in culinary circles, and he was earning a decent wage, enough, at least, to indulge his passion for extravagant clothes and his burgeoning social life. At work he remained professional and ambitious, completely focused on using his charm and skills to become *chef de cuisine* once again. And the opportunity to take sole charge of his own kitchens soon arrived, with an offer from the stupendously wealthy landowner William Lloyd and his beautiful second wife Louisa. The Lloyds were the owners of Whittington Castle, Aston Hall and Chigwell House, three substantial country estates around Oswestry, two hundred miles from London on the Welsh borders. While not as grand as the Sutherlands, the Lloyds appeared to be generous and appreciative employers and, most importantly, it was Alexis's chance to start climbing the ladder again. A spell in northern Shropshire would do no harm at all to his future prospects.

And so in 1832 Soyer made his first excursion north of London, through the Midlands to Aston Hall, the Lloyds' main residence. He journeyed by the old Holyhead mail, which left the Swan With Two Necks in Lad Lane in the early evening and ploughed on through the night via Towcester, Dunchurch, Coventry, Shifnal and Shrewsbury, before depositing him, weary and dishevelled, at the Queen's Head near West Felton, right on the edge of the Aston estate, just before two o'clock the following afternoon. After a restorative brandy, it was a short walk with his boxes to the gates of Aston Hall.

Once he was settled, it didn't take long for Soyer to make his presence felt. The Lloyds were thrilled with the talents of their new acquisition, whose classic haute cuisine caused a sensation in a rural county where, pre-railway, even the gentry were still, as the writer Surtees called them, a 'leg-tied tribe'. Alexis may no longer have had easy access to all the fresh and imported delicacies that the London markets had to offer, but he was delighted with the quality of the Welsh lamb and game, the local cheeses and the freshwater fish available from the waters of the Perry, Dee and Severn. His cooking quickly became the envy of the Lloyds' social circle, and William and Louisa were not only bountiful hosts, but delighted in sending out the amusing Frenchman as a roving culinary consultant when their friends were entertaining too.

Soyer's celebrity gave him an unusual status – though clearly not in a comparable class to his masters, he was never entirely the servant either. Everyone quickly got to know his name, guests to Aston Hall would always make a detour to the kitchen to chat, flatter his talents, taste some experimental dish currently in development, or ask for the recipe of a favourite creation, which – unlike many chefs then and now – he was always happy to give out. Not only did his metropolitan cachet place him in a social middle ground, but his conversation, his stories of life in great London houses and his general exoticism meant that he was often invited not only to supervise the catering, but join in the subsequent dinner.

One private residence where he lent his services was at Chirk Castle between Oswestry and Wrexham, a massive and magnificently dour fortress build by Edward I. It was owned by a dashing young soldier, Thomas Myddleton Biddulph, who was keen to add Soyer to his acquisitions. '*No one* could cook like Soyer could,' he recalled years later. But the chef was not for poaching, and, like everyone else, Biddulph had to be satisfied with invitations to Aston Hall or borrowing him on occasion. Another of the Lloyds' circle who appreciated Soyer's cookery was the improbably named Sir Watkin Williams Wynne of Wynnstay, master of a 100,000-acre estate near Ruabon with a huge, deer-stocked park and lake designed by Capability Brown. The wealthy Sir Watkin had once been MP for Denbighshire, but was such a political lightweight that his Westminster colleagues gave him the nickname Bubble. Country pursuits and house parties were more Bubble's thing, and on 1 March he would celebrate St David's day by entertaining the local sportsmen with a hunt gathering. Soyer, as a new arrival of great curiosity value, was invited to join them, but became the victim of an unkind practical joke when the huntsman deliberately unbagged a dog instead of a fox. Alexis, not knowing either the customs of English fox-hunting or the difference between a fox and a dog from half a field's distance, immediately ploughed after the animal, to the huge entertainment of everyone watching. If that wasn't humiliating enough, Alexis's horse then stumbled and pitched him into a hedge, completing his mortification.

For the gentry Soyer proved a pleasing diversion, but his real friends were drawn from a humbler social circle. One of them, Charles Pierce, Myddleton Biddulph's steward at Chirk Castle, would become a close and lifelong friend. Pierce, at twenty-five just three years older than Alexis, later became steward of the Russian Embassy and, inspired by Soyer's publishing success, wrote a modest domestic manual called *The Household Manager*. Also included in Alexis's Oswestry circle were two former apprentices he had known in Paris, now working at other large houses in the area. As Aston Hall was three miles from town, he made his local the Queen's Head, and there he and Charles would regularly hold court with rowdy sing-songs and – of course – lengthy drinking sessions.

Life was good for Alexis in Shropshire. He enjoyed the Welsh border country, he was constantly maturing as a chef, and it was at this time that he began to develop the flair for invention that would bear such immensely profitable fruit in the years ahead. Always looking for new ways to modernise cooking methods and smooth out the practical problems of running a large domestic department, he would puzzle over each technical hitch until he came up with a new gadget or design modification to cope with it. With a clear-sighted logic he contrived a range of ingenious little labour and timesaving devices which he would then bestow on his friends. His relationship with the Lloyds remained cordial – they would remain in friendly contact years after his departure. Mrs Lloyd would chatter to him in French while Soyer lost no opportunity to flatter her taste and judgement, displaying early signs of the sycophantic streak that would become more exaggerated over time. Best of all, during the summer season he would travel with the Lloyds' entourage to their house in Upper Brook Street, off Grosvenor Square, giving him a welcome dose of London life and a chance to catch up with Philippe and other friends. And it was on one such trip, three years into his employment with the Lloyds, that he first met Emma Jones.

It was at the start of the 1835 season when Alexis decided, for reasons unknown, to have his portrait painted. He was recommended to approach a Flemish artist called François Simonau, who had a studio near Fitzroy Square. Simonau had arrived in London with his brother Pierre some twenty years earlier, and while Pierre had established a successful lithographic business, François had opted to concentrate on portraiture. Within a few years he had built up an impressive client base and regularly exhibited at the Royal Academy. He also tutored Pierre's small son

Gustave, who was destined to become one of Europe's greatest archi-tectural artists. Pierre and Gustave had returned to Brussels in 1828 but François, by then married to an affluent English widow, had opted to stay in London.

The fact that Simonau was accustomed to painting the élite of English society did nothing to discourage the young chef from approaching him but, far from being affronted, the fifty-two-year-old artist was amused by Alexis's presumption, and Alexis in turn was entertained by Simonau's 'somewhat peculiar disposition'. Instead of offering to do the picture himself – in fact Alexis was unlikely to have been able to afford him – Simonau passed him over to his pupil and stepdaughter Emma, a talented artist in her own right who was just starting to take on her own commercial commissions. She had already developed a good line in quick crayon sketches, which, thanks to the influence of the colourful Count d'Orsay, who was a superb portrait sketcher, were becoming increasingly fashionable among the aristocracy.

In the *Memoirs*, Volant coyly asserts that Soyer's purpose in com-missioning the picture was to send it to Paris, 'we believe to an old love', as a visual marriage proposal. Whether or not this was fanciful invention, poor Adelaide was forgotten the minute Alexis, kitted out in his portrait finery, met Emma – and with his characteristic impetuosity promptly fell in love. For one thing Emma offered a complete contrast to the women Alexis had previously encountered – from the rich wives he had catered for, to the servant girls in the restaurants and households he had worked in, and the actresses and show girls in the theatres he loved to frequent. Emma was not just pretty and demure, but bright and funny, highly talented and, thanks to her careful education, able to banter with him in flawless French.

The attraction was mutual. Alexis was not just tall and striking, but exuberantly charming and witty, as well as an outrageous flirt, easily able to make a girl believe she was the only woman in the world who existed for him. An initial sitting was arranged for the following day, and Soyer managed to spin out the following meetings for as long as humanly possible. He needed to; at the time twenty-one-year-old Emma had another suitor. But Alexis quickly saw him off with his single-minded pursuit, which included dedicating to her a stream of terrible but rather touching poetry. '*O vous, Emma, o vous, que mon coeur aime, Enfant gâté d'Apollon et des arts,*' began one flowery ode, penned on 13 May 1835, and leaving her in no doubt of his admiration. '*Hier au soir, belle amie!!! Pour vous voir – oui, en vain –*' began another, written a year later and showing that there had been no cooling of his ardour. On another occasion, while out of London, Alexis sent Emma a box of local tulips, only to receive a tart reply. 'Miss Jones is quite astonished at the liberty M.S. has taken, in sending her such a present without her request, and consequently, by the next mail, he will receive a box and and his flowers back; and it will be useless for him to send any more, as she will return them in the same manner.' The box duly arrived, but when the chef took off the cover, expecting to find a pile of wilted blooms, he saw instead an exquisite painting of the flowers arranged in a pretty nosegay. It was a painting he kept for the rest of his life, and one of those he exhibited after her death to raise money to launch a soup kitchen in Spitalfields.

The question of marriage inevitably arose. By now, as a head chef in a large country house Alexis was earning enough to take on the responsibility of a wife, but perhaps not someone of Emma's middle-class background and expectations, and Simonau, despite his liking for Soyer, made it clear that he would not allow his precious stepdaughter to throw herself away on 'a mere cook', whatever his growing reputation or prospects. Alexis realised he must leave the Lloyds and return to London on a permanent basis if he was to pursue the courtship seriously. He would have to prove his steadfastness and commitment if he was to overcome the objections to his union with Emma. He swiftly found a post as head chef for another well-known gourmet, Archibald Kennedy, the Marquess of Ailsa. The genial marquess lived with his wife at St Margaret's House, a splendid residence set in vast parklands on the Thames at Twickenham, which for Alexis's purposes was ideal, being within easy reach of Emma's home. And so, having made the appropriate arrangements, Alexis spent his last winter at Aston Hall, finally leaving Oswestry in the spring of 1836.

As usual, it did not take Soyer long to ingratiate himself at St Margaret's. Like the Sutherlands, Ailsa owed his huge wealth to large land holdings in Scotland, and the family seat, Culzean on the south Ayrshire coast, was an exquisitely beautiful castle perched romantically on a cliff edge. However, Ailsa, a passionate Liberal, spent more of his life in London than on his Scottish estates, where he was actively engaged in behind-the-scenes politics. At sixty-five, he was a representative peer, a Fellow of the Royal Society and the Grand Master Mason of Scotland – the Kennedys had been prominent in Scottish freemasonry since the middle of the eighteenth century. Ailsa had been among the minority of peers who had steadfastly voted for the Reform Bill, and he continued to support the Whigs' drive for the abolition of slavery in the colonies and the improvement of working conditions in factories.

To enable him to stay late at Westminster and enjoy the London social scene, Ailsa had built himself an impressive town house in Privy Gardens, in the centre of Whitehall, but the weekends he spent at St Margaret's, where he would entertain in style. A regular presence in the kitchen, he would spend hours with Soyer, poring over menus, recipes and remembrances of great dishes and great banquets. Again, it was a relationship that would last. Years later, Ailsa would invite Alexis to seek rest and solace as a guest in the restorative peace of St Margaret's following Emma's funeral, insisting that he brought his bereft father-in-law along too. It was possibly Ailsa who introduced Soyer to freemasonry, which he pursued for the rest of his life. And the marquess certainly helped to spread Soyer's reputation as he bragged about having the best chef in London.

But most importantly, it was through Ailsa's association with the new Reform Club that Alexis got the biggest break of his career. As a dogged campaigner for the Reform Bill through its long and tortured progress through Parliament, Ailsa was part of the circle of radicals who had felt, in the aftermath of the changes wrought by the Act, that it was about time the Whigs copied their Tory rivals at the Carlton Club and established a London club of their own. For the Reform Act, in extending the franchise, had fundamentally changed the nature of the party. No longer solely the preserve of privileged, landowning Whigs, it was now as much a party of businessmen, lawyers and soldiers. The newly diverse membership needed a social and political rallying point, or as Louis Fagan, the Reform Club's first official biographer, grandiloquently phrased it, a 'recognised centre of English Liberalism'.

Established the previous year, the Reform Club's first home was in a tall narrow town house in Pall Mall and, right from the start, the founders had realised that home comforts such as a well-stocked library and quiet drawing rooms, but most particularly the quality of the food it offered, would be critical to the club's success. If the social wheels were to turn properly, if ideas were to be developed and alliances forged, then the atmosphere had to be one where the members would have every encouragement to linger, where they would feel relaxed and inclined to dine at leisure. The members would all be accustomed to dining extremely well at home, and so the quality of dinners at the club would have to compete with those available at their own firesides. Successful public banquets would also be crucial for the club's reputation, when it entertained cabinet ministers or visiting foreign dignitaries. To begin with, the committee contracted out these formal dinners to the assembly rooms at the rear of Horns Tavern, on the edge of Kennington Common. But soon it was clear that a dedicated, imaginative and flexible chef was needed: someone to provide large numbers of excellent meals on a daily basis as well as cater for the big events; someone to help give the club prestige, justify the large subscriptions and better encourage the members to dine together regularly. Their first choice, one Auguste Rotivan, lasted just three weeks before he buckled under the pressure of work and resigned. For the next appointment, the committee had to get it right.

Although he had been with the Marquess of Ailsa for just a year, Alexis immediately saw that this was the job he had waited for all his life. This was his chance to boost his fame, not to mention fortune, by following in Ude's footsteps. Soyer also recognised that such a position would provide him with a platform for his other ambitions. And so he persuaded Ailsa to use his influence with the club authorities to lobby for his appointment. Not that he necessarily needed such a distinguished guarantor – he knew that there was no one else in London better qualified for the job. Ailsa was loath to let Soyer go, but recognised that this was a superb opportunity for him. And with his Whitehall *pied à terre* situated so close to the club, at least Ailsa knew he could continue to enjoy Alexis's cooking during the week. He promoted Alexis's interests with his usual generosity, and in 1837, at the age of twenty-seven, Soyer took up the position of *chef de cuisine* of the Reform Club, to which institution he would devote all – or almost all – his energies for the next thirteen years. And with such an undeniably impressive job secured, the last of the Simonaus' objections to his marriage with Emma collapsed, and he was finally free to book St George's for the long-awaited nuptials.

3

'The glory of the edifice'

Thursday, 28 June 1838 – Coronation Day – dawned wet and windy. By the time the doors of Westminster Abbey opened at 7 a.m., the lines of shivering ticket-holders had been queuing in the cloisters for a full hour. And everyone had to wait – there were no exceptions, irrespective of rank, age or infirmity.

Three hours later, when Victoria finally emerged from Buckingham Palace, the rain had stopped, and watery sunbeams were starting to break through the clouds. Under five feet tall, even in her embroidered coronation slippers, the diminutive monarch looked suitably magnificent in the dazzling crown jewels, her dumpy figure tightly corseted into a virginal white gown that was barely visible beneath the weight of her crimson, gold and ermine robes. She was attended by a total of thirty-two ladies-in-waiting, and the splendour of her clothes and entourage was matched only by that of her glittering carriage, drawn by eight grey horses, which the young composer Felix Mendelssohn, witnessing the spectacle while on holiday from Leipzig, described as 'golden and fairy-like, supported by Tritons with their tridents, and surmounted by the great crown of England'.

Victoria had opted to follow her Uncle William's example and dispense with the tedious coronation banquet in Westminster Hall. Instead, she was spending the entire £70,000 budget on a grand regal, military and diplomatic procession, which would be witnessed by up to 400,000 spectators. The majority of these had arrived from out of town the day before, and 'the uproar, the confusion, the crowd and the noise' were, according to another observer, Charles Greville, indescribable. 'Horsemen, footmen, carriages squeezed, jammed, intermingled, the pavement blocked up . . . The town all mob, thronging, bustling, gaping and gazing at everything, at anything, or at nothing.' Green Park was 'one vast encampment, with banners floating on the tops of tents and still the roads are covered, the railroads loaded with arriving multitudes'. He conceded, however, that the great merit of the coronation was precisely that it had been designed for the enjoyment of the people. The theatres and pleasure gardens were all giving away free tickets that night, and to 'amuse and interest *them* seems to have been the principal object'.

But the procession was undoubtedly the highlight of the celebrations, and a circuitous three-mile route had been mapped out that snaked along Constitution Hill to Hyde Park Corner, down Piccadilly, St James's and Pall Mall to Trafalgar Square and Whitehall. Escorting the royal carriage, in fresh new uniforms, were the Royal Huntsmen, the Yeomen Prickers and Foresters and the Yeomen of the Guard, and following it was the cavalry. It took until a quarter past twelve for Victoria, accompanied by Harriet, Duchess of Sutherland, her Mistress of the Robes, and the Earl of Albemarle, the Master of the Horse, to reach the Abbey, and nothing more brilliant could be conceived, wrote Mendelssohn, 'than all the beautiful horses with their rich harness, the carriage and grooms covered with gold embroideries, and the splendidly dressed people inside'. Among the participating ambassadors joining the procession was the former French commander Marshal Soult, Wellington's old foe, who got a particularly loud cheer from the crowds in a rare gesture of pro-French generosity; and Austria's Prince Esterhazy, who got a similar cheer on account of his extraordinary uniform, which was so heavily encrusted with pearls and diamonds – even down to his boots – that people marvelled at how he could walk under its weight.

The rareness of a mid-week public holiday, the excitement of the crowds and the lavishness of the parade all contributed to the sense of new beginnings that the rosy-cheeked young queen seemed to usher in. Since her accession a year earlier, the papers had been full of praise for what Wellington had referred to as Victoria's 'charm, dignity and grace', which made such a striking contrast to the boorish behaviour of her dissipated Uncle William. Finally, here she was in the flesh, smiling and nodding, an unspoiled girl of eighteen radiating the promise of a fresh start. Mendelssohn, mingling with the crowds outside the Abbey, had clearly got caught up in the emotionally charged atmosphere as he described the instant that Victoria stepped from her coach. 'The mass of people was completely hidden by their waving handkerchiefs and raised hats, while one roar of cheering almost drowned the pealing of the bells, the blare of the trumpets, and thundering of the guns, and one had to pinch oneself to make sure it was not all a dream out of the Arabian Nights.'

Along Pall Mall, the clubs had ensured that their façades were lavishly decorated for the occasion, and in a rare burst of gallantry members had invited in the ladies to take advantage of the best views from the upper balconies. On the lower levels the sash windows were lifted out of their frames to enable people to lean out a little further and wave their scarves and banners over the heads of the ordinary spectators on the street. 'Every balcony was a parterre,' reported *The Globe*, 'and every window was a bouquet of loveliness and beauty.' The Reform Club was also keen to capitalise on the Mall view, even though the members had vacated the site three weeks earlier in preparation for the demolition of the old club house and erection of a bigger, purpose-built version. So the committee instructed the architect for the project to assemble a giant scaffold across the east and western sides of the empty building, which, when decorated and filled with benches of elegantly dressed ladies, would resemble the stands of a medieval joust.

Pairs of numbered tickets for places on the scaffold, which could hold six hundred women in spite of the vogue for ever-widening skirts, were strictly controlled by the club secretary, Walter Scott, who kept a special book in his office that each member had to come in and sign 'in his own handwriting', in order to qualify for the ballot, which was ceremonially drawn at noon on the Saturday before the coronation. Fortunately the temporary club house, Gwydyr House, a rented Georgian mansion around the corner in Whitehall, was also on the queen's route, and so the Reformers had two vantage points onto the procession. To allow members to avoid the crowds, Gwydyr House opened at six in the morning on Coronation Day, but to enable Soyer to cater in the hopelessly inadequate kitchen facilities for the two thousand members and guests that were expected to eat later on, no breakfasts were supplied after 10 a.m.

In the gardens around Gwydyr House, a large bandstand had been built for the reception of young Johann Strauss and his Viennese dance band, a team of twenty-eight hand-picked players judged the finest Austria had to offer. Strauss had managed to generate a world-wide craze for his joyous dance compositions since putting together his first orchestra in 1825, and his waltzes, polkas and galops were being energetically copied at balls and in dance halls around the country. To cash in on the coronation festivities, he had arranged a mammoth seventy-two-concert tour of England, and the Reformers had pulled off quite a coup to secure him for the day itself – although at £30 for the afternoon they paid quite a premium for the privilege. However, Herr Strauss did not disappoint; among his own works that he conducted were the overtures of *Pré aux Clercs* and *Masaniello*, as well as *Pot-Pourri* and *Le Bouquet*.

After the first passing of the procession, when *The Globe* dutifully reported that 'scarfs, handkerchiefs and hats were waved as Her Majesty passed', the Reformers and their guests were treated to a suitably majestic buffet. The details of the day's arrangements, written on the front of Scott's ticket book, had referred to the provision of a 'Cold Collation', but Alexis had scribbled out this phrase, with its dreary cold-meat-and-salad connotations, substituting instead the more flamboyant *Déjeuner à la Fourchette*, in imitation of the stylish plate-and-fork garden parties currently in vogue on the continent. Feeding all 2,000 diners in the period before the queen's return journey to the palace was his first real logistical trial as the club's new culinary star, and he was anxious to impress his employers. As Volant commented, it was 'no joke for a young *aspirant* and a foreigner to face some fifteen hundred members of the aristocracy, whose refined appetites were on the *qui vive* to taste with severe criticism the productions of the youthful artist'.

Fortunately, the whole showy coronation trumpery had appealed to his innate theatricality, and the lavish budget he was given enabled him to give full rein to it. The long buffet tables were piled with snowy napkins, decorated with wreaths of flowers and set against a backdrop of dramatic *pièces montées* – the intricate sugar ornaments featuring the theme of the day, with a selection of carriages, gilt crowns and other carefully crafted regalia. The dishes mixed the staples of solid English cuisine with more baroque French classics: *Galantine de volaille, Truffes au vin de Champagne, Turban of Larks à la Parisienne* and *Pâtés de Pithiviers* – all designed for easy consumption by elbow-to-elbow diners. There were delicate fish in clear aspics, succulent pigeons wrapped in vine leaves, salmon in pastry cases and tiny butter croustades filled with lobster, oysters and carefully blended pâtés. Alexis was an inspired salad maker, who also firmly believed in their important medicinal qualities. He mixed together the most exotic leaves but preferred to keep each salad simple, sticking to just three or four ingredients for each – endive was a great favourite, plus yellow tansy flowers, sorrels and *barbe-de-capucin*, a wild blue chicory which had to be carefully blanched to remove any trace of bitterness. He took care to herb, season and dress the dish just seconds before being taken to table, to keep the balance and freshness of the flavours perfect. 'What is more refreshing than salads,' he would write later, 'the nice, fresh, green and crisp salad full of life and health, which seems to invigorate the palate and dispose of the masticating powers to a much larger duration?'

Always a stickler for using produce only in their proper season, Soyer was lucky: the coronation was just in time for the last of the spiny-leafed roman artichokes and fat white asparagus from Paris, as well as the best of the English salads and red berries from Covent Garden. Hungerford market and Billingsgate provided excellent fish; Gloucester salmon, sturgeon and trout, not to mention Yarmouth lobsters, prawns, flounders and red mullets. Spring chickens, pullets and capons, goslings and pea-fowls made up the poultry dishes, and he was able to use expensive black plovers eggs – which he rated so highly above the common hen variety that he would pay three shillings each for really fresh ones. Black Piedmont truffles, foie gras, and other French delicacies were purchased from Hedges & Butler in Regent Street, and with them Soyer worked his magic, producing a stunning array of elegant but easy-to-handle dishes to be nibbled by the revellers. For the sweet-toothed there were pistachio meringues and tiny cups of apricot nougats, apple flans, madeleines, creams and bavaroises, flaky mille-feuilles layered with cream and rasp-berries, sweet vol-au-vents filled with peaches, greengages and cherries, and baked frangipane puffs filled with a rich crème pâtissière. The next day's *Morning Chronicle* was rapturous. It pronounced Soyer's meal a 'very splendid' affair, planned 'upon the most liberal and extensive scale'.

While the Reformers mingled in the garden with their strawberries and champagne, tapping their feet to the latest galop, for the queen inside Westminster Abbey, things had also progressed relatively smoothly. The thousand-year-old communion service, the anointing under the cloth of gold, performed to the Anthem of Solomon, the benediction, the homage, the throning, and finally, the crowning itself. With precision timing, the moment the Archbishop of Canterbury placed the crown on the young monarch's head, the peers replaced their coronets, the bishops their mitres and the heralds their caps; the drums and trumpets sounded, the tower cannons were fired, and a massive roar from the crowd could be heard as far away as Lambeth and St James's.

There had been some tricky moments during the marathon five-hour service. Lack of rehearsal meant that some key players fluffed their parts; the Bishop of Durham lost his place and started the Litany too soon, while the Bishop of Bath and Wells turned over two pages at once, missing out a crucial bit of the service. Victoria had to be hastily summoned back from a brief period of supposedly quiet contemplation in St Edward's Chapel – although Disraeli, wandering in later, found the altar covered with sandwiches and open bottles of wine. When the frail, eighty-year-old Lord Rolle tripped over his robes on his way up to the throne, he tumbled down all the steps to the bottom while Victoria could only watch in horror. And she didn't escape unhurt herself – the Duchess of Sutherland claimed the peers gave her a headache by clumsily knocking her heavy crown while paying their homage instead of just touching it lightly, and when the Archbishop insisted on jamming the ruby ring of state onto her fourth finger, when it had been designed for the little one, he badly bruised it. The orb was given to her too soon, and was so heavy she could barely carry it, and on the way out her eight young attendants jerked the train of her dress painfully. But these mishaps were invisible to the crowds outside, and as she made her exhausted progress back to the palace, she knew the event had been a triumph. After a break for dinner, and to bath her favourite dog Dash, she was out on the balcony until midnight, watching the fireworks in Hyde Park.

Revels continued into the evening across the country. Local papers spent the night busily compiling statistics about just how many hundreds of thousands of pounds of roast beef and plum pudding had been donated by the rich to the working-class poor in their area, which was duly guzzled in hundreds of street parties, dinners, fêtes, picnics and hoolies. In Topsham, the townspeople consumed four bullocks, several sheep and 2,000 pounds of pudding in just two hours, while in Cambridge one giant picnic attracted more than 15,000 people, who in the course of the afternoon gorged their way through 7,029 joints of beef, mutton, pork, veal and bacon, 4,500 two-pound loaves of bread, 125 gallons of pickles and 1,608 plum puddings.

At Gwydyr House, as in the other clubs, the celebrations continued well into the night, with innumerable loyal toasts to her majesty taking their toll. *The Globe* reported that 'the club building, the occupiers of which had excelled almost every other club in the display of ladies in the balconies during the morning, was not less distinguished by its illuminations at night.' These ostentatious decorations chiefly consisted of a huge crown, a wreath, and the name V*I*C*T*O*R*I*A picked out 'on a colossal scale' in jets of gas.

Clubs have clustered around Pall Mall for centuries. In their simplest incarnation, as regular meeting places for select groups to gather together for card-playing, debating or simply drinking, they grew out of tavern clubs, such as Wood's – favoured by Pepys – and coffee-houses, most famously Tom's and Will's, where men disinclined for an early night would congregate after the theatre to socialise without the encumbrance of women. The first subscription club, opened in the eighteenth century, was the Albion Hotel at number 86, but politics didn't emerge as a principal *raison d'être* for a club until the last quarter of that century, when the clientele of White's Chocolate House began to use their favourite rendezvous as the informal headquarters of the Tory party. As an antidote to White's, the Whigs, led by Charles James Fox, developed their own club, the exclusive Brooks's in St James's Street, which quickly became the party's feverish election headquarters.

In the first half of the nineteenth century the number of clubs multiplied rapidly, and among the most fashionable were Crockford's, the Union (launched to celebrate the 1801 union with Ireland), the Guards, the Oxford and Cambridge, the Carlton, the Travellers' and the Athenaeum. In a single decade, from 1832 to 1842, the majority of the opulent club houses which still line Pall Mall were built, their fashionable Italianate façades presenting 'an almost uninterrupted line of temples dedicated to social intercourse and the interchange of ideas'. The irony of the clubs' popularity was not lost on Louis Fagan, the Reform's first biographer, who noted that while the English had a reputation abroad for being the most taciturn of people, the unique nature of the West End clubs surely proved they were actually the most talkative folk in existence.

By the 1830s Brooks's, the traditional preserve of the Whiggish aristocracy, was considered neither large enough for the expanding party or appropriate any more, its louche environment of drinking and gambling being at odds with the new atmosphere of purpose and industry in the Liberal movement. More to the point, Brooks's didn't really want to embrace all shades of Liberalism, but preferred to retain its exclusivity. When Edward Ellice, MP for Coventry, an extreme radical who had managed the extraordinary feat of working as a Liberal whip throughout the life of the Reform Bill without becoming heartily disliked by all his colleagues, suggested to the Brooks's committee that it might consider expanding its membership by 600, the committee less than politely declined. The only answer, decided Ellice, was to start an entirely new club.

In fact the Reform was not the first club to be established by a group of disaffected Liberals – that distinction went to the shortlived Westminster Club, set up in 1834 by radical MPs Daniel O'Connell and John Wilks.

Although it only lasted for two years before collapsing with debts of £1,000, it attracted some interesting members, including an unknown but ambitious twenty-eight-year-old Liberal named Benjamin Disraeli. When the club's committee wrote to Disraeli, politely reminding him that his subscription of £15. 15s. was overdue, it received a cheque by return and a curt request that his name should be withdrawn from the list of members, 'as my engagements have not permitted me to avail myself of the Westminster Club'. A year later when, having switched parties, Disraeli stood as a Tory candidate for Taunton, the hostile Devon press accused him not only of having Whig sympathies, but of belonging to a Liberal club. 'It's a club I never heard of,' Disraeli lied shamelessly, 'and I never belonged to a Reform or Political Club in my life.'

The Westminster had failed to make an impact because its particular political balance had never fully satisfied either the Whigs or the radicals. Ellice was able to learn the lessons of the Westminster by striving to unite both ends of the Liberal spectrum, and also to bag 'nineteen-twentieths' of its membership list. Ellice – nicknamed Bear because as a Hudson's Bay Company director his wealth came from the Canadian fur trade – established his own committee, which met at his home in Carlton House Terrace early in 1836. By the first week in May, the essential elements of a new club were in place: committee members and trustees had been finalised and premises rented at 104 Pall Mall, a narrow but deep town house recently vacated by the Countess of Dysart, which was conveniently situated between the Carlton and Travellers' Clubs. The club's official opening was on 24 May – loyally chosen because it was Princess Victoria's birthday – and the event was advertised in all the daily papers, along with the Reform Club's stated intention: 'To promote the social Intercourse of the Reformers of the United Kingdom'. Further, it should 'consist of One Thousand Members, exclusive of Members of either House of Parliament, and of Foreigners admitted by the Committee'. By the time the advert appeared, however, the club had already filled its full complement of members, and still had another four hundred to be balloted. Annual subs were set at ten guineas, or you could opt for life membership at £65.

Right from the start, the determination of the founders to make the Reform 'the best club in town' relied as much on the provision of creature comforts as of intellectual stimulation. 'It will be like the Athenaeum – a good *dining club*,' wrote Sir William Molesworth to his mother. 'It is much wanted. Brooks's is not Liberal enough, too expensive, and not a *dining club*.' Rotivan's departure at the end of June was therefore a significant problem, and the club remained without a permanent *chef de cuisine* until Soyer's arrival the following year. In any case, the cramped dining room at 104 Pall Mall held only fifty members at a sitting, which was hardly adequate for a venue with ambitions of becoming a fine dining club.

In fact, with 1,300 members (the numbers had risen swiftly) excluding honorary, supernumerary and life members, it was soon realised that the whole house was far too small to accommodate even a third of the members comfortably. In the middle of January 1837, Ellice suggested that the narrow old club house should be demolished, and a large modern building, in keeping both with the other clubs in Pall Mall and the political ambitions of the Reformers, should be purpose-built. This could be achieved by leasing an extra parcel of land, roughly fifty feet by a hundred, adjacent to the club, which had recently been freed up by the demolition of three old houses. The management committee agreed, and at a meeting on 1 February resolved to begin negotiations with the Crown's administrators – as all the land on the south of Pall Mall from Waterloo Place to St James's Palace formed part of the Crown estate. Two architects, George Basevi, a club member, and Edward Blore, were engaged to inspect the ground and draw up plans based on the committee's ideas, which they duly submitted a fortnight later. The committee, however, then started dithering, with letters regarding various modifications going backwards and forwards. Eventually, with the Reformers' ambitions getting bigger and grander by the week, they decided to widen the competition and invite seven architects to submit plans for a payment of £50 each, with £100 going to the one whose design was chosen. Among those invited to tender were several architects with club experience, such as Sydney Smirke, who had designed the Oxford and Cambridge with his brother Robert, Decimus Burton, who had laid out the Athenaeum, and Charles Barry, who had built the Travellers'. On 3 June a dedicated building committee of seven members was established, which included Ellice and which would oversee all aspects of the project for the next six years.

As the committee's ambitions grew, so did the projected cost, from an initial estimate of £12,000 to more than £37,000 by the time a floor of bedrooms had been added for the convenience of out-of-town members – making it the first club to provide living accommodation – and numerous other luxurious additions, designed 'to produce a clubhouse that would surpass all others in size and magnificence'. The extra parcel of land they had secured meant that the frontage could stretch to 140 feet

– the width of the Athenaeum and the Travellers' combined. After a protracted wrangle over fees, with the prospective architects all arguing for the usual five per cent of the budget but eventually settling for a one-off sum of £1,689, and a further increase of the budget to £44,000, Barry was finally selected as the successful candidate on 27 November, his plans being considered, on balance, to be 'the best and fittest'. Barry's plans were by far the most well developed and meticulously drawn; he had used every inch of ground available and provided precise sketches and measurements for every chamber, down to the sizes of the baths and cupboards, with artistic illustrations of the finished rooms to aid the imagination of those committee members who were unfamiliar with architectural plans.

Things finally started to move forward. Within a month, the final amendments to Barry's plans, which included roofing the courtyard to create a stunning central hall, were accepted. By May, building contracts were being considered from a dozen firms, whose estimates ranged from £38,400 to £42,852, with a further £6,450 needed for a state-of-the-art kitchen, the expensive oak library fittings and other incidentals. The contract finally went to Grissell & Peto – Peto being a club member. The committee also allowed £2,000 a year to cover the costs of leasing a temporary home for the club during the building work, and Gwydyr House was quickly engaged for the purpose. On 7 June 1838 it was announced that 104 Pall Mall would close on the following Sunday. It was not to reopen for another three years.

In many respects the suave, immensely gifted Charles Barry was the obvious choice to design the Reform Club. Five years earlier he had completed his first major commission, the neighbouring Travellers' Club, to which he had given his now trademark neo-classical, palazzo frontage. His interpretation of the Renaissance style was one that, with adaptations, would influence a large proportion of the nation's public and commercial buildings throughout the middle decades of the century. At forty-two years old he was the most powerful architect in London, having just beaten off almost a hundred competitors to secure the most prestigious contract in the country – and the biggest budget ever allocated to an English building project – to rebuild the burned out Houses of Parliament, a mammoth project that would preoccupy him for the next fifteen years and eventually earn him a knighthood. For the New Palace of Westminster, the government had insisted on a more traditional English style, something strong and dignified – preferably something Elizabethan

– which it was felt would echo the country's history at a prosperous and forward-looking point, and imbue the Mother of Parliaments with a sense of national pride, morality and even mythology. And so Charles Barry sensibly recruited the precocious but brilliant young Augustus Welby Pugin, the leading authority on Gothic, to design these quasi-historical elevations. But with the Reform Club, he was on his own territory, working in the Italianate genre at which he excelled.

Barry's taste for Palladian lines was, however, purely aesthetic, and inside his classically inspired palaces he was an advocate of the very latest technology in the building process. This suited Alexis perfectly, who immediately saw that here was a chance to exercise all his ingenuity in the arrangement and fitting out of the club's enormous basement. This was a far cry from inventing little gadgets in Shropshire. Here was a unique opportunity to create an entirely new style of modern, machine-driven, super-efficient kitchen. Cool-headed Barry, respecting Soyer's extensive experience, was impressed by his practical suggestions for the construction of the ideal catering department, and intrigued by the excitable Frenchman's flood of wild ideas, which included rows of ovens run by temperature-controlled gas flames, fish slabs 'refrigerated' by running ice water and of steam-operated mechanical spits and food lifts. At a time when even the grandest kitchens were relatively simple affairs – high-ceilinged chambers lined with smoking ranges and cumbersome copper boilers, where joints were still roasted by clockwork bottle-jacks or primitive smoke-jacks powered by the flue of the fire, Soyer's ideas were revolutionary indeed. Over the next three years the fertile genius of the architect and the practical ingenuity of the young chef would combine to produce the most famous and influential working kitchen in Europe.

While Barry was withdrawn and dour, and Soyer brash and voluble, in fact the two had more in common than talent and vision. Both men were social climbers, easily impressed by men of rank. Both were from relatively humble backgrounds (Barry was the son of a government stationer) but destined to spend their working lives serving those of extreme wealth and privilege. And both men were hugely ambitious in the projects they took on, but had the energy to match their commitments, regularly rising at four in the morning to get through the day's work. Barry clearly warmed to Alexis, enjoying the younger man's undeniable gallic charm. 'Foreigners especially made their way with him,' said Barry's son Alfred in a biography of his father, 'for he always liked the greater freedom and liveliness of Continental manners and character.' There was still a social distinction between them: Barry, as an architect, was a member of the educated professional classes and a gentleman, while Alexis, as a chef, even a highly valued and indulged one, remained firmly trade. But Alexis – partly because of the infectious enthusiasm of his character, and partly because of his French background, which put him slightly outside the rigid class boundaries – felt he could ignore any such barriers and cajole Barry into adopting his radical plans for the all-important culinary department.

Barry, for his part, was a good delegator when he believed in the talent of his associates. Just as he had given Pugin free rein to design not just the elevations but all the interiors of the Houses of Parliament 'from thrones to umbrella stands', the same was true with Alexis and his subterranean empire. 'The enthusiasm and knowledge of M. Soyer were allowed full scope,' confirmed Alfred Barry. For Barry, it must have been a relief to hand over some of the work when his time was so much occupied with the great parliamentary project. And Soyer, given the chance to design his own, purpose-built, virtually no-expense spared, state-of-the-art kitchen, was willing to move heaven and earth to get it right.

Work on the site finally began in the summer of 1838. Ten months later, after various minor alterations, Barry was able to report that things were progressing to his 'entire satisfaction' and that the roof would be fitted by November. This complacency was short lived, however. Technical problems, dithering on the part of the committee and two accidents – both falls from the timber scaffolding, one of which permanently disabled a bricklayer – all caused delays. In January 1840 Barry requested an extra £1,307 in order to sink a well and erect a six horse power steam engine, which would not only warm and ventilate the building, but power a lift, able to move coal and heavy objects to the upper storeys. The Bank of England and GPO buildings had recently installed the new steam technology, and Barry was keen to emulate their success. Alexis was also anxiously pressing Barry for the engine to be fitted, as he had plenty of ideas for how to utilise the steam power.

During the first months of 1840 Alexis was kept busy with his duties at Gwydyr House, which included catering a special members' dinner to celebrate the queen's marriage to her cousin Albert of Saxe-Coburg-Gotha on 10 February. But between his shifts at Whitehall he managed to interview a stream of contractors and small manufacturers about the feasibility and costs of his various innovations for the new club house. In March his final list of specifications for the cooking apparatus and kitchen fittings was eventually sent, via Barry and the building committee, to a shortlist of seven suppliers, and the contracts were awarded in May. Despite the spiralling costs, few of the extra expenses requested were denied. The final contracts for the kitchen and gas fittings, lifting machines – including steam-driven dumb waiters to carry hot food two floors up from the basement to the main dining hall, known as the Coffee Room – the lighting and the steam apparatus, amounted to more than £3,000. Although Alexis did not receive any formal recognition in the building committee minutes for his kitchen design, no one ever disputed the extent or originality of his input. Barry, Fagan, the press and public all gave him his due, and Soyer would spend the next few years fully exploiting the brilliance of his inventions.

Throughout the summer, there were 220 workmen at any one time on the Pall Mall site, and one of the biggest and most complicated areas of activity was in the kitchens. Each day Alexis would dash backwards and forwards from Gwydyr House as often as he could, to chivvy on the workers with jokes and edible bribes and so ensure the smooth implementation of his designs. The building committee minutes record that one newly installed kitchen range had to be taken out and another fitted 'on the plan adopted at Christ Church, Oxford', and in November a further £63 was allowed for more changes, including the addition of a steam table, but otherwise all went well. By the onset of winter, the club building's Portland stone façade was in place, the ornate exterior friezes, modelled on the Acropolis, had been cast, and the committee was ready to pick out designs for the china plates.

On the first day of February the building was ready for the servants to move in and start the long preparations for a grand opening at the end of April. The staff had to learn how to handle the new technology, work out their service stations and systems, and ensure everything was in place, from the bedlinen to dustpans, salt cellars and teaspoons. With the introduction of bedrooms for out-of-town members wishing to stay over, the kitchens had now to be prepared to provide breakfasts as well as luncheons and dinners – upwards of 20,000 covers a year – not to mention the never-ending stream of coffees, drinks and snacks. Although he had more than enough to attend to in his own department, Alexis took a close interest in every aspect of the club – a problem that would at times cause considerable friction with other staff and members of the committee.

Everything was ready on time, and the doors of the new club house were formally opened to the members on 24 April 1841. Those who had waited impatiently to inspect the new premises started with a tour of the ground floor. From the steps outside the porter's lobby, they saw first the 'splendid hall, from thence to an elegant saloon, an appropriate visitors' waiting-room, a comfortable morning-room, a very fine Parliamentary library, a most commodious, large, and beautiful coffee-room, second library of general reference, and a very magnificent drawing-room'. Then they were guided around the other five floors, taking in the comfortable bed chambers, the ultra-modern bathrooms, the marble-lined galleries and landings, the committee, card, smoking and strangers' rooms, the offices and the barber's shop. The most popular port of call, however, was always the magnificent kitchen department in the basement, where a massive £674 had been spent just on the *batterie de cuisine*. All in all, the members judged that the £87,435 final bill for their new headquarters – treble that spent by any other club – was well worth the outlay. However, the costs had stretched the club's finances to the limit. When Barry submitted his own revised bill, which came to nearly £4,000, payment was refused until the claim went to arbitration. Even when Barry won his case there were more delays from the cash-strapped committee until the cheque was personally guaranteed by the chairman, Lord Marcus Hill, and three other wealthy members.

Alexis could not wait to get into the building and take over his gleaming culinary domain, which from the moment of its completion, says Fagan, was 'pronounced by connoisseurs to be unrivalled'. The design was undeniably superb. The main kitchen was simply the focal point of a series of interconnecting chambers, all separated by doorways but built without doors, enabling Soyer, a stickler for precision timing, to keep an eye on all that was happening from a few key vantage points. 'The minute index-hand did not pass more regularly over the face of the clock,' wrote an observer, 'than the assistants of Soyer revolved around him as the centre planet of their system.' Key to the whole conception, however, was the sophisticated control of temperature, via the manipulation of fire, water, gas, steam and ice. In a dedicated roasting kitchen, for example, were two mammoth ranges, complete with huge iron jacks and spits, each one capable of roasting a whole sheep. To maximise the value of the vast amount of fuel gobbled up by these ranges, the walls of this furnace were also lined with the latest French boiling stoves, charcoal grates, hotplates, large pastry and small soufflé ovens, a six-foot steam closet and a hot water cistern supplied from a 100-gallon boiler. To shield the rest of the kitchen from the blistering heat, Soyer designed huge tin-plated screens, six feet tall and two feet deep, that moved around on castors. When placed in front of the fire, these screens – which were also fitted with insulated recesses to act as food warmers – reflected back almost all the generated heat. They were so effective that Soyer often used them as a party piece – flinging them open so that his visitors would jump in shock, entirely unaware that they had been standing so close to such an intense fire.

In the central kitchen, where the main food preparation took place, a cast-iron closet was placed in the middle of an elm work table, the interior temperature accurately controlled by the application of steam from a valve running underneath. The fireplace in this kitchen, reserved for the roasting of game and poultry, was tall but shallow, with a clever pull-out grate designed in such a way that the coals stacked up vertically, giving a larger cooking area and making it easier to clean. The walls of this kitchen were also lined with stoves, ovens, and large, deep, hot water bain-maries for soup and sauces. Around these principal kitchens were dedicated anterooms designed with equal care. There was a boucherie for the preparation of the raw meat, separate meat and game and sauce larders – kept at a constant 35 degrees – a pastry and confectionery department, a vegetable kitchen and scullery. There was the *chef de cuisine*'s large and comfortable private office, complete with a large desk, hearth, tables and easy chairs, not to mention a selection of Emma's paintings and a large cabinet filled with fine wines and spirits. There was a room and pantry for the butler and a dining room for the kitchen maids. Even the passageways were put to good use, for extra storage, for the steam and hand-operated lifts, and for the large sloping fish slab, which was kept cool by a clever system of running iced water over the fish via a shower-pipe, and for the kitchen clerk's high desk, from which he took down orders from the floors above via a system of speaking tubes, then supervised their delivery and worked out the bills.

But Soyer's technical *pièces de résistance* in the main kitchen were his two gleaming gas stoves. These wonderful machines afforded the chef, he later wrote, 'the greatest comfort ever introduced in any culinary arrangement'. The Reform stoves were placed on either side of a traditional charcoal fire and served by separate gas pipes. Each stove was then further divided into five pan-sized compartments, each one having an individual gas supply and brass cock, so they could be used and regulated independently. For chefs, the idea of a clean, smoke-free, coal-free, controllable fire was an almost unimaginable boon. Cooking with gas had been heard of before – a Moravian chemist called Zachaus Winzler had experimented with a prototype stove as early as 1802 – but the first English gas cooker had only recently been developed, and it would not become a widely available commercial product until after a range of models were displayed at the Great Exhibition in 1851. Even then, public mistrust of gas appliances continued for some time. Apart from the safety concerns associated with gas, in the early years there were few places with a consistent supply of the fuel. However, here Alexis was lucky, for Pall Mall had been the very first London street to be lit by gas lamps in 1807, and by the time the Reform Club's foundations were laid, the street had well-established supply lines to Frederick Winsor's Gas Light & Coke Company – the first centralised gasworks in the world.

Alexis summarised the chief attractions of his gas stoves at length.

You obtain the same heat as from charcoal the moment it is lit, it is a fire that never requires making up, is free from carbonic acid which is so pernicious, especially in small kitchens, and creates neither dust nor smell (except when gas should neglectfully be not properly turned off). And by my last improvement it is also now quite free from smoke. With the aid of my new octagonal trivet I can place nine stewpans over without the fear of upsetting either, some only simmering and others boiling at the same time, which is invaluable . . . The gas stoves also tend to greater economy, as they are not lit till the moment wanted, then only the quantity required, and may be put out the moment it is done with. I think it a great pity that they can only be fitted in London and other large towns daily supplied with gas, but it is there it is most required, as the kitchens are smaller than in country houses, no heat whatever being created in the smallest kitchens by the use of gas stoves.

Not only was gas fully controllable and economical to boot, but it did away with filthy coal, perfect for a man unusually obsessed with issues of order and cleanliness. 'Cleanliness is the soul of the kitchen,' was his oft-repeated motto, and the ease of washing was at the forefront of all his kitchen and utensil designs. Far more importantly though, gas finally did away with the carbonic acid, a by-product of the huge quantities of charcoal previously burned, which was not just 'pernicious' to the health of full-time cooks but frequently fatal, as the carbon monoxide fumes gradually destroyed their lungs in the hot, deliberately enclosed atmosphere. Alexis's hero, the great *cuisinier* Antonin Carême, who had died ten tears earlier at the age of fifty, was one of many professional chefs who had put the decline of his health down to the effects of the acid – before stoutly declaring, with a swaggering panache worthy of Soyer himself, 'Charcoal kills us, but what does it matter? The shorter the life, the greater the glory!'

Soyer remained a passionate and influential advocate of the benefits of this revolutionary form of cooking. He gave a lengthy interview on the subject of gas to *The Builder* and would later write about the benefits of gas in books and articles. He would use huge open-air gas ovens at public dinners, in soup kitchens to produce great coppers of broth, and he even designed his own gas cooker – manufactured and marketed as the stylish but unpronounceable Soyer's Phidomageireion. He even presided over some formal trials at the Royal Naval School in Greenwich, in which equal quantities of mutton were simultaneously roasted in gas and conventional ovens. *The Mechanic* magazine reported that the twenty-three joints roasted in the gas oven lost less than nineteen pounds in weight during the cooking process and cost just ten pence in gas, while the same number of joints roasted in the conventional ovens lost thirty-four pounds in weight and consumed a hefty 102 pounds of coke and thirty pounds of coal.

Soyer was exceptional in being both a brilliant *chef de cuisine* and a genuinely talented inventor. All his life he would have several ideas in development at any given time, and a number of his inventions became significant commercial successes. They were often simple solutions – as the best ideas are. Mechanical kitchen timers, tendon separators, plug strainers, cafetières – many of his ideas would become kitchen com-monplaces. And the Reform Club kitchens, naturally, became the laboratory and showcase for all this creativity.

Visitors to the kitchen loved Soyer's ingenious attention to detail. The way the larder walls and vegetable boxes were lined with slate for coolness, and the dressers had lead-lined ice drawers, with little funnels at the bottom for the drainage of the melted ice. The way the meat safe could be shut, via a complicated system of cords and pulleys, by a jerk of the elbow when your hands were full. The way almost everything was on wheels, so that even the smallest kitchenmaid could move things around. The way the marble mortar had been sunk into a dresser top, to allow the cooks to take both hands to the pestle. There was a place for everything, and everything was in its place. To solve the perennial Victorian problem of blocked drains, every sink contained one of Soyer's sink trap bells, a small pierced copper dome attached to a rod and chain that stopped any debris from falling into the pipes. Even the pillars had been fitted with spinning carousels of tin-lined compartments, so that the most frequently used herbs and seasonings were always to hand. Soyer was particularly proud of his beautiful elm preparation table, the underside of which had been fitted with knife drawers, slide-out chopping boards and copper buckets that were filled with water and cloths for sponging away blood and mess. The table was deliberately small – just twelve feet long – and was cut into twelve irregular sides, in order to accommodate a dozen cooks 'without anyone interfering with each other'. 'I consider too large a table to be as bad as too large a kitchen,' Alexis explained to a puzzled guest, 'as much time is lost in the cleaning, and more in running about for articles required for use.'

No wonder the fame of the new Reform Club, despite its magnificence, was quickly eclipsed by news of this extraordinary model kitchen. Barry's exquisite marble lobby; his elegant parliamentary library, the oak shelves lined with the creaking new leather-bound volumes; his graciously proportioned and decorated morning, dining, committee and drawing rooms barely got a look-in compared to the interest generated by the basement. *The Spectator* raved about 'the matchless culinary arrangements' and a report in the *London Gourmet* gave a classic example of how public attention had effectively been hijacked by one of the club's servants.

The Reform Club very closely resembles the other distinguished clubs at the West End . . . but it is by the possession of its famous *kitchen* that this club has gained a peculiar notoriety; a kitchen which baffles the conception of those who are accustomed only to ordinary culinary arrangements. The 'genius loci' is M. Alexis Soyer, whose occupation is that of chief cook to the club, and whose invention the general arrangement of the kitchen seems to have been. The gastronomic art, certainly, never before had so many scientific appliances at its disposal.

Another reporter went even further, imparting to Alexis almost mystical qualities.

It is in the lower regions, where Soyer reigns supreme, that the true glories of the Reform Club consist. Heliogabulus himself never gloated over such a kitchen, for steam is here introduced and made to supply the part of man. In state the great dignitary sits, and issues his inspiring orders to a body of lieutenants, each of whom has pretensions to be considered a *chef* in himself. Soyer is indeed the glory of the edifice.

Curious members and their guests flooded into the basement to view both the famous kitchen and the celebrity chef at his *batterie de cuisine* – in fact the basement became as much a social focal point as the drawing room for as long as Alexis remained at the club; in 1846 he claimed to have received 15,000 visitors in his domain over a ten-month period. Although all the attention gave a huge boost to his already healthy vanity, the flood of requests for guided tours became so intense that Soyer was forced to delegate most of them to François Volant, the French friend and drinking partner whom he had recently employed as an ad hoc secretary and fixer. The most important guests, of course, he would make time for and, dressed in his whites and now trademark red beret, he would laugh and joke and show off to them, feeding them foie gras and other titbits as tantalising *amuse-gueules*. As almost every member of the government dined at the Reform at some stage, the most influential politicians of the day invariably found their way into the kitchen, and Alexis, with his fool's licence, would put on his motley and treat them to an inimitable mix of deference and comedy. When the prime minister, Lord Melbourne, commented archly on the number of pretty girls Soyer employed in the kitchen, the chef replied, 'Well, sir, we want no *plain* cooks here.' Volant later described a typical scene.

When Soyer himself showed the place, it was curious to watch him, with his red velvet hat and spoon in hand, explaining to elegantly dressed ladies, and to the best blood of the aristocracy and nobility, his various methods of concocting soups of exquisite flavour, or his different styles of producing his dishes of fish, game, poultry, etc., at the same time giving full proof of his power over the art, by handing round either some *properly* made mulligatawny, or a basin of filleted sole *à la maître d'hôtel*, sending home the tasters positively rabid for their dinner, and wishing Soyer could be divided into as many pieces as the calf's head for his mock turtle, that they might each have a bit of him in their cookery department. Sometimes he would suddenly plunge his finger, diamond ring and all, into what appeared to be a boiling cauldron of glue, pass it across his tongue, wink his eye, and add either a little more salt, pepper, or some mysterious dust, known possibly only to great *artistes*, to make it palatable. Then, again, he would whisper, chucklingly, 'I've a dish for Lord M— H—, for six o'clock, or a potage for Sir J So-and-so at eight o'clock; *let us taste it.*'

As the fame of the kitchen spread abroad it became as fashionable for distinguished overseas visitors to visit Soyer's kitchen as it was to attend Vauxhall Pleasure Gardens, or The Bazaar in Baker Street, a collection of life-size wax models being displayed by another eccentric French national, eighty-year-old Marie Tussaud. The visiting Vicomtesse de Malleville gave a detailed description of the kitchens in the *Courrier de l'Europe*, in which she managed to capture the dramatic intensity of the kitchens when in full swing – the heat and noise and steam, and the dozens of white-clad minions rushing about their business, but always with constant and obedient reference back to the *chef de cuisine*.

Unlike in a theatre, we see no naked walls behind the scenes – no tattered draperies – no floors strewed with sawdust. This fine apartment is the kitchen – spacious as a ballroom, kept in the finest order, and white as a young bride. All-powerful steam, the noise of which salutes you as you enter, here performs a variety of offices: it diffuses a uniform heat to large rows of dishes, warms the metal plates, upon which are disposed the dishes that have been called for, and that are in waiting to be sent above; it turns the spits, draws the water, carries up the coal, and moves the plate like an intelligent and indefatigable servant. Stay awhile before this octagonal apparatus, which occupies the centre of the place. Around you the water boils and the stewpans bubble, and a little further on is a moveable furnace, before which pieces of meat are converted into savoury *rôtis* – here are sauces and gravies, stews, broths, soups, etc.; in the distance are Dutch ovens, marble mortars, lighted stoves, iced plates of metal for fish, and various compartments for vegetables, fruits, roots and spices. After this inadequate, though prodigious nomenclature, the reader may perhaps picture to himself a state of general confusion . . . If so, he is mistaken. For, in fact, you see very little, or scarcely anything, of all the objects above described; the order of their arrangement is so perfect, their distribution as a whole, and in their relative bearings to one another, are all so intelligently considered, that you require the aid of a guide to direct you in exploring them, and a good deal of time to classify in your mind all your discoveries.

The man who devised the plan of this magnificent kitchen, over which he rules and governs without question or dispute, the *artiste* who directs by his gestures his subalterns tricked out in white, and whose eye takes in at a glance the most difficult combinations in the culinary art – in a word, the *chef* by whom every *gourmet* admitted within the precincts of the Reform Club swears, is M. Soyer . . . Allow him therefore, to give you the history of his discoveries and improvements; let him conduct you into the smallest recesses of his establishment, the cleanliness of which would shame many a drawing-room . . . Let all strangers who come to London for business, or pleasure, or curiosity, or for whatever cause, not fail to visit the Reform Club. In an age of utilitarianism, and of the search for the comfortable, like ours, there is more to be learned here than in the ruins of the Coliseum, of the Parthenon, or of Memphis.

Soyer, uniquely among the clubs, was the only servant to be mentioned in every contemporary newspaper account of the Reform, and the wits were soon suggesting that his cooking did more for party unity than any Liberal dogma. If the founders of the club soon wearied of so much attention being focused on their chef, rather than their principles, there is little evidence of it in the early years of his culinary reign. On the contrary, Soyer's cooking remained as ingenious as his kitchen appliances, and in the first four years of his tenure the succession of new soups, delicate entrées and imaginative desserts that he introduced to the main bill of fare met with widespread approval.

By the beginning of 1842 Alexis felt, at the age of thirty-two, that he had it all: total authority in his beautiful white kitchens, a superb reputation that was spreading through Europe, a substantial salary, plus regular and lucrative offers of freelance work, which included numerous commissions to design other kitchens on the Reform model. To put the icing on the *gâteau*, Emma had finally announced, after five years of marriage, that she was expecting their first child.

4

Elizabeth Emma Jones was born on 5 September 1813, to Richard and Elizabeth Jones, a wealthy London couple. The Joneses already had a son, christened Newton, and Emma would be their last, as Richard died shortly before her fifth birthday. By the time of her father's death the precocious Emma was already considered something of a prodigy. She excelled at music and drawing, French and Italian masters were engaged and found her a willing and capable student, and before long her widowed mother was pouring all her energies into the careful cultivation of her daughter's talents.

Just a few months after her husband's death, Elizabeth took Emma to see François Simonau, who was supplementing his commissions with a small but prospering art school in Commercial Road. Initially, Simonau was reluctant to take on such a tiny student, but the child seemed genuinely talented and he eventually agreed. After six months, the pushy Mrs Jones was anxious to secure more of the master's time for little Emma, and offered to compensate Simonau for all the other students' fees if he would drop them and concentrate exclusively on her daughter. He gave in – on that and every other matter, it seems, for within three years Mrs Jones had married him. They tied the knot on 24 October 1820, in Lambeth church. Strangely, Elizabeth reverted to her maiden name of Newton for the ceremony, thereby declaring herself a spinster rather than a widow in the register – despite the contrary evidence of her two small children, who were both in attendance as witnesses. There are several reasons why she might have done this. It was possible that she was trying to circumvent a financial penalty in Richard's will that came into force on her remarriage. However, it is more likely that Emma's mother had never been legally married to her father – and so in spite of being referred to as Mrs Jones, genuinely was a spinster. It might also explain the unusual choice of Newton for her first-born's Christian name. After the wedding the small family moved to new lodgings in Greek Street, Soho.

As well as harbouring artistic ambitions for her daughter, Elizabeth was also busy promoting Emma's musical talents, and managed to hire the Duchess of Kent's piano teacher, Jean Ancot, to give her lessons. Perhaps his services were acquired on a quid pro quo basis, as a few years later Simonau submitted a portrait for exhibition at the Royal Academy entitled *Monsieur J. Ancot, Composer and Professor of the Pianoforte*. Ancot was a friend of both the fat and jolly Rossini, who was enjoying his first international successes with *The Barber of Seville*, and the thin, tubercular Weber, who had recently completed his romantic masterpiece, *Der Freischütz*. A few years later Emma played a passage from *Der Freischütz* to the great man himself, and Weber was said – perhaps feeling the pressure under the gaze of a proud mama – to have been impressed enough to have encouraged her to become a professional musician.

At first Elizabeth agreed with Weber, feeling that too much close drawing might prove injurious to the health of her little girl. However, it appears that she changed her mind after an incident during a restorative family holiday on the continent. Emma happened to look out of a window in Dunkirk one morning to see some other children blowing bubbles. She went outside to look more closely, and was so enchanted by the picturesque scene that she picked up a piece of charcoal and quickly sketched it on a wall. The drawing was so well executed that when her mother and stepfather saw it, they agreed that art should be her main occupation in the future, with music relegated to a genteel hobby. Emma made a painting from the charcoal sketch which was sold, a few years later, for the equivalent of around £4,000. With art now her principal study, she improved rapidly and was said to have finished more than a hundred portraits 'with surprising fidelity' by the age of twelve. In total she would complete more than four hundred works, exhibiting twelve at the Royal Academy in Piccadilly between the ages of ten and twenty-one, thirty-eight at the British Institution in Pall Mall, and fourteen at the Society of British Artists gallery in Suffolk Street. In addition she exhibited several works at the Louvre.

Emma was also deemed quite a wit, and she certainly shared a love of practical jokes with Alexis. Her only surviving written work is a satire on the 1830s vogue for etiquette books, which affected to lay down rules for every exigency of modern life, from what colour gloves to wear at a ball, to tips on how to hold your cutlery. One such manual, published in 1834, specified the thickness of the bread to be served at family meals (no less than one and a half inches thick). 'There is nothing more plebian,' it declared, 'than *thin* bread at dinner.' Emma's parody, entitled *Fashionable Precepts for the Ladies*, inverted all the norms of reasonable behaviour for comic effect. However, today her humour seems not only leaden but stuffed with inverted snobberies of her own. She exhorts any woman striving for social acceptance to 'deviate from Nature' in all particulars. 'To speak naturally, to act naturally, are vulgar and commonplace in the last degree,' she states, before describing how a truly fashionable woman will walk in a stilted fashion and blush at the slightest excuse, restrict her reading to novels and magazines like the low-brow *Theatrical Inquisitor* and allow her discourse to turn solely 'on the unfashionableness of ordinary life'. There's no evidence that her work ever found a publisher. Alexis, however, no stranger to excessive verbiage himself, was no doubt as charmed by her writing as he was by her paintings.

The marriage began well. The young couple took lodgings at 26 Charing Cross Road, and the first few years passed in a happy rush of work: Alexis dashing between Whitehall and Pall Mall as the new club house took shape, and Emma painting and studying beside François. Two weeks before the wedding, Adelaide Lamain had died in the Rue St Nicolas, Paris, at the age of thirty-one, after handing over guardianship of six-year-old Jean to a close friend. While Alexis would have been saddened by the death, the news may have taken a while to filter through to him. There is nothing to suggest that he had continued to support his little family in Paris, or even kept in touch with them beyond the first few years. There would have been few opportunities to visit France as he worked hard to establish himself in England, and written communication was equally difficult: Alexis struggled enough, and Adelaide was unlikely to have been much more literate. There was certainly never a question of Jean being sent to join his father, and Soyer had long since considered himself free of his youthful entanglements.

The year 1839 was marred by two more deaths, first of Emma's mother, Elizabeth, and then Alexis's brother Philippe, at the age of just forty, two days after Christmas. By then Alexis's father Emery was also dead, and his mother, Marie, had remarried a prosperous farmer, a widower called Pierre Travet from the neighbouring town of Crécy. On her marriage Marie had moved from Meaux into Travet's house in the Market Place, and it was here that Alexis took Emma to visit after their wedding, and where Emma painted her new mother-in-law in a composition called *The Farmer's Wife*. And it was here that Philippe's health had collapsed during a summer visit with his family. Tuberculosis had been exacerbated by years in charcoal-fumed kitchens, and the disease had reached an advanced stage before chest pains, night sweats and severe breathlessness restricted him to bed. By the end of August he was spitting up blood, and had lost so much weight that it was clear that he was too weak to be moved. His stepfather Travet finally summoned the town notary and an array of neighbours to witness a will, in which Philippe left his property to his English wife, Elizabeth Williams, and their five children. As head cook to the Duke of Cambridge for so many years, Philippe had managed to accrue a significant estate, including a house in Wilton Street, to which his widow later returned. Although Philippe and his wife had spent much of the last few years at the duke's residence in Hanover – all of their children were born in Germany – the brothers had remained close, and Alexis was devastated by his death. He never lost his terror of tuberculosis, the 'white plague' that would later claim his other brother Louis, particularly as it was associated with the respiratory problems that afflicted every chef. He often feared that he, too, was doomed to an early grave.

After her mother's death Emma invited Simonau to join them in the Charing Cross Road flat, where they lived with her maid, Sarah Vaughan, and a lodger, a Frenchman called Louis Lowil. The 1841 census also lists Alexis's brother, Louis, as living in the house, although he may simply have been visiting. By this time Emma had moved away from working in crayons and water-colours to more serious oil paintings; her reputation as an artist was growing and, once Simonau had completed the household, the two artists began making short tours around Britain and Europe to promote her work further. Few of her paintings, which the critics agreed were boldly executed and coloured, survive, but with titles like *The Blind Boy, The Crossing Sweeper* and *The Kentish Ceres*, it's unlikely that they strayed far from the romanticised, sentimental compositions that remained fashionable throughout Victoria's reign.

It was a highly unconventional arrangement – a married woman travelling without her husband, commercially promoting her own work – but it was successful. Simonau was the ideal chaperone, and with Alexis working late into the night at Gwydyr House or Pall Mall, he hardly required a traditional wife with a meal waiting for him at home. Perhaps it was a relief to know that she was occupied during his own long absences. Although he enjoyed the domesticity of his married life with Emma, and particularly enjoyed entertaining their friends, he was not a man to expect his wife to give up a promising career to wait on him. On the contrary, he was proud and supportive of her talents, and ferociously sensitive to any slight, real or imagined. After several unsuccessful attempts to get more of her paintings exhibited at the Royal Academy, in early 1840 Emma had written to Sir Martin Archer Shee, the Academy's president, asking if he could use his influence to help her. The request was innocent enough, but offended Sir Martin's keen sense of protocol, and after a long delay he sent back a note to say that his position did not give him the privilege to influence the admission or rejection of works of art sent for exhibition – that decision rested entirely with the council. The letter was curt and dismissive, and Alexis was furious. Possibly, he was concerned that Madame Soyer, wife of a cook, had become less attractive to the snooty Academy than the talented stepdaughter of the revered Simonau, and he never forgot the snub. Years later he was still scribbling rude doggerel about art critics and, specifically, Royal Academicians, who, he said, would rather trample on talented artists than protect them. '*Le vrai génie devant vous deploie-t-il ses travaux / Au lieu de l'existence il y trouve le tombeau,*' he wrote bitterly after Emma's death, in a poem called '*Aux Royaux Académiciens*'. He could clearly hold a grudge. In fact in the next two years Emma exhibited twice more at the Royal Academy – a painting of children fishing entitled *The Juvenile Anglers*, and a portrait of one of Alexis's most enthusiastic private patrons, the wealthy Warwickshire baronet, Sir George Chetwynd.

The atmosphere in the new club provided an ideal milieu for Soyer's burgeoning talents as a networker. Although parliamentarians still dominated the membership list, in the four years since the club's inception many Liberal-minded intellectuals had also been elected, whose public status was based on achievement rather than birth. In addition to the landowning political acolytes of Lord Grey – who once boasted that his Cabinet owned more acres than any other in history – Reformers were now drawn from the Church, the services and even the professions. The Reform was the first club to welcome merchants and industrialists, and also – uniquely in clubland – happily took Nonconformists, Roman Catholics and Jews onto its books. The engineer Isambard Kingdom Brunel, the sculptor George Rennie Jr, the club's own architect Charles Barry and the horticulturist Joseph Paxton were all early members. Authors and journalists were also drawn to the Reform: Douglas Jerrold,

William Makepeace Thackeray, George Augustus Sala and John Delane, the pioneering editor of the *Times*, among them. These and all the other members became regular diners at the club, and Soyer – never one to hover in the background if his jovial company was required – forged valuable relationships with many of them.

He was also cementing friendships with the leading figures of his own profession, notably the wealthy Ude, who was busy piling up his cash at Crockford's. The two men shared more than a reputation for gastronomic genius and a past life that included leaving France in a hurry; they shared a sense of humour, extreme garrulousness, and an eccentricity of dress and manners that amused most but alienated some. Despite the devotion of his employer, the Earl of Sefton, and his followers at the clubs where he worked, many distrusted Ude's sharp tongue and nouveau-riche lifestyle, and his critics claimed there was always something of the charlatan about him. The Cockney journalist Renton Nicolson wrote 'there was a vast deal of humbug' about Ude – which was a bit rich, coming from a man whose most successful publication, *The Swell's Guide to the Great Metropolis*, was a barely disguised directory of London brothels.

Soyer's relationship with Ude, as well as containing genuine affection, held significant benefits for both parties. Ude may have been the reigning king of kitchens, but he was getting old, and Soyer was unquestionably the coming man. It was a shrewd move for Ude to associate himself with the next big thing, while it did no harm to Alexis to be the acknowledged heir of Ude's considerable culinary legacy. 'Music, dancing, fencing, painting, and mechanics possess professors under the age of twenty years, but pre-eminence in cookery can never be attained under thirty,' Ude had written years earlier. To him, Soyer was just about coming of age.

Ude and Soyer also shared the tendency to allow their respect for their social superiors to slide, on occasion, into cheeky irreverence. Just as Soyer would attract trouble at the Reform for rudeness to members who annoyed or patronised him, so it was for Ude at Crockford's, who once insulted a diner who dared to quibble over an extra sixpenny charge levied on a beautifully finished fish sauce. 'The damned *imbecile* apparently believes that the red mullets come out of the sea with my sauce in their pockets,' he declared contemptuously. And both men at times came under suspicion of sharp practice with regard to the vast quantities of luxurious ingredients that poured into their kitchens each week. And it wasn't just a question of skimming, or juggling the bills to make them tally. There were undoubtedly plenty of wine merchants and grocers anxious to influence the *chef de cuisine* who were prepared to offer generous gifts and hospitality in return for a lucrative supply contract.

Ude was once sued for serving grouse at the club in July – as it was a full month before the legal start of the season, it proved that the birds had been poached. The litigious Marquess of Queensbury, who was horrified to find the offending bird on his plate, insisted on the case going to Bow Street court, where the chef was duly fined five shillings. Cheekily, Ude put the grouse on the menu yet again the following day – this time turned into a highly seasoned ragoût with mushrooms and truffles – and when Queensbury objected, claimed he was simply using up the left-overs. Soyer clearly learned from Ude's experience and when, at the beginning of August 1849, a member complained about the absence of grouse from the Reform menu, Soyer quickly replied that it was club policy not to buy game before the legal time.

Ude lived in considerable splendour in a house in Albemarle Street, midway between Bond Street and Berkeley Square, which was packed with valuable art, lavish plate, rare china and *objets de vertu*. He shared the house with his wife, with whom he quarrelled loudly and continually, and a menagerie of pet dogs, cats and parrots. The noise they made was legendary. Ude also, in a strange reversal of social norms, let out the top floors to William Arden, the second Lord Alvanley, after the spendthrift baron and superannuated dandy had been forced to sell off his family estates in Cheshire to settle some gambling debts accrued at White's. The arrangement worked well, as the portly, good-natured Alvanley, once a great drinking pal of the Prince Regent, and who could also claim a distant kinship with Shakespeare's mother, was quite as batty as his landlord. He told friends that the constant racket from downstairs was strangely reassuring to him and, more importantly, as a noted gourmand, he adored Ude's cooking. His straitened circumstances had done nothing to diminish the peer's appetite for outrageously expensive dishes, of which favourites included a *Suprême de Volaille* which required twenty birds to create one portion, as he insisted that only the bite-sized oysters, or *noix*, from the undersides of the carcasses were tender enough to eat.

While Ude was both notoriously rich and notoriously stingy, once a year, on 25 August, he would throw caution to the wind and celebrate his birthday by hosting a spectacular dinner party for around two dozen friends and disciples. In 1841 Alexis and Emma found themselves in receipt of such a precious invitation. 'As it was the first to which I had been invited, I was very anxious to go,' Alexis wrote later. 'About a week previous, so strong was my wish to be present at this feast, I asked the committee to grant me leave of absence from duty for one evening, and they kindly acceded to my request.' Ude always expected his guests to be highly honoured by their inclusion at this select epicurean experience, which was served at precisely 5.30 p.m. and to which latecomers were barred. Tradition also dictated that expensive birthday presents were to be delivered several days prior to the event, and the Soyers, mindful of this, duly sent across one of Emma's recent productions, *La Jeune Fermière*, a charming painting of a country girl carrying a wicker basket of chickens to market on her head, which was worth an extremely generous £40. (After Emma's death, when Alexis was frenziedly trying to buy back all her work, he was furious when Ude refused to sell it back – despite his offering him fifty guineas for it.)

This year, however, the dinner turned into a fiasco. The soup – a superb *bisque d'écrevisses* – had scarcely been finished, and the Madeira was still on its first round of the table, when a hapless guest trod on the paw of Vermilion, Madame Ude's favourite pooch, which precipitated not just a quarrel between the host and hostess, but a fight among the dogs, and in turn some vicious bites. Then a pile of valuable plates – bought at auction from the Duke of York's estate – were cracked when the guest carving the joint placed them on a spirit-warmer when stone cold. Finally, a second dog choked on a piece of venison which another guest had secretly thrown under the table to him, and despite Madame Ude's attentions, it later died. The evening was so awful that, in Soyer's eyes at least, it became hilarious, but it took all his wit and charm to cajole Ude back into a good temper.

Soyer shamelessly basked in the praise and attention that his work at the Reform Club was now bringing him. He ironed out the inevitable teething problems that the operation of such a large kitchen involved, he continued to entertain the great and the good in his inner sanctum, and he began another lifelong habit – courting the press, so that a stream of admiring descriptions of his underground kingdom kept his celebrity well stoked. He was so busy at this period that even Emma found him increasingly hard to pin down. So rarely was he home that she took to dropping into the club if she needed to see him. On one occasion, having waited in his office for more than an hour, she became so impatient that she sketched a quick self-portrait on the wall, rang the bell, and told the maid that she couldn't wait any longer. Instead, she said – pointing to the wall – she had left her calling card. When Alexis finally returned he was so pleased with her quick wit that he put a frame around the sketch and a pane of glass over it, turning the joke into a permanent fixture.

Alexis did not confine his sense of fun to the basement. He persuaded the Reform's committee that a fitting reward to the staff for their part in the successful launch would be to turn over the new club house to the servants for one night only, in a sort of variation on the ancient carnival convention of Twelfth Night bringing about playful role reversals. On the last day of Christmas, choristers and church functionaries had traditionally been given the opportunity to mock the liturgy and order the senior clerics around during the Feast of Fools, while in the domestic sphere the inversion of authority saw masters waiting on their servants. Soyer's idea was to substitute for the customary below-stairs Christmas party a grand ball, complete with the finest food *à la Soyer* and a first-rate band, to which the maids, cooks, clerks and waiters could invite their own guests, dress up like the toffs and dance the night away. After some resistance from 'over-nice members' who did not wish to be deprived of their privileges for an evening, the committee agreed, and the date of the ball was fixed for Twelfth Night, 1842. The weeks leading up to it were ones of feverish anticipation, according to Volant, with the female portion of the staff preparing their muslin gowns and headdresses with as much care 'as if each of them were going to be married'.

On the day, the members vacated the club house early, to give the staff plenty of time to decorate the place with evergreen garlands, bowls of flowers and extra lights, to lay the tables and install the bandmaster and his men before going off to dress. 'This ball of course was the gossip of the members of the club,' said Volant, 'and so excited the curiosity of their wives and daughters that, in the course of the evening, carriage after carriage set down parties of ladies with cards of *laissé passé*, to have a peep, and, if possible, criticise the innovation so creditable to the Reformers, thus giving enjoyment to their servants and their friends, altogether about 150 persons.' The festivities only wound up shortly before 4 a.m., when a scuffle broke out between men who had made a little too free with the claret. There are no specific references to the ball to be found in the committee minutes, which has made some historians doubt the veracity of Volant's account. But if it was exaggerated – or even fabricated – then the legend still served to add lustre to the story of Soyer's tenure at the great club.

With life at the Reform Club and Charing Cross Road running smoothly and Emma happily expecting their first child, Alexis began to think of ways to capitalise on his growing reputation and expand his business interests. He was doing well at the club – not only was he on an excellent salary (the *chef de cuisine* bowed only to the club secretary in being the best-paid officer of the establishment) but the club permitted him to take on trainees, or 'improvers', both men and women, who paid a handsome £10 a year each for the privilege of working beside the great man. And of course there were plenty of fringe benefits for a man in his powerful position. However, Alexis wanted to diversify, to investigate the bigger commercial opportunites that were available to him rather than simply rake in the perks of the job. He established a company, A. Soyer & Co., with an office just a few yards from home at No. 5 Charing Cross Road, and his first enterprise was to publish a huge lithograph of the Reform kitchens. The picture, called *The Kitchen Department at the Reform Club*, was commissioned from a young architect called John Tarring, who later became an acclaimed designer of London chapels. It was three feet long and nearly two high, and by a clever demolition of the connecting walls showed a cross-section of the entire kitchen department, with the text underneath detailing the function of each chamber and the new inventions that filled it. To kick-start sales Soyer took subscriptions from club members, charging a guinea for a coloured copy and half a guinea for black and white. There is no evidence that he sought permission from the club committee to exploit their property in this way, but his subscription book still exists in the Reform Club archives, and shows that the members indulged him by ordering plenty of prints and writing complimentary comments in the margins. He even managed to get his lithograph reviewed in *The Spectator*:

> This is a curious print, and unique of its kind: it presents on a large scale a coup-d'oeil of the matchless culinary arrangements of the Reform Club, the various offices for which extend over the whole basement of the building. To show them at one glance, the partition-walls are cut away, and a bird's-eye view is given of the several kitchens, larders, sculleries, and batterie de cuisine: the different functionaries are all at their posts, and the accomplished chef, Monsieur SOYER, is in the act of pointing out to a favoured visitor the various contrivances suggested by his ingenuity and experience. With a plan of the building, there are references to a minute explanatory account of the uses of the multifarious apparatus here exhibited, for the admiration of the scientific gastronome and the envy of rival artistes.

The press interest ensured that the prints also sold well outside the club, and Alexis had soon cleared 1,400 copies at a huge profit. The lithograph continued to sell for many years, and was the first indication of the commercial acuity that would lead to ever more ambitious projects. His first entrepreneurial foray into the business world had proved highly encouraging.

As the culinary reputation of the Reform picked up momentum, Soyer became anxious to ensure that the kitchens provided a supply of hearty but affordable suppers for the less well-off members, as well as more luxurious options for gourmets. He therefore ensured that solid, traditional club dishes for those wanting comfort food rather than haute cuisine were always available. Joseph Hume, the radical former MP for Middlesex, regularly dined off a slice of meat from the main joint for a shilling, and the novelist William Thackeray once broke an important dinner date to stay at the club, seduced by the promise of his favourite boiled bacon and cabbage *à la Soyer*. In July 1842 the committee decided that a full roast supper should be had for as little as 1s 6d, although this rose to two shillings the following year. For the same money you could order lunch from a selection of cold meats, although any extras cost more.

Despite his common sense approach to the problems of large-scale catering, Soyer was not entirely free from the tantrums and affectations traditionally associated with the culinary artist. Who knows to what degree the *Punch* correspondent was exaggerating when he reported: 'We understand that the *Chef de Cuisine* is so extremely sensitive that he had been known to shed tears if a person ordering a basin of mutton broth has asked for the pepper, because the mere demand seems to throw a doubt on M. Soyer's powers of seasoning.' In the same piece another anecdote harnessed recent political events to poke fun at Soyer's already inflated sense of his own importance.

At a recent house-dinner a member of the committee held in his hand the resignation of M. Soyer, which was to have been peremptorily given in if a new arrangement of beef collops had been in the smallest degree objected to. By some this step may have been regarded as unconstitutional; and it is probable that M. Soyer had in his remembrance the extreme step taken by EARL GREY to ensure the passing of the Reform Bill, when he caused it to be given out that he had in his pocket a *carte blanche* for the creation of Peers. The collops, however, on coming to a division, were perfectly successful, and their principle unanimously approved.

In early August the club was visited by Prince Albert's father, Ernest, Duke of Saxe-Coburg. Like most tourists on a visit to London, he was keen for a tour of the Reform's famous culinary department, which Soyer was delighted to host. The men conversed easily in French, and the duke was reported to be impressed, not just with Soyer and the technical brilliance of his kitchen system, but with Emma's work, examples of which lined the walls of Alexis's office. He invited Soyer to join him on the next stage of his journey to Brussels, where he was to visit his brother Leopold, King of the Belgians. Ernest clearly wanted Alexis to entertain as well as cook for him during the passage, and promised to introduce him to Leopold, telling him that as a great connoisseur of art the king would appreciate seeing Emma's paintings. Alexis was thrilled, and although Emma was nearing the end of her pregnancy, she urged him to go. For a grocer's son from Meaux to become a duke's personal travelling companion was exciting enough, but the possibility of gaining royal patronage for Emma's work as well represented a wonderful opportunity. He didn't need much persuading – Emma's confinement was still at least a fortnight away, he could stay with Simonau's brother Pierre in Brussels and, Emma told Volant, her husband was in need of a holiday from the club. He left London with the duke's suite in late August, leaving his wife putting the finishing touches to a new work, *The Organ Boys*.

Two days later, after a run of scorching weather in London, the air pressure intensified and thunderclouds gathered throughout the afternoon, leaving Emma hot and uncomfortable. With just her maid and pet greyhound for company, she left her oils and listlessly amused herself with pencil sketches. When the servant wanted to leave early to go to the theatre, she begged her to stay behind. To compensate her for the missed night out, Emma drew the maid playfully embracing the dog, promising to turn it into a full portrait after her confinement. Then, in an absent-minded doodle, she sketched out a delicate design of her initials entwined in a laurel wreath and surrounding a palette. The storm that finally broke that night was so violent in its intensity that Emma, her husband was later told, was frightened into an early labour. There were complications, help was slow to arrive and, by sunrise, twenty-eight-year-old Emma – and her baby – were dead. Distraught, Simonau immediately summoned Volant for a crisis meeting about how to break the news to Alexis. As he was highly excitable at the best of times, they were genuinely frightened of how he might react if he discovered the truth while alone in a foreign city. In the end they decided to try and delay the full horror of discovery until his return, and sent a carefully worded letter explaining that Emma had been prematurely confined, that mother and child were unwell, and that he should rush back. The next day the men changed their minds, and decided that Volant would go to Brussels ahead of the letter, break the news as gently as possible, and bring him home.

Volant left immediately but, once in Brussels, he had not even reached Pierre Simonau's address before he bumped into Alexis in the street, strolling with another companion towards the house to prepare for dinner. Astonished to see the friend he had only just left in London, Soyer immediately suspected something was wrong, but Volant, trying to parry until he could get Alexis indoors, made up a lame story about having chaperoned two young girls of his acquaintance to a boarding school – 'which will give me the pleasure of going back with you'. The three men walked on in an awkward silence, but Volant's anxious face betrayed him, and before they had gone far Soyer grabbed his arm. 'Now my dear fellow, are you not the messenger of death?' By now they were almost at the house, and Volant, in tears, managed to prevaricate just long enough to get Soyer inside before the chef started to shake him. 'For Heaven's sake, speak; is she dead?' Alexis cried. Volant finally admitted the truth.

'It would be superfluous to describe the state of Alexis's mind,' Volant wrote sixteen years later. 'Suffice to say that he attempted to snatch a knife from the dinner-table, but M. Simonau, his son, and Mr V—, dragged him into the garden, where it took two long hours to bring him to a sense of reason.' As soon as he had calmed down sufficiently the two men set off for Ostend. The speedy packet crossing was helped by fine weather and there were so many people on board who knew Alexis that he was forced to stay calm. By the time the boat train arrived at London Bridge station, where another party of anxious friends were waiting for him on the platform, he was 'a great deal better than could have been anticipated'. More friends had gathered at the house in Charing Cross Road to comfort Simonau, and the reunion was an emotionally draining one; Alexis became inconsolable once again, and it was only with the greatest difficulty that they could prevent him lifting the coffin lid to gaze at Emma and the dead baby.

In spite of his grief, the next morning Soyer began to take practical matters in hand. He paid a hefty £73 for a plot of land at the fashionable new Kensal Green Cemetery and began to sketch out designs for an ostentatious stone monument that was already taking shape in his mind. Three days later, the funeral took place, attended, said Volant, 'by numerous friends and admirers of the deceased lady'. Her artistic legacy brought her some generous obituaries in the morning papers. *The Times* commented on her prolific output, referring to her numerous drawings and sketches as well as her hundreds of finished portraits, and to her critical success both at home and in France.

> No female artist has exceeded this lady as a colourist, and very few artists of the rougher sex have produced portraits so full of character, spirit, and vigour, and that boldness and breadth of light and shadow which constitutes one of the highest triumphs of art. She was exceedingly clever in recognising the character of those who sat to her, so that her portraits convey the mind as well as the features of the sitters, their thoughts and sentiments.

It particularly praised her painting of the two young boys selling lemons, which had recently been engraved by Gérard of Paris for a mezzotint and likened her style to that of the great seventeenth-century Spanish master, Murillo, which she achieved 'without the subserviency of imitation, nor the stiffness of copy'. The anonymous writer was clearly a friend of Alexis's – perhaps young Thackeray, who at thirty-one was just starting to make his name as a freelance journalist, most notably in *Fraser's Magazine* and *Punch*. The last comment certainly betrayed a familiarity with the club – which Thackeray certainly had, having been a member since 1840. 'There are a number of Madame Soyer's paintings at the Reform Club-house,' it concluded, 'which will well repay a visit from those who have a taste for genuine merit and real nature.' But the other papers were generous too. The *Morning Chronicle* claimed she was even more successful in France following the exhibition of the *The Young Israelites*, and *La Revue des Deux Mondes* and *La Capitole* both noted her passing with regret.

Soyer received a flood of sympathetic correspondence from friends, colleagues, former employers and aristocratic admirers. The Duke and Duchess of Cambridge sent an elegant note of condolence, as did the Duchess of Sutherland. The Duke of Saxe-Coburg wrote from his home in Gotha to thank Soyer for sending him a drawing of Emma and some engravings of her portrait of *The Young Israelites*, which he had requested, and to offer his condolences – hoping that time would soften his sorrow over her premature loss. The most generous and practical note, however, was the first, sent to Simonau the day after Emma's death, from Soyer's old friend and master in Twickenham, the plump and cheery Marquess of Ailsa.

To M. Simonau

St Margaret's, 2nd September

Sir, – I very deeply deplore poor M. Soyer's and your loss. If I could render him any service, I should be happy to do so. He is most welcome to come here, and you with him, and stay as long as you please. –

Your most obt. servant.

Ailsa

It was just what Alexis and François needed – a complete break from London, from the demands of the Coffee Room and the management committee, from the house in Charing Cross that was still packed with Emma's paintings and possessions, and from the constant demands of well-meaning but exhausting visitors. The two men accepted immediately and, after securing permission for a lengthy leave of absence from the club, left for the luxurious seclusion of St Margaret's straight after the funeral. They stayed for several weeks, while Alexis, to pass the time and assuage his grief, which was perhaps exacerbated by a sense of guilt that he had not spent enough time with his young bride, worked and reworked his grand design for Emma's memorial. In the event it would take two years and a vast amount of money to complete, and become one of the grandest cemetery monuments in London.

Within a few weeks of the funeral Alexis was back at the club, working harder than ever. Perhaps long hours at Pall Mall seemed preferable to a cheerless hearth and his father-in-law's grief. One of the practical problems left by Emma's death was his lack of a secretary – embarrassed by his lack of education in general and his poor spelling in English in particular, his wife had gradually taken over responsibility for almost all of his correspondence. Faced with a mountain of paperwork and a problem that was not going to go away, Alexis resolved to improve his writing skills and employed a teacher, a Mr Lewis from the Strand, to give him four lessons each week. But his natural impatience, coupled with an already heavy workload, made the process dull and trying, and after a few months he gave up, the only lasting result being a more flamboyant signature. Instead he began to employ secretaries on a regular basis – William Watts, who would stay with him for many years, handled the bulk of the work, while Volant took on any business in French.

By the end of the autumn, Soyer had rallied sufficiently to resume something of his old social life – he even started revisiting the theatres and opera halls of his bachelor days. His old love of pretty dancers and actresses came back too. He had always been attracted to creative and spirited women, and in the theatrical world he could both admire their talent and feel at home in the classless milieu they inhabited – fêted by society for their artistry, financially independent, and yet still, like him, salaried servants when all was said and done. And at thirty-two Soyer was young, handsome, famous and rich enough to be an attractive proposition for almost any of them. Although determined never to marry again, having declared that he could never find another woman like Emma, he was soon distributing his favours widely, or as one friend put it, 'roving like a bee from flower to flower'.

No one particular woman caught his attention for long, however, until one May night in 1844, when he visited one of his favourite theatrical haunts, Her Majesty's in the Haymarket, to see a production of a grand ballet in six scenes, *Ondine*, or *La Naïade*, produced by the French dancer, Jules Perrot. The title role had been created the previous summer for the tiny Italian dancer, Fanny Cerrito, who had captivated the ballet-loving public with her sensational *pas de l'ombre* – an impossibly dainty passage danced in moonlight, in which the ethereal ballerina, to illustrate her character's transition from spirit to mortal, at first tries to seize but then recognises and finally dances with her own shadow. The audience went wild, one witness describing Cerrito's water nymph as 'a delicious creation, with all the loveableness of the woman combined with the airiness of the fairy'. Her performance even inspired a brief fashion trend. In one dream sequence, which Fanny choreographed for herself, four attendant nymphs waved scarves around her, at one point enveloping her in pink gauze, and before long pink scarves 'in Iris or zephyr gauze' were being worn over evening dresses all over London.

While twenty-eight-year-old Cerrito was not a conventional beauty (she had short legs, an ample bust and was plumper than most ballerinas), or even a conventional dancer – instead of belonging to any recognised school, one critic observed, she seemed 'to improvise everything she does' – there was so much youthful strength and exuberance, so much natural grace and beauty to her movements, that she mesmerised every audience she danced for. She could, it seemed, inject heartbreaking pathos or infectious humour into every *jeté*. She had already conquered much of Europe with her vigorous performances before spending two years as prima ballerina at La Scala. In 1840, she had added the English to her admirers after dancing in a short piece called *Une Nuit de Bal* at Her Majesty's. Immediately declaring her one of the most gifted dancers in Europe, the *Morning Post* had raved about her unique style.

Her eccentric movements, rapid as a meteor, with complete abandon and still perfect precision – the long flying intervals betwixt the moments at which she touches the ground, and the marvellous steps she executes in a slanting position – are feats which must be beheld, and which baffle description . . . We never beheld any adept in the choreographic art who evinced more complete forgetfulness of the prying spectators below. Bursts of applause and bursts of laughter followed one another as she swept the stage.

Ondine was revived on 4 May 1844, with Fanny receiving a roaring ovation, like 'a pent-up torrent of greeting and congratulation' wrote one critic, as she slowly appeared in a sea-green costume, rising Venus-like from a shell in the centre of the stage. The same witness stated that she received the protracted applause 'with the innocent air she so prettily assumes upon such occasions, acknowledging the compliments of the house with a meek gravity of manner and half-frightened look which, as she manages it, is indescribably prepossessing and attractive'.

She had put on a little weight since the first production, but her performance, all agreed, was as brilliant as ever, including the magical *pas de l'ombre*. So much so that a sizeable part of that night's audience returned the following Tuesday to watch her again. The next few performances, however, didn't go quite to plan – first of all the lights went out, leaving the stage in darkness while some 'noxious fumes' spread out from the orchestra and stalls, causing much of the audience to start sneezing. The next Saturday it was the turn of the artificial moon to break down just before the *pas de l'ombre*, and when Fanny tried to substitute another dance there was nearly a riot – the audience was not prepared to be fobbed off with a mere tarantella. Perrot had to step forward and apologise for the unexpected '*éclipse complète*', which at least made the front row laugh and defused the tension. All the teething problems were ironed out in time for the 8 June performance, however, when Queen Victoria and Prince Albert brought along, among other guests, Tsar Nicholas I of Russia, who had expressly requested to see *Ondine*. What is not known is exactly which of these few performances was the one that captivated Alexis Soyer, although knowing what a practical joker he was, he would no doubt have relished the disastrous shows as much as the perfect ones. But whichever one he attended, by the end of the evening he felt himself wildly in love again. And this time the relationship with Fanny – in various forms – would continue for the rest of his life.

5

'CHÉRIE, CHÉRIE, CERRITO!'

On 3 July 1846, the Reformers organised what Louis Fagan later described as 'one of the best and most noble entertainments which any club ever gave'. Fagan was perhaps too partisan, but it seems that many of the newspapers concurred, because their lengthy descriptions of the event – a banquet given in honour of Ibrahim Pasha, the Egyptian army commander and conqueror of Syria – all agreed it was of 'consummate splendour'. And despite the banquet's political importance, it was Alexis Soyer's triumphant achievements that, as usual, claimed most of the paragraphs.

Ibrahim Pasha was the son of Mehemet Ali, the warlike Albanian soldier who had declared himself Egypt's hereditary ruler after Napoleon's hasty retreat had left a dangerous power vacuum in the country, and Ibrahim's subsequent military exploits had become as legendary as his father's. More than a decade earlier he had used Ali's armies to seize both Palestine and Syria, and was within marching distance of Constantinople before an Austro-British alliance finally forced him out of Turkey. Despite this earlier action against him, the British had great respect for his leadership. More pertinently, with his eighty-year-old father's mental powers in decline, at the age of fifty-seven Ibrahim was poised to take over as Egypt's regent, and the British government was keen to court him as a potentially valuable ally in the East.

The Pasha's reasons for visiting London were not entirely clear, and his highly publicised trip fell somewhere between a state visit and a private holiday. He was cordially received by Queen Victoria as a royal prince and war hero, and tours and functions were laid on in his honour, while the curious public responded to his charming manners and exotic

Oriental entourage by gathering in large excitable crowds wherever he was expected to appear. Displaying an unflagging energy and enthusiasm to see all things modern and British, the short, stout figure of Ibrahim, with his smiling, smallpox-scarred face, seemed to pop up everywhere. In London he visited most of the major public institutions, including the Horticultural Society's world-famous gardens in Chiswick where Joseph Paxton had begun his dazzling career twenty years earlier. He travelled north by train from Euston to Birmingham, where he bustled through what seemed to the puzzled citizenry like every last button, bed, pen and glass factory, workshop and showroom in the manufacturing district. Then he rushed off on day trips to see Warwick Castle and Leamington Spa.

As he progressed further north – waving to the crowds from his railway carriage – he visited schools, went down coal mines and toured the cotton mills. In Manchester the bemused locals dubbed him 'Abraham Parker' as they followed him around town, spreading scandalous rumours that he had brought five wives with him. But the culmination and great highlight of Ibrahim Pasha's visit to Britain was the grand dinner held for him at the Reform Club in Pall Mall. The invitation had initially been delivered to him in the East, by none other than Rear Admiral Sir Charles Napier, Commander of the Channel Fleet, and the occasion was declared by the club committee, with suitable pomposity, as 'a mark of respect to a stranger, illustrious alike for his talents and his position, and to do special honour to him, for the facilities afforded to the English traffic during the events in Syria and for the improvements which had been effected by him and his father in Egypt'.

More than 150 members attended the banquet, with many more crowding into the building to watch the formalities, and the event stretched the facilities of the new kitchens to full capacity. As the Pasha arrived promptly at ten past seven, attended by the only male non-members allowed into the building – his chargé d'affaires, Consul-General and the Secretary of the Ottoman Empire – they were greeted by a small group led by Sir Charles and Lord Palmerston, while the band of the Scots Fusiliers Guards struck up 'The Sultan's March'. The saloon was already crowded with expectant members, while the surrounding corridor was thronged with their elegantly dressed wives, determined to make the most of a very rare invitation into the club. They took their places in the grand dining room – and at exactly half past seven Napier and Palmerston ceremoniously led his Highness to the seat of honour between them, to the tune of 'The Roast Beef of Old England'. The band then took up their positions at one end of the hall and launched into a selection of 'favourite Turkish airs' for the rest of the marathon banquet. The choice of Turkish airs to serenade their Egyptian guest was rather tactless considering his failed invasion, but he no doubt appreciated the general stab at Orientalism.

On the tables the diners found a menu – to be reproduced in the newspapers the next morning – that was extraordinary in its scale, originality, luxuriousness and complexity. In his basement office Soyer, carefully dressed, coiffed and adorned with the diamond rings that he now sported, had been preparing, with some excitement, to supervise the proceedings above stairs, before being presented, as the magician of the feast, to the Pasha. However, just before setting off he was warned that some of the sous chefs were creating trouble – it is not exactly clear what was going wrong, but a mutiny was the last thing he could afford. Weeks of meticulous planning, not to mention his reputation as an organisational genius, were in danger of serious damage. Furiously, Alexis had to strip off his finery, put his aprons back on and supervise the kitchen staff himself, barking orders and revving up the pace. The flip-side of his geniality was a temper capable of whipping even the most recalcitrant minions into line. In the event, the dinner passed off perfectly.

As the members seated themselves at the tables, they viewed, as the *Illustrated London News* would later describe it, 'a splendid ensemble . . . principally illuminated from silver candelabra arranged along the centre, alternating with vases of the choicest flowers. According to Eastern fashion, the centre of the tables was filled with pipes, grapes, and other choice fruits in profusion.' The meal began, according to custom, with a selection of exquisite soups – considered by all epicures to be the essential, health-giving *apéritifs* of any great dinner. They included consommés such as *Potage à la Victoria*, a delicate veal broth garnished with blanched cockscombs; *Potage à la Colbert*, a vegetable soup flavoured by glazed Jerusalem artichokes laboriously cut into pea-sized balls, and *Potage à la Comte de Paris*, a sherry-coloured, intensely flavoured meat soup filled with macaroni ribbons and delicate chicken quenelles. As the tureens were cleared, and as the noise levels rose to compete with the band, the members moved on to the most delicate dishes, the hot fish. Turbot *à la Mazarin*, lightly poached and served with a delicately beautiful pink cream sauce made with butter and lobster roes; pan-fried trout in a sherry sauce; a pyramid of whitings, deep fried and served *à l'Egyptienne* in tribute to the guest of honour, and wild salmon from the River Severn – which Alexis considered the very best – line caught that morning and brought in on the afternoon train, to be pounced on by the kitchen staff and immediately scraped, gutted, washed and prepared in a simple cream gratin.

Then came the dishes for the main service, carefully arranged on the crisp white damask cloths – two, four or six platters of each item laid out in perfect symmetry. These included a choice of *rôts*, such as young, tender turkeys, no bigger than chickens, their necks skinned but heads left intact, tucked under their wings. There were also hares in a red-currant sauce, capons with watercress, plump white ducklings, spit-roasted and served with the juice of sour bigarade oranges. The first *relevés* were also waiting: an almighty baron of beef; haunches of mutton roasted *à la Soyer* and saddle of lamb *à la Sévigné*, served with veal quenelles, stewed cucumbers and asparagus purée. There were also more elaborate *removes*, such as *Chapons à la Nelson*, a complex dish which involved gluing truffle- and mushroom-stuffed capons into pastry crous-tades shaped like the prow of a ship – complete with sails, portholes and anchor – and fixing them into waves of mashed potatoes. Soyer adored these elaborate culinary trompes l'oeil, and at the same banquet produced for the first time his *Poulardes en Diadem*, this time the pastry croustade resembling a jewelled crown, stuffed with roasted chickens, boiled ox tongues and glazed sweetbreads. He adorned them with *attelettes* – another Soyer innovation – newly commissioned gold and silver skewers with carved tops representing fantastical animals, birds, shells and knights' helmets. The *attelettes*, or *hatelets* as the popular electroplated copies were called, were the equivalent of culinary jewellery, and would be strung with crayfish, truffles and quenelles before being stuck into the dish as the ultimate sparkling garnish.

Never one to pass up a marketing opportunity, Soyer exploited the extensive press coverage that he knew the banquet would garner to launch another of his new inventions, a huge earthenware dish in the shape of a Chinese pagoda, which had one large central well and was surrounded by smaller ones, each covered with an elaborate lid. The design traded on what he had observed of Londoners' current craze for all things Oriental – '*Chinese* quadrilles, *Chinese* fashions, exhibitions furi-ously *Chinese*' – and the idea was simple: the large pot would contain the meat or fish, while the satellite dishes were filled with a range of sauces suitable for it. Alternatively, for less formal occasions, the big pot could house the main dish, and the surrounding ones the vegetables. Heated silver sand was stowed in a secret compartment to keep the food hot.

Alexis was inordinately proud of the design of his cumbersome *plat d'entrée*, which he had had manufactured exclusively for him by George Smith, a potter with a small workshop in Conduit Street, and he was assiduously selling them via the Reform Club.

The next service heralded the *entrées*: spring chickens, lamb, veal, rabbit, ham braised in Madeira, the chef's signature dish – Mutton Cutlets Reform – not to mention pâtés, rissoles, the feather-light vol-au-vents perfected by Carême, curried lobsters, salads and vegetable dishes – peas and green beans in beurre noisette. The *entremets* made their appearance at the second service too, among them elaborate fruit jellies and ices, meringues and charlottes, tarts of praline and apricot, or almond and cherries. But these puddings were merely an overture to the extraordinary confections that followed, the *pièces montées* with which Soyer sought to show off his design flair and skills in the ancient and dying art of the decorative *pâtissier*. One of the most admired of these dishes was the *Gâteau Britannique à l'Admiral* – placed in front of and in honour of the chairman, Lord Napier. This cake took the form of a huge man-of-war flying both the English and Egyptian flags. The hold was filled with a cargo of iced peach mousse and fresh fruit, and Napier was called on to do the honours and serve the Pasha. The performance amused Ibrahim, reported Fagan, because 'as the ice in this unique preparation melted it absorbed the solid-seeming hull of the man-of-war, which indeed was constructed of nothing stronger than sponge cake. As the gallant sailor was in the act of helping the remainder of the ice, the vessel collapsed into a wreck – to the company's lively amusement.'

Even more of a conversation-stopper than the ship, the star of Soyer's menu was his greatest creation to date, *La Crème d'Égypte à l'Ibrahim Pasha*, which was clearly influenced by – and could easily match – the famous sugar confections produced by the great Carême himself and invented expressly for the occasion. A detailed description was published in the *Morning Post*. 'The dish consisted of a pyramid about two and a half feet high, made of light meringue cake, in imitation of solid stones, surrounded with grapes and other fruits, but representing only the three angles of the pyramid through sheets of waved sugar, to show, to the greatest advantage, an elegant cream *à l'ananas*, on the summit of which stood a likeness of Mehemet Ali, drawn on a round-shaped satin *carton*, the exact size of the top of the cream.'

'Soyer's novel production challenged the admiration of the whole company, and especially of the Pasha, who certainly felt flattered by the attentions of the chef,' wrote Fagan. The portrait was immediately recognised by the Pasha, who picked it up, and, 'after showing it to several of his suite, placed it in his bosom'. Then 'Ibrahim's next surprise was when he perceived under a glass a highly finished portrait of himself, inclosed in a frame. Soyer having been sent for by the party, was highly complimented by the guest, who expressed himself anxious to know how such a perfect likeness of his father had been produced, and how his own was so correctly drawn in the cream.' Alexis was delighted to explain that they had been copied from some drawings done by Horace Vernet in Alexandria. The head on the cream was delineated on wafer-paper, which, being placed on the damp jelly representing the glass, dissolved, so that nothing remained of the paper but the appearance of the water-colour drawing. The imitation of the gilt frame was made with *eau-de-vie* of Dantzic and gold water mixed with jelly, the gold leaf of which formed the frame. Seeing the Pasha's delight in the art work, no one dared to cut into it, and so 'although as good for food as it was pleasant to the eye, this *chef d'oeuvre* of Soyer's art remained untouched until the end of the banquet'.

Finally, the soiled tablecloths were removed altogether, and only the greasy wine glasses and the silver *épergnes* remained in front of the replete and half-cut diners. A party of professional glee singers, led by the appropriately named Mr Jolly, sang grace – in this instance William Byrd's elegant choral piece, '*Non nobis Domine*' – as a way of winding up the culinary part of the evening before the speeches. These were led by the chairman, who called on the company to refill their glasses with large Irish bumpers before proposing the usual loyal toasts – Victoria, then Albert, then the Prince of Wales and the rest of the royal family – which were loudly cheered. Then Napier proposed the toast of the evening – 'The health of Ibrahim Pasha, and prosperity to Egypt!' – which called for much more glass filling. Napier went on to praise Ibrahim's gallantry in wartime and leadership in peacetime, concentrating on his achieve-ments for Egypt but also his benign governership of Syria, in which he had promoted agricultural reform and patronised the arts, and thanked him and his father for their honourable treatment of all Englishmen in Egypt throughout the last war. Again, this called for the glasses to be raised in a toast of 'three times three', and after a suitable return of thanks from the Pasha, via his interpreter Mr Nubar, Lord Palmerston – who as foreign secretary in the 1830s had forged the Austro-British alliance that had forced Ibrahim's troops out of Turkey – rose to propose yet another toast. This one, with all past grievances put aside, was for the Pasha's father, and to the future of British interests in Egypt, which again was toasted three times by the increasingly voluble guests. (So many glasses and plates were smashed by the drunken members during the evening that one of Alexis's friends sent him some comic doggerel verses about the event entitled 'The Fall of China'.) The toasts, speeches and cheers carried on and on until the Pasha, no doubt exhausted, retired to the drawing room for coffee, where, in a very unusual move, several of the ladies were presented to him. He left shortly after 11 p.m., after ensuring that Mr Nubar communicated his obligations to the club for the magnificent entertainment they had given him.

The banquet for Ibrahim Pasha, while one of many that Alexis created during his club career, was probably his finest hour at the Reform. 'The repast was most sumptuous, and did the highest credit to the skill and taste of M. Soyer, the *chef de cuisine*,' said the *Illustrated London News*. *The Globe* went further, declaring, albeit with its tongue firmly in its cheek, that 'The impression grows on us that the man of his age is neither Sir Robert Peel, nor Lord John Russell, nor even Ibrahim Pasha, but Alexis Soyer.'

While such culinary triumphs enhanced Soyer's reputation and cemented his career at the Reform, his love life was not prospering. A year before the Ibrahim Pasha banquet, his great love Fanny Cerrito had devastated him by marrying another artiste: the brilliant violinist, dancer and choreographer, Arthur St-Léon. Since he had first seen Cerrito on stage in the summer of 1844, Soyer had been utterly captivated by her exuberance and beauty. He took every opportunity to see her perform, and wooed her with his usual blend of persistence, extravagant praise and bad poetry. Cerrito had all the artistic talent and temperament that Alexis adored in women, and while she made it clear that Alexis was far from her only suitor, Fanny was clearly flattered by the attentions of this famous and handsome young widower. At thirty-four Alexis was a decent catch for the twenty-eight-year-old Fanny, and as a pair of hard-working, ambitious and talented foreigners busy sustaining high-profile careers in London, they had much in common.

Fanny Cerrito was in fact one of the few women in London who could, in her own right, match Alexis in every department. She was as successful as he was – more so, as her talents were being fêted right across Europe, her triumphant performances earning rapturous reviews wherever she danced. She was also earning a fortune – at the peak of her career, and with all the major opera houses desperate to secure her services, she could virtually name her price. Three years earlier she had broken all records by securing the highest salary ever offered to a dancer – 20,000 florins, around £2,000, for the winter season at the Karnth-nerthor Theatre in Vienna, plus four exclusive benefit performances. Following a long-standing theatrical tradition, she was also stockpiling a valuable collection of jewels, sent – often anonymously – by the wealthy admirers who packed the 'omnibus boxes' that flanked each side of the stage. Unlike Alexis, who spent lavishly and showed little financial prudence, Fanny was shrewd with money and, knowing the brevity of a dancer's career, was determined to secure her future. While it was her pushy father, Raffaele Cerrito, who officially negotiated her contracts, Fanny's input was considerable and she wasn't averse to using her feminine wiles to parry for better deals. So much so that in 1845 Alfred Bunn, the manager of Drury Lane, who had been trying, unsuccess-fully, to secure her services for years, complained bitterly that Fanny was 'forever coquetting with one manager to exact higher terms from another'.

Physically, Fanny's unconventional beauty derived as much from her extraordinary strength and energy as from her features. She was fair-haired and blue-eyed, and while some found her face a little heavy-featured, there were plenty of others ready to concede its loveliness. Her lack of height was compensated for by her voluptuous figure; her full bust and plump arms were considered of 'rare beauty' and although the *Morning Post* once rudely commented that her body 'was not quite of the de Medici elegance in its lower extremities', other critics praised her shapely legs. The most detailed description of her appearance came from a French poet and novelist, the scarlet-waistcoated dandy Théophile Gautier, who as theatre critic of *La Presse* submitted a lengthy piece about the dancer in July 1846.

La Cerrito is blonde: she has very gentle and tender blue eyes, and a pleasant smile which is possibly a little too much in evidence. Her shoulders and bust have none of that skinniness which characterises those *danseuses*, all the substance of whose body seems to have sunk into their legs. Her rounded and well-covered arms do not offend the eye with sad anatomical details, and they unfold with grace and flexibility. Her charming figure gives no hint of the fatigue of the classroom or the sweat of training. She might be a young girl who only yesterday was snatched from her family and pushed on to the stage. Her foot is small, well arched, the ankle delicate, and the leg well shaped. Her only shortcoming – whether this be an illusion caused by her belt being fixed too low, or whether her body is really a little too long – being that her figure is divided by the waist into two perfectly equal halves, which offends the rules of human proportion and is particularly unfavourable to a dancer. In short, all in all she is young and attractive, and makes a good impression.

It is interesting that to Gautier – as to many others – Cerrito still gave the impression of being a young girl, when in fact at that point she was almost thirty. This girlishness was something that Fanny had deliberately cultivated and valued highly, indeed from the age of seventeen she had consistently lied about her age – first subtracting two years and later on four – a deception she got away with by dint of her tiny frame and coquettish manner. She perfected what one perceptive witness identified as a 'sly humility', whereby she would look shocked and almost frightened by the rapturous receptions she received while blushing prettily, a display which was entirely contrived but seemed to drive the men wild. She exploited her sex appeal further by displaying her legs in daringly short costumes whenever possible, and was particularly fond of showing off her generous bosom. After her London début in 1840 the *Morning Herald* sniggered about her 'contempt for the superfluity' of cloth and some years later, when Fanny was performing *Giselle* in St Petersburg, the dowager empress was moved to comment that the Italian ballerina seemed 'slightly addicted to abbreviated drapery', a hint which resulted in Fanny having two tucks let out of her costume.

This tendency to showiness in dress delighted Alexis, of course, who, inspired by the achingly fashionable Count d'Orsay, whom he called 'the *arbiter elegantinum* of our day', rejoiced in increasingly dandyish costumes himself. Since Emma's death Alexis's penchant for extravagantly colourful clothes had grown rather than diminished, and he had begun to spend quite considerable sums at the tailors. He developed a trademark look that involved having all his garments cut on the bias – 'à la zougzoug', as he called it – giving each ensemble a bizarre, lopsided appearance. Even his hats were made to sit at a slant on his head, his cigar case and the handle of his cane were obliquely slanted, and his business cards were die-cut into parallelograms. (The cards read 'Alexis Soyer, London, Paris' – although there is no evidence that he was keeping a flat in Paris at the time.) Given Fanny's penchant for risqué outfits, the couple must have made quite a sight when they went out together. They were both vivacious companions and incorrigible flirts, but most importantly, Alexis relished Fanny's intelligence and humour – like him, she was quick-witted and sharp. She loved food and fancied herself as something of a gourmet, although her career and easy tendency to put on weight made her cautious about her diet. She also drank wine, although not excessively, and Alexis loved to provide her with excellent vintages to sample.

Alexis was also good-humoured and relaxed enough to indulge Fanny in some of the less appealing aspects of her artistic temperament. She could be vain, impatient, imperious to the point of arrogance, sometimes insecure, and unswervingly jealous of her main rivals, the equally brilliant – and significantly more experienced – prima ballerinas Marie Taglioni and Fanny Elssler. Capricious outbursts were frequent and often petty, when she imagined (wrongly) that other ballerinas were being given precedence over her. Once, after smarting for days at some negligible privilege given to Taglioni by the management of Her Majesty's, Fanny returned a complimentary ticket for an upper-tier box when she realised she would be seated near to the older dancer, declaring cheekily that she was 'much too young to be exalted to the skies before her proper time'. On another occasion she refused a second curtain call when she thought Fanny Elssler had received more bouquets. Most strikingly, she made a point of 'taking on' her rivals by appearing in the very roles they had just triumphed in, often only a few days after their last appearance. It was a brave and reckless policy, and while, critically speaking, she didn't always come off best, it certainly worked in terms of creating controversy in the press and keeping her name on everyone's lips.

The apogee of this manufactured rivalry had come in 1843, when both Fanny and Marie Taglioni were engaged for the Carnival season at La Scala, Milan. Ballet fever had swept through the city and the Milanese quickly divided into 'Cerritisti' and 'Taglinisti', each determined to prove the supremacy of their favourite dancer. As one newspaper reported: 'Discussion of ballets and ballerinas has now become a matter of state, and little more is needed to make it the fashion to pirouette and dance in the street. Whether you are reading your newspaper, taking your soup, drinking your coffee, or refreshing yourself with ice-cream, the gauntlet of challenge is cast at your feet.' The ballerinas occasionally shared the bill but generally danced on alternate nights, and the contest was a close one, judging by the critical reception of each performance, the wild enthusiasm of the audience and the number of bouquets that were flung onto the stage. The final dance-off came at the tail end of the season, on 20 March. The crowd were in good spirits after the programme opened with a superb performance of the opera *I Lombardi*, and the composer, Giuseppe Verdi, was called up for a rapturous curtain call. But the ballet was the main event of the night – and Fanny was the first to dance, followed by Taglioni. Both performed brilliantly. By the time the audience let them go it was almost three in the morning and, as they had each received storming ovations, had to concede a draw. At Fanny's final performance two days later, it was reported that the final curtain call garnered a total of 836 garlands and 1,494 bouquets, one of which contained no fewer than 2,576 camellias. Even Fanny's ego had been sated and by the time she reached London that May, the news of her Italian triumph had preceded her, adding to the excitement of her return – and the box office receipts at Her Majesty's.

By the early 1840s, speculation about Fanny's virtue and marriage-ability had already been rumbling on for years. Her beauty and talent had assured her plenty of admirers among the aristocratic men who filled the expensive boxes on either side of the stage. At this time it was customary for some of these privileged patrons to be allowed backstage in the interval between the opera and the ballet, where, on the lookout to recruit fresh mistresses, they would flirt with the prettiest artistes. Fanny's infatuates at various times included the Duke of Beaufort, the Earl of Cardigan, Prince Paul Esterhazy, Louis Bonaparte and even Ibrahim Pasha – who called her 'the Sultana of the Beautiful Eyes' and asked her to accompany him back to Egypt. But Fanny was determined not to join the crowded ranks of kept women. Although she was a flirt she seems to have resisted any affairs so far, and while happy enough to distribute her favours platonically – to Alexis and to others – for anything more she was holding out for marriage.

At the height of her popularity in 1842, the papers had been full of inaccurate rumours of a forthcoming marriage. In August a scandal sheet called the *Satirist* reported that twenty-six-year-old Fanny was 'meditating matrimony', and that 'if the prominent nose and greasy black hair of the *inamorato* are to be trusted, with a loving countryman of her own. All happiness to the lively little Neapolitan who has so cleverly thrown dust in the eyes of the old *roués* of the omnibus!' Yet just a week later the same paper was predicting a match with an Englishman called Medhurst, which it claimed would be 'the unkindest cut of all' to certain of her admirers. The following year, the paper finally hit on the man who would eventually prove successful – Arthur St-Léon – a twenty-two-year-old Frenchman whom Cerrito had already danced with on a number of occasions. St-Léon was certainly an extraordinary talent. The son of a well-respected dancer and director of fight scenes at the Paris Opéra,

Arthur had been something of a musical prodigy. Having studied with Mayseder and Paganini he gave his first professional performance as a violinist at the age of thirteen, and the following year he débuted as a dancer, executing an exquisite *pas de deux* in the German ballet *Die Reisende Ballet-Gesellschaft*. He was also a gifted choreographer, and on occasion he combined all three disciplines – in his ballet *Le Violon de Diable* he managed to accompany himself on the violin as he danced his own steps. As a choreographer St-Léon would go on to create *Coppélia*, still the most frequently performed ballet in the world, and to invent the first system of dance notation, but in 1841, when he met Fanny Cerrito, he was still establishing himself as a leading character dancer and concert violinist, with regular tours all over Europe.

St-Léon and Cerrito had danced together several times before St-Léon's London début in 1843, but it was during that season that their dancing partnership had really taken off. St-Léon had been an immediate hit, and *The Times*, reviewing his performance, called his dancing 'the sport of a young Hercules . . . so amazing were his tours de force that he at once won the acclaim of a public which in general abhorred the presence of male dancers.' More importantly, the exuberant energy of his style had proved an ideal complement to Cerrito's. When *The Times* concluded that 'the vigour . . . he exhibits, the immensity of his pirouettes and other feats seem to mark him as the founder of an entirely new style of dancing', they could have been talking of Fanny. Three weeks after St-Léon's London début Fanny danced in a benefit performance for him, and soon afterwards they were paired in a triumphant revival of the ballet *Alma*.

Before long the couple were an established dance partnership, and although an off-stage friendship had blossomed, when their marriage was announced, Alexis was not the only one to be shocked. The more cynical elements of the press detected a hint that Cerrito had only deigned to accept St-Léon after abandoning hope of a more socially elevated suitor. 'It appears she has found to her cost,' sniped one report, 'that the omnibus cads only pay in bouquets.' In fact there was some truth in the suggestion that Fanny had been holding out for a more illustrious husband – or at least her parents had. Raffaele and Marianna Cerrito, with little understanding of the English social scene, had spent years labouring under the delusion that Fanny would one day marry one of her high-born suitors. At first they had moved to quash the St-Léon rumour, insisting that Fanny would continue her career for several more years, after which she would have accumulated a substantial fortune and could marry anyone she wished, 'an artiste only excepted'. Such a snooty put-down of St-Léon was hardly appropriate from the Cerritos – after all Raffaele was only a soldier, hardly a major step up from a dancer. But the ambitious Cerritos clearly thought no match too ambitious for their daughter.

'Captain' Raffaele Cerrito was in fact a retired second-lieutenant from Napoleon's hastily recruited revolutionary Italian army and a man whom one newspaper editor described, when a young man, as having 'a forthright manner, short-cut hair, bush moustache, and soldierly bearing'. Fanny, born on 11 March 1817, was the Cerritos' second child, Marianna having given birth to a son, Joseph, two years earlier. The family home was a humble house on the Pedamentina San Martino, a narrow alleyway leading up to a large monastery high above the bay of Naples. While no prodigy, Fanny – christened Francesca Teresa Giuseppa Raffaela – had loved to dance as soon as she could stand upright, and early on fixed her sights on a career as a dancer. By all accounts she was impatient and strong-willed even as a child, and hated being disciplined, but she had flexibility, energy and grace, and by sheer perseverance convinced her parents that ballet was her vocation. From then on they poured money into her classes until she was accepted as a pupil at the renowned School of the Royal Theatres in the centre of Naples. By the age of fifteen, such was her progress that she not only graduated early but skipped all the ranks of the *corps de ballet*, and made her début as principal ballerina in a comic ballet called *L'Oroscopo* at the Teatro del Fondo in July 1832.

The critics immediately applauded the originality and singularly energetic style of '*la volupte ingénue*', and from then on the Cerritos embarked upon a peripatetic life, accompanying Fanny as she travelled around Europe to fulfil increasingly lucrative engagements. They made an embarrassing entourage – Marianna was an ill-educated nag 'with little grammar, no talent, and an untiring tongue' according to the American journalist Charles Rosenberg. But Cerrito *père* was even worse. Initially the family had hired an agent called Benelli to negotiate Fanny's contracts, but soon Raffaele took over himself – he liked to control the money and fancied himself a shrewd manager. In reality he was more of a liability, the worst sort of show-business parent, constantly demanding more money and more concessions for the daughter he termed '*La Divinità*'. The theatre managers dreaded having to deal with him, considering him nothing more than a greedy, ignorant hanger-on, but Raffaele insisted on chaperoning Fanny to the theatre each night before pretentiously declaring after each curtain call that '*Nous* avons dansé magnifiquement ce soir.' He also courted the critics for good reviews and was not above dangling his daughter before any love-struck writer who might put his pen at her service. Peter Borthwick, who wrote for the *Court Journal,* found himself a victim of this ruse when he realised that all of his many invitations to visit Fanny at home had come not from the charming girl herself but her meddling father. When he left the *Journal* he also got his marching orders from Captain Cerrito, on whom, one friend reported, Borthwick later 'vented his spleen in unmeasured abuse'.

Despite her humble background and awkward relations Fanny seems to have been accorded a slightly higher measure of respectability than most dancers of her day, probably because of her refusal to become a society mistress. Unlike Marie Taglioni or Carlotta Grisi she was regularly admitted into English polite society, and was even befriended by aristocratic women such as Jane Saunders, the Countess of Westmorland. Many years later Lady Dorothy Nevill, the political hostess and horticulturist, would write in her *Reminiscences* that 'Taglioni . . . was not generally received. Cerrito, however, I perfectly well recollect seeing at Mr Long's, at whose house in Grafton Street one used to meet all sorts of clever and interesting people, for he had the especial gift of collecting together notabilities of every sort. I was introduced to this famous dancer, who looked very pretty and demure and made an excellent impression upon everyone.'

And so Fanny, like Alexis, inhabited that strange social limbo reserved for the Victorian celebrity – their talent and conversational skills affording them entry into some of the most elevated circles, but only on the unspoken assumption that it was not quite on an equal footing with the other guests. They had to understand they were being welcomed only for their novelty and entertainment value. His celebrity, economic independence and public life meant that Fanny was not subject to many of the middle-class restrictions that had impeded Alexis's early courtship of Emma, and the two could see each other regularly. While Raffaele and Marianna immediately made it clear that Soyer – a mere cook – was as unwelcome a candidate for their precious daughter's hand as St-Léon, Fanny, who grew more pragmatic about her marriage prospects as she entered her late twenties and was, in any case, strongly drawn to Alexis, was more receptive to his advances. It was true that she had once told a journalist bluntly that when she married she expected her husband to be able to maintain her, rather than to support him, but she lacked the social ambitions of her parents, and so Alexis fitted the bill perfectly.

Alexis had introduced Fanny to Simonau soon after that rapturous first night in May, and the two got on well, so much so that by the following summer Alexis and his father-in-law had persuaded her to sit for a portrait. Fanny's English was still poor but her French was improving rapidly, and the relationship was easy and informal enough for Fanny to feel comfortable turning up for sittings in the large dishevelled flat the two men now shared in Leicester Square, and where Simonau preferred to work if he could avoid travelling to his clients' homes. These quarters were described by Volant as 'covered with pictures by poor Emma Jones', the main studio being 'a mixture of something of everything – works of art, old china, bronzes, old furniture, pictures, and drawings; besides, the bed was not made up, a feather-bed and mattress lying on the floor, and on a beautiful drawing room table lay carrots, onions, leeks, and cabbages, *pele-mele* with the scrap of mutton the servant was getting ready'. What Fanny must have thought of this mausoleum is not recorded. It was not that the widowers could not afford better lodgings, but they were busy men, and without their wives the domestic niceties had been neglected. After Emma's death, Soyer would never again set up a conventional household.

In the event Simonau produced one of the best of the many wonderful portraits painted of Fanny Cerrito, in which he toned down the ballerina's heavy brows, gave her an elegant white neck, rosebud lips and a serene gaze. She wears a ruched white gown and richly embroidered shawl and is proudly seated beside the trophies of her recent triumphant winter season in Rome. There are some specially struck commemorative medals, and a gold coronet, made by the jeweller Serretti and set with a huge central emerald flanked by two large rubies, each of the gems surrounded by diamonds. The crown, said to be worth more than 500 scudi, was commissioned by a group of admiring noblemen who had watched her perform from the proscenium boxes of the Teatro Alibert, and presented to her on her last night. The love-struck Soyer haunted the studio during Fanny's sittings, trying to distract her with a stream of jokes and poems and outrageous compliments, and if the scene reminded Simonau of when, eight years earlier, the exuberant chef had wooed his dead stepdaughter, he declined to comment on it. Alexis was so thrilled with the finished painting that he paid for it to be lithographed, although it seems he stopped short of trying to sell copies of it, as he had the one of the Reform Club kitchens.

As part of his campaign of courtship Alexis also began writing a comic ballet for Fanny. He called it *La Fille de l'Orage* – The Daughter of the

Storm – and dedicated it 'without permission to she who is universally *chérie, chérie Cerrito!*' Less a ballet than a satirical pastiche of the melodramatic scenarios that were dominating the London stages at the time, it parodied the excesses and artificialities of these dances and was filled with spirits, gods, storms, and all the ludicrous special effects associated with the romantic ballet. He preceded it with an introduction in which the writer imagines Cerrito moved to tears by reading the plot. There is even an imaginary opening performance, in which the ballet is received with catcalls and demands from the audience for their money back, until the author, driven insane by failure, is carried off to Bedlam. Soyer calls his author the 'amateur' but clearly identifies himself through a description of his gaily coloured trousers, of '*couleurs mirobolantes*'. It is possible that Soyer asked his friend Thackeray to read through the work before presenting it to Fanny, for a few years later, when Alexis appeared in Thackeray's novel *Pendennis* as the thinly disguised French chef, the novelist had given his excitable character the name of M. Mirobolant.

However, even with Thackeray's editorial input, *La Fille de l'Orage* was a pretty terrible piece of work. The dialogue was lively enough and there were plenty of humorous flourishes, but it was also full of weak jokes and appalling puns, and the dance itself, as Volant tactfully put it, was 'replete with choreographic difficulties and not entirely suited to the London boards'. Of course Alexis never seriously intended it to be staged, he just wanted to entertain Fanny and stand out from the other backstage Johnnies who wooed her with more conventional offerings. It read like a conversation – which is hardly surprising as Soyer probably dictated it – and was full of in-jokes. The rival suitor (clearly St-Léon) was characterised as 'a very small man, though a very great dancer' who kept clamouring for a part ('*tragique, tragique pour moi*'), and Fanny's mother as a domestic drudge obsessed with dinner ('Six o'clock, don't be late . . . I'll do that Italian dish I promised you'). Despite its insularity, however, Soyer was clearly proud enough of his first literary labour to include it in his first book, *Délassements Culinaires*, which was published the following year.

Alexis also found other inventive ways of courting Fanny. He created a new dish for her, *Cerito's* [sic] *Sultane Sylphe à la Fille de l'Orage*, a huge conical meringue and ice cream confection topped with one of his new silver *attelettes*, this one with the stick designed *à la zoug-zoug* (of course) and topped by a dainty ballerina. Cerrito had had a dish named after her before; a chef in Rome had created the *Bomba alla Cerrito* following her début in the city, but that one had turned out to be a bit of a disappointment. It looked wonderful, like an ostrich's egg with the head of a bird emerging from it, but on closer inspection it proved to be nothing more exotic than a ball of rice surrounding the body of a thrush.

In September, when Emma's elaborate and extremely expensive memorial was finally ready, it was Fanny who accompanied Alexis to the inauguration ceremony. This was an impressive affair, as befitting such an ostentatious monument, and for decades to come the massive stone figure of Faith, rising twenty-one feet from the ground and carved by the renowned Pierre Puyenbroeck of Brussels, a court sculptor, was the grandest monument in Kensal Green cemetery. 'It consists,' wrote Volant, 'of a pedestal about twelve feet in height, surmounted by a colossal figure of Faith, with her right hand pointing towards heaven, and the left supporting a golden cross. At her feet, lightly floating upon clouds, are two cherubim, the one holding a crown over the head of, and the other presenting a palm to, the deceased, who is represented on a beautiful medallion executed in white marble, and surrounded by the emblem of eternity.' The image of Emma on the medallion was a portrait by Simonau, and beneath it was a carving of a palette and brushes, surrounded by laurels and topped by her initials, taken from the sketch she had made the morning before her death. Also at Faith's feet Soyer created, with typical ingenuity, an eternal flame, the gas flue neatly hidden behind a cherub's head. To surround this funereal extravaganza Alexis had employed William Rogers, 'a great artist in wood carving', to design and build an elaborate railing, a great swirling mass of branches with the word 'Soyer' etched into the thickest bough.

The artist and journalist George Augustus Sala, who with the Marquess of Ailsa and many of Soyer's other friends and patrons attended the service, remembering the affair in his autobiography, was unsure whether it was Douglas Jerrold, Thackeray or Monckton Milnes who had suggested the epitaph *Soyez Tranquille*. But for once in his life Alexis was not amused by a bad pun, and opted instead for a complete contrast to the splendour of the monument itself by choosing the simple, touching inscription, TO HER. However, Alexis was rarely able to leave anything alone, and twelve years afterwards, having been told by the chaplain of the cemetery that the surname Soyer made people assume she was French, added the words: 'England gave her birth; genius immortality.' Alexis had spent an astonishing £500 on the monument, not to mention the £46 he had had to pay for the two adjacent plots of ground he had needed to build it on, it had taken two years to complete, and now he was determined that the service would dignify the memory of his late wife.

It is therefore extraordinary, even by Soyer's often dubious standards of taste, that he arranged for his current girlfriend to play a key part in the ceremony, by laying a funeral wreath upon the pedestal. The wreath was made up from a laurel chaplet, which had been placed on Fanny's head by the Archduke of Austria on the stage of La Scala, and after the unveiling, Soyer had the wreath placed, along with Emma's palette, in a shallow display case carved into the back of the monument and covered over with glass. The *Morning Post* alone picked up on the dancer's presence: 'Amongst the parties present at the inauguration we perceived the fair Cerito, bestowing upon the shrine of her sister artist a wreath *funéraire*, made from a crown placed upon her head in La Scala, at Milan, before several thousands of her country people. Such feeling impressed all with the highest respect for that fairy child of Terpsichore, and deserves a distinguished place in the history of art.'

Straight after the ceremony Fanny left London and headed south for some engagements in Bath, Bristol and Brighton, before embarking on another tour of Italy. She travelled with her family, as usual, two supporting ballerinas and St-Léon, who as well as partnering Fanny had lined up some violin recitals. In fact on this trip it was his solo performances that attracted much of the praise, the *Brighton Herald* reporting that he had an 'exquisite delicacy of touch' and could make his instrument 'do everything, and then more, to assuage the thirst for harmony which evidently inspires him'. Alexis, perhaps on a whim, perhaps overcome with jealousy at St-Léon's increasing importance to Fanny, perhaps determined to persuade the Cerrito parents of his seriousness, decided to follow the party down to Brighton. He took 'some very acceptable presents', but received a frosty welcome from Marianna Cerrito and, ultimately, a final rejection of his proposal from Fanny.

Whether Fanny's parents had to pressure her into turning Alexis down is not known, although she was still very much under their influence. What is likely is that the commercially driven Raffaele had realised what a uniquely strong artistic – and therefore money-spinning – partnership Fanny and Arthur made together, and it was this that eventually persuaded him to promote the match. As the Cerrito–St-Léon bandwagon progressed through Bologna to Rome, it had become clear that together they made an unbeatable team, and that theatre managers would be prepared to pay virtually anything to secure their services. Houses were packed, and critics and audiences were united in their enthusiasm.

By the time the party reached Venice, Fanny had accepted St-Léon. They married on 17 April 1845, near the home of the groom's parents in Les Batignolles, Paris, and in contrast to Alexis's quiet wedding eight years earlier, Raffaele ensured that it was a splendid affair. 'Never, indeed, was a theatrical union more fashionably attended,' wrote one correspondent. 'The *acte de mariage* bore the names of some distinguished persons as witnesses . . . [and] a splendid banquet followed the ceremonies.'

Just how far Fanny's parents had influenced her choice of husband is impossible to say, but whatever enthusiasm the bride and groom had once had for the marriage quickly waned, and the union was a miserable one. Possibly sensing potential problems even at the outset, and feeling the need to protect her money from falling into St-Léon's hands, Fanny had turned her considerable fortune over to her parents, which already included an estate near Venice that alone produced an income of 6,000 francs a year. She kept only her jewellery. As for her friendship with Alexis, even her marriage did not end the relationship. Although they would often spend long periods apart, Soyer remained constant in his devotion to Cerrito, and she would remain a fixed, albeit secretive, presence in his life.

6

'COOK AND DRESS TEN EARS . . .'

Alexis's first excursion into the world of letters was hardly promising. In early 1845 Jeffs of Burlington Arcade had published, in French, *Délassements Culinaires*, a three-shilling collection of poems, novelettes and reflections on English life. It included a fantasy dream sequence called *Le Rêve d'un Gourmet*, the execrable *La Fille de l'Orage* and an eccentric essay on foot-binding and other Chinese traditions that masked a lengthy plug for his *Plat Pagodatique*. He was proudest, however, of a horribly sycophantic piece, *La Crème de la Grande Bretagne*, written in the form of a mock recipe, which contrived to mention almost all of his female patrons via a list of ingredients which included 'a Smile from the Duchess of Sutherland, a Mite of Gold from Miss Coutts, a Figment from the Work of Lady Blessington, a Ministerial Secret from Lady Peel, Piquante Observations of the Marchioness of Londonderry, and a gentle shower of Reign from Her Most Gracious Majesty'.

Soyer sent review copies of *Délassements Culinaires* to his friends in the press and achieved some reasonable reviews in *The Spectator* and *The Times* – one critic considered it a decent blend of 'poetry, pastry and politics'. However, the initial print run of 250 copies did not sell out and there was to be no second edition – nonetheless, as late as 1852 Alexis was still claiming that one would be appearing 'shortly'. (Jeffs did eventually persevere with a reprint of *La Crème de la Grande Bretagne*, which was made available in both French and English for a more modest one shilling and sixpence.) The failure of his first book had not put Alexis off the publishing world; on the contrary it had shown him that you did not have to be a literary scholar to write a book. In fact you did not need to write at all if you had a crack team of researchers and secretaries to shape your ideas for you. All you needed was the right concept and the renown and drive to promote it. Freed from the daily grind in the kitchens – his carefully drilled team could now easily handle the day-to-day requirements, with Alexis merely supervising important dinners between six and eight in the evening, and showing around the most distinguished guests – Soyer was ready for a new commercial project. He wanted something to enhance his reputation beyond the club, and to mark him out as, if not an equal to those he cooked for, then at least something more than a servant. He also needed a distraction from the distressing news of Fanny's marriage that April.

Naturally enough, friends had long been encouraging him to cash in on his growing reputation by revealing some of his secrets in a cook book, and although he later claimed to have resolved that his 'few ideas, whether culinary or domestic' should never encumber a library, of course in truth he loved the idea of putting his recipes and opinions into print for the education and edification of householders and their domestic staff. What was more, he could see the commercial potential of such an enterprise, as cook books were enjoying a period of heightened popularity. This was principally owing to the success of a middle-aged Suffolk spinster called Eliza Acton, whose pithily titled volume, *Modern Cookery in All Its Branches: Reduced to a System of Easy Practice, for the Use of Private Families*, had just appeared to huge acclaim, and become a national bestseller within a few weeks of publication. Cookery books had been published in England since the fourteenth century, but it was Acton's *Modern Cookery* that took the genre to new heights, with its comprehensive scope and unprecedented accuracy.

A stream of domestic manuals and recipe collections had been produced since the middle of the 1830s, designed to assist the burgeoning middle-class population – or at least their cooks – to provide better-quality meals, whether for private dining or when entertaining guests. Dinner parties as a recreational activity were increasingly *de rigueur*. They gave hosts the opportunity to impress their guests with fresh fish fetched from the coast and other country delicacies brought to London either by train or on the swift new macadamised roads. The growing availability of mass-produced dining goods such as cut-glass finger bowls and silver-plated cutlery – all of it elaborately engraved, embossed or chased – with which to deck out tables, put stylish entertaining within growing numbers of people's reach. And the books most fitted to help people achieve this social success were not the great French works on classic cuisine and gastronomy by Carême or Brillat-Savarin, but more practical volumes, which tended to be written by women – either well-intentioned lectures by gentlewomen for those lower down the social scale, or domestic cooks imparting the fruits of their long experience. Acton, however, fell into neither category. The forty-six-year-old daughter of an Ipswich brewer, she was an unsuccessful poet whose London publisher, Thomas Longman, had reportedly rejected a long laboured-over manuscript with the words: 'It is no good bringing me poetry! Nobody wants poetry now. Go home and write me a cookery book, and we might come to terms.'

And the literal-minded Acton, who began with no culinary expertise at all, had taken him at his word and produced the most all-encompassing, logical and precise cookery book the public had yet seen. Such was its immediate success that by the end of the following year *Modern Cookery* had already run to six editions. What made the book so different from its rival offerings was its scientific approach. Eliza was the first food writer to give a list of ingredients, with exact quantities and instructions for the cooking time needed – all laid out as neatly as a chemical experiment. She gave detailed instructions on developing basic kitchen skills such as boning, trussing and carving meat; raising and icing cakes and thickening sauces. Most of all, the book was entirely comprehensive, its recipes covering every aspect of domestic cookery, from soups and sauces, to fish, meat, poultry, salads, vegetables, bread, cakes, soufflés, puddings, pickles and drinks. Although she was essentially writing for housewives whom she would have expected to employ a cook, she herself tested out every recipe at home in order to guarantee its accuracy. And although she was of a very different cast of mind to Soyer, they shared many basic culinary principles – including a love of economy and a detestation of waste, an absolute insistence on using only the freshest of ingredients, however humble, and a natural understanding of the importance of balanced nutrition. In her twenties Acton had spent some time living in France (there were persistent rumours that she had had an illegitimate child there) and she had learned to respect the frugal but healthy French peasant cookery that Alexis had been raised on. Although she resisted importing French recipes into her books, which remained solidly English, like Soyer she wanted all Englishwomen to learn the rudiments of cooking properly, and share the 'universal culinary skill, or culinary knowledge at the least', of their French sisters.

Acton's success naturally inspired many others. Alexis soon heard that a rival chef and acquaintance, forty-year-old Charles Elme Francatelli, was also planning to publish a substantial book, of around 1,500 recipes, to be called *The Modern Cook*. The handsome Francatelli, who had been born in England to Italian parents but studied in France – he claimed to have trained under Carême himself – had returned to Britain and followed a similar career trajectory to Soyer: moving from the kitchens of various noblemen to that of a club, in his case following in Ude's footsteps to that lavish aristocratic gambling den, Crockford's. In the early 1840s he had been chief chef and *maître d'hôtel* to Queen Victoria and Prince Albert, but he had loathed the foul-smelling, badly ventilated conditions in the Buckingham Palace kitchens, which had yet to be modernised. Worse, the pay could not compare to the riches offered by the London clubs, and Victoria's frugal upbringing combined with Albert's delicate stomach meant that both preferred plain, bland food, which rarely stretched Francatelli's considerable skills or creativity. The result was that Francatelli left the royal household after just a year, heading back to clubland, initially to the Coventry House Club. He later succeeded Alexis as *chef de cuisine* of the Reform Club, where he would spend seven undistinguished years. Although Francatelli had made his career cooking for the aristocracy, he, like Alexis, could not fail to be aware of the contrast between the staggeringly extravagant banquets he provided for the rich, and the poor-quality, meagre rations the bulk of the population had to subsist on. According to Henry Mayhew, chronicler of London's working poor, a piece of bread and an onion was a popular dinner for a labourer at this time, while meat was a luxury and not even tea and milk were daily staples for many. People developed little tricks to stave off hunger pangs, as W. B. Tegetmeier's *Manual of Domestic Economy* recognised, when it advised a core part of its readership: 'If you are very poor, and have not enough to eat, do not drink cold fluids.' Like Soyer, Francatelli's social conscience would become sharpened by the acute distress he saw all around him, and he would also go on to write cook books for the poor as well as handbooks for the wealthy, once claiming that he could 'feed 1,000 families a day on the food wasted in London alone'.

Clearly, there was plenty of overlap between Francatelli's areas of interest and Soyer's. Alexis, his competitive spirit roused, determined that however cordial his personal relationship with Francatelli, he would try to top his sales by running a spoiler – and beat Francatelli into the bookshops. Furthermore, his culinary work would be on an altogether grander and more elaborate scale than Francatelli's or Acton's – in fact, he would create an entirely new system of cookery. If Francatelli offered 1,500 recipes, Soyer would offer 2,000. Let Acton exhaustively probe and test every instruction – he already knew how to cook.

He set to work at once – or rather, he put his staff to work. After all, they had been drilled to copy the methods that he had honed over the years until they could perform them as well as he. And so he simply appointed the first kitchenmaid, 'a very clever [girl] who had been some years under his tuition, and knew well the composition of all his soups, sauces, entrees, etc', to transcribe carefully the order and methods used. It was probably no accident that this unnamed but crucial helper was a woman, and therefore – bearing in mind her pivotal role in the creation of the book – no threat to Alexis. However competent a deputy she was, and however talented a cook, she could never become a *chef de cuisine*. A female cook might become head of a large private kitchen, but never a professional one such as in a gentlemen's club, where the few women employed in the kitchen remained on the lowest rungs of the ladder. Thackeray, who was spending a considerable amount of time in Soyer's cosy office-cum-parlour during his evenings at the club, may have been making an ironical reference to this important distinction in *Pendennis*, when he had his fictional chef Mirobolant arrive at Clavering Park with 'a professed female cook' among his aides, 'who had inferior females under her orders'.

Alexis ensured the accuracy of the transcribed recipes by asking his chief apprentice to test them out. Soon there were more than two thousand sheets of recipes for him to select from and edit into the bulk of what would become his first major book, to which he would add, in his inimitably eccentric way, a host of other material: prefaces, essays, directions, observations, opinions, digressions, diagrams, inventions, kitchen designs, menus, portraits, letters, reviews and puffs. Once it was completed, he personally delivered the manuscript to his publishers just ten months after beginning the project. And Alexis was to have no truck with modest titles about modern cooks or family cookery; for this masterpiece of culinary wisdom he coined a new moniker for himself that would stick with him throughout his life – *The Gastronomic Regenerator*.

Like Acton and Francatelli, Soyer claimed that this 'simplified' work was 'suited to the income of all classes', yet in reality Alexis did not even attempt to adapt the bulk of the dishes in *The Gastronomic Regenerator* to a domestic environment. He decided to leave others to fight each other for dominance over the new niche market – providing manuals for the dinner party-giving bourgeoisie. Soyer would go for the high end of the market instead, concentrating on rich food for the tables of the super-rich. Of course, there would be something to draw in the aspiring reader too: a section of 'Kitchen at Home' recipes using cheaper ingredients, simpler methods and reduced portions, but these were essentially designed to maximise sales. His core interest was in teaching the world to create dishes worthy of a duke, and so his recipes were not scaled down in either luxuriousness or quantity – his black pudding recipe called for six pints of pig's blood and even a simple sponge cake required thirty eggs. Indeed the bulk of the recipes were specifically dedicated to 'The Kitchens of the Wealthy' and the instructions were clearly intended to be passed down to the experienced staff of large-scale establishments, who would have the vast stock pots and numerous other implements demanded for such work. Even the cost of the volume – a substantial guinea a copy – put it beyond the reach of all but the most prosperous middle-class households.

To further boost the book's snob appeal and underline his own vast acquaintance among royalty and the upper classes, Soyer prefaced the work with a frontispiece featuring the Duke of Cambridge's coat of arms and a fulsome dedication to his (and Philippe's) erstwhile employer, and followed it up with two densely typed, double-column pages listing his patrons – those 'distinguished persons [who] have honoured the author with their approbation'. This was virtually a gazette of English dukes, duchesses, countesses, marquesses, earls and lords, plus a fair smattering of foreign princes, barons and counts. Listed by rank, mere admirals, generals, knights and MPs found themselves at the end of a very long list, and Alexis clearly hoped to swell the subscription list by appealing to their vanity as well as their purses. An actual book of subscribers, for both the kitchen lithograph and *The Gastronomic Regenerator*, was kept in Soyer's office at the Reform, and brandished before visitors who came to see the chef *in situ*. Among the eminent autographs he attracted was Giuseppe Verdi's, who signed it in July 1847 while visiting London for the opening of his opera *I Masnadieri*. Beside his signature Verdi sketched the opening bars of the soprano aria made famous by Jenny Lind, '*Carlo vive di caro accento, melodia di paradiso*'.

But as ever with Soyer, brass-necked sycophancy and opportunism were tempered with humour. In his tongue-in-cheek preface he declared that native gallantry forced him to write the book following requests from several distinguished ladies of his aquaintance, 'to whom I have always made it a rule never to refuse anything in my power'. He had held out for so long against the project, he went on, because of a distressing experience in a superb library in a splendid baronial hall. After browsing through the works of Milton, Locke and Shakespeare he had found a monstrous and impressively bound nineteenth edition of an unknown but voluminous work, and had opened it up in excitement, only to find . . . a recipe for oxtail soup. The disappointment had made him vow that his own ideas should never encumber such a sanctuary, but now he presented his book on condition that the reader would put it 'in a place suited to its little merit, and not with Milton's sublime Paradise, for there it certainly would be doubly lost'.

For the recipes themselves he claimed to have hit on a new method of presentation. Instead of arranging them as a succession of complete dinner menus, or bills of fare, he presented a group of each style of dish in turn, in the order in which they appeared from the kitchen, thus making 'the whole contents of my book one regular bill of fare'. And while the rest of the material in *The Gastronomic Regenerator* displays little in the way of organising principles, within the recipe section he generally sticks to his plan, with only the very occasional discursive ramble away from the subject in hand. Alexis was not the first to categorise his recipes other than as a series of menus; as early as 1814 Beauvilliers (who clearly inspired Soyer) had divided up his cook book by the main protein element – i.e. fish, game, beef etc – but the recipes are clear and readable, many still exquisitely mouth-watering, although in spite of protestations to the contrary, even the most modest recipes in the 'Kitchen at Home' section generally assume a considerable degree of kitchen knowledge.

As in all classic cookery, key to the success of most dishes is the saucing, 'the great test of culinary civilisation', according to the *Morning Chronicle*. Soyer kicked off with a selection of simplified 'foundation' sauces – stocks, béchamels, veloutés and demi-glaces that any chef would be familiar with today, before moving into more sophisticated territory. Next come dozens of soups, from clear light game consommés to complex vegetable *potages* filled with light chicken quenelles and – with a nod to his patron – *Potage à la Marcus Hill*: a delicately reduced veal stock with a sorrel and lettuce chiffonade. The star of the soup section is undoubtedly his recipe for turtle soup, which he considered 'the leading article of English cookery'. Certainly, turtle was the status symbol soup of choice at all fashionable dinner parties, prized as much for its value and skill of creation as for its delicate flavour. The turtles were imported live from the West Indies and Ascension Island, and such luxury did not come cheap. Lewis Carroll called it 'beautiful soup so rich and green' and in *Hard Times* Dickens made his stingy factory-owner, Josiah Bounderby, complain that the discontented, starving workers wanted to eat 'turtle soup from golden spoons'. Queen Victoria, however, once admitted to Wellington that she loathed the stuff as much as insects and

Tories. Soyer claimed that while the 'great complication' of the recipe generally made it impracticable for the private establishment, he had simplified it enough to make it accessible to any chef – although his first paragraph of preparatory work alone would strike terror into the heart of most domestic cooks.

> Make choice of a good turtle, weighing from one hundred and forty to one hundred and eighty pounds, hang it up by the hind fins securely, cut off the head and let it hang all night, then take it down, lay it upon its back, and with a sharp knife cut out the belly, leaving the fins, but keeping the knife nearly close to the upper shell; take out the interior, which throw away, first collecting the green fat which is upon it, then remove the fins and fleshy parts, leaving nothing but the two large shells, saw the top shell into four and the bottom one in halves, then put the whole of the turtle, including the head, into a large turbot kettle, and cover them with cold water (or if no kettle large enough blanch it in twice), place it upon a sharp fire and let boil five minutes, to sufficiently scald it, then put the pieces into a tub of cold water, and with a pointed knife take off all the scales, which throw away, then take out carefully the whole of the green fat, which reserve, place the remainder back in the turbot kettle, where let it simmer until the meat comes easily from the shells and the fins are tender, then take them out and detach all the glutinous meat from the shells, which cut into square pieces and reserve until required. Fricandeau and a few other entrées were sometimes made from the fleshy parts, but the stringy substance of that mock meat is not worth eating, and few stomachs can digest it.

Alexis goes on to give several variations of the soup, including a clear, more easily digestible version without the turtle meat, which is, he says, 'held in the highest estimation among real epicures and when artistically prepared is indeed worthy of the name of a luxury', and a mock turtle soup, made with whole calves' heads rather than turtle, and sherry instead of the more traditional Madeira. 'Forcemeat and egg-balls were formerly served in this soup,' he concludes crisply, 'the latter in imitation of turtles' eggs, but better imitations of bullets, and almost as indigestible; the omission of them will, I am certain, prove beneficial, for whether the stomach be strong or delicate it will not bear loading with ammunition of that description.'

And so on to '*Poissons*' – via lessons on fish-cleaning techniques and how to kill an eel humanely. He is happy to recommend Dublin Bay haddock as, although this fish used to be difficult to procure fresh, nowadays 'the rapidity of steam conveyance by sea and land, brings it almost alive into the London markets'. As with all his recipes, copious quantities of cream, butter and egg yolk are used to emulsify, thicken and enhance the dishes. To accompany poached turbot he recommends putting 'one pint of cream on the fire in a good sized stewpan, and when it is nearly simmering add half a pound of fresh butter . . . then add a liaison of three yolks of eggs'. So the fat content was vast, in keeping with current fashions in Victorian fine dining. But portions were smaller than they are today and even wealthy people burned more calories than most twenty-first century citizens by walking longer distances, and by living in colder houses. Although there was a growing awareness that obesity could cause health problems, it would be more than a decade before the *Cornhill* journal published a series of articles about the 'ills of corpulence' and the first weight-for-height charts began to appear in popular magazines.

From fish to *hors d'oeuvres* 'or dishes to be handed round the table', then the *removes*, a selection of elegantly sauced meat and game 'made' dishes – i.e. in sauce – and the *flancs*, a range of impressive fillets, loins and other joints designed to complement the côtelettes, escalopes and croquettes of the entrée course. One of the *removes*, a leg of mutton slow cooked for a full seven hours, he prefaced with the outraged exclamations of a friend, renamed 'John Bull', who claimed that such a nonsensical recipe, 'which I am sure no one upon this soil will ever follow, or disgrace their tables with', should only be written in the cook's native tongue, 'so it could offend no one'. Soyer charmingly acquiesces, and the recipe for *Gigot de Mouton de sept heures* is printed entirely in French.

Prefacing a section called 'Of Roasts for Second Course', Alexis gives directions on wringing a bird's neck, before stressing that while 'near two thirds of our animal and volatile food is daily roasted', few cooks pay enough attention to a deceptively sophisticated art. In a kitchen such as the Reform, Soyer would have employed at least one dedicated and specialist roasting chef, but he recognised that this was not a resource available to many. So he lectures on timings and temperatures, larding and basting – which he considers to be, generally, a bad thing. 'I have never during the last six years suffered any bird to be basted in my kitchen,' you can almost see him wagging his finger, 'with the exception of rubbing a piece of butter over the breast of poultry or game as soon as the skin becomes set.'

For the roasts, as with every other dish, whether referring to capons, green geese, pea fowls or turkeys, a rigid sense of culinary decorum held sway. In his instructions for truffled turkey, for example, Soyer sternly instructed the householder to select a *small* bird, 'for what would look noble in the first course would appear vulgar in the second'. Similarly, in the section of 'Savoury Dishes for Second Course' – which included such outré items as a boar's head with pastry tusks, truffle eyes and flowers stuck 'tastefully' in the ears – the etiquette attached to the ingredients used, and their places on the dining table, was just as carefully prescribed. 'The large pieces, such as pâtés of game, galantine of turkey, poulardes, boars' heads, etc., are in smaller dinners placed at the bottom of the table to face the roasts, but in a dinner of six or ten entrées they are served as flancs. All others . . . by making them smaller may be served as savoury entremets, in a corner dish.' This was still some time before polite society finally jettisoned the formal table layouts of *service à la Française*, where you helped yourself from the selection of (invariably cold) dishes that happened to have been placed next to you, for the pleasures of being served a progression of hot dishes *à la Russe*, a concept that was still being pioneered by another dandyish gourmet, the Russian ambassador to Paris, Prince Alexander Kourakine.

A long section devoted to vegetables covered the wide selection of exotic produce available to the wealthier 1840s housewife at Covent Garden market: black and white truffles, asparagus, sea-kale, salsify, Jerusalem artichokes, endive and sorrel. Alexis recommends French red kidney potatoes as the best variety, being not too mealy or too waxy, and eulogises about lentils, rarely seen in England but popular in France, which he calls (incorrectly) 'the only dish of vegetables that we have inherited from the ancients'. And while he constantly refers to how things are done in France (with the implication that they are done better), and what is and is not in vogue in France, he recommends not just Périgord and Piedmont truffles but the ones still then to be found in Hampshire.

But it is on the subject of the '*Entremets*' that he is the most opinionated. He opens the section devoted to an exquisite range of *tartelettes, gâteaux, tourtes, flans, crèmes, Génoises* and *meringues* with a long discourse on pastry-making, in which he pays generous tribute to one of his culinary heroes (while cleverly placing himself on a par with the great man): 'It is only within the last twenty years that it [the art of making pastry] has attained any degree of perfection, which is partly due to the talent and intelligence of my illustrious compatriot and confrère,

CARÊME, who has left little or no room for innovation in that vast field of culinary delight.'

However, he then observes that the fashion for the colossal sugar pieces that had made Carême's name was on the wane. And very properly too, he adds – 'Simplicity, the mother of elegance, being now the order of the day'. Which was a bit rich coming from a master of fruit-filled cakes and puddings disguised as ships, turkeys, mushrooms, pyramids and goodness knows what else. Indeed the book's final recipe section was dedicated to those mock dishes designed to cause the 'greatest hilarity at table', including a fake boar's head with dried cherry eyes and lashes of sliced pistachio, a forty-egg sponge swan covered in white icing, and a faux-ham joint sprinkled with crushed ratafias. Soyer was the acknowledged master of these culinary practical jokes, which appealed hugely to the less sophisticated side of his humour, and his favourite was a ghastly confection, named in honour of the Duchess of Sutherland, called *Petits Poussins en Surprise à la Sutherland*. It consisted of three buttery sponges filled with marzipan cream and shaped to look like a trio of plucked and trussed chickens – complete with pastry claws.

In 'Savoury Dishes for Second Course' Soyer inserted one of his signature dishes: *Salade de Grouse à la Soyer*, a highly decorative *flanc* of lightly cooked grouse pieces doused in a creamy dressing and placed on a sharply flavoured salad surrounded by a border of hard-boiled eggs. He couldn't resist adding a lengthy footnote describing the first time he had produced the dish, which was at a private dinner for a group of noblemen and gentlemen. The diners had made a wager as to who could produce the best dinner – Soyer or 'a rival artiste from a celebrated establishment in Paris, where they had previously dined'. Naturally, the effect caused by this novel dish won the day, and Alexis was called out to celebrate the triumph, when 'over several rosades of exquisite Lafitte, the salad was christened *à la Soyer* by General Sir Alexander Duff, who presided over the noble party'. However, it was another signature dish, and one that he named not after himself but after the club, which was to cement his reputation as a culinary innovator for generations to come, although this creation was not given the anecdotal fanfare of the *Salade de Grouse à la Soyer*.

Soyer had been successfully serving *Côtelettes de Mouton à la Reform* in the dining room for years, but this was the first time his recipe for the increasingly popular dish had been committed to paper. Recipe number 698 revealed the secret of this celebrated dish – later to become Lamb Cutlets Reform as the English taste for mature mutton gave way to one for young lamb. The method was prefaced by a recommendation to use sheep from the South Downs rather than Wales, as he considered them leaner and more intensely flavoured as a result of their heathy diet. He directed the reader to cut the meat into cutlets with a portion of bone remaining at the fat end – into a modern chop, in fact – and an illustrative woodcut demonstrated the correct technique. The instructions then described the correct way to coat the meat with a fine blend of breadcrumbs and lean ham, how to arrange the broiled chops as a crown fixed into a bed of mashed potato, and the creation of the famously piquant Reform Sauce. This was an immensely complex compound of various stocks and secondary sauces, consommé, herbs, vinegars and 'preserved tomatas', all boiled and blended and reduced to just the right consistency. The preparation of this one sauce required the labour of many hands to purée and blend the various ingredients, and kitchenmaids could spend whole mornings rubbing it through the hair sieves and fine muslins known as tammies.

To modern eyes the whole calves' heads, swans and turtles, the lambs' tails and feet, and the pints of pigs' blood, are virtually unthinkable raw materials for a meal. To see recipes beginning with instructions such as 'Cook and dress ten ears', 'Procure eight lambs' tongues' or 'Roast six woodcocks underdone' may as well place the food of *The Gastronomic Regenerator* in the twelfth century as the nineteenth. Yet many of the techniques Soyer uses are French culinary classics, and his easy conversational style and real expertise – always worn lightly – can tempt the present-day cook into fresh interpretations which often stand up well. This is particularly true of the 300 simplified recipes in the book, designed to compete with Francatelli and Acton for the attention of the more modest householder. Although, with Alexis perhaps over-mindful of the need to make use of cheaper cuts and leftovers in this part, the 'Kitchen at Home' section relies rather heavily on stews, ragoûts, hashes and curries.

At the end of the book Soyer added yet another batch of miscellaneous material – and kept adding to it with each new edition. There was a minute description of his Reform Club kitchens, printed on the pretext of offering a simple guide 'for fitting up the kitchens of the wealthy', which included detailed diagrams of his state-of-the-art equipment, and a pull-out scaled down copy of the lithograph he had commissioned and marketed so successfully four years earlier. There were floor plans for a series of other 'model' kitchens too, including a cottage kitchen and a bachelor's kitchen. To the 1848 edition he even added a ship's kitchen, which he had created the year before for a newly built merchant steam-ship called *The Guadalquivir*. In a galley just seventeen feet long and eight wide he had managed to cram in a vertical range, smoke-jack, screen, spits and dripping pan, bain-marie, three charcoal stoves, a hotplate, gridiron, steam boiler, bread oven, hot closet, fuel store and work table – not to mention a complete *batterie de cuisine*. He fitted shelf blocks to stop pans falling off the walls, and strips of India rubber across the rows of ladles to stop them rattling. Most ingeniously, he invented a moveable balance grating – a swinging iron trivet fixed above the stove between two upright rods – which stopped the saucepans spilling out their contents during stormy weather. The kitchen was made up by Bramah, Prestage & Ball in Piccadilly, but destroyed, along with the ship, just two years later.

While there was unlikely to be much demand for this maritime invention, Soyer had been unable to resist showing it off. This was also evident in his inclusion of the floor plan of his own kitchen, which was, he said, although compact, big enough for 'any man cook . . . to dress a first-rate dinner'. He gave it the title 'My Kitchen At Home', he explained, in order to 'shelter myself from culinary criticisms, because every man is, or ought to be, allowed to do anything he likes "at home".' This comment was even cheekier than most readers would realise, as Soyer did not possess a kitchen of his own. After renting various small places after Emma's death in 1842, he had moved into his father-in-law's large, chaotic Leicester Square flat. The kitchen only came into being a few years later, when the journalist George Augustus Sala, a guest at one dinner, described it as tiny but beautifully fitted up, and 'as complete in its way as the wonderful kitchen and annexes which he had arranged for the Reform Club'.

Soyer was very nearly caught out in the lie by one determined fan, an attractive Irishwoman called Elizabeth Boyd. According to Volant, this woman became determined to view this model of domestic comfort for herself, and decided that in order to gain access to Soyer she would first ingratiate herself with Simonau, knowing the men were still close, by commissioning him to paint a twenty-guinea portrait of her. She duly turned up, unannounced, at the flat early one morning to find the place in seeming chaos, unframed pictures by Emma and Simonau piled up against every wall, the beds unmade, the furniture in disarray and, on a beautiful drawing room table, a pile of vegetables and a scrag of mutton. According to Volant, the nosy visitor, horrified to discover that Soyer lived in such a place, had the cheek to follow Simonau into the small back room which served as washroom, kitchen and servant's quarters, and watch the old man as he prepared a humble *potage* for himself and his son-in-law. 'You see, madame,' he apparently teased her, 'we are very domesticated; we do everything at home; besides, we foreigners cannot live without good soup and some relishing stews: these are as much the half of our lives, as roast beef and plum-pudding are to the English.' Just then Alexis came home and, instead of admitting defeat, had the quick wits to continue the fiction by declaring that while he would love to show Miss Boyd his Kitchen At Home, it was *out of town*, at his place in the country and, being a bachelor, he could hardly invite her down to see it. Whether or not she swallowed the deception, a flirtation began between them; Simonau did indeed paint her picture, and the relationship culminated in a lengthy poem from Soyer in his usual terrible doggerel. The five interminable love-and-yearning verses of *À La Belle Irlandaise* detail the 'black-eyed virgin's' many physical charms, including a cheeky reference to her voluptuousness – as with Emma and Fanny, Soyer clearly appreciated the more well-upholstered damsel.

Concerned with every aspect of successful dining, over the years Soyer had become exasperated by a common Victorian problem – that of the inexperienced, nervous, or simply maladroit social carver, who mangled and disfigured the beautifully prepared joints and birds that the poor chef had burned his fingers sending up. And so he used *The Gastronomic Regenerator* to unveil his solution – which was nothing less than an entirely new method of carving. In a droll essay he illustrated the problem with the example of the essayist Launcelot Sturgeon's man of fashion, whose ineptness with the knife had sent a bird flying into the lap of an expensively dressed female guest. 'With admirable composure, and without offering the slightest apology, he finished a story which he was telling at the same time, and then, quietly turning to her, merely said, "Madam, I'll thank you for that turkey".' According to Soyer, the correct way to carve was, naturally enough, *à la zoug-zoug* ('in everything I dislike a straight line . . .') and he provided lettered diagrams and complicated instructions on how to hold the knife, slice the meat, and even spoon the gravy. His method was, as one frustrated *Morning Chronicle* reviewer called it, 'apparently successful though unintelligible'. Soyer even invented an entirely new, carver-friendly joint – a saddleback of venison, devised with his butcher, a Mr Grove of Charing Cross, which became quite popular. (Dickens' wife, Catherine, was a big fan.) He later tackled the problem from another angle, coming up with a new gadget, the Tendon Separator, a sort of cross between heavy-gauge scissors and springed secateurs, designed as an aid to the tricky business of dissecting poultry and game at table. He had the utensils manufactured by his old friends at Bramah, Prestage & Ball of Piccadilly and took the rare step of visiting a patent agent in Lincoln's Inn Fields to register the design. He then commissioned a full-page illustration for the fourth edition from Walmsley and as usual had no compunction about trying to flog this 'most serviceable of instruments' to his large readership.

Soyer also turned *The Gastronomic Regenerator* into a treasury of extremely practical lessons in those areas where he felt that British cooks performed particularly badly. These include detailed directions for larding joints in the French style – from selecting the right bacon for the best lardons (firm, quite fat, and not at all red) to using a larding needle to make chequered rows of beautifully marbled meat. There are also strict instructions on how to make a good pot of coffee while still being economical – in lieu of the execrable brew usually on offer – which was supposedly provided by his housekeeper, Irma de l'Ombre, who attaches her signature to the recipe for added authenticity and in exchange for which, Soyer claims, she would receive a new gown. A series of memos provides insider's shopping tips and regular injunctions to eat foods at the peak of the proper season. These are endearingly housewifely, even gossipy: we learn, for instance, that plovers' eggs are his favourites, so much so that he has been known, at the beginning of the season, to pay three shillings and sixpence each for them, whereas of red mullets he exclaims 'we had none this year except at a very extravagant price'. He tells us that crabs are best in May, but oysters are not so good until September; that Medway smelts are the best, the Yarmouth and Carlisle ones being too large; and that while out of season produce can be bought at a great expense, it does not repay in flavour its exorbitant price. 'Make but few preserves,' he counsels, 'only those that are indispensable: you will have a continual enjoyment of earlier stock, as Nature closely watches our wants and liberally supplies our wishes. The real gourmet, though anxious to produce novelty, never attempts to over-force the produce of the various seasons.'

While most of Soyer's thoughts on the correct preparation of food follow the traditional rules of classic cookery, the odd subversive thought creeps in. He counsels professional cooks to over-season dishes rather than under-season them, for example, contrary to 'the expressed opinion of every other previous publication', and his logic for this, if flawed, is at least original: 'Your employer can correct you by saying there is too much of this or that, and you can soon get it to his taste; but while you fear over-seasoning you produce no flavour at all; by allowing each guest to season for himself, your sauce attains a diversity of flavours. The cook must season for the guest, not the guest for the cook.'

For general interest, there are menus of his most triumphant banquets, 'pull-out' engravings of more complex dishes, his own designs for *attelettes* and jelly moulds, tables of kitchen utensils, and even the transcription of a conversation in French between Soyer and his great patron at the Reform Club, Lord Marcus Hill. In this *Dialogue Culinaire*, dated 14 May 1846, Hill plays the starring role, naturally enough, coming out with a stream of witty and wise culinary *bon mots* with which the obsequious Soyer can only concur. His lordship notes, for example, the difference between a gourmand and a gourmet – '*l'un mange sans déguster, l'autre déguste en mangeant*': one eats without tasting, while the other tastes while he is eating. It is left to Soyer to play up the romantic Frenchman stereotype with the observation that a gastronomical gathering with no ladies present would be like 'a garden without flowers, a sea without waves, a squadron without sails'. It took *Blackwood's Magazine* to point out that as chef to an exclusively masculine organisation, 'of which a principal object was to prove that female society was far from being indispensable to man . . . a thorough-going club-man would very soon drive a coach and four through the Regenerator's polite eloquence'.

Perhaps most eccentrically, at the end of *The Gastronomic Regenerator* Alexis chose to fill a page with the self-portrait that Emma had finished just before she died, alongside a short but loving biography, and a tribute to her talent. Even at the distance of four years, and despite the speed with which he had embarked on a new relationship, Alexis was clearly still smarting about the perceived slights his wife had once received at the hands of Archer Shee, and parts of the account read more like an emotional outburst than a measured eulogy. Neither had he forgiven Ude, who had recently died, for his refusal to sell back the painting of the market girl carrying a basket of hens given to Ude prior to his disastrous birthday party. He made a point of commenting that 'in the fullness of my own individual regard for her memory and of her rare gifts, I have for some while been adding to my collection, and at any expense, all those of her paintings which may come within my reach . . .' He had recently managed, he added, to purchase back a painting called *Buy-A-Broom Girl and Boy*, from the Saltmarsh collection. Alongside his own encomium (which is a little shaky on dates) to the woman he described as being 'of a most amiable and cheerful disposition, a kind friend, excellent and affectionate wife, too modest to set much value upon her works, leaving the palette to attend to her household duties', he reproduced some letters of condolence. Naturally he chose those from his most socially elevated patrons, notably the Duke of Saxe-Gotha, the Baron de Knesbeck and the Duchess of Sutherland. He also reprinted some of Emma's obituaries, including those from *La Revue des Deux Mondes* and *La Capitole.*

As well as this most personal of material, Alexis had no qualms about including purely commercial puffs in his magnum opus. His expansive endorsement of various kitchen products were perhaps disinterested – such as the footnote that gave a handsome plug to the 'stone bottles and apparatus for preserving fruits invented by Mr James Cooper, of No 7, St John-street, Clerkenwell . . . I have used them upon several occasions and for different descriptions of fruit, and have never met with any system that so well preserved the freshness of the fruit, or which is more simple in its operation.' But he certainly accepted cash for the advertisements at the back of the book, in which he raved about such items as Arney's Patent Jelly and Blancmange Powders ('There is an economy in the cost, economy of time, and a certainty of having a brilliant jelly at any time'), and Captain White's Curry Paste and Powders ('The several ingredients are so well proportioned, that [it] possesses a delicacy of taste not always to be met with in India') – not that Soyer had ever set foot on the subcontinent. Over time, successive editions would contain advertisements for his own bottled sauces, books and stoves.

The Gastronomic Regenerator finally appeared in the second half of June 1846. Review copies, along with ingratiating letters, were despatched to editors such as William Harrison Ainsworth, the Lancashire novelist and editor of *Ainsworth's Magazine*, and Douglas Jerrold, one of the founders of *Punch* magazine and a biting social satirist whose work Alexis relished – 'no man caught the dazzling fire of Jerrold's sarcasm better than Soyer', wrote Volant. So Soyer sent him a letter congratulating 'the earnest and talented pioneer to many of those great movements effected and in operation towards the comfort of the poor'. Such an approach was unlikely to thaw the serious-minded Jerrold, but overall Soyer's policy worked brilliantly, and the book was received with pages and pages of universally positive reviews.

Soyer had just failed to beat *The Modern Cook* into the bookshops – Francatelli's dedication was dated 21 February, and his first notice, in the *Literary Gazette*, appeared shortly after Easter. But they appeared close enough together to be linked by some of the newspapers, such as *The Times*, which considered the bulky and 'important' volumes to be

'equally excellent', although differing in form according to the personality of each chef. Francatelli wrote in a 'grave and business-like fashion,
never tempted into digression, never moved into metaphor'. Soyer, on
the other hand, like Tristram Shandy, found digressions to be the
sunshine. 'He can afford to garnish his prose with the flowers of fancy,
as his material dishes are crowned with *croustades* and *atelettes*,' wrote the
reviewer. 'He handles with equal ability the quill of Pegasus and the
larding-needle, and records with the former the achievements of the
latter, in a strain of enthusiasm and heroic sensibility that are not to be
surpassed even in the odes of a poet laureate.' There was no doubting
which book the writer preferred, as he fell over himself to praise Soyer's
'matchless modesty, his courteous urbanity, his devotion to the fair sex,
and his occasional touching and highly imaginative digression'. He was
equally impressed by Soyer's industry as his authorship, and mused at
length on how he had managed to produce the book while running the
club kitchens and masterminding a stream of banquets.

> For ten months he laboured at the pyramid which the remotest
> prosperity shall applaud; and during the whole of that period he was
> intent upon providing countless meals at the Reform Club which a
> living generation have already approved and fully digested. Talk of the
> labours of a Prime Minister or Lord Chancellor! Sir Robert Peel was
> not an idle man. Lord Brougham is a tolerably busy one. Could either,
> we ask, in the short space of ten months . . . have written the
> Gastronomic Regenerator, and furnished 25,000 dinners, 38 banquets
> of importance, comprising above 70,000 dishes, besides providing
> daily for sixty servants, and receiving the visits of 15,000 strangers, all
> too eager to inspect the renowned altar of a great Apician temple? All
> this did M. Soyer.

The *Morning Post* praised both his delicacy – 'Everything gross is
excluded, and the more nutritious portions of food are alone preserved,
in such forms as to please the eye and the palate, without embarrassment
to the digestive process' – and his range. 'In one portion of his book he
provides materials for the dinner of an emperor; in the other . . . he
enables the smallest private family, or even the solitary bachelor, to live
well on small means.' Mindful of its core readership, it strongly recommended his simpler recipes to those who were tired of conventional
dinners 'composed of everlasting chops and steaks'. The *Morning Advertiser*, more realistically, declared Soyer 'a wit and a wag of the first order',

The Sun dubbed him 'the mighty gastronomic magician' and the *Morning Herald* cheekily declared that 'We had no idea that so much good could emanate from the Reform Club, and lived in the belief that their dinners were as dull as their dogmas,' before declaring that with M. Soyer as caterer they could dine in amity even with a Radical, a Repealer, or a Chartist. 'Every recipe,' it concluded, was 'an epic, every dish a picture, and every sauce a study'. *The Globe* opened its facetious review by demanding an appropiate public recognition of his services. 'When Napoleon first started the distinction of the "Legion of Honour", Moreau ridiculed it by proposing to confer a *casserole d'honneur* on his cook. But we beg to propose some "Soyer testimonial" without any joke at all.' Most ludicrous was the overheated analogy, extended over several pages, by one eager hack at *Blackwood's Magazine*, who compared Soyer's career and talents to that of the Duke of Wellington, and declared that soon an entire army of his culinary converts would be 'marching and countermarching, cutting and skewering, broiling and freezing, in blind obedience to the commands of the Regenerator'.

The Gastronomic Regenerator was not just a critical success. In less than twelve months more than 2,000 copies had been sold at a guinea each, with reprints and new editions coming out every few months. As with the lithograph, the Reformers subscribed generously and provided thought-ful tributes. 'Soyer regenerator . . . who would be without such a book,' wrote club member Thomas Hall on 24 November. 'It enhances the value of the *chef de cuisine* of The Reform Club and has introduced quite a *reform* in the Arts of cookery. Poor Ude is dead, Carême also, Soyer lives, need I say more.' By 1850 Soyer was already on the ninth edition, and many more followed. While Alexis did not pocket all the money – he had split the publishing costs, and therefore the profits, with a business partner called Alexander Symons – he was still making a tidy sum from it. With his salary from the Reform Club, plus the fees he was raking in from his 'improvers', it all amounted to the enormous income of around £1,000 a year, which was particularly impressive when one considers that the club's butler earned around £75 per annum, and a top chef anywhere else would be fortunate to earn anything over £100.

Whenever new editions were published over the years, Alexis could not resist tinkering with the body of the text. He would increase and improve the recipes, correct errors, put in tables and woodcuts, include more favourable reviews and add more little sections on his favourite hobby-horses, so that the work became less a comprehensive work than a mixed bag of his current preoccupations. For the fourth edition, impressively published within nine months of the first, he added some recipes sent in by fans, or rather 'communicated by amateurs' as he pompously put it, 'which are not deficient in good taste'.

He also added a detailed engraving of what he called his *Bouquet de Gibier*, or 'Sporting Nosegay', a variation on the festive hamper idea that he had sent to various of his patrons that Christmas. The 'bouquet' consisted of a ten-foot-tall arrangement of laurel, holly, mistletoe and evergreen branches into which several dozen freshly shot birds and game had been artistically entwined: wild ducks, grouse, partridge, snipes, peewits, woodcocks, plovers, leverets, rabbits, pheasant, widgeons and teal. Soyer had presented these monstrous trophies to, among others, Viscount Melbourne at Brocket Hall and Lady Blessington and Count d'Orsay at Gore House. He had even sent one to Louis Philippe, the King of the French, at the Château des Tuileries in Paris. All had been politely acknowledged, and their responses were duly copied into *The Gastronomic Regenerator*. D'Orsay had apparently declared that Landseer would have appreciated the artistic novelty, while the king sent a handsome letter of thanks (reprinted in full) declaring that such a welcome and graceful present from a foreign country had never before penetrated through France to the palace of its kings, and that he planned to have a similar bouquet carved in wood to adorn the grand sideboard of the banqueting hall. The letter was sent to Alexis via the French ambassador, along with a diamond and pearl pin in the shape of a bouquet. As for his employers, the Reform Club committee must have been baffled as to what to do with this showman-cook who, it must have seemed, not only upstaged their serious political work, but now – with his impressive Imperial connections – even their diplomacy, at every turn.

7

'A BROTH OF A BOY'

To the south of Arbour Hill, between the imposing Royal Barracks and the River Liffey, is Dublin's Esplanade. On 5 April 1847, it provided an ideal location for a late gala luncheon, and by three o'clock a well-dressed group had gathered expectantly beside a newly erected and rather unusual canvas and board pavilion. The ridge pole had been decorated with Union flags and some jaunty bunting for the event and in the crisp spring breeze they could be heard flapping furiously above the muted buzz of conversation.

The hundred-odd guests, led by the Duke of Cambridge, in whose kitchen Alexis had begun his English career, comprised the cream of Dublin – and Irish – society, among them the Earls of Meath, Charlemont and Roden, the Earl and Countess of Donoughmore and the Lords Brabazon and Duncannon. They joined a considerable contingent from England, including eminent members of the government, the clergy and the medical profession. The military establishment was represented by a clique of captains, colonels and field marshals, including Lord William Paulet, whose patronage would assist Soyer so much in the Crimea; and the great military engineer Sir John Burgoyne, who had just been appointed by the prime minister to head a new Irish relief commission. The crowd of ordinary Dubliners who had gathered from Phoenix Park to watch the event were kept well away from the VIPs by the expediency of stout new railings.

This 'large and brilliant assemblage' was there by the invitation of Alexis Soyer, famous *chef de cuisine* of London's Reform Club, who wished them to sample his latest creations. They were not expecting to participate in one of the splendid, multi-course banquets that had made his name, but on the contrary, to see what he could do with a restricted budget and the most basic ingredients – and to gauge the success of his experiment with mass catering on an unprecedented scale. For at the height of the worst potato famine ever to strike the Irish mainland, Soyer's Famine Soups, a range of carefully devised compounds, were being held up by many as the long-awaited lifeline for the hordes of starving peasant farmers who were now dying in their hundreds of thousands.

On the dot of three o'clock the guest of honour arrived – the Lord Lieutenant of Ireland, Lord Bessborough. But far from throwing open the doors of the pavilion, as planned, to unveil to the amazement of the crowd the scientific ingenuity of Soyer's Model Soup Kitchen, his excellency, who in fact had only weeks to live, proved too weak to leave his carriage. Instead he was served a bowl of soup by Alexis himself, and 'expressed his perfect satisfaction at its excellence' before being driven home, when it was left to the chef, with his usual panache, to lead his curious guests into the wooden pavilion.

At forty-eight feet long by forty wide, the enormous soup kitchen occupied 2,000 square feet. Once inside, the VIPs were suitably impressed with the highly organised, conveyor-belt feeding system that Soyer had created. There was a large door at each end of the room, and in the middle a dais, on which stood a massive thirteen-foot, 300-gallon soup boiler on wheels. Beside it was a bread oven, capable of baking a hundredweight of bread at a time, and both were heated by a single fire contained within a sunken coal pit. Around the boiler eight six-foot-wide iron *bains-marie* used the residual heat to keep a further 1,000 gallons of soup warm, and at each end were a carefully designed array of chopping tables, storage tubs, drawers and shelves. Around the roof pillars were circular tin boxes to house condiments, and in each corner of the huge room ventilation safes doubled as storage areas for the meat, vegetables and grain. Under the eaves, vast water butts held 1,792 gallons of water. Against three of the walls long tables, eighteen inches wide, were cut with rows of holes, each just big enough to hold a white enamelled bowl, and to each bowl a metal spoon was attached by a fine chain. Tin water boxes, placed at ten-foot intervals along the trestles, were furnished with sponges for the helpers to rinse out the bowls between each sitting. It was all as carefully thought out as the time and labour-saving techniques Soyer had introduced in the Reform Club kitchens, only simplified and enlarged.

The concept was simple enough. The destitute would assemble outside the pavilion, where officials would herd a hundred at a time into a queuing area marked off by cordons arranged in a zig-zag formation (naturally it had to be *à la zoug-zoug*). When a bell rang, these hundred would file through the front door into the kitchen, passing beneath a portrait of Queen Victoria, to take up positions at the tables, and eat their soup before leaving through the other doorway, where they were issued with a portion of bread or biscuit to take away with them. The bowls would then be washed and refilled, and exactly six minutes after the last peal the bell would ring again to admit the next group, giving a throughput of 1,000 diners per hour. (In fact, the kitchen was soon serving up 8,750 meals a day, where 5,000 had originally been projected as the maximum possible.) A further 3,000 portions were to be given away at the door, in exchange for tickets, or distributed to outlying parishes on donkey carts. These were specially adapted with small coppers and 'fires attached' so that the soup arrived at the villages while still hot. And to show just how simple it was, Soyer made his guests experience the process for themselves. The next day the *Dublin Evening Herald* reported on how the trial had gone.

Shortly after three o'clock those invited, ladies and gentlemen, were admitted through the labyrinth, to the amount of one hundred, and all took up their posts at the table on which the bowls were placed and the spoons attached with a slight chain, and it was most gratifying to see with what appetite all, from the peer to the private citizen, hastened to gratify their palate as well as their curiosity with the several foods prepared, in all six varieties, made strictly after the recipes in M. Soyer's book, and such as will in future be cooked for the use of the poor recipients. In seven or eight minutes the party retired, and gave place to one hundred of the male and female poor from the Mendicity Institution. Grace having been impressively said by the Very Rev. Dean Tighe, the poor creatures were served with their meal, and having finished, their expressions of gratification were unbounded. They had five minutes for the discussion of their meal, consisting of one quart of the food, and on leaving the room everyone was furnished with a fine biscuit to eat at their leisure.

After all had departed the public were admitted, and all seemed much pleased. About six o'clock the poor people who were but spectators outside the rails were invited in and supplied abundantly. At night the kitchen was illuminated, and continued an object of attraction during the evening. The kitchen will be open for public inspection for a few days.

So Soyer had, on the surface at least, pulled off another triumph. Each one of his illustrious guests declared his soups excellent and his system flawless – they were astonished that he could achieve so much with such limited resources. The small matter of how tasteful this jamboree would appear – complete with flags, illuminated lights and grateful, grovelling paupers – to the rest of the population did not seem to bother him. Sir John Burgoyne may have expressed the private sentiments of others who attended when he likened the sight of the poor being put on display and made to eat with chained spoons as treating the destitute 'like wild animals'. As far as Alexis was concerned, he was filling the bellies of thousands of starving souls every day, with a brand new system that could be replicated across the nation.

While Soyer's highly publicised journey to Ireland – sponsored as it was by the British government – was a highly political, even inflammatory one, Alexis had little time for the politics of famine management. He saw starving people, he knew what it meant to be one step away from hunger, he knew he had the right blend of skills, contacts and practical imagination to help, and he set about doing so. The idea that he was being used as a propaganda tool by an increasingly panic-stricken administration did not, initially at least, occur to him. As a Frenchman he had little understanding of the long and bitter history of Ireland's clashes with the British, a struggle that many believed had led directly to the catastrophe that was now enveloping the country.

At the heart of the island's problems was the crushing poverty of the vast majority of the population, coupled with its total dependence on the potato. The poverty could in large part be put down to centuries of British colonisation, which saw the bulk of the fertile land formed into great estates owned by absentee landlords – principally English aristocrats. These landowners pressed their farm managers to squeeze every penny of profit from the land, by extracting maximum rents from their tenants and by producing crops which only stayed in the country long enough to be bagged up for export to more prosperous markets abroad. As these estates were viewed purely as income-generators, the landlords had no interest in investing any of their profits back into Ireland, which they viewed as one vast, heathen, boggy health hazard, never to be approached unless absolutely necessary. Therefore, although many built gracious mansions to display their wealth, few visited their Irish estates, and gradually the island's infrastructure and indigenous industries declined until, by the end of the eighteenth century, Ireland had become the most backward nation in northern Europe. By the mid-1830s three-quarters of the labouring classes were out of work. On top of this a huge growth in the population had made the land more and more densely populated. As rents continued to rise, a complicated system of sub-letting tinier and tinier parcels of land (often as little as half an acre) to the increasingly impoverished tenants meant that subsistence farming relied more and more heavily on the potato.

Potatoes had been cultivated in Ireland for centuries. Whether or not Sir Walter Ralegh was responsible for introducing the first Virginian varieties, he certainly grew them on his Munster estate, and by the end of the seventeenth century economists were advocating that large crops of the versatile tuber should be planted all over the country, ironically as a preventative *against* famine. Gradually, the potatoes became the staple food of the working population, specifically the 'lumper' potato, a variety that grew so large and prolifically that a family of six could produce enough of the crop to feed themselves for a year on a quarter of the land that would be needed to grow grain. Packed with calories, protein and vitamin C, it was an excellent source of nutrients, seed potatoes were cheap, the crop was easy to nurture and needed few tools, and the yield was not only filling and tasty but required no more processing to make it edible than a domestic fire, a pot for boiling water, and a basket to strain them in. Those families lucky enough to have a pig could fatten it on the peelings, then use the manure to fertilise the potato plot. Eventually, two million acres of Ireland were given over to potatoes and three million people ate nothing else, bar salt for seasoning and the odd cabbage leaf. Men consumed an incredible average of fourteen pounds every day, women and children more than ten pounds, and many passed their lives without so much as touching a loaf of bread or much of anything else. Indeed, small-scale fishing was only really practised in the west of the country, and even there fishermen relied on potatoes for the bulk of their subsistence. Ovens were a scarcity, and the only grain that was grown was for selling, not eating – just as the pig was generally raised for market rather than private consumption – as it was grain and bacon that paid the rent and saved the farmers from eviction. Always a hovering threat, evictions soared at times of national crisis as landowners, finding them-selves legally obliged to contribute to the local poor relief scheme for each of their hungry tenants, preferred to 'clear' them from the land the moment they fell into arrears.

For the population of a nation to be so reliant on any single crop was potentially dangerous, but potato crops were particularly vulnerable to the weather, as unlike grain they could not be dried and preserved almost indefinitely against lean times. They were also susceptible to fungal diseases that could wipe out entire crops in a matter of days. Indeed there had always been periodic failures of the harvest, roughly one every twenty or thirty years, with each one leading to scarcity and widespread hardship. But the near disaster of 1845, when a third of the national crop was lost, followed by the ruination of ninety per cent of all potato fields the following year, would lead to the greatest single humanitarian disaster to befall Europe in the nineteenth century.

The first year of famine had been bad enough for the English – wet weather had wrecked much of the native corn harvest, and the draconian Corn Laws, which imposed heavy duties on cheap imported corn, had made bread an inaccessible luxury for many. But England had an expanding industrial base, an effective infrastructure, and a relatively strong social safety net to help those most badly affected. Ireland, run from London by a succession of self-interested administrations, had none of these things, and when the potato blight *Phytophthora infestans* appeared in the first weeks of September 1845, it was the presage of a hellish five years of starvation and death to follow.

Phytophthora infestans was a new disease that had spread from the United States to Europe, rapidly travelling across Flanders, France, Switzerland and Germany. In Ireland, fears had been allayed by an excellent first crop in early August and so, although the blight was first reported in September, alarm did not spread until the following month, when the main autumn crop was lifted and found to be diseased. Although some areas had been spared by an early frost, a third of the late crop was lost, making it the worst harvest for a hundred years. Misdiagnosed as a form of wet rot by botanists, it would be more than thirty years before an antidote was developed. Meanwhile panic and confusion spread, the poor went hungry and, worse, had to watch in agony as Irish-grown grain, enough to feed 1,250,000 people in Britain, was exported from various ports under armed military guard.

As the news reached England, public reaction was mixed. While some were shocked by the scale of the disaster and stirred into relief efforts, others interpreted the biblical scale of the famine as God's punishment on the Irish, either for persisting in their errant popery, or alternatively for the perceived indolence and complacency of the peasant population. The prime minister, Sir Robert Peel, reacted by creating huge road-building and other public works schemes, which provided 140,000 jobs but did not pay the labourers a high enough wage to keep pace with the rocketing price of food. He also arranged for £100,000 worth of American corn to be sold cheaply to those in most need, but so inadequate were Ireland's ports, roads and railways that there was little hope of the grain ever reaching those it was intended for. They had been well-intentioned measures, but showed a shocking lack of understanding of the scale of the calamity.

While losing a third of the 1845 crop had been bad enough, the following year was catastrophic. At first the seed had thrived, and visitors travelling through the country reported fields packed with the dark green leaves and purple blossoms of healthy potato crops. Then, on 3 June 1846, the first signs of blight appeared on a few farms in County Cork. Near the end of July, it resurfaced in a few more towns. Soon, the familiar sulphurous stench of the rotting plants filled the air. Overnight the leafy stems formed brown spots, then quickly went black, withered and stank. In desperation, families rushed into their potato patches and ripped off the stems, hoping to prevent the disease from affecting the small potatoes still buried under the earth. But it was too late – when they pulled up a tuber it would be black and putrid and disintegrate in their hands. As their entire year's food supply turned into slime before their eyes, all they could do was wring their hands and pray. The disease spread at a rate of eighty kilometres a week, aided by a strong prevailing wind, until the entire country was affected. 'Within the last three days the blight has committed dreadful ravages,' wrote one eye-witness, 'and is now so decided that we can no longer flatter ourselves with even a chance of escape; it is north south, east, and west of us.'

With so many newly destitute to cater for, local relief committees soon collapsed under the increased demand for food. Skibbereen, a small town in County Cork, came to represent all the horrors of the famine. There, the first deaths were reported on 24 October, and by Christmas dozens more were waiting for burial. The artist James Mahony, visiting Skibbereen for the *Illustrated London News* in January 1847, drew graphic pictures of skeletal figures huddled forlornly outside semi-derelict stone huts, or sitting inside on dirty peat floors, shoeless, foodless and fireless. To add to their misery, that winter was one of the most severe on record. 'I saw the dying, the living and the dead, lying indiscriminately upon the same floor,' he wrote, 'without anything between them and the cold earth, save a few miserable rags upon them.' Malnutrition and weakened immune systems also led to outbreaks of highly infectious and often fatal diseases – typhus, yellow fever and dysentery were rife, while children were particularly susceptible to diarrhoea, measles and tuberculosis.

'Famine fever' described most of these complaints, and killed not just the poor but thousands of the doctors, clerics and relief officers who came into contact with them. At least a quarter of a million died from fever during the famine, on top of the 1,100,000 deaths from starvation. Wood to make coffins soon ran out – not that anyone had the cash to buy them – and so the dead were flung into deep open pits that remained uncovered until they were full.

Throughout these horrors, the British government's reaction remained directed by self-interest, wilful ignorance, political and religious dogma and the sort of obstructive, pettifogging bureaucracy that characterised the Victorian civil service and gave Charles Dickens so much ammunition for his satirical attacks. Eventually, in May 1846, and contrary to the wishes of his own party, Peel repealed the hated Corn Laws to abolish food tariffs, a move that effectively cost him the premiership. Although it was an essential move to alleviate a desperate situation, the wave of unpopularity this action brought him within Westminster was hardly surprising – a quarter of the peers in the House of Lords had Irish interests. Lord Palmerston, for example, who became foreign secretary in Lord John Russell's Whig cabinet following the swift collapse of Peel's Tory administration, owned a large tract of land in County Sligo. But instead of sending any food relief to his hundreds of starving tenants, he eventually shipped them off, some naked and all famished, to Newfoundland, to fend for themselves in the port of St John's. Eight died on the passage, and the rest spent the first winter begging on the dockside. When news of their condition came back home, even the English were shocked enough to force Palmerston to make a statement in the House of Commons. The repeal of the Corn Laws was still not nearly enough in itself to provide immediate support for the dying in Ireland and, with public pressure mounting, Russell finally acknowledged that more must be done, and urgently. He allowed the Board of Works to take on more labourers for more pointless relief works – mainly building roads that started nowhere and led nowhere – although the eightpenny daily wages were still too low to feed a family, and most of the men were by now too weak and ill to work effectively.

In the meantime private charities were starting to make a difference. Journalists and philanthropists travelled through Ireland and their horrified reports from the field finally began to stir people into fundraising efforts. A group of London-based businessmen, led by bankers Lionel de Rothschild and Thomas Baring, set up an organisation called the 'British Association for the relief of the extreme distress in the remote parishes of

Ireland and Scotland'. Launched with a £2,000 contribution from Queen Victoria, the organisers quickly gathered in £435,000. Churches mounted collections, money came in from around the Empire, America sent more than a hundred ships loaded with food aid, and Irish immigrants in the States remitted thousands of dollars to families back home. Finally, even Russell, who deplored the idea of state intervention and greatly feared the setting up of a dependency culture, recognised that 'the pressing matter at present is to keep people alive' and that 'soup kitchens appear the most immediate relief'. A number of small-scale soup kitchens were being run by proselytising Protestant groups hoping to turn their Irish brothers away from Catholicism with the lure of free food. Since November the Quaker Central Relief Committee in Dublin – without the evangelical agenda – had been quietly distributing meals in a more organised way from makeshift soup kitchens in some of the most distressed areas, and by January 1847 their Cork kitchen was dispensing over 1,300 pints of soup a day, plus free turnip and parsnip seed.

Having seen what could be done, the same month the government finally agreed to change tack and abandon the useless public works schemes for more direct aid. But the Quaker kitchens, while excellent, were not productive or economical enough to supply the quantities of food needed to keep hundreds of thousands of starving people alive. And this was where Alexis Soyer came in.

By the middle of the 1840s Alexis had been established in the echoing marble halls of the Reform Club for nearly a decade. Each day he had access to suppliers of the most expensive delicacies that Europe had to offer with which to tempt the palates of his sophisticated diners. Almost by definition a club such as the Reform provided, to its famous chef as well as its members, a luxurious retreat, a thick-carpeted, velvet curtained, hushed cocoon where you could feel safe and insulated, temporarily at least, from the outside world. But Alexis was not one to be institutionalised, or to lose sight of the desperate poverty of many of those he walked past on his way to Pall Mall every day. He may have dressed outlandishly but by preference he ate simply and lived simply. Neither did he become so blasé about the luxuries at his disposal that he forgot that they were available only to the very privileged. By the time the public were waking up to the enormity of the crisis in Ireland, Soyer had long been concerned with helping the working classes whose lack of the most basic skills in cookery and household management struck him as deplorable. Unlike the French housewife, he found that English women, when he visited their homes, displayed very little resourcefulness when it came to feeding their families from limited resources, a theme he would explore at greater length in his *Shilling Cookery for the People*, published in 1854 with such unflattering chapter titles as 'General Ignorance of the Poor in Cooking'.

He was equally concerned with feeding those who could not, for whatever reason, feed themselves at all. For some time he had acted as an unpaid consultant to various poorhouses and hospitals, including the Brompton Road Consumption Hospital in Knightsbridge, showing the trustees how to adapt and streamline their kitchens, ordering procedures and cooking methods to maximise the quality and quantity of the food they provided. And he gave cookery lessons to the well-heeled ladies who wanted to make and distribute soup to the poor in their immediate neighbourhoods, which was a popular charitable hobby at the time. As a result of these classes he had spent a considerable amount of time devising and testing various soups and panadas – thick porridge-like pastes – that could provide nourishing and reasonably tasty meals for the poor at a minimal cost per head.

Gradually, the idea for an entirely new sort of soup kitchen emerged in his mind, run on a far more efficient and scientific model than had ever been attempted before. Soup kitchens, of course, were nothing new. Voluntary organisations, funded by private donations and established with the exclusive intention of feeding the hungry in the area in which they operated, with food cooked and consumed on the premises, had been running in London for decades. They were particularly common in the East End, usually run by and for immigrant communities anxious to show their neighbours that they could provide for their own, and that they were not significantly adding to the burden of the poor rates. One of the first, La Soup, had opened on Brick Lane in 1797 to give aid to the large number of starving French Huguenot silk weavers who had settled in Spitalfields after escaping Catholic persecution across the Channel. Initially a thriving artisan community, the arrival of cheap, mass-produced, imported silk from abroad had gradually driven these skilled workers and their families into destitution, and various Protestant chari-ties felt an obligation to help. Jewish soup kitchens also sprang up in the area, and a few Jewish charities would eventually raise enough money to create purpose-built, institutional kitchens – the first opened in Leman Street in 1854 – but in the mid-forties they were still in the main small, informal and inefficiently run affairs.

Soyer had seen how these kitchens operated, and with his mania for organisation had seen how easily they could be redesigned to save time and money and yet massively expand their productivity. He also saw how his ideas could be replicated to help the starving millions across Ireland. Getting too closely involved in an existing kitchen was probably not a good idea; he ran the risk of treading on too many sensitive charitable toes, but he could, he reasoned, use his celebrity clout and contacts to start up and promote an entirely new one. And once the idea had crystallised – and with Ireland heading into deeper and deeper crisis – he plunged into action. On 10 February 1847 he despatched a batch of letters to *The Times*, the *Morning Advertiser* and various other papers, outlining his ideas for a large-scale 'model soup-kitchen' to be established simultaneously in London and Dublin, funded by public subscription, with a view to feeding large numbers of the destitute on an unprecedented scale. If successful, they could be the first of a chain of such kitchens. To set the ball rolling, Soyer pledged a generous £30 of his own money. The response was immediate and liberal, and within a few days he had received, by his own reckoning, 'several hundreds of letters' offering both money and encouragement. There was enough cash for him to take his plans to the iron foundry of Bramah, Prestage & Ball, who were busy perfecting the design for his tendon separators, where a prototype of his Subscription Kitchen for the Poor, complete with his newly designed steam apparatus, was immediately commissioned.

On 17 February he followed up his original letter with another lengthy report in *The Times*. In it he asked the editor to publish two new recipes which, he said, 'if closely followed, would confer an immediate benefit, not only on the poor, and various charitable institutions, but also on the labouring population of the United Kingdom'. Alexis wrote that he regretted the delay – although it had only been a week – since the publication of his last letter, but he had been caught up in various experiments on the different ways of thickening his soups, trying out 'various kinds of farinaceous ingredients, produced and imported into this country; and likewise with some of the immense varieties of vegetables, cultivated with so much success in this favoured soil; but which, generally speaking, are not sufficiently appreciated, or used to the greatest advantage by the industrious classes'.

The first recipe, 'the result of my first economical study to produce a cheap and wholesome soup', was for two gallons of a thin vegetable concoction flavoured with a tiny amount of meat and dripping and thickened with flour and pearl barley. He made a point of showing just how mean you could be with the ingredients, using just two ounces of

H. ALLEGORICAL.—TOMB OF EMMA SOYER.

'To Her'. Emma's monument in Kensal Green Cemetery, which cost Soyer £500. The whole monument is over 20 feet tall and the gas flue which fed an eternal flame is cleverly concealed behind a cherub's head. The ornate wooden railings by William Rogers, which had Emma Soyer carved into the boughs, were removed in the 1920s.

Clockwise from top Meaux-en-Brie in the nineteenth century. The old stone bridge linked the commercial and residential districts of the town; a self-portrait by Emma, painted shortly before her death in 1842; Emma's portrait of Alexis, now hanging in the Reform Club. Alexis wears his trademark red beret and is eating his favourite dish – truffled chicken; the ballerina Marie Taglioni in La Gitana, painted by Emma Soyer in 1839. Within a few years of Emma's death, Taglioni would become Fanny Cerrito's main professional rival.

'M. Soyer, At Home'. An idealised image of a small soirée chez Soyer, used in *The Gastronomic Regenerator*.

The upper level of the saloon of the Reform Club in 1841, on one of the rare occasions when women were admitted.

Soyer directing operations in the new Reform Club kitchens, shortly after its opening.

The triumphant banquet for Ibrahim Pasha, on 3 July 1846. An occasion of 'consummate splendour'.

The opening of Soyer's Model Soup Kitchen on Dublin Esplanade, 5 April 1847. The central boiler could hold 300 gallons of soup, while a series of iron *bain maries* kept a further 1,000 gallons warm.

'King Soyer resigning the Great Stewpan'. *Punch* reacts in classic mock-epic style to Soyer's surprise resignation from the Reform Club, May 1850.

Prince Albert at the York banquet in 1850, which was hosted by the city mayor to drum up support for the Great Exhibition. Overseen by Soyer with a budget of 1,000 guineas, the queen's consort is dwarfed by the ludicrous decorations the chef commissioned from Alfred Adams.

Soyer overseeing the roasting of a baron of beef by gas, for the Grand Dinner of the Royal Agricultural Society's twelfth annual festival in Exeter, 18 July 1850.

Left Lady Blessington's salon at Gore House, shortly before Soyer took over the lease. Pictured in the foreground are (from the left): William Thackeray, Mrs Norton, Rev Dr Lardner, Edward Bulwer Lytton, Count d'Orsay, Benjamin Disraeli, Lady Blessington, Daniel Maclise, Lord John Russell and Charles Dickens. *Below* The sheer volume of visitors to the Crystal Palace in the summer of 1851 caused chaos and gridlock on the streets of London. Illustration by George Cruikshank.

The meadow attached to the Symposium gardens which Soyer transformed into *Le Pré D'Orsay*. Among the risqué marble statues you can see the Grotto of Ondine, where visitors had to dodge past a permanent shower of water at the entrance – or hire an umbrella for sixpence. In the distance, at the back of Gore House, is the 40-foot shell which Soyer planted with rare blooms.

The inaugural Metropolitan Sanitary Association Dinner, held in the Baronial Hall on 10 May 1851. The guests ate turbot and drank champagne, and Dickens proposed a toast to the Board of Health.

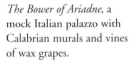

Various rooms inside the Symposium, drawn by Sala for inclusion in Soyer's souvenir catalogue, *The Book of the Symposium, or, Soyer at Gore House.*

Left *La Salle de Noces de Danaë*, a room in which a cascade of gold and silver teardrops seemed to shower down from the ceiling.

The Bower of Ariadne, a mock Italian palazzo with Calabrian murals and vines of wax grapes.

The *Grotte des Neiges Eternelles*, a North Pole cave with a stuffed fox and real ice stalactites.

La Forêt Péruvienne, a moonlit forest featuring a warm breeze and real palm trees.

dripping, a quarter of a pound of meat, and the mere offcuts of vegetables – he actually specifies just fifteen celery leaves, the 'peeling' of two turnips, and the green part of two leeks – i.e. the parts that are perfectly nutritious but 'the whole of which, I must observe, are always thrown away'. And yet he describes the cooking of these scratch ingredients with as much care as he would outline the preparation of a delicate Dover sole or Reform Sauce. The onions are carefully sweated, the beef cut up small enough to give every portion a shred, the flour well cooked through, the whole simmered carefully for three hours, and seasoned with salt and a spoonful of sugar for sweetness. 'The above soup has been tasted by numerous noblemen, members of Parliament, and several ladies, who have lately visited my kitchen department, and who have considered it very good and nourishing,' he couldn't refrain from boasting, before printing a table of costs:

Quarter of a pound of leg of beef, at 4d. per lb	1d.
Two ounces of dropping-fat, at 4d. per lb	½
Two onions and other vegetables	1d.
Half a pound of flour, seconds, at 1½d. per lb	¾
Half a pound of pearl barley, at 3d. per lb	1½
Three ounces of salt, with half an ounce of brown sugar	¼
Fuel	1
Two gallons of water	0
Total	6d.

'The above expenses make it come to ¾d. per quart in London; but as almost everything can be had at much less cost in the country, the price of this soup will be still more reduced,' he added. 'In that case a little additional meat might be used; and by giving away a small portion of bread or biscuit, better support would be given to the poor at a trifling cost, and no one, it is to be hoped, hereafter, would hear of the dreadful calamity of starvation.'

The second recipe was, he claimed, even cheaper and quicker to produce, and could easily be made up in quantities of even a hundred gallons at a time, if the maker used whatever vegetables he could get his hands on, from sorrel and parsnips to mangel-wurzels, 'all cut in a slanting direction, which facilitates greatly the cooking'. He recommended that the cook improvised some sort of stirring utensil, such as a piece of wood 'the shape of a cricket bat' that could reach the bottom of such a big copper cooking vessel. Such quantities called for '12lb of solid meat, or 18lb with the bones' – 'legs or clods of beef, with a portion of cow-heels, are excellent for the purpose; but any kind of edible meat, from beef to doe venison, would do' – plus twelve pounds of onions, twenty-four pounds of vegetables, twenty-five pounds of flour, thirty pounds of barley or rice (more if it was of poor quality), nine pounds of salt and three pounds of brown sugar. When well cooked, 'the proper thickness is easily ascertained when the soup hangs lightly on the back of the spatula or ladle', he added. It was his first carefully considered recipe for real mass catering, and came in at under a pound for a hundred gallons of it.

He hoped, he added, that the soup providers would, while sticking to his basic principles, vary their ingredients as much as possible, in order to provide their clients with some variety in their diet, 'which acts as generously on the digestive organs as a change of air does on the convalescent' and to stop racketeers – such as were operating in Ireland – from hiking up the prices of the ingredients he specified. There was also a third reason. 'For should the soup be approved of, and become a chief article of consumption for a certain time, such a receipt would be quite useless in some parts of the country where the ingredients could not be obtained; my sincere devotion to this important cause being to take every possible advantage of every kind of nutritious substances, animal and vegetable, and fish, and to convert them, by study and judgment, into a wholesome and cheap aliment for the millions.'

Alexis then went on to say that he had received so many generous contributions from the public since the publication of his last letter that he had already started to put his theories to the test. 'I have been able, already, to begin one of those kitchens on a small scale, where from 40 to 50 gallons of soup can be easily made, and quickly distributed to 200 or 300 poor, in an ordinary-sized London house . . . A correct drawing of my large plan for making and supplying 20,000 persons, is also in a very forward state.'

The 'test' kitchen he was referring to was in the East End, where the previous Saturday he had conducted his first experiment, 'to relieve the sufferings of that industrious but distressed class of society, the Weavers of Spitalfields'. The fact that it was starving French Protestants who had been the first to benefit from his charitable efforts was hardly surprising – however well he was integrating into English life, these were still his compatriots and co-religionists, and he had been profoundly shocked by the poverty and abject misery he had found in Spitalfields. He had been shown around the district by one Rev. Joseph Brown, the pastor of St

Matthias church, who, knowing the famous chef's background, cleverly judged him to be the right man to help him to help his parishioners, and had effected an introduction through mutual friends.

In yet another lengthy letter to *The Times*, written from the Reform Club and published four days later, Soyer described in some detail his walk with Brown around the parish. The tone was spare and direct, his usual flowery style for once forgotten in the urgent drive of the narrative.

We found in many of the houses, five or six in a small room, entirely deprived of the common necessaries of life – no food, no fire, and hardly any garment to cover their persons, and that during the late severe frost. In one of the attics we visited we inquired of a woman how they subsisted. Her husband, she said, had no employment during the last four months, and that they merely lived on what he could get by begging in the streets; she added, that she and her children had not tasted a bit of food for twenty-four hours, the last of which consisted of apples partly decayed, and bits of bread given to her husband, which food we may consider, if even plentiful, to be pernicious to health. The only piece of furniture in that gloomy abode of misery was the weaving machine, now at rest, and which, in time of prosperity, was used to provide food, and made, if not a wealthy, at least a happy home for those now wretched and destitute families . . .

After having witnessed such distressing scenes, I immediately proposed that my Subscription Kitchen for the Poor, which was being made at Messrs. Bramah and Prestige's [sic] factory, should be erected, without any loss of time, in the most populous district of Spitalfields, where there are no less than 10,000 poor people in one parish, and hardly any wealthy families among them to give them relief.

Within a couple of days the foundry had finished, delivered and installed Soyer's Parochial Model Kitchen for the Poor Weavers of Spitalfields, which was duly opened under the official patronage of the Bishop of London. The first day, sensibly enough, consisted of a controlled run-through to iron out teething problems, and Alexis for once refrained from informing the press until after the event – when, of course, he could boast of its great success.

I am happy to inform you, Sir, that my first experiment, made last Saturday, has been most successful, having been able to make a most excellent peas panada and meat soup in less than one hour and a half, and that at a very moderate expense – the quickness and saving of which are partly owing to the contrivance of my new steam apparatus, and which food was distributed, without any confusion, in less than twenty minutes, to about THREE HUNDRED AND FIFTY children, who were selected for the occasion from the different schools, the remainder of the food, with bread, being given away to many poor families in the neighbourhood.

The kitchen, he went on, would from now on open daily, providing a quart of food or soup, and a quarter of a pound of bread, for just one penny, with nothing given away 'except to those who are proved to be quite destitute', although he didn't say exactly how he intended to means-test the waifs and paupers at the door. Other details, though, had been carefully worked out – information about the issuing of tickets and receiving of subscriptions would be made known by advertisements, and a monthly catalogue published, detailing income, expenses, a list of subscribers, the quality of the ingredients consumed and a list of the poor relieved. Donors who wished to remain anonymous could provide a 'private mark' rather than a name, to keep the records in order. Soyer proposed that donations should not exceed a guinea, as 'I am aware that every nobleman, gentleman, and tradesman have to support their own poor', but that contributions below that figure would be thankfully received, 'and disposed of with the greatest economy'.

In fact only £147 was raised at this juncture, making Soyer's own contribution by far the largest single donation. While his friends and patrons had swollen the subscription list for *The Gastronomic Regenerator* to an impressive two thousand names, only twenty contributed to his soup kitchen appeal. But it was still enough to get the ball rolling. Later he would attempt to swell the coffers by holding an exhibition of 140 of Emma's paintings and drawings, many borrowed from their owners, at the Prince of Wales' Bazaar, which he rented at his own expense and decorated with lavish flower arrangements. He called the show Soyer's Philanthropic Gallery and produced beautifully designed admission tickets (like his business cards, cut as rhomboids) and a comprehensive catalogue carrying lengthy descriptions of the provenance and merit of each painting. These included such personal exhibits as a portrait of his mother, painted on a trip to Meaux, and a drawing of her maid and greyhound which Emma sketched on the morning before her death. *The Times* was particularly taken with the catalogue, which it described as 'an amusing book per se' and a 'fund of pleasant anecdotes', and declared that the portraits gave the saloon a comfortable feeling, 'as if the walls were peopled by lively good-humoured personages'. With typical over-optimism, Soyer had hoped to raise enough from the exhibition to start a new soup kitchen in every parish, but it was not a great success. Despite a dazzling launch attended by his old employer, Harriet, Duchess of Sutherland, the Countess of Blessington and a host of other luminaries, fewer than three hundred people visited it, raising a total of just £259. 11s. 10d. – enough to provide 50,000 free meals, but no new premises. The truth is that Emma was not, in fact, a particularly well-known artist, or her paintings of the highest order, so few would have been attracted for the aesthetic experience. In additon, people do not like to be pushed into giving to charity, and many still genuinely believed that the poor starved through ignorance and laziness. His patrons at the Reform Club, who may have been happy to indulge Soyer with subscriptions to his litho-graph and cook books, would have found the spectacle of their cook publicly taking it upon himself to feed the London indigent, while Parliament was abjectly failing to do so, acutely embarrassing. It was no wonder that they stayed away in droves.

One of the many aristocrats Soyer tapped for cash was the loyal Duchess of Sutherland, herself an influential philanthropist and Poor Relief Committee member who had an abiding fondness for Soyer, with whom she would, to his great delight, chat away easily in French. Bearing in mind the speed with which Soyer's innovative plans to feed the poor on an even grander scale came to the attention of the government, it was likely to have been the duchess who encouraged the relevant departments to take his ideas seriously as a partial solution for the Irish crisis. However it happened, Alexis would later recall that 'I was requested to lay my plans before the Lords of the Treasury, and being approved of, I willingly accepted the invitation of erecting my model kitchen in Dublin, instead of London, as I at first intended.'

In fact, Soyer was probably more of a godsend to the government than even he realised. His experiments in Spitalfields fell in the same fortnight as the passing of a new Irish Relief Act, which dealt specifically with soup kitchens: how they would operate and who would be eligible to use them. Despite their reluctance to abandon a *laissez-faire* economic approach and provide direct food aid, the previous month the government had finally done a U-turn and caved in to the inevitable. The public works scheme had failed miserably, the Irish landowners were clearly not prepared to take responsibility for their tenants, and so for the duration of the crisis the people simply could not feed themselves, and must be fed by the state. However, if the government was going to help out, they certainly were not going to be generous, and the cheapest food possible was to be found. Soyer's soups, with their miniscule quantities of meat, floury padding and vegetable peelings (only Soyer advocated that the outer layer of the vegetable was worthy of cooking too – 'that which has hitherto only increased the malaria of our courts and alleys by its decomposition'), served from hastily erected factories that could each feed many thousands in a day, was exactly what they needed.

Within a few days, the *Sunday Observer* announced that Soyer had been officially appointed 'Head Cook to the people of Ireland, with ample instructions to provide his soups for the starving millions of Irish people'. Lord Bessborough, the Lord Lieutenant of Ireland, had written to the Reform Club requesting the committee to grant their chef a temporary leave of absence so he could rush to Ireland and set up his Model Kitchen, and by the end of the month Sir Randolph Routh, head of the commissariat department, was able to write to Charles Trevelyan, the most senior civil servant to oversee relief spending, that 'Soyer is on his way!' Thackeray also gave his friend's enterprise a generous fanfare in *Punch*. 'M. Soyer deserves to be called the Gastronomic Regenerator of Ireland. His receipt for cheap soup is the best practical suggestion which has been yet made for the relief of that unlucky island,' he wrote, before suggesting, with dubious taste, a mass cull of English game to provide his soups with extra protein.

Initially at least, Alexis's reception in Ireland was also positive. 'We learn that the Government have resolved forthwith to despatch M. Soyer, the *chef de cuisine* of the Reform Club, to Ireland,' announced the *Cork Examiner* on 26 February.

Pursuant to this wise and considerate resolve, artificers are at present busied day and night, constructing the necessary kitchens, apparatus, &c, with which M. Soyer starts for Dublin direct to the Lord Lieutenant. His plans have been examined both by the authorities at the Board of Works and the Admiralty, and have, after mature consideration, been deemed quite capable of answering the object sought.

The soup has been served to several of the best judges of the noble art of gastronomy at the Reform Club, not as soup for the poor, but as a soup furnished for the day in the *carte*. The members who partook of it declared it excellent. Among these may be mentioned Lord Titchfield and Mr O'Connell. M. Soyer can supply the whole poor of Ireland, at one meal for each person, once a day. He has informed the executive that a bellyfull of his soup, once a day, together with a biscuit, will be more than sufficient to sustain the strength of a strong and healthy man . . . To the infant, the sick, the aged, as well as to distant districts, the food is to be conveyed in cars furnished with portable apparatus for keeping the soup perfectly hot. It would be premature to enter into further details. M. Soyer has satisfied the Government that he can furnish enough and to spare of most nourishing food for the poor of these realms, and it is confidently anticipated that there will soon be no more deaths from starvation in Ireland.

Soyer's claim that a bellyful of his soup would sustain a strong man was an extravagant, even reckless one. While his well-fed patrons at the Reform might have considered a small cupful before dinner as perfectly palatable, Alexis knew little solid science about calories or real subsistence survival – despite his general good sense in other matters of nutrition – and considering that each portion of soup could contain no more than half an ounce of meat and fat per head, plus whatever carbohydrates and vitamins could be extracted from the thickening agents, it's no wonder that his detractors immediately pounced on this claim as arrant nonsense. However, it wasn't entirely clear whether Soyer was claiming that such a meagre meal would sustain a man in good health for good or, as was more likely, that it would merely keep him alive and active in times of famine. One of his loudest critics was another chef, one Monsieur Jaquet of Johnson's Tavern in Clare Court, who declared in a letter to *The Times* that with so little meat in it, Soyer's soup was less soup for the poor than simply poor soup, 'an innutritious compound as will only tend to weaken and destroy the constitution'. Having no intrinsic value, he finished, it should not be used as an experimental food on the destitute poor of Ireland. Embarking on a protracted correspondence with him, Alexis replied with spirit that not only had the government seen fit to approve his soups, but that he now had three versions of it 'on taste', two with meat and one without, and he defied Monsieur Jaquet 'to tell which was which'. Flesh was not meant to be the primary source of nutrition, he declared. 'The meat I consider of no more value than the other in-gredients, but to give a flavour by properly blending the gelatine and the osmazone, for in compounding the richest soup, the balance of it is the great art.' Jaquet countered by saying that if an independent scientific analysis of a portion of Receipt Number I proved that there were adequate nutrients to sustain life, then he would apologise. Needless to say, neither party commissioned such an analysis. Soyer dealt just as robustly with his other critics. When a woman calling herself *No Cook* wrote that she had tried the recipe for her family of nine, and found that it cost three-halfpence rather than three-farthings a quart, and accused Soyer of a 'great injury to the poor by misrepresenting the price of necessities', Alexis argued with her maths and offered to show her how to make it properly. And as for those who challenged him to live on the stuff himself, he declared that he had. 'For the last three weeks I have made so many soups, and continually tasting of each, that I have actually fed on it (barring the biscuit) and I assure you, sir, that all the nobility and gentry, now daily visiting me, say that I look as well as ever.'

Despite the growing scepticism, Alexis was delighted and highly flattered by his dealings with the government. The ragged boy from Meaux-en-Brie was being consulted, courted even, by men at the acme of English government, including the prime minister himself. These politicians were, it seemed, beginning to see him as the saviour of Ireland – and by implication, bearing in mind the increasing gravity of the situation – themselves. For everyone had heard of Alexis Soyer, and if Alexis Soyer could be seen by the English public to be providing enough food to feed the starving in Ireland at a minimal cost to the taxpayer, perhaps the tide of public opinion would turn in the government's favour. And if, in his enthusiasm to impress the new Whig administration with both the efficiency of his system and the rigid economy of his recipes, Alexis lost sight of exactly how much food really was needed to sustain adequately a man in dire need, and how to present his revolutionary kitchen to the establishment with suitable tact and decorum, these troubles were for the future. In the short term, Alexis provided the government with his soup kitchen plans and, as instructed, proceeded to Ireland in great haste. He took with him George Warriner, a loyal and lifelong friend who accompanied him on many of his travels abroad. It was also Warriner who, a few days after the publication of the first famine recipes in *The Times*, had rushed into the Reform Club kitchen, red-faced and breathless, to declare 'Dripping's up!' There had been a run on the cheap fat since Soyer had recommended it and, joked Warriner, 'If you had told me that you intended publishing your receipts, I could have gone into the market, and bought tons of dripping; and we might between us have pocketed a few hundreds.' Of course Warriner was aware that Alexis abhorred any hint of racketeering, and in any case knew little and cared less about cash when there was glory to be had.

Once in Dublin, says Volant, Soyer 'began his task in a very energetic manner'. He made a point of employing local men and set up a short-term, makeshift soup depot in the coach-building yard of a Mr Tonge, of Great Britain Street, while the main pavilion on the Esplanade soon buzzed with engineers, timber merchants and workmen. Soon realising that his original estimate of a two-week trip was unrealistic – in fact it took four to complete the Model Soup Kitchen – on 11 March he asked Lord Bessborough to write to the Reform Club requesting an extension to his original leave of absence. The members of the club committee immediately agreed that the project would continue to 'benefit by his supervision'. Then, on 1 April, Alexis himself wrote to the committee, asking for yet more time, he estimated until 'the end of next week' – in order to get everything up and running satisfactorily. Somehow, three weeks before the opening he also managed to find time to make detailed amendments to the fourth edition of *The Gastronomic Regenerator*, adding a new preface and table of contents, more recipes, a long plug for his tendon separators and the thank you letters for his *Bouquet de Gibier*, which displayed rather an extraordinary facility to switch his focus between the abject wretchedness of the famished masses he was seeing all around him in Dublin, and the superficial business of gadgets and nosegays and diamond pins.

As soon as Alexis's famine recipes had appeared in *The Times*, industrious scribes around Ireland had been busy copying them out and circulating them to anyone who might be able to produce them. On 10 March, one Robert White sent a manuscript to an associate entitled '*M. Soyer's Soup Receipts for the use of the Irish poor, copied with a view, should an opportunity offer, of their being used for the benefit of the poor labourers at and about the Arigna mines, County Roscommon*'. Alexis realised that this information needed to be disseminated across the country as quickly as possible. So while the Dublin kitchen was still under construction he managed to put together a small sixpenny booklet, just fifty pages long, entitled *The Poor Man's Regenerator*, which was published shortly before his return to England in April. In it, he recorded all his famine soups, panadas and other economical recipes for the poor, with a penny from each pamphlet going to charity. Whether he was compensating himself for his unpaid labours, or saving people the effort of copying out his recipes is moot, but *Soyer's Charitable Cookery*, as it became known, was well enough received, and, wrote one critic, 'deserves a corner in every poor man's library'. This rather missed the point, as the book was intended as a textbook for charity workers rather than a manual for the labourers themselves (who were lucky to own a Bible, never mind a library), and it was soon being used as a principal source of information in soup kitchens around the island. Perhaps surprisingly, given all that Alexis had seen and learned during his mission, in the book's foreword, entitled *Address to the World in General, but to Ireland in Particular*, he seemed to subscribe to the view that the Irish sufferings owed more to the will of God than any deficiencies of man. After describing the horrors he had witnessed during his visit, he declared, 'What are the efforts, even of a civilised nation, against the will of the Almighty? With me you will justly answer useless.'

Meanwhile, in London there was a split between continuing support for Soyer among the people – ballad sheets about the colourful chef and his Irish mission were being sold in the streets – and the press, which was now moving from admiration of the government for sending its own favoured *chef de cuisine* as the chosen servant to feed the starving Irish, to outright ridicule. Even *Punch*, usually a strong supporter of Alexis (affectionately dubbing him a 'broth of a boy'), began to have doubts about the power of his soup to stave off the effects of starvation. By April, the magazine was hinting that 'a gentleman of taste, who had dipt rather deeply into M. Soyer's soups, says the Irish would certainly relish the soup all the more if there was a bit of Irish Bull in it'. *Punch* was still being flippant, but other journals began to launch far more serious attacks on him.

That same month *The Lancet* took up Jaquet's attack on Receipt Number I and published a vitriolic piece – submitted by an anonymous author on Athenaeum notepaper who adopted the nom de plume of *Medico* – which dismissed Soyer's remedies as nothing better than 'soup quackery', promoted by a changeable, incompetent and niggardly government, 'at one time adopting public works, at another preaching a poor law . . . and then descending to M. Soyer, the chief cook of the Reform Club, with his ubiquitous kitchens and soups, at some three farthings the quart, which is to feed all hungry Ireland'. As the rich were using M. Soyer and his soups as a salve for their consciences, continued the author, 'with a belief that famine and fever may be kept at bay by M. Soyer and his kettles, it is right to look at the constitution of this soup of pretence, and the estimate formed of it by the talented but eccentric self-deceived originator'. Receipt Number I, continued *Medico*, contained less than three ounces of solid nutriment to each quart of soup *à la Soyer* – and everyone knew the debilitating effects of a liquid-only diet. Using some fairly unimpressive dietetic science he went on to create a crude equation between how much a healthy man needed to defecate each day, and from that deduced how much he needed to consume.

Organic chemistry proves to us that the excretae from the body of a healthy subject by the eliminatory organs must at least amount to twelve or fourteen ounces; and organic chemistry will not, we fear, bend to the most inspired recipes of the most miraculous cookery book, to supply the number of ounces without which the organic chemistry of the human body will no more go on than will the steam-engine without fuel. M. Soyer, supposing each meal of his soup for the poor to amount to a quart, supplies less than three ounces, or less than a quarter the required amount, and of that only one solitary half ounce of animal aliment, diluted, or rather dissolved in a bellyful of water. Bulk of water, the gastronomic may depend, will not make up for the deficiency of solid convertible aliment. No culinary digesting, or stewing, or boiling, can convert four ounces into twelve, unless, indeed, the laws of animal physiology can be unwritten, and some magical power be made to reside in the cap and apron of the cook for substituting fluids in the place of solids, and *acqua pura* in place of solids in the animal economy.

It seems necessary to bring forward these facts as M. Soyer's soup has inspired the public mind with much satisfaction – a satisfaction which, we venture to say, will never reach the public stomach. Marquises and lords and ladies may taste the meagre liquid, and pronounce it agreeable to their gustative inclinations; but something more than an agreeable titillation of the palate is required to keep up that manufactory of blood, bone, and muscle which constitutes the 'strong, healthy man'.

Even the Irish papers seemed to turn against Alexis. While the *Dublin Evening Herald* had reported so favourably on the opening of the Model Soup Kitchen, journalists from the city's other papers saw things in a very different light. The *Dublin Evening Packet* poured scorn on what it saw as the patronising attitude of the wealthy and the inappropriate air of celebration. 'His Excellency the Lord Lieutenant was there . . . the ladies Ponsonby and many other fair and delicate creatures assembled; there were earls and countesses, and lords and generals, and colonels and commissioners, and clergymen and doctors; for, reader, it was *a gala day, – a grand gala.*' Warming to his theme, the writer referred to the charitable subscription Alexis had requested from each guest, to be distributed to worthy causes by the lord mayor. 'Five shillings each to see paupers feed! Five shillings each! To watch the burning shame chasing pallidness from poverty's wan cheek! Five shillings each! When the animals in the Zoological Gardens can be inspected at feeding time for sixpence!' The correspondent for the *Freeman's Journal* was equally enraged by the sight of the Union flag 'flaunted in triumph from the top of the soup kitchen'. Then again, he added sarcastically, perhaps it was 'its natural and most meet position; the rule of which it is the emblem has brought our country to require soup kitchens, – and no more fitting ornament could adorn their tops. All the parade I could have borne,' he continued, 'but indefensible was the exhibition of some hundreds of Irish beggars to demonstrate what ravening hunger will make the image of God submit to.'

Equally damaging was the publication of a ten-page pamphlet, published simultaneously to the damning edition of *The Lancet*, written by Queen Victoria's own doctor, Sir Henry Marsh, and excerpted in many of the newspapers. Without deigning to mention Soyer by name, he effectively agreed with *Medico* that a diet of 'soups and other semi-liquid articles' was, by definition, unhealthy, not least because it could not be chewed. 'These pass away too rapidly from the stomach,' he wrote, 'are swallowed too hastily, and violate a natural law in superseding the necessity of mastication . . . Food, to be at once sustaining to the labourer, and preventive of disease, must have bulk – must possess solidity – must not be rapidly digestible, and must contain, in varied proportions, all the staminal ingredients of nutriment.'

The growing number of attacks was not only bewildering and painful to Alexis, who had never encountered such viciousness before, but completely undermined the government's high-profile change of tack. Something had to be done to save face, and eventually an independent report *was* commissioned, to examine the efficacy and value for money of Soyer's Famine Soups. Produced by the Royal Dublin Society, it was written by a member of the Chemical Committee, a Professor John Aldridge, and presented at the society's Agricultural Evening Meeting on 6 April. Aldridge had spent some time at the Model Soup Kitchen, interviewing Soyer and analysing and sampling his recipes before submitting his report, and Alexis clearly used all his charm to win over this potential antagonist. In the end Aldridge's findings, while generally positive for Alexis, were often non-committal and sometimes barely intelligible. Comparing four of Soyer's soup recipes with one from St Peter's Parish, one from St Anne's Parish and one from the South Dublin Union Poorhouse, he concluded that:

The real pecuniary value of the foregoing soups do not differ by any means as much as might be supposed from their nominal cost per gallon. Thus, the South Dublin Union Poorhouse soup is really as cheap as M. Soyer's soup No 5, although the one is said to cost 4d a gallon and the other 6d. And the pecuniary value of M. Soyer's soups, Nos 2, 4 and 5, may be perceived to be just the inverse of their nominal cost. M. Soyer's fish-soup No 6, is peculiarly deserving of remark, being the most nutritious and the cheapest of all those under consideration.

'M. Soyer agrees with me,' added Aldridge, 'as to the danger of feeding the poor chiefly upon liquid aliment,' and went on to look at the value and composition of Alexis's other charity dishes, such as his Savoury Hominy, Rice Panada and Peas Panada. The first two he deemed to be cheaper but less nutritious than wheaten bread, but the last one he found 'a remarkable contrast: it is only one-fourth the price of bread, while it is fully five times as nutritious'. The only improvement he could suggest was the addition of a few more onions – 'and that solely on chemical principles. Moreover, I can bear testimony, from personal experience, to the exceedingly palatable nature of the dish, when prepared in the manner recommended by M. Soyer.' Aldridge also supported Alexis's views that the labouring classes should be taught to seek out and cook whatever natural resources – such as fish and wild seeds – could be found in their locality; that 'the flesh of cattle is not essential to human food' and that 'by frying a small quantity of meat, its flavour may be diffused through a large bulk of boiled vegetable matter . . . a principle in the preparation of food which, I think, is most important and should not be neglected.' The words could almost have come from Alexis's own mouth.

Finally, Alexis's charm offensive was rewarded with a generous acknowledgement of the chef's creativity and co-operation at the end of the report.

I feel myself called on to return my personal thanks to M. Soyer [wrote Aldridge] as well as to Mr Warriner, who accompanied him to this country, for the assistance they afforded me . . . In every respect they have assisted my enquiries in the most liberal and unreserved manner. And in the name of the Irish people I thank M. Soyer for I what I believe to be his purely philanthropic intentions towards them. He has given to us two boons of no ordinary value, – a model dispensing kitchen of great ingenuity, and a method of economic cooking far superior to any to which the poorer order of our countrymen have hitherto been accustomed.

Although ostensibly exonerated by the Aldridge report, Alexis, bruised from the attacks in the press and having already overstayed his intended visit by five weeks, was ready to return to London. A few days after the gala opening, his Model Kitchen was officially purchased by the government and on 24 April handed over to the women of the South Union Relief Committee of Dublin to run. He and George Warriner finally left Dublin on 11 April after seven weeks in Ireland. The night before his departure around thirty of his Dublin patrons and allies held a formal dinner for him in the Freemasons' Hall, complete with loyal toasts, votes of thanks and the presentation of an elegantly engraved snuff box as a memento of his philanthropic expedition. Once he was back in London, there was another meal in his honour, this time at the London Tavern, which was attended by 150 supporters. 'The dinner was of a most *recherché* description,' commented Volant, already forgetting the contrast between the cheap, chained-up bowls Soyer had just left behind and the 'table service of gold and silver' that was supplied by the banqueting house. 'It was a most fitting ovation to the unbought talents of the chef.'

Following Alexis's departure from Ireland, soup kitchens were gradually set up all over the country. However, in some areas – including the town of Skibbereen – they only came into operation in mid-June, far too late for many thousands of men, women and children. Also, despite the wide circulation of Alexis's carefully worked out recipes, the quality and quantity of the food provided varied enormously between the different distributing committees. Some of the 'poor soup' served up made Soyer's dishes look like luxurious abundance. Eventually, the relief commission ordered a daily ration of at least one pound of meal per adult, a carbohydrate compound that could consist of varying amounts of maize, rice and oats, according to availability, which was then boiled up with water to form a primitive porridge or 'stirabout'. It may have been a far cry from what Soyer had had in mind, but it was food, and it was finally getting to the hungry. By July the entire populations of some counties were being fed on government rations, and there were three million meals being distributed a day, at a cost of 2d. a head. Although providing food through soup kitchens proved a better system than taking the emaciated men off the land – where they could at least have been sowing seed for the following harvest – to work on pointless public building projects, riots occasionally flared up as a protest at what the people saw as the demeaning way the new regime operated. Yet however imperfect it was, the system worked, the mortality rate immediately plummeted, and at a fraction of the cost of the public works scheme.

However, the government had only ever regarded the soup kitchens as a temporary measure to stave off the worst after-effects of the 1846 crop failure. As the autumn of 1847 looked set to produce a tolerably successful harvest, many in England asserted that the famine was over, and that Ireland was returning to 'normal'. Towards the end of August the soup kitchens began to close down, and by the end of September they had disappeared altogether. This was a tragedy as, far from being over, the famine would continue for another three years, causing the death of many more hundreds of thousands. The dismantling of the soup kitchen network was one of the greatest disasters of all.

Despite the bitter controversy surrounding his mission to Ireland, Soyer did not come back – as some suggested – with his tail between his legs, and thereafter bury himself in the Reform Club basement. On the contrary, and in spite of the pasting he had received from some parts of the press, his experiences in Ireland proved to him just how much he could achieve with the right amount of energy, commitment, publicity, common sense and a few basic resources. Before long he bounced back, as bumptious as ever, and soon found that his expertise was respected and his advice sought by all sorts of charitable institutions. The Royal Agricultural Society asked him to contribute articles to their journal on famine relief, potato substitutes and charitable soup-making for the kitchens of large country houses – declaring that 'a hint from M. Soyer would no doubt make this soup equal to mock-turtle soup, at a trifling expense'. When asked to rewrite the RAS's existing *Cottage Tract on Cookery*, he sent them in answer a copy of *The Poor Man's Regenerator*.

On 28 September, *The Times* published what Alexis called a 'brief statement' (although with him brief was always a relative term), in which he announced that his system had proved of 'paramount importance, both as regards the large quantity of superior food that could be produced, and the immense saving that could be effected'. He claimed that local poor relief boards could halve their costs if they adopted the principles of his Model Soup Kitchen, and backed up the statement by saying that the ratepayers of the North Union of Dublin paid 3s. 4d. in the pound, while those of the South Union – the catchment area of his kitchen – paid only a shilling, which 'speaks volumes in favour of my system'. He added that since the opening of the kitchen, Messrs Brown & Co. of Great Suffolk Street, Dublin, had also installed a new patent steam-plate oven, which could bake 1,000 four-pound loaves every twelve hours, using just three bushels of coke, saving a further twenty-five per cent on the cost of bread. Finally, he added the statistics from 6 April to

14 August. In four months the kitchen had served almost three million pounds of food at a cost of £7,768, 'including coals, expenses of house, carriage, labour etc'. Under the old system of preparing food in different depots, he asserted, this would have come to £15,536 – i.e. twice the price.

With that Soyer managed to brush aside the claims that his rations constituted anything other than 'superior food'. His charitable urge to save more of the hungry poor was stronger than ever. During 1847 two new soup kitchens had been established, in Leicester Square and Farringdon Road, as well as the original Spitalfields site, but the failure of his art exhibition meant that Soyer could not carry the financial burden alone. He therefore arranged to hand over the Leicester Square and Farringdon Road kitchens to the Quakers, although he was loath to loosen the reins at the Spitalfields kitchen (perhaps because of the Huguenot connection) and in the end shared responsibility for it with the Duchess of Sutherland and her various charitable helpers. The ever-loyal Warriner, who that autumn made Soyer godfather to his new son, Alexis, was always there to offer practical support. And unlike some of his more impulsive undertakings, Soyer's passion for philanthropic endeavour would remain with him to the end of his life.

8

'OUR EYES SPARKLE AND
OUR PALATES YEARN'

The mid-forties represented a time of extraordinary commercial as well as philanthropic activity for Alexis. Now in his thirties he was at the peak of his fitness, unencumbered by any family commitments to keep him from working and playing hard, and his booming celebrity made him a very attractive proposition for manufacturers wanting to promote any new-fangled culinary products or contrivances. And Soyer was certainly not above cashing in on any star endorsements in the offing. The small offices of A. Soyer & Co., at 5 Charing Cross Road, an address he shared with a firm of opticians called Wilkins & Hall, swarmed with inventors and entrepreneurs anxious to get the great chef to lend his name to their latest projects.

Wisely, Alexis generally chose to stick with established companies, and was keen, as an experienced inventor himself, to be involved in the development of the products he was to be associated with. His relationship with Bramah continued to flourish, leading to the launch of two new ranges, a Cottager's Stove, and later Soyer's Deluxe Kitchen Range. Both were based on Reform Club designs but adapted for completely different domestic environments; the large range facilitated seven different types of cookery – roasting, baking, boiling, broiling, braising, stewing and frying, while the small stove could not only bake, boil and roast, but heat the iron, dry the linen and warm the front room into the bargain. Although never a great businessman, on these occasions Alexis had the nous to ensure that the designs remained his property, with Bramah producing them under licence. Later on Bramah did buy the design for the Deluxe Kitchen Range, while the Cottager's Stove was sold to a rival company, Deane & Dray of London Bridge. Deane & Dray later manufactured several other products for Alexis – Soyer's Baking Stewing Pan, which came in two-, four- and six-quart sizes, and Soyer's Improved Baking Dish, which incorporated a 'vegetable drainer and cullender saucepan'.

The nature of his business relationships changed as Alexis gained experience and his career progressed. Sometimes the small firms he worked with acted merely as selling agents, sometimes as manufacturers, sometimes they simply paid to use the Soyer brand name, and sometimes they became partners in one of a number of small, ad hoc companies that Soyer set up in this period. It is impossible now to unravel all of his commercial undertakings, which were often as chaotic as the rest of his life. In Kelly's trade directory he is listed as having links to at least a dozen different companies and business addresses in the 1840s and 1850s, most of them set up for just one – often short-lived – enterprise. Overall it chimes with a picture of a man with a butterfly brain spilling over with enthusiasms that rarely lasted the course. And fame and novelty were clearly stronger spurs than money, in spite of the pleasure he took in spending it, as with all these companies Soyer never sought to limit his liabilities, and while he got around to registering the designs of a few of his inventions, he rarely got as far as the patent office.

There was one exception to this – in 1853 he tried to patent an invention concerning 'Improvements in Preparing and Preserving Soups' called Soyer's Osmazome Food. This was a concentrated and supposedly nutritious compound made to resemble the sort of caramelised juices that are left in the saucepan after meat has been roasted – effectively an early form of liquid stock cube. He had earlier defined osmazome as 'that liquid part of the meat that is extracted by water at blood-heat', found principally 'in all adult animals having a dark flesh, and to a very small extent in those having a white flesh, such as the flesh of fowls'. The concept of osmazome was not new to the Victorians – Brillat-Savarin had described it as where 'the principal merit of a good soup resides', but Soyer was certainly the first man to try and bottle it. Typically, however, he failed to file the final paperwork in time and his application duly expired.

Often mercurial in his enthusiasms and slapdash in his methods, Alexis could also be a poor judge of character – mixing business with pleasure and being guided by affection rather than hard-headed pragmatism would lead to some disastrous decisions, eventually costing him friends, a vast amount of money and eventually his hard-won reputation. However, at least one business relationship forged at this time was to prove a long and fruitful one, both professionally and personally. Charles Phillips was a gas engineer, whose small company, Smith & Phillips, was based in Snow Hill. It was still a decade before Robert Bunsen was to come up with his ingenious little burner, but as the availability of gas was gradually increasing, forward-thinking companies were looking at ways to harness the new fuel to heat and ventilate houses, and also as a substitute for coal in kitchen ranges. Smith & Phillips was one such company and, knowing of Soyer's famous experience of installing gas cookers at the Reform Club, decided that he was just the man to have on board. For his part, Alexis appreciated the company's modern approach, and eagerly embraced the opportunity to spread his enthusiasm for cooking with gas into the domestic arena.

To begin with, Alexis put his name to one of Smith & Phillips' small ovens. It was called Soyer's Celebrated Roaster, ran the advert, 'in justice to that great master of the Culinary Art', and was a snip at just £1. 15s. But Charles and Alexis had already set their sights on bigger things, and soon afterwards a large and decorative modern kitchen range was launched, complete with its own separate boiler and priced at a gigantic £22. Called Soyer's Phidomageireion (meaning 'thrifty kitchen' in Greek), it was one of the very earliest domestic gas cookers on the market, and the accom-panying literature by Smith & Phillips – who did own the patent to their invention – was clearly inspired by Soyer's customary sweep of super-latives. The Phidomageireion, it said, 'so highly appreciated by MONS. SOYER (who certainly is eminently qualified to judge of the practical utility of this apparatus, as being equally well adapted for the cooking of the varied French dishes, as for the more substantial English ones) is acknowledged, by the best judges in gas matters, to stand unrivalled'. The Phidomageireion's unique selling point – apart from the rarity of its use of gas – was a small window near the pilot light underneath the boiler, so that the user could clearly see whether or not the gas was burning, thus saving wastage and, more importantly, improving safety:

> by precluding the possibility of explosion ever taking place, an incon-venience to which all previous gas apparatus for cooking are liable . . . This system is evidently of the utmost importance, as a means of preventing accidents, and also gives an opportunity, if necessary, of cleaning the burner with great facility. In fact the whole of the apparatus is truly simple and convenient, possessing the advantages of

ROASTING, STEAMING, BOILING, BAKING, BROILING, FRYING, STEWING &tc, with a certainty of PERFECT VENTILA-TION and a . . . CLEANLINESS INCREDIBLE to all who have only seen defective cooking apparatus.

The ability to regulate the heat, the thriftiness of being able to turn off the fuel supply the minute the food was ready, and the capacity to keep cooked food warm without spoiling, were all praises of gas previously sung by Soyer and now repeated in the Smith & Phillips blurb. Knowing that the high price of the Phidomageireion would put it beyond the reach of many, the partners also made a point of targeting the pub and restaurant trade by inviting the owners of club houses, inns and dining halls to a daily demonstration at the company's showroom on Skinner Street, 'where its value can be fully appreciated, and proof given that it requires only to be seen in action to promote its general adoption'.

In fact the Phidomageireion would not make Soyer's or Phillips' fortune – it was far too advanced for its time. Kitchen range and oven technology did gradually improve throughout the 1840s, but only a minority of more enlightened housewives – like Charles Dickens' wife Catherine – installed the latest equipment, and it would be another forty years before the first power station for domestic consumers opened the way for widespread gas cookery. Even by the turn of the century only a quarter of homes had cottoned on to the benefits – which by then included wipe-clean enamel surfaces, see-through doors and new 'grills' that could toast any food placed under them. In essence these 'cookers' were much the same as Soyer's, but they came far too late for him to profit by them. Soyer did, however, learn about the hugely persuasive power of daily showroom demonstrations to shift units of stock, a lesson that would become extremely valuable later on. He also began a lifelong friendship with Charles Phillips – in fact it was Phillips' son, another Charles, who would eventually travel with him to the Crimea.

Another prosperous businessman to enter Soyer's life at this stage was a fellow freemason, David Hart, whose many enterprises included a small engineering foundry in Trinity Square, which made several of Alexis's little kitchen gadgets – Soyer's Egg Cookery Apparatus (a mechanical egg-timer), and a similar contraption, for timing meat, called the Alarum. Hart made the pieces from Soyer's designs, which were then sold through A. Soyer & Co. Alexis was initially very impressed with David Hart who, although ten years older, displayed the drive and dynamism that attracted him to his various business associates. As their affairs became more entangled, however, the relationship would sour, with catastrophic consequences for Alexis.

David Hart hardly needed Soyer's business – he was already making a fortune through wines and spirits. The Harts, a prominent Jewish family originally from Cornwall, had been importing rum from the West Indies since the early eighteenth century and in 1804 David's father, Asher Laemle ben Eleazar, had changed his name to Lemon Hart and established his own hugely successful brand of rich, sweet Jamaican rum. The family moved to London in 1811 to expand the business further, and soon won the contract to supply Lemon Hart rum to the British navy. By 1849, David, who had inherited the business four years earlier, was said to be supplying the navy with 100,000 gallons of rum a year. He had also inherited his father's shipping and other interests, which stretched from Tower Hill to Deptford, and lived in nearby Leytonstone in considerable splendour with his wife Mary and thirteen children. The association with Soyer had probably originated with his cousin Jacob James Hart, who in partnership with his uncle Lemon had established links with various London clubs, including the Reform, supplying them with fine wines from the company's base at 59 Fenchurch Street. It was through this connection that Jacob had befriended Palmerston, a prominent Reformer, who later appointed him Consul-General for the Kingdom of Saxony when the partnership with Lemon broke down. David, in taking over Jacob's club contacts, would have inherited the relationship with the Reform's influential chef with it.

On the face of it, David, with his inherited wealth and large family, had little in common with Alexis beside a knowledge of fine wine and a drive to be successful. Especially as Hart, unlike Soyer, was a tough operator who saw no sentiment in business and for whom the making of money was a serious matter. Yet both were outsiders, men who, however rich or successful they became, would never be socially acceptable outside their own milieu – Soyer because of his calling, his lack of education, his poor background and his very *Frenchness*, Hart because of his Jewishness. For however rich he was, Hart would always be 'trade' – as Jews were still, in the 1840s, barred from higher education, from the professions and from politics. Benjamin Disraeli, the flamboyant MP for Maidstone and Tory high-flyer, was the exception to the rule, but he had only managed to enter Parliament by virtue of the fact that his parents, despite remaining Jewish themselves, had had him baptised at the age of twelve – a move which led many to condemn the family for crass opportunism. It would be a dozen years before Lionel Rothschild, the first Jewish

Member of Parliament, was legally able to take his seat in 1858, and more than a quarter of a century before Jews were permitted to study for degrees at Oxford and Cambridge. So while economically successful Jews like David Hart became more middle-class, more 'establishment', more secular (he even married a Gentile), whatever good works they did – and Hart, like Soyer, did much for charity – they would always be kept within their own spheres, and not allowed to get 'above' themselves.

Despite this new focus on commercial enterprises, Soyer was keen to stress to his masters at the Reform that he was not neglecting the day job. He often boasted that during the ten months of creating of *The Gastronomic Regenerator* he had also produced 25,000 club dinners, thirty-eight important banquets and given kitchen tours to 15,000 strangers, figures that rather ignored the reality that Alexis delegated almost all of this work to his capable lieutenants – with the exception of supervising the most important dinners, banquets and visits. Volant, by now working full time for Soyer, was speaking of himself, with clear exasperation, when he wrote of having to entertain the majority of the visitors to the Reform kitchen, 'It is an actual fact that the gentleman upon whom devolved the duties of secretary to Soyer, had to neglect his business very often to pay polite attention to Lord This, or Count That, who had called, sent in their cards, and begged permission to see the improvements of the renowned model kitchen.'

There is no doubt that Alexis was stretched to the limit. The famous banquet for Ibrahim Pasha, which had required such meticulous planning and which filled so many rapturous column inches, was produced within days of the launch of *The Gastronomic Regenerator*. One of Soyer's admirers, the bullish Fox Maule, MP, who as Lord Panmure would play such a crucial role in Soyer's success in the Crimea, was both a guest at the banquet and a subscriber to the book, and from his Angus estate wrote to a friend a few days after the event: 'The bill of fare at the Reform Club was worthy of the great *Soyer*. Pray call at Ridgway's, and desire him to send me two copies of his book by Saturday next's Dundee Steamer.'

But by far the most interesting feast Alexis masterminded at the club during this period was a legendarily ostentatious private dinner, held on 9 May 1846, for Osbourne Sampayo, an extremely wealthy club member, and nine of his gourmet friends. It was a dream commission – as Sampayo not only allowed but encouraged the chef to give full rein to his creative ambitions, giving him *carte blanche* to create the most innovative, opulent and exquisitely rendered feast of his career. No expenditure was to be spared in the compilation of the menu – indeed the high cost was not incidental but the point of the exercise. 'The *Diner Lucullusian à la Sampayo*,' reported *The Times*, 'was ordered with a magnificent contempt of expense. No money was to be spared in obtaining the most novel, luxurious, and rare compounds that ingenuity could discover or gold procure.' And Soyer needed no further encouragement to test the limits of his skill and ingenuity. Volant later recalled that 'our *chef* almost believed himself inspired while producing it'. Great discussions took place – with Sampayo going so far as to visit some of the suppliers a number of times in advance of the dinner to double and treble-check the quality of their produce. The final bill of fare, an extraordinarily sumptuous collection of more than two dozen of his most extravagant dishes, makes quite some reading:

Potage à la Comte de Paris
Potage à la purée d'Asperges
Saumon de Severne à la Mazarin
Rougets gratinés à la Montesquieu
Le Chapon farci de Foie gras à la Nelson
Saddleback d'Agneau de Maison à la Sévigné
Les Olives farcies
Thon marine à l'Italienne
Salade d'Anchois historiée
Sardines à l'Huile de Noisette
Sauté de Filets de Volaille à l'Ambassadrice
Petites Croustades de Beurre aux Laitances de Maquereaux
Côtelettes de Mouton Galloise à la Reforme
Turban de Ris de Veau purée de Concombres
Rissolettes à la Pompadour
Les Dotrelles aux Feuilles de Vigne
Le Buisson d'Écrevisse Pagodatique, au Vin de Champagne à la Sampayo
Les grosses Asperges vertes, sauce à la Crème
La Gelée de Dantzic aux Fruits Printaniers
Les Petits Pois nouveaux à l' Anglo-Français
Les grosses Truffes à l'Essence de Madère
Les Croquantes d'Amandes Pralinées aux Abricots
Le Miroton de Homard aux oeufs de Pluviers
La Crème mousseuse au Curaçao
La Hure de Sanglier demi-glacée, garnie de Champignons en surprise
Les Diablotins au Fromage de Windsor

As always, there was a heavy bias towards some of Alexis's favourite ingredients – truffles, foie gras, plovers' eggs – and his most cherished creations, including Mutton Cutlets Reform, his capon stuffed into a huge pastry ship's prow, and his mock boar's head garnished with meringue mushrooms. The new creation for the night, however, was named in honour of the host: *Le Buisson d'Écrevisse Pagodatique, au Vin de Champagne à la Sampayo*; a concoction of Champagne and truffle-stewed crayfish. The dish cost an enormous seven guineas – two months' salary for the average vicar – four of them going on two large bottles of Périgord truffles. Soyer had in fact organised yet failed to deliver another spectacular dish, based on the French custom of eating specially fattened ortolans. These miniscule songbirds, no bigger than a plum, were traditionally captured alive and force-fed for several weeks until they had tripled their weight, then drowned in Armagnac before being roasted and eaten whole – bones, beaks, entrails and all. The diners draped large white napkins over their heads to keep in the aromas, to hide the mess and – some said – their faces from God. Soyer had planned to prepare the birds in an entirely new way, however, using truffles. He was a huge fan of truffled food – truffled chicken was his favourite dish and Emma had painted him merrily tucking into a great plate of it – and he stuffed truffles into almost everything. But the essence of this idea was to reverse the culinary norm and stuff the actual truffle – with the ortolans. 'An ortolan can hardly be truffled, but I will undertake that a truffle shall be ortolaned!' one journalist, describing the preparation of the dinner, imagined him declaring. It was a dish of unimaginable opulence, but in the event he was foiled by the weather – the two dozen ortolans he had ordered from Paris failed to arrive on time. Disappointed, he later gave a detailed description of exactly how he had planned to prepare them.

Having already procured twelve of the largest and finest truffles I could obtain, it was my intention to have dug a hole in each, into which I should have placed one of the birds, and covered each with a piece of lamb's or calf's caul; then to have braised them half an hour in good stock made from fowl and veal, with half a pint of *Lachryma Christi* added; then to have drained them upon a cloth, placed a border of poached force-meat upon the dish, built the truffles in pyramid, made a purée with the truffle dug from the interior, using the stock reduced to a demi-glace, and poured over; roasted the twelve remaining ortolans before a sharp fire, with which I should have garnished the whole round, and served very hot.

Although his Parisian suppliers may have let him down, the London tradespeople, who received their final instructions a week before the dinner, did him proud. Grove's, a Bond Street fishmongery, provided him with the mullet and the salmon, which was caught in the Severn and rushed straight from Gloucester to London by train, arriving – still alive – at the Reform's kitchen door at exactly seven o'clock. Alexis immediately gutted and boiled them, 'being just ten minutes before the dinner was placed upon the table', so they could be eaten 'in their greatest possible perfection'. Alexis later described the Sampayo bill of fare in *The Gastronomic Regenerator*, which came out just a few weeks after the dinner, where he also gave credit to all his suppliers – the rest of the fish came from Jay's in Hungerford Market, and the poultry from Bailey's in Davis Street and Townshends in Charles Street. 'The foies gras and some very fine fresh French truffles came from Morel's; the hors-d'oeuvres from Hedges and Butler, Regent Street. The saddleback of lamb came from Newland's, Air Street, Piccadilly; the Welsh mutton from Slater's; and the young green peas and a very expensive dessert came from Lewis Solomon's, Covent Garden.' So many purchasing details – notwithstanding the surprising admission that he had bought in one of the desserts, albeit from a specialist confectioner – were given not to advertise the shops, he said, but to prove how much trouble a 'real gourmet' will go to to furnish his table. In spite of the missing ortolans the meal was a culinary triumph, the final cost working out at £4.4s. per head – around £300 in today's money – excluding the wine.

Of course Sampayo could have shown his respect for the great chef by spending the same sum, not on dinner for nine friends, but on soup for 10,000 starving silkweavers instead. His gathering certainly marked the apogee of vulgarly excessive consumption at the Reform Club, and perhaps in the country, and was, as Alexis admitted himself, 'the most *recherché* dinner I ever dressed'. Perhaps the flashy host, the 'mysterious and too exclusive' Sampayo, and his guests deserved the drubbing they received in *The Times* for the over-indulgence of such preternaturally sensitive palates.

A memorable dinner was given at the Reform Club . . . upon the 9th day of May of the present year, to a select party of ten highly-gifted connoisseurs; none of your gobble-and-gulp people, who, in their melancholy ignorance, swallow a *potage à la Comte de Paris*, or a *rissolette à la Pompadour*, with the same frightful nonchalance as a sailor will devour his pea-soup, or a rustic bolt his bacon; but creatures of ethereal natures, devotees of what the painters call 'high art', men who feed their bodies only to give elasticity and vigour to their souls . . .

And so with his work at the Reform, the success of his book, the promotion of his stoves and other products, and his charitable work, there was more than enough going on to keep Alexis fully occupied. Details of his social life at this period are sketchy, but we know he was still a keen habitué of the theatre and the ballet and, despite his heartbreak over Fanny's marriage, revelled in suddenly finding himself a good catch – still slim and handsome, famous, successful and only in his mid-thirties – he was a very attractive figure to the beautiful actresses and dancers whose company he undoubtedly solicited. He was also becoming rather well-off, and enjoyed his money. Always one to spend rather than save, he delighted in increasingly outlandish clothes and liberal entertainment, with always, always plenty of champagne. He gave generously to others, and was the first to put his hand in his pocket on hearing any hard luck story. Whatever the cause, he would casually instruct Volant: 'Well, my dear boy, if it is all right, put down a sovereign for me.'

Such willing charity and visible consumption, coupled with a certain unworldliness over financial affairs, inevitably attracted mountebanks and hangers-on. Volant relates the story of one such fly-by-night, a French conjurer called Philippe who was making a success of his magic act in London that summer – just the sort of character to have appealed to Alexis's love of showmanship. Alexis quickly formed a close and easy friendship with Philippe, who, said Volant, 'speedily discovered that his new friend Soyer had a few thousands in the Bank of England'. And Philippe, just as swiftly, saw to it that the money was spent – on railway shares. Philippe had been ploughing his own earnings into railway shares since his arrival in England in the expectation of making a killing before his return home, and it wasn't hard to convince Soyer to do the same, in spite of the fact that he was known to hate gambling. But, after all, this seemed like a solid speculation, and to begin with Philippe had been very successful. 'At that period [he] was on the winning side, and used to show his luck, and boast how easy it was to get a fortune by steadily playing for the rise of shares.' So they decided 'that in all future transactions Philippe and Soyer would share and share alike in the purchase or sale of railway shares, and divide the difference'.

The spread of the railways in the early 1840s had fed an enormous and still growing speculative spree, with investors in the grip of 'railway mania' pouring whatever money they could into the latest railway company to launch a prospectus. While these private companies initially tried to raise the money locally to wherever their line was being built, it gradually became clear that London was where the big money was to be found. Soon the joint stock company method was abandoned for the stock market, and a free-for-all began as the new tracks snaked their way up, down and across the country. The situation was exacerbated by the 'cheap money' available at the time – the bank lending interest rate had been cut to three and a quarter per cent, and the Bank Charter Act of 1844 had helped to create stability and confidence in the pound. Once the queen herself had travelled from Slough to Paddington on a railway train, any residual public anxiety about their safety, or their respectability, had vanished. By November 1845, 620 schemes, with a capitalisation of £563,000,000, were before Parliament, while another 643 were awaiting registration or a prospectus, and it was estimated that more than 5,000 miles of new track would be built by the end of decade. Everyone wanted to cash in.

Some of these new railway companies had no revenues and no clear idea of what their business model would turn out to be. Their investors were just as naive. Like Philippe and Alexis, most were private individuals sinking their savings into a once-in-a-lifetime opportunity, having never invested in the stock market before. The bubble could not last, and sure enough, the combined effects of a loss of confidence in the domestic economy, the vast numbers of too-small, badly managed railway companies, and the external drain of gold to America finally brought share prices crashing down. By Christmas 1845 whole fortunes were wiped out as the share prices fell to a fraction of the heights they had achieved. By 1848, even the best companies had lost fifty per cent of their net worth. Philippe and Alexis, like thousands of others, lost almost all they had invested. At the end of just a few months, Alexis found himself poorer by almost £1,000, and, when the last £150 debt was called in, discovered that Philippe had disappeared without trace, leaving him to settle the bill. In total, and in just a few months, they had lost over £2,000 – roughly £150,000 in modern money. Yet Soyer took even such a big hit well, and dictated a good-natured letter of forgiveness to Volant, which was duly forwarded to Philippe when he resurfaced. In the *Memoirs* Volant prints a translation of the letter, which shows the chef in generous, typically sentimental humour, only mildly mocking, and displaying a mind, as usual, racing from subject to subject.

You are a naughty fellow. You came to see me, not finding me at home, you ought to have written; but believe me, my good friend, notwithstanding the misfortune weighing heavily upon us – more particularly upon me, because I never had a wish to speculate in anything, being satisfied with the produce of my humble talent, whilst, on the other hand, you are a sublime genius perhaps a little too exalted, leading you to heavenly dreams, but that time has not yet arrived – I hope however, that we shall have to live and love each other for a long time to come on this earth. *N'importe* what may happen, be always Philippe; and I swear, on my honour, that Soyer shall always remain Soyer. Do not lose your courage, my good friend, you and I are one; together we shall form a colossus, capable in a short time, to overthrow a thousand adversities . . . London is full of people, advertise well, and Christmas will put us on our legs again.

Despite his recent romantic and financial setbacks, Soyer remained cheerful and friends recorded that 'an unceasing love of pleasure marked his life'. His office, that attractive and convivial little parlour in the middle of the Reform Club kitchens, provided a sanctuary from the pressures of the outside world where he could spend long evenings entertaining his friends in style. He took particular pleasure in testing out his latest culinary creations on the private guests he invited there, constantly trying to outdo himself in terms of flavour and ingenuity. These occasions were hugely enjoyable, with Alexis extracting full drama from the process – literally making a meal of it. Volant, who as a friend as much as an employee was often party to these entertaining events, recalled them affectionately.

We would walk into the room that was hung around with his wife's beautifully executed paintings, and where some of his own extraordinary inventions were seen upon a little square table near the window . . . Then would Alexis unlock a mystical cabinet, full of all kinds of rare liqueurs, wines, and brandies, huddled together with his different sauces, and books, emanating from a brain continually on the rack for new potages, sauces, or *entrées* – and, wonderful to say, never failing to find them – and place on the table for us to enjoy, with something *piquant* and *appetissant*, a bottle of wine, which made our eyes sparkle and our palates yearn for a dozen of it. At last would come forth the new and much looked for dish. We would taste it, whatever it might be, look at him, and taste again, and pronounce, as judges of what was good, Soyer to be 'never a traitor; but, most assuredly, a *traiteur* of the class A1'.

On nights out Alexis would look as magnificent as any of the Reform Club members above stairs as he swanned through the kitchen, having changed out of his working clothes and red beret into his zig-zag dress suit, complete with zig-zag top hat, hollow-heeled boots (one of his own inventions – they held his coins) and white kid gloves over his diamond rings. He also wore a versatile gold-braided waistcoat, and a cravat that could be folded in different ways to create 'half a dozen fashions, and all *comme il faut'*. In one of his pockets there would be a gold toothpick and a stash of the parallelogram business cards that he dispensed so liberally. And then he would sally forth to Her Majesty's or Drury Lane, more often than not with an attractive woman on his arm, where his celebrity and long-standing admittance into London's theatrical circles meant that he rarely had to pay to see anything. On occasion, after pulling strings to secure some highly sought-after tickets for a member and his wife, he would join them for the performance: 'I got three tickets, for you, Madame and me,' he wrote to one grateful Reformer. (He also mixed socially with club members at Masonic functions – he had been a freemason since his days with Ailsa – and clearly relished being in the one club that did not discriminate against his class or calling.)

After the opera or the ballet he might meet friends for dinner and some wine-fuelled songs. His favourite haunts included an elegant and overpriced eatery called Dubourg's, near the Haymarket, where, according to George Augustus Sala, the cunning French cooks would 'send you up pheasants and partridges *en papillote; filets* with mushrooms or truffles, culinary gewgaws that shall cost five shillings the dish'. But Soyer could get fine French cooking at home, and anyway his private tastes remained simple, so at Dubourg's he would simply enjoy a glass of cognac and a chat about the old country with the proprietor, before moving on to less pretentious surroundings. En route, even in his finery, he might indulge in the cheap street food he had loved in poorer days, and could be seen walking along the street eating two-pennyworth of fried fish – presumably having removed his white gloves first.

By two in the morning he would be at the Provence Hotel, the Cyder Cellars, or Evans's Late Supper Rooms in Covent Garden – also frequented by Thackeray – where customers descended a flight of stone steps to a smoky basement called the Cave of Harmony, which was in fact a large, raucous music hall and café serving simple, alcohol-absorbing meals of fatty chops, sausages, grilled kidneys in gravy, Welsh rarebit and baked potatoes. Here the exclusively male clientele would stay until the early hours, cheering and heckling the professional glee singers and comic acts while knocking back the cheap booze – stout, pale ale, punch, grog, hot whisky and water. Or he would arrange a gathering of a dozen or so 'men of talent' in the private room at the back of a tavern called Frost's in Bow Street, which only closed when the last customer staggered home to bed. There he would hold court, much as he had in the days of his rowdy sing-songs with Charles Pierce and their Welsh cronies at the Queen's Head in Shropshire. He kept his audiences laughing with his by now finely chiselled (and no doubt embellished) anecdotes of his early life, and with his heavily accented tenor voice he would offer up a solo of one of his favourite songs, such as the army anthem '*Vive le Militaire!*' before taking a self-deprecating bow and declaring, his accent further thickened by wine, 'Ah my boys! You are all good friends to me, I *nevare* can return your compliments.' Describing his regular rendition of another favourite, '*Pan, pan, pan, voilà mes amis*', 'Who that has heard [it] can ever forget,' declares Volant, his 'rich, racy, unctuous, exuberant style?'

It was at Frost's, one snowy night, that he surreptitiously stole two fresh roasting birds that one of the company happened to have brought along with him, whipped down to the kitchen and swiftly fricasseed them. He then persuaded the man to stay for some supper he had ordered for himself and eight others – brushing aside his claim that he had already eaten at Jaquet's *à la mode* beef-house – before serving him up a dish of his own fowl. Oblivious to the deception, the friend enjoyed the dish so much that he paid 2s. 6d. for a round of brandies before discovering, to his annoyance, that he had effectively been twice conned. Soyer 'positively screamed' at the joke. The tables were partially turned, however, when another friend invited him to a birthday dinner and ensured that on the table was a dish of rabbit curry – knowing it to be one of Alexis's favourites – that the friend had cooked himself, using a recipe from *The Gastronomic Regenerator* which called for the addition of stewed onions and streaky bacon (a recipe Alexis repeated, with minor variations, in two more books). Sure enough Alexis chose some of the curry, and eventually had three helpings of it, loudly declaring it to be the most delicious dish he had ever tasted, before his friends laughingly told him that he praised himself, as the recipe which he had failed to recognise was his own.

In the summer of 1846 he travelled to a small gathering in Windsor organised by Alphonse Gouffe, the Queen's head pastry cook, who was throwing a weekend of birthday celebrations at his lodgings within the castle. Most of Gouffe's colleagues and friends being either German or French, the occasion rang with a certain continental 'freedom and gaiety'. Soyer took his secretary-companion Volant along with him. The pair travelled by coach, and while walking from the drop-off point to the castle were caught by a sudden outburst of rain. The ever-efficient Volant pulled out the umbrella, but on putting it up realised that there was a huge tear right across the top. Never ones to pass up a visual gag, the men decided to carry on with the umbrella up, huddling beneath it and talking earnestly as if nothing was amiss, until people began to stop and laugh at the two outrageous Frenchmen parading around town, soaked to the skin underneath a ridiculously inadequate umbrella.

After an evening of dinner, songs, cards and a late supper, the following morning the party set off for a day at neighbouring Virginia Water, the enormous man-made lake on the edge of Windsor Great Park. Spanning 130 acres and providing an idyllic seven-mile stroll around its picturesque circumference, the lake, complete with its gushing waterfall and Corinthian pillars newly imported from North Africa and artfully arranged to look like a ruined temple, utterly enchanted the chef, who loved its rarefied atmosphere and romantic prospects. He called it the *Paradis Champêtre* of England, and in time it would become a holiday home and a refuge for him – the old Wheatsheaf Hotel on the south side of the water providing a welcoming second home whenever he needed privacy, or at times of exhaustion, depression or illness.

When the others returned to the castle to prepare for that evening's dinner and ball, Alexis and Volant walked around Windsor where they spotted another heavily moustachioed Frenchman who was having trouble making himself understood to his interpreter. Soyer stepped in, and had soon befriended Ernest Bourdin, a well-known and extremely prolific Parisian editor, printer and publisher of original art, maps and books. Ignoring both castle security and house party etiquette, Alexis invited his new friend to join the group for the celebrations, much to Bourdin's delight and Madame Gouffe's annoyance. The publisher, it transpired, was also the literary editor of Frédéric Fayot, one-time secretary to and later biographer of Alexis's great hero, Carême, and now author of a culinary bestseller of his own – *Les Classiques de la Table*. Alexis clearly hoped that Bourdin would publish his own books in France. This was not to be, but Bourdin did pass a copy of the awful *Cream of Great Britain* on to Fayot, and Alexis was thrilled to receive back a generous and complimentary letter from the great man.

Around this time Soyer tried to institute a kind of celebrity chef club – a bi-monthly gathering of six top chefs, at which each would present two completely new dishes to a panel of six independent judges, who would award a silver platter to whichever was deemed 'the newest, lightest, and most delicate'. An annual pamphlet entitled *Gastronomique Innovation* would then publish the winning recipes. The first meeting took place at the newly built Royal Hotel, a large and comfortable railway hotel in Slough, whose proprietor, an Italian named Dotesio, ensured that the enormous modern kitchen was placed at the disposal of the competing chefs. The august gathering included Alexis, two royal chefs, Philippe Moret and John Hutin, a M. Comte, head chef of the Dowager Baroness Rothschild, then later the Duke of Cambridge (following Soyer's brother, Philippe), and the head cook of the hotel. The twelve participants duly sat down to eat and, after an excellent course of soup and fish, prepared to examine the first round of original dishes. Soyer ensured that his came last, and it was carried in with all due ceremony by Dotesio himself. Labelled *La Croustade Sylphe en surprise à la Cerito* [sic], when Dotesio lifted off the huge silver dome the company was astonished to see a carrier pigeon fly out, and just as quickly disappear through an open window. The platter, however, proved to have a false bottom, and when it was lifted out the diners were duly served with variations on two of Soyer's favourite dishes – *salade de filets de grouse à la Bohémienne*, and some sponge-cake chops, served with meringue mushrooms and resting on a sauce of creamed peaches.

It is not known whether Soyer's menu won the Slough competition, but it did win him a wager. A few days earlier, he had made a bet with some of his cronies that he could send part of a dish, made by himself, from Slough to London faster than the fastest railway train – as fast, in fact, as the new electric telegraph. Therefore, as soon as his *Croustade Sylphe en surprise à la Cerito* was placed on the table, a telegraph was sent to his friends, who were waiting at a prearranged meeting place, to the effect that the 'aerial' was on its way. And sure enough, within fourteen minutes the 'principal part of the atmospheric dish' arrived, with a paper attached to one of its legs with a message on it. 'Please to pay the *chef-de-cuisine* of the Reform Club the sum of £50 . . . and make the cheque payable to A. Soyer.' Alexis had gone to huge trouble to make the elaborate joke a success – although his *Gastronomique Innovation* was less so, and the invited chefs, perhaps non-plussed by his prank, never met for a follow-up.

Such fun came to a temporary halt when Alexis became preoccupied with his Dublin project, and his ongoing work for the London soup kitchens. But nothing dampened down his social life or extra-curricular activities for long. His fame was certainly secured – indeed, hadn't his friend Thackeray just called him 'the immortal Alexis Soyer' in the year's most talked about novel, *Vanity Fair*? The narrator of the novel, a satire on London society that was currently being serialised in *Punch* magazine, had been made to declare, with a sly reference to his Irish adventures, that M. Soyer could 'make more delicious soup for a half-penny than an ignorant cook can concoct with pounds of vegetables and meat'. No self-respecting home would be without its copy of *Punch* prominently displayed, and now it was selling many more thousands of copies a month on the back of *Vanity Fair*'s success, while everyone in London was discussing Thackeray's gold-digging anti-heroine, Becky Sharp. To be mentioned in *Vanity Fair*, therefore, was to reach the pinnacle of contemporary celebrity. Indeed sales of the story were only matched by Dickens' latest offering, *Dombey and Son*, and would far outstrip those of the novels of the Yorkshire brothers Ellis and Currer Bell, the mysterious and fiercely passionate talents behind *Jane Eyre*, published in October, and *Wuthering Heights*, which appeared shortly before Christmas. (These dark works simultaneously delighted, appalled and intrigued London society – at least they did until the scandalous discovery the following year that the Bell brothers were, in fact, women – the Brontë sisters.)

Of course *Punch* – mainly through its most prolific contributor, Thackeray – had been reporting on Alexis's activities for years, and would continue to do so for many more, via numerous reports, squibs and cartoons. Thackeray delighted in weaving compliments to or caricatures of the chef into many of his works. In November, via *Punch* again, he wrote a spoof letter to a fictitious academic committee at Cambridge University, in which he argued that a new scientific chair should be established for the study of eating. The supposed author, an ill-educated cook called 'Corydon Soyer', declares that eating could be described as both a physical and moral science – 'physical, [as] it acts on the health; moral, on the tempers and tastes of mankind'. In another veiled stab at Alexis's activities in Ireland, Thackeray has the preposterous Corydon declare that the 'Soyer Professorship of Culinarious Science' would equip the young ecclesiastic leaving Cambridge to teach the inhabitants of 'a distant and barbarous province' how to improve their diet and live more harmoniously.

Such ridicule – albeit affectionate – sums up Thackeray's complicated attitude to Alexis. Both now in their mid-thirties, they shared a real friendship, based on an energetic social life, a passion for the theatre, a sense of humour and – increasingly – a tendency to heavy drinking. While Thackeray never dressed as outrageously as Soyer, his great height and flowing white hair gave him an air of elegant raffishness, and he had a sneaking admiration for the outright dandies like Alexis and Count d'Orsay, 'those knights of the broadcloth and shining fronts'. They could converse easily in French, and Thackeray enjoyed Soyer's eccentricity while respecting his skill and industry. Both men had lost adored wives young – Emma to a premature death and Thackeray's wife, Isabella, to madness, although it was the deprivation of their wives that enabled them to enjoy such hectic, rackety nights together. Both worked hard but were imprudent with money – Thackeray too had lost £500 he could ill afford on railway shares.

Thackeray, who was perpetually hard-up until the success of *Vanity Fair* (he had had to borrow the subscription fee to join the Reform), was perfectly happy to accept Alexis's generous hospitality, all those delicious dinners by the fire in his comfortable basement parlour saving him the price of a formal meal above stairs, and the two men often invented new dishes together, experimenting with extravagant and exotic sauces until the early hours of the morning. Sala, who when working for Alexis often observed the two men together, later recalled that Thackeray had for Soyer 'the friendliest of feelings and genuine admiration to boot; since the mercurial Frenchman was something more than an excellent cook – that is to say, Alexis was a man of sound common sense, a practical organiser, a racy humorist and a constant sayer of good things.' Alexis, for his part, 'almost worshipped' Thackeray.

However, Thackeray could never quite forget Soyer's humble beginnings, his lack of education, his vocation as a 'mere' cook. Perhaps because Thackeray himself had at times been regarded as little more than an impecunious hack, he was acutely aware of class snobbishness and very sensitive to being patronised himself. He was a gentleman, a university man, a member of the Reform rather than a servant of it, and it was a gulf between him and Alexis that could never be entirely bridged. So Thackeray, in regularly pointing up Alexis's faulty English and ridiculous clothes, failed his friend in spite of his fondness for him, by seeing him as someone slightly less than himself – as so many others would throughout Alexis's life.

9

'Sir Oracle'

The following year continued Alexis's remarkable run of commercial success. While 1848 saw autocratic monarchies and authoritarian governments topple across Europe, Marx and Engels launch their blueprint for a communist future and yet another cholera epidemic rampage across London, Alexis Soyer was preoccupied with bottled sauces and fizzy drinks. He had attempted to break into the groceries market a few years earlier with three new products – Soyer's Diamond Sauce, designed to accompany 'cold or hot meat, poultry, game etc', a clumsily titled condiment called Kalos Geusis (Greek for 'beautiful taste' – although often misprinted as Halos Genesis) and Versailles Sauce, a sort of flavoured mayonnaise. All were manufactured by the company of Messrs William Clayton & Co. of the City of London, and sold in quart and pint bottles through the Italian warehouses across the city. However, Clayton & Co. failed to market the sauces vigorously and Alexis, preoccupied with *The Gastronomic Regenerator*, did not pick up the trail until the warehouses were left with unsold stock, the distribution network had gone cold and he was forced to withdraw from the market.

While this first incursion into the sauce market was not a success, neither did it cost Soyer much, and it laid the foundation for what, two years later, would become a hugely successful collaboration with a pickle manufactory in Soho Square being run by the shrewd young partnership of Edmund Crosse and Thomas Blackwell. In the *Memoirs* Volant does not even mention the Clayton sauces, stating simply that Soyer's first 'successful' effort in reference to sauces was made in 1848, when, 'to the delight of all lovers of piquant flavour', he launched Soyer's Sauces – with a spicy version for gentlemen and a milder one for ladies, price 2s. 6d., 'which went off amazingly.' Whether Alexis simply recycled the 'piquant flavour' from his Diamond Sauce recipe we cannot know, but he certainly wasn't the man to let a good recipe go to waste, and Crosse & Blackwell – to protect their exclusive 'Soyer' branding – had shrewdly bought the licences to all of his early sauces, although they only seem to have produced the Kalos Geusis.

It seems that after the dismal débâcle with Clayton, Soyer had at first intended to control the manufacture and sales of the sauces on his own, but he soon realised that he needed professional help if he was going to make any real money out of the venture, and Crosse and Blackwell were the obvious partners for him. Not only was their company fast becoming the market leader in preserved foods, but they had the manufacturing capability, a solid reputation for quality, the relevant advertising and distribution networks set up and, crucially, the marketing drive that Clayton's had so clearly lacked. Having been burned once, even Alexis would be more careful next time.

As with Smith & Phillips, Alexis would have liked the creative energy, the big plans and the forward-looking approach of Crosse and Blackwell. The men had met at the age of fifteen, when they had been taken on as young apprentices at West & Wyatt, an old-established Soho company which could trace its roots back to the first years of the eighteenth century. The original West & Wyatt were oilmen – dealers in sweet oils and foods preserved in oil – and the company also produced crystallised fruits, pickles and preserves from its factory at 11 King Street. Both boys came from prosperous retail families – Blackwell's family were Holborn druggists and the Crosses had been trading around Ludgate Hill for three hundred years – and they quickly became friends as well as colleagues. So much so that when William Wyatt announced his retirement in 1829, Crosse and Blackwell decided to buy the business.

Once established in King Street, Crosse and Blackwell directed their energies into expanding the company's range of preserved products to include up-market game pâtés, liqueurs, honey, marmalade and con- serves, vinegars, curry powders and pastes, soups and sauces. By 1839 they were able to expand the factory at King Street and build a grand new house in Soho Square, which had a store on the ground floor and enough living space for both men and their families to live above the shop. As a specialist firm, using the latest canning and preservation technology, Crosse & Blackwell was soon being appointed to supply exploration parties and military expeditions, and orders began to flood in from India and other expat enclaves around the world. These were high-priced, luxury foods rather than utilitarian goods, expensively packaged in beautifully embossed tins, elegant wooden boxes and Wedgwood porcelain jars. To provide the right image for such opulent provisions the partnership needed to recruit the right men to provide the recipes – not simply skilled chefs, but well-known names who would give the products that must-have feeling of quality and luxuriousness – so that while housewives might not be able to afford the services of a celebrity chef, by buying his bottled sauces they could feel they were lending their own dinners a sprinkle of his sophistication. In time, therefore, it was not just Soyer whom the partnership employed to devise new products, but Francatelli (as ever hard on his heels) and a range of ex-Napoleonic French chefs, plus an Italian cook called Qualiotti, who marketed the first commercial version of the old Indian mustard and turmeric condiment called pickle lila – rebranded as piccalilli. The success of Crosse and Blackwell's approach meant that over time the company would grow to become one of the biggest food manufacturers in the world, with factories, breweries and canneries all over London.

And so Soyer's Sauces, 'the most novel and delicious of all modern social inventions', were launched in the middle of April 1848. Needless to say the publicity material boasted of the sauces' many applications. Used neat, sauce was an ideal accompaniment to cold meat, when mixed in with the juices from a roast it became a sort of early gravy browning; it could be added to hashes for an extra dash of flavouring, or made into a makeshift béchamel as an all-purpose sauce. On receipt of their crates of samples, Soyer's friends in the press were, as always, generous. 'Amongst the very few good things for which we have been indebted to the French during the last few weeks, is to be reckoned a new sauce from the laboratory of Professor Soyer, of the Whig College, commonly known as the Reform Club,' ran a *John Bull* leader. 'We beg to acknowledge receipt of a specimen, which arrived a few days since at our office, with a communication highly characteristic of the learned Sauce-er. John Bull is not addicted to kickshaws, but gratitude compels him to notify the pleasure which he derived from his last steak, seasoned as it was with the specimen above referred to.' The literal-minded *Morning Post* decided, rather unhelpfully, that the sauce was 'piquant without being pungent, and of the highest flavour, without conveying any definite taste . . .' but the *Morning Advertiser* declared Soyer 'a real benefactor to society' and *The Sun* 'the great Napoleon of Gastronomy'. Even Disraeli found time to praise the new sauces in the *Morning Chronicle*, causing *Punch* to quip that the busy parliamentarian should use it on his bills to make them more palatable – before teasing Alexis for promoting cannibalism by the outrageous act of producing sauces 'for ladies and gentlemen'. With so much positive coverage sales could hardly fail to receive a kick-start. The only teething problem seemed to be that some considered the bottles to be too big, as only a small sprinkling of the condiment was needed, and too expensive at a hefty 2s. 6d., so Alexis swiftly brought out a smaller bottle for a shilling less.

It seems likely that at first Crosse & Blackwell did not buy the recipes from Soyer, but as his 'principal agents' manufactured and distributed them on his behalf. The same is true for his next and biggest hit, the Soyer's Relish, launched in 1849 with a swaggering strapline declaring it to be 'an entirely new and economical condiment, adapted for all kinds of viands, which, by those who have tasted, has been pronounced *perfect*'. It is impossible to know the composition of the Relish now, or what made it so popular – beyond the hype – although Soyer did once confide the recipe to Sala, who wrote down the 'prescription' before promptly losing it. But years later he did recall that it was chiefly composed of what the Victorians referred to as the 'stinking rose' – garlic. Again, the newspapers did not let him down. If they had raved about Soyer's Sauces they were now ecstatic about his Relish – which came in attractively designed half-pint flagons with figure-of-eight labels bearing a bereted Soyer and the Gothic letters *AS*. *The Observer* considered that 'at present we do not know of any person who administers more assiduously and effectively to our corporeal wants – at any rate, to the most craving of them – than the renowned Soyer . . . we see him now compounding a sauce, which undoubtedly will prove a "relish" to the most used-up of palates.' Another review declared the Relish 'the best promoter of the appetite, and the most agreeable adjunct to the festal table of any sauce hitherto in use'. 'The greatest reform wrought by *The Gastronomic Regenerator* is his second achievement in the palatable form of a new companion to the universal dinner-table, entitled *Soyer's Relish*,' announced another. 'After its delicacy of flavour, its chief recommendation is apparent in its wholesome qualities; and its cheapness consists in its various capabilities, since it is equally available for FISH, MEAT, POULTRY or GAME. As an incentive to the appetite it is invaluable, and is pronounced by celebrated epicures to be the most *recherché* sauce hitherto devised.' Much of the overblown praise smacks of Soyer's own pen, and busy hacks, then as now, may have been grateful for a fulsome press release to crib from.

As for the Relish's much lauded wholesomeness, this cannot be established from such a distance of time, but Crosse & Blackwell, despite its upper crust reputation, was not above adding some distinctly unwholesome additives to its products. This was, after all, the period when the unregulated adulteration of food had reached terrifying proportions, leading to regular cases of chronic gastritis and even fatal food poisonings. These were more serious than the old Regency vices of padding coffee with burnt corn and flour with chalk, spinning out sugar with ground glass and recyling tea leaves. The desire for consistency of products, and to make them go further and last longer, had led to the addition of some very nasty chemicals – strychnine, cocculus indicus and copperas in rum and beer, sulphate of iron in tea, sulphate of copper in pickles, bottled fruit, wine and preserves, and lead chromate in mustard and snuff. Before the widespread availability of canned and bottled foods it had been impossible for the government to regulate what went into loose food, but with the new branded goods, such as those produced by Crosse & Blackwell, action could be taken to protect the public from many of the worst effects of these poisons. In July the first Public Health Act created local boards to monitor commercial food preparation, and in 1850 Thomas Blackwell was forced to give evidence to a parliamentary inquiry into the adulteration of foods. He admitted to the committee members that his firm had added copper salts to preserved fruits and vegetables to boost their 'greenness', and iron compounds into their red sauces for potted meat, 'not realising,' he said, 'that they were so objectionable'.

By the summer of 1850 it was clear that the huge and sustained sales of the Soyer products called for a proper legal agreement between Alexis and the partners. And so in August the company's lawyers drew up a contract in which Alexis granted Crosse & Blackwell sole and exclusive rights to prepare and sell Soyer's Sauces and Soyer's Relish – and agreed not to disclose the recipes to any third party. He also agreed to allow the company to use his name in any proceedings taken against anyone who might try to cash in on the Soyer brand by producing rival products under the same name, and gave them first refusal for any future compositions he might invent – excluding drinks – provided they picked up the option within three months.

In return, the company agreed to pay a royalty for each bottle of Alexis's sauces that they sold. Using rather a quaint formula, it was agreed that Soyer would be responsible for printing the labels for the bottles of sauce – bearing a periodically up-dated portrait – for which the company would reimburse him reasonable expenses, and pay him a further sum as the labels were used. The sum fixed on was four shillings per dozen for the half-pint bottles of Soyer's Sauce and, bearing in mind the much greater quantities sold, one shilling per dozen for Soyer's Relish, the money going up proportionately for bigger sized bottles. Crosse & Blackwell further undertook to spend £50 a year on advertising for at least the next two years.

It is interesting to note in the small print that while Alexis granted Edmund and Thomas, and 'their executors, administrators and assigns', the right to market his sauces in perpetuity if they so chose, Crosse and Blackwell only undertook to pay Soyer 'during his lifetime'. It may have seemed an inconsequential detail at the time, perhaps Alexis did not even notice it, but it was an inequity with significant financial implications. Bearing in mind that all three sauces continued to sell well for many years after his death – the Relish alone was manufactured until 1920 – that small clause deprived Alexis's estate of more than sixty years' worth of royalties. It was further proof of how Soyer's carelessness over money and lack of attention to financial details meant that savvier businessmen could easily get the better of him in such matters. It was the inventiveness – and the praise – that mattered to Soyer, not the amassing of wealth.

The contractual stitch-up did not damage the relationship, however, professionally or personally – eight years later Crosse & Blackwell would also manufacture Soyer's final concoction, the Sultana's Sauce, inspired by his time in the East, and Crosse, in particular, became a trusted advisor. It was to Edmund that Alexis hurriedly entrusted his most valued possessions – Emma's precious paintings – when he set off for the Crimea, and it was Edmund whom he appointed as sole executor of his will.

Alexis swiftly followed up the success of the sauces with the launch of a sparkling drink. Artificially carbonated waters had been produced and packed in commercial quantities since the late eighteenth century (Schweppes had begun to produce soda waters in 1792), but for years these had been seen as essentially medicinal drinks, their great benefits being that they were both non-alcoholic and unadulterated – no small recommendation when the water supply was contaminated with cholera and a host of other diseases. It took time, however, for flavourings to be introduced, and the first references to a sparkling lemonade being sold commercially date from the early 1830s. But the popularity of carbonated fruit beverages grew quickly, especially after the removal of glass excise duty in 1845 reduced the price of the bottles, and by the end of the 1840s there were more than fifty fizzy drink manufacturers in London where twenty years earlier there had been just ten.

Never one to miss a trick, Soyer had been experimenting with fizzy lemonade for a while, so when he was approached by Charles Codd, the owner of a London drinks company called Carrera Water Manufactory & Co., an exciting new opportunity opened up. Carrera made a 'cooling beverage' called Tortoni's Anana, which had an uninspiring flavour and equally uninspiring sales. The factory and distribution network were well established, however, so when Codd offered Alexis partnership in the launch of a completely new drink, with *carte blanche* to create his own formulation, he could not resist the chance to reinvent and rebrand it. After much trial and error, he came up with a novelty that was, according to Volant, who could have been writing the press release (and possibly did), 'composed of the juices of the most delicious fruits, mingled with the scientific dash of a master-hand: the saccharine tartness of the raspberry, the mellow flavour of the apple, a bare suspicion of quince, merely an idea of lemon, and all creaming in effervescence. Ganymede never made such nectar for the gods, in all his Olympian revels.'

In common with all commercially bottled variations of lemonade, Alexis would have used a base of citric acid, described at the time as 'concrete acid of lemons', and essential oil of lemon with a flavoured sugar syrup, the mixture being topped up with water and impregnated with carbon dioxide gas. However, to make his variation unique, he spiced it with cinnamon and coloured it with a chemical pigment called 'lake' – and in so doing gave the novelty-hungry Victorians their first blue drink. It may not have been subtle, but Soyer was quick to recognise its excellent properties as a hangover cure – or, as he more delicately expressed it, its capacity to settle upset stomachs, to cool and tranquillise the nervous system 'no matter how nervous', and provide a refreshing drink that would soothe the stomachs of those 'fasting in the morning, after a late ball, or evening party'. As with all carbonated liquids at the time, the drink had to be packaged in Hamilton bottles, which were long, thin and contoured with pointed or egg-shaped bottoms to ensure they were stored on their sides and the corks kept moist, the only way to stop the pressure of the internal gases from shooting the corks out of the necks. The thick green glass was embossed with the legend Soyer's Nectar, and diamond-shaped paper stamps over the seal gave Alexis's latest business address, 40 Rupert Street.

The Nectar, which came in six- and ten-ounce bottles, was officially launched in July, three months after the Relish, with a heavy advertising campaign. Alexis promoted it in the same way as he had the sauces, sending crates of free samples to all his media cronies, along with a letter boasting of its vast improvement on any other beverage currently for sale, and adding the tip that 'the addition of a little brandy or wine would be excellent for winter'. He did not have to wait long for yet another bundle of ecstatic reviews. On 13 July *The Sun* declared: 'It beats all the lemon-ade, orangeade, citronade, soda-water, sherry-cobbler, sherbet, Carrara-water, Seltzer, or Vichy-water we ever tasted.' *The Globe* dubbed Soyer the 'Emperor of the Kitchen', and duly recommended the addition of a tot of rum. On the 29th even *The Lancet*, the medical journal which had attacked his famine soups so viciously, published a piece on the drink's health-giving properties: 'It is a delicious beverage and always, in the summer months, will afford gratification to thousands. The man who can thus, as in many instances, add to the enjoyments of the community, at a moderate cost, must be regarded in the light of a public benefactor,' it enthused in an extraordinary U-turn. Anonymous poems praising the drink found their way to Soyer – most in doggerel every bit as bad as his own – and it also found favour with his usual aristocratic patrons. After his first sip the King of Hanover apparently ordered six cases a month. The Duke of Cambridge recommended its effervescent taste, and the Duchess of Sutherland loyally considered it 'excellent and refreshing'. Even Alexis's hero and fellow dandy, the Count d'Orsay, claimed Soyer's Nectar was yet more proof of Alexis's good taste and declared that all at Gore House enjoyed it.

Sales boomed, and the Nectar continued to sell well for some years. A few years later the journalist Henry Mayhew reported that numerous drinks sellers, who during the summer months filled the East End with wooden carts from which they sold glasses of ginger beer and foaming lemonade made from pump water and a variety of noxious powders, were also selling a nasty-sounding fake Nectar, 'in imitation of Soyer's'. This compound had more sugar and less acid than the lemonade, but was also cinnamon-flavoured, bright blue and – due to its fashionableness – never sold for under a penny. This trade, among London's poorest citizens, was never going to dent Soyer's more sophisticated market, but the progress of the real Nectar was not entirely smooth. Just a few months after its launch a rumour began to circulate that Alexis actually had nothing to do with the drink at all – he had simply lent his name to it for a fee. It could not have helped that he was so publicly involved with such an enormous array of projects at the time – not even the great Soyer, said his critics, could spread himself that thinly.

Quick to respond, Soyer paid for a damage-limiting advertisement to be printed in all the morning papers, rebutting the allegation.

A rumour has got into circulation that M. SOYER, in consequence of numerous engagements, does not attend to the manufacture of [Soyer's Nectar]: such is not the case. The ingredients are manufactured every morning, under his *personal* superintendance, at his factory, Rupert-street, and afterwards bottled, with the addition of aerated water, at his factory, Whittlebury-street, near the Euston-square station, which he has established for the sake of obtaining the purest water in London, from the Artesian Well belonging to the North Western Railway Company.

In fact, as in the Reform kitchen, Soyer's 'superintendance' was more in the breach than the observance, and 'his' Whittlebury Street factory was in reality a Carrera site (production later moved to High Holborn). Nonetheless the advertisement was enough to quieten the rumour, and sales continued unimpaired. The Nectar was particularly popular as a mixer, and Alexis, who with some justification could be called the pioneer of the English cocktail, published a variety of recipes for 'Nectar Cobblers' and other glamorous, boozy compounds.

The success of the Nectar attracted the attention of speculators keen to invest in such a popular new product, and Soyer and Codd were soon approached by a stockbroker who was so anxious to become involved that even before any agreements were signed he had placed £1,000 at the firm's disposal in the London and Westminster Bank. This was big money – almost £80,000 in modern terms – just for a gesture of good faith, and Soyer and Codd could not help being impressed. However, the goodwill did not last long. After some internal dispute the new investor took over control of the financial side of the business, 'which naturally caused discussion, and ultimately the break-up of the affair'. In 1850, Soyer – perhaps now bored by the whole business – sold his concern in the company for £800, a healthy sum on top of the running profits he had already received, and a useful amount of capital (the equivalent of more than £60,000) to invest in a new, much bigger enterprise that was beginning to take shape in his mind. Carrera, which by now had harnessed other brightly coloured drinks to the 'Soyer' brand under licence to A. Soyer & Co. (including a garish, saffron-tinged lemonade, an orange-flavoured version, a 'Persian' sherbert drink, a soda and a ginger beer), continued trading until 1855. The Nectar had a second lease of life when Codd's grandson, John, relaunched the company in 1885 as Soyer and Company Limited. As well as the original Nectar, John Codd produced Soyer's Nectar Lemonade and Soyer's Nectar Soda Water, but his company lasted only five years before going into liquidation.

One of the reasons Alexis let go of the Nectar so easily was because another of his inventions had struck gold – the money was already rolling in and, if he would only devote enough time and dedication to promoting it, it clearly had the potential to make him a fortune. The exact origins of Soyer's Magic Stove are unclear. It was certainly Alexis's company, A. Soyer & Co., that perfected the design and commissioned it from Gardner's, a reputable lamp manufactory operating from premises a few doors down from the office on Charing Cross Road, then set about marketing and selling it as the latest brainchild of the great chef. But whether Alexis actually invented the stove is far from certain. Volant, whose memory was often unreliable but who was working closely with Alexis at this period, claimed that it was a mysterious Chevalier Lemolt who approached Alexis with an ingenious miniature stove of around six inches in height and diameter, which was powered by a small spirit lamp connected to it via a blowpipe. When the spirit lamp was lit, the vapour it produced was forced through the blowpipe into the stove unit, where it connected with a reservoir of methylated spirit to produce a flame of 'intense heat, double that of a charcoal fire'. This strong flame was then directed through a flue on the top of the unit, and could be regulated by moving a valve at the end of the tube. A frying pan, saucepan, kettle or coffee pot could then be placed safely on the top. The whole apparatus weighed just over three pounds and represented a genuinely inventive breakthrough at a time when even the most sophisticated cookery still involved filthy charcoal fires and plenty of dirty, heavy, dangerous work.

Perhaps Lemolt showed Alexis something that provided the chef with the idea for the Magic Stove, but it seems more likely that Soyer simply took over his prototype wholesale. After all, his inventiveness had always tended towards mechanical contraptions rather than creations which needed a proper working knowledge of the physical sciences, and on several occasions he was to prove himself quite capable of passing off other people's work as his own – despite Volant's insistence that he remained uninterested in anything that did not 'spring from his own brain'. And it seems that Lemolt took a share of the profits – indicating that he was prepared to give up ownership in exchange for cash. Whatever deal was finally struck, 'M. Soyer at once perceived the importance of this little apparatus,' says Volant, 'and very shortly afterwards, it was brought out, with valuable improvements, as Soyer's Magic Stove.'

As usual, Alexis would keep tinkering with these 'improvements', which included trimming the size of the stove even further, refining the decorative design of the metal trellis work, and adding a large plaque on the side declaring that the stove had been registered in February 1850. In fact two versions of the Magic Stove were registered, the first on 29 August 1849, along with a large new domestic range called Soyer's Modern Housewife's Kitchen Apparatus, and the second the following February, both times by Alexis and his now regular partner, Alexander Symons, trading under the name of A. Soyer & Co. The basic model was sold for £1. 15s., while at the top end of the scale you could buy an entire deluxe travelling kit, called the Camp Kitchen, or Magic Kitchen, 'expressly adapted for the Overland Route'. This was a tin chest, small enough to stow under a carriage seat, which held a stove and a complete set of miniature pans, utensils, dishes and plates, cutlery, a spice-box and coffee pot, with a tray to stand everything on. It contained all you needed to produce a complete meal for a dozen people, and all for £5. Other, smaller versions of the Magic Kitchen right down to a 'pocket' size for individuals, also became available.

Soyer milked the Magic Stove for all it was worth. The genuine novelty and utility of the invention enabled him to give the papers a really good story, and they quickly picked it up. 'The ever-inventive Soyer has just produced a complete *bijou* cooking apparatus,' enthused the *Morning Post* in May, before going on to give a detailed account of the workings of the tiny copper furnaces, flues, burners and the spirit reservoirs that made up the device. It declared, rather unconvincingly, that the stove was so exceptionally clean in its operations that a lady 'may have it among her crotchet or other work', and that the size and ease of use of the miniature kitchen meant that every man could become his own cook, and that henceforth 'no bachelor's chambers, no traveller' would be without it. The portability of the apparatus was a theme picked up by many. The *Morning Advertiser* was thrilled to find that it could conveniently be carried in its owner's hat. The *Morning Chronicle* thought it would be particularly valuable for 'the angler by the side of the mountain stream', and then carried out a successful motion test in a railway carriage. *The*

Globe predicted great benefits to 'emigrants and tourists' and *The Sun* to 'soldiers, sailors and sportsmen'. And *The Sun* was right – in 1850 the navy equipped Captain Austin's expedition to the Arctic with several Magic Stoves. Austin was travelling in the footsteps of Sir John Franklin, who had vanished without trace during his search for a North-West Passage five years earlier, in the hope of finding some clues to the fate of the doomed explorer and his large crew. Austin and his own men became trapped fast in the icy Crozier Channel throughout the winter of 1850 and, with a finite store of heating fuel, the stoves would have provided a comforting way of spinning out their rations.

Soyer had finally come out with a truly useful modern convenience which attracted many long-standing fans. They included Sala, who later wrote in his memoirs that during his long career as a foreign correspondent he never travelled without one. Alexis himself, a few years later, would find himself perching a Magic Stove on a fallen capital of the Acropolis, before cooking up an elegant Athenian *petit déjeuner à la forchette*. The stove also found a following with walkers who fancied a hot meal during their rambles. Alexis, prior to the launch, had himself tested it on a group of friends whom he invited to join him on a special picnic. He ensured that his guests had worked up an appetite by making them trek through some isolated fields to the middle of nowhere, before letting them unpack the luncheon baskets to discover that he had brought only raw provisions. Waiting until they were suitably annoyed by such a mean prank, he then held up his arms, theatrically called forth his 'spirits' from the deep – i.e. his spirit stove from a hamper – and produced for them a delicious cooked lunch.

In the first year of production alone he turned over between £5,000 and £6,000 worth of business, and Gardner's could barely keep pace with demand. The little office in Charing Cross Road swarmed with buyers, suppliers, journalists and the plain curious. Each day, an invited audience, drawn from the press, aristocratic friends and carefully selected members of the public, filed in to see Alexis's cooking demonstration on the Magic Stove. Dressed to the nines and full of comic patter, he would stand behind a drawing room table, on which the stove and a range of ham, chops, eggs, herbs and other ingredients had been assembled, and proceed to illustrate the range and versatility of his contraption by conjuring up such complex dishes as *Filets de volaille à la maître d'hôtel*, *Foie de veau au jambon*, and *Rognons de moutons aux fines herbes*. With his usual panache he then offered the fragrant dishes to his admiring audience, to be washed down with claret, champagne, and of course his own delicious Nectar.

Soyer would take his roadshow on a series of successful tours round the provinces, and once sent George Warriner on a promotional trip to France. A newspaper called *La Patrie* reported how an Englishman had been stopped by a customs officer, who told him that the apparatus he was carrying was clearly hardware, and he was not allowed to bring it into the country. Warriner assured the officials that the box was, in fact, his kitchen, and seeing them looking sceptical 'quietly fixed the stove, lit a brass lamp, produced . . . one or two raw côtelettes ready egged and breaded, threw them into a microscopic frying-pan, and served them up in about a minute, to the great astonishment of the spectators'. The *douaniers* were suitably impressed, and Warriner was allowed to bring in his stove.

But even Soyer drew the line at some publicity stunts. In August he met a flamboyant character called George Burcher Gale, a former actor and naval lieutenant who had become a notoriously reckless hot air balloonist. Gale had invented a crazy new type of balloon called the Prince of Wales Aerostatic Machine, which was supposed to make aerial firework displays safer. It worked on the principle of two swinging cars instead of one, which fitted into each other. Once the aeronaut was in the air, he would lower the outer car – which held the fireworks – by a rope and pulley system, and then discharge the fireworks over the heads of the awestruck crowds. Gale would further thrill his audiences during these performaces by leaping acrobatically between the cars. Clearly a show-man after Soyer's own heart, Gale immediately recognised the publicity potential of cooking himself a meal while up in his balloon, and begged Alexis for permission to take up a Magic Stove. Soyer sensibly declined, insisting that the stunt was far too dangerous as the spirit-fuelled flame could easily touch some part of the balloon or basket with disastrous consequences. He refused with tact and charm, telling Gale that he would 'not find many customers for stoves in the clouds'. When Gale persisted, claiming it would make a capital advertisement, and that he had never had an accident in a career of more than a hundred ascents, Alexis declared that such a run of luck should make him even more cautious, 'as immunity from danger for a while might lead to unwise neglect of precautions'. Soyer's injunction was unusually prescient. Three weeks later Gale was killed during a performance in Bordeaux as he was attempting to descend on the back of a horse strapped to a platform suspended beneath a balloon. He was not the first aeronaut to attempt the 'equestrian ascent', but two years later similar stunts were banned in

England, as the animal-loving English were outraged by the cruelty involved in swinging horses around the sky.

As part of this all-consuming drive to find more outlets for his concoctions, and to fill every niche in every relevant market with his inventions, Soyer was also determined to cash in on the enormous and continuing success of *The Gastronomic Regenerator* by attempting another bestseller. His last literary production, his *Charitable Cookery*, or *Poor Man's Regenerator*, had not been designed to sell in large numbers. Published to coincide with the opening of the Model Soup Kitchen in Dublin, the slim, pocket-sized textbook had been intended only for those wanting to run an efficient soup kitchen. It simply described the model soup kitchen, some stoves, some soup recipes, some basic meal and cooking techniques, and dedicated the last page to a list of the benefactors of the Leicester Square kitchen. But his time in Dublin did, indirectly, supply Alexis with the idea for his next major book. In April 1841, at the London Tavern dinner thrown to welcome him back to London and honour his achievements in Ireland, he had particularly enjoyed the company of a married couple called Baker, who resided in domestic harmony in St John's Wood. The Bakers became close friends, and Alexis enjoyed many evenings at their home – in time he would even take a house in nearby Marlborough Hill. Deprived of the comfort of his own family hearth – although he had moved from Simonau's chaotic flat into his own lodgings, it hardly compensated for the lack of a wife and family – he admired the warm and comfortable home that Mrs Baker created, and their lengthy conversations on cookery and household management formed the basis for his next work, which in 1849 would be published as *The Modern Housewife or Ménagère*.

Having now written for the very richest and the very poorest in society, Alexis aimed this manual squarely at the middle classes. It consisted of nearly a thousand new recipes. These were not simply dishes for the wealthy cut down in scale – a criticism that could be levelled at much of the middle-class section of *The Gastronomic Regenerator* – but one that really addressed the needs and aspirations of those who wanted to live well on a less elevated income. By the late 1840s the good livings to be made from manufacturing, colonialism and other lucrative sources meant that the upwardly mobile middle ranks were increasingly anxious to define their new stations, to establish respectable households and develop social graces. As a result, etiquette books and household manuals began to sell by the million, offering newly affluent housewives advice on everything from establishing domestic routines, managing servants and provisioning and furnishing their homes, to sourcing good food, planning dinner party menus and cooking.

Soyer decided he could help out – and not just with the cooking. Despite being free from the responsibility of maintaining a family of his own, he still held fixed views on a host of domestic matters. He may not have run a nursery, established a laundry or organised a child's birthday party himself, but he confidently instructed his readers how best to do so. The bulk of the book, though, was devoted to recipes, and to present them in a novel way he hit on the clever device of using an epistolary framework, his fictional correspondents being two middle-aged house-wives, the rather superior Hortense (based on Mrs Baker), a capable matron living in the imposing-sounding Bifrons Villa, St John's Wood, and Eloise, her mousy friend, whose reduced financial circumstances have led to an early retirement to the country. Eloise occasionally visits Hortense, when the communication changes from letters to rather stilted dialogues.

Almost all of the letters are from Hortense to Eloise, as she lectures her friend, with an air of almost comical condescension, on how to transform her home into a carbon copy of her own. In line with middle-class mores, Hortense is constantly keen to exercise restraint and economy at all times – while naturally deploring meanness. Hortense's views perfectly reflected Soyer's own attitudes to careful husbandry. While he may have been the undisputed master of the big-budget dinner, and relished being given free rein to create the most extravagant, no-expense-spared ban-quets for his rich clients, Soyer believed that everyone in society should eat as well as they possibly could within their given budget. For those with smaller incomes, it was simply a question of exercising enough ingenuity to furnish their tables superbly. The Soyer that could spend seven guineas creating a dish of crayfish and champagne was not incompatible with the Soyer who could devise a hundred ways with brisket – both were challenges that excited his imagination and stretched his creativity.

And so in *The Modern Housewife* the focus is on making the best use of leftovers and cheap cuts, on the virtue of recycling joints, cakes, and even the fat used for deep-frying. In common with prevailing tastes there is a tendency to favour heavy red meat dishes, particularly mutton and beef, although the most popular (and inexpensive) remained pork and its derivatives. 'No animal is more used for nourishment and none more indispensable in the kichen,' declares Hortense, 'employed either fresh or salt, all is useful, even to its bristles and its blood; it is the superfluous riches of the farmer, and helps to pay the rent of the cottager.'

Where Soyer diverged from other contemporary cook books was in devoting a large proportion of his recipes to vegetable and salad dishes, which the carnivorous Victorians often shrank from providing in abundance. Neither did they eat much fish, beyond salmon, oysters, haddock and skate, yet Soyer included a great many fish recipes, and believed that a fish diet was essential to good health. In fact this was a recurrent hobbyhorse of Alexis's – he could never understand why the English, surrounded on all sides by such excellent stocks of fish, failed to take full advantage of such a cheap and plentiful supply of delicious food. 'Of all aliments that have been given to the human race for nourishment, none are more abundant or more easy to procure than this antediluvian species,' declares Hortense, 'and yet of how few do we make use, and how slight is our knowledge of their habits.' Soyer had begged the Irish to eat more fish during the famine, and he continued to preach the virtues of eating fish in each of his books.

In *The Modern Housewife* Soyer took pains to ensure that the recipes were achievable in households without the luxury of an extensive *batterie de cuisine* or unlimited labour. Although the existence of a reasonably comprehensive staff is taken as a given – a cook, a few maids and a manservant at the very least – Hortense makes it clear that these are recipes she has mastered herself, and that when the cook takes over, it is under her tuition and supervision. This claim does not seem beyond the bounds of possibility. Whether Soyer intended it or not (and as the character was based on a friend it is unlikely), running through Hortense's undeniably sensible advice is a slightly disagreeable insinuation that if Eloise and her husband had only managed their affairs better, they would not now be in such straitened circumstances.

The letters, interspersed between sections of recipes, allow Soyer to play around with his usual mix of sound advice and useless information, unaccountable digressions, terrible puns and excellent tips on which foods provide best seasonal value in the 'London market'. The staple Soyer tropes are there – the dodgy history lessons (most ingredients, it seems, were 'known to the Romans'), the wild flights of fancy, and the comical anecdotes. There are the plugs for his own products – Hortense's letters shoehorn in recommendations for his Nectar, his Bramah stove, his tendon separators and *The Gastronomic Regenerator* – and outings for most of his personal hobbyhorses, from gas cookery to the importance of training middle-class girls in the practical business of housekeeping rather than giving them a merely 'ornamental' education. In general the prose is clear and elegantly phrased, and while the letters may ostensibly be from the pens of Hortense and Eloise, in reality you can hear the voice of Soyer addressing you, loudly and humorously.

A subsequent edition even gave Alexis the opportunity to insert a little puff for his Magic Stove when the fictional Hortense boasted to Eloise of her 'newly-invented Magic lamp-stove', on which she personally cooked Mr B's cutlets, eggs, ham and bacon at the breakfast table. Hortense's letter was accompanied by an illustration of the device, which was set up on a white cloth next to an appetising saucepan of chops, and carried an explanatory footnote.

> This is, as you see by the engraving, a very neat and portable cooking apparatus; the heat is given by the vapour of spirits of wine passing through a flame: it will cook cutlets or boil water in as short a time as the best of charcoal, and to the sportsman on the moors must be of great utility; with the sautepan everything can be cooked as on a charcoal fire, and with a small saucepan anything that may be required in the room of the invalid, where the heat of a fire would not be allowed.

Again in partnership with Alexander Symons, Soyer had the book published by Simpkin & Marshall and *The Modern Housewife* came out on 7 September 1849. It was an immediate hit, and would remain in print for the next fifty years. The first impression of 3,000 copies sold out within a few days, as did a second edition of 6,000, printed a fortnight later. A total of 16,000 were snapped up within the first six months, and sales showed no sign of slowing. The reviews were, as usual, glowing. *The Spectator* wrote that '*The Modern Housewife* is the most dramatic of cookery-books; carried on by dialogue, correspondence, and a certain artful arrangement by which two-thirds of an epic – "action" – is introduced into the didactic work.' *The Times* considered some of the transitions between dialogue, correspondence, recipes and comic scenes 'somewhat violent and sudden', but was essentially enthusiastic. 'It is at once a grave essay in prose, and a most felicitious poem; it deals with that undoubted reality the human stomach, yet with a pen essentially romantic and imaginative. It is at once didactic and dietetic, dramatic and culinary.' The *Literary Mirror* dubbed Soyer 'Sir Oracle', and the *Morning Post* wrote that 'Henceforth no cook, no countess, no scholar, no scullion, no philosopher, no feeder, will think an establishment complete where the "Modern Housewife" is not present.'

Soyer ensured that the Scottish and Welsh papers received copies, and his diligence paid off handsomely. 'He writes fluently,' said *The Scotsman*, 'tossing off a paragraph as adroitly as he would a pancake, and garnishing his sentences with figures of speech as profusely as his model housewife does her cold meat with parsley. He is by turns philosophical, scientific, historical, picturesque, dramatic, and poetical.' *The Principality* declared that, 'Like its author, this book is without a parallel.' Even the local newspapers weighed in – with the *Bath Herald* ('sound and economical'), *Manchester Examiner* ('read, mark, learn and inwardly *digest*'), *Norfolk News* ('a very unique performance'), *Bristol Mirror* ('really invaluable') and dozens of others joining the chorus of praise. Only one review slammed the book, an anonymous piece in *Fraser's Magazine*, the monthy literary and political journal whose reputation had been built on contributions from such literary luminaries as Samuel Taylor Coleridge and Thomas Carlyle. The attack, which appeared in August 1851, following the twenty-first edition, declared Soyer's art little more than 'quackery', and offered the view that 'Mons. Soyer's *Modern Housewife*, otherwise insignificant, becomes very important as an engine of social mischief, likely to retard the progress of the science it pretends to expound, on which the greatest of our social blessings – health – so very much depends.' The article was as vicious and personal as the attacks that had rained on him in Dublin, and showed that the easy-going Frenchman whom his friends declared was liked by all was far from it – and for whatever reason had made at least one outspoken enemy.

Sales continued unaffected and in December 1851 an American version appeared, with editions in both New York and Philadelphia. But for the United States market the text was edited by 'an American Housekeeper' who, while abstaining from 'any attempt to gild the refined gold of M. Soyer' by the addition of his or her own words, chose to iron out the bulk of Soyer's now characteristic mass of eccentric footnotes and digressions', and with them much of the book's charm. However, the recipes themselves remained untouched, with only one American classic, crab soup, added. As in the UK, the reviews were superb, drawing praise from such diverse publications as the *Protestant Churchman* and the *Brooklyn Daily Freeman*, which ended its piece with a very modern injunction: 'Don't take our word for it, but try it for yourselves.' Even the dour *American Whig Review* pointed out that Soyer was now so famous in America that the mere attachment of his name to the book would ensure its instant popularity.

As usual Soyer tinkered with the copy before each new edition, adding more recipes, new sections (including one on 'The Physiology of Tarts'), more letters from the 'ladies', usually bragging about the flattering reception their little culinary correspondence had attracted from the public, which Hortense at least had the grace to credit to the 'iron tongue of the press', which indeed had been more than helpful. In 1853, in a preface to mark the 30,000th copy, readers were informed of a change in Hortense's fortunes. A 'too bold speculation' had reduced the couple to relative poverty, and forced Mr B to take a job on the railways. But the ever resourceful Hortense, having forsaken Bifrons Villa and St John's Wood for the less rarefied air of Camellia Cottage, Rugby, writes to Eloise that, as 'adversity gives birth to genius', she has applied herself to thrifty living and managed to buy 'an ox-cheek and palates, an ox foot boiled, two sheep's heads, twelve sheeps' brains, one ox kidney, twelve onions, a few leeks, carrots, turnips, a little thyme, bayleaves, a few cloves, salt and pepper' all for 3s. 6d. Always ready to recycle previous work that he felt had not had a sufficient airing, Soyer then included *The Poor Man's Regenerator* – to suit Hortense's new circumstances. It seems the real Hortense, Mrs Baker, had also lost her good fortune; Volant records that she died 'in a hospital' – effectively meaning she was destitute – some years later.

How great was the influence of Hortense and Eloise in America remains unknown, but in Britain it was considerable. The famous and flamboyant dermatologist Erasmus Wilson, who paid for the massive obelisk known as Cleopatra's Needle to be brought from Alexandria to its current home on the Thames Embankment, wrote to Soyer to tell him that he considered the section on food for children to be 'one of the most valuable pages I have ever read on the subject of Diet, and . . . calculated to confer an everlasting benefit on society'. He referred to Soyer's wisdom again in an important treatise on healthy skin, and recommended that *The Modern Housewife* should become the study of anyone 'on whom the proper rearing of children in any way rests'.

Two years after its first appearance, a small menu book called *What Shall We Have For Dinner? Satisfactorily Answered by Numerous Bills of Fare for from Two to Eighteen Persons* was published by Charles Dickens' wife Catherine, under the pen name of Lady Maria Clutterbuck. The pamphlet consisted of 164 suggested bills of fare for a variety of occasions, from family meals to dinner parties, plus a few recipes. Most of the menus were regular Dickens family favourites, and typical of their period, income and class. Catherine had clearly consulted a range of contemporary cookery writers such as Eliza Acton, Sarah Hale and

Christian Isobel Johnstone, but her chief influence – which she happily acknowledges – was Alexis Soyer. She adopted Soyer's innovative saddle-cut joint for big dinners and freely borrowed his recipes – for cod rechauffé, salmon curry, loin of mutton, broccoli au gratin, maître d'hôtel butter and sauce *à la maître d'hôtel*. Some she copied virtually verbatim, others she re-interpreted – in a later edition she used Soyer's cheese soufflé as a fondue base, and adapted his recipe for broiled rump steak by dredging it with seasoned flour rather than powdered biscuit and shallot powder. Such small adaptations said more about the pantry goods available to home cooks, who did not have the resources of a professional kitchen to hand, than about differences of personal taste.

More importantly than the minutiae of the recipes, Catherine Dickens' book highlighted the common values shared by the Dickens family, Soyer, and a growing number of their contemporaries. Generosity was important but economy was also a positive virtue. (Having experienced extreme poverty, Charles Dickens was always cautious about money, and carefully supervised Catherine's domestic budget.) Soyer has Hortense declare that dishes created from leftovers should be made 'out of those parts which are rarely or never used in this country by the middle classes'. And Catherine clearly agreed – although less of a fan of offal than Alexis, in her household expensive cuts were kept for special occasions, and each menu combined joints with made-dishes in fairly equal ratios, providing ample choice while limiting expense. As Alexis recommended, Catherine exercised thrift by the extensive use of pork and all its by-products, and she, too, clearly loved fish. Just as Alexis had once told Lord Bessborough that he thought the Irish peasantry, by fertilising their soil with fish meal to grow potatoes, chose to 'manure the land with gold to reap copper', so Charles Dickens had long advocated that many of the nutritional (and financial) deficiencies suffered by the working classes could best be alleviated by the consumption of more fish, and he and his wife certainly put their theory into hearty practice.

Dickens, who was just two years younger than Alexis, grew to know and respect the chef's views on other matters too – both men either served on or gave evidence to various government committees on health and sanitation. In 'The Water-Drops', a story Dickens wrote for his campaigning weekly magazine *Household Words*, one of his characters testifies accurately to another Soyer preoccupation – the unhealthy hardness of London water: 'M. Soyer (evidence before the Board of Health) says you can't boil many vegetables properly in London water. Greens won't be green; French beans are tinged with yellow, and peas shrivel. It don't open the pores of meat, and make it succulent, as softer water does. M. Soyer believes that the true flavour of meat cannot be extracted with hard water.'

While *The Modern Housewife* cemented Alexis's renown as an author, his freelance work as a master caterer also regularly took him away from his cosy Reform Club parlour. On 7 July 1849 he created a celebratory dinner for Michael Thomas Bass, the wealthy Midlands brewer, to celebrate his recent entry into Parliament as a Liberal MP. A few weeks later he travelled to Grendon Hall in Atherstone, Warwickshire, the seat of his old friend Sir George Chetwynd, whom Emma had painted years earlier, to oversee a banquet to celebrate the christening of Sir George's six-week-old grandson. Turtle soup, ortolans, quails wrapped in vine leaves, Severn salmon, a haunch of venison, a huge christening cake, strawberry and pineapple ices and his much loved mock wild boar cake all featured among the dozens of dishes on the lavish bill of fare, and after the meal Soyer, rather cheekily, 'had the honour of presenting the infant with a proof copy of his new work on Cookery'.

The most prestigious catering event of the year, however, he was forced to miss due to ill health. Prince Albert was now thirty years old and had spent the last decade striving to find a useful public function independent of his role as royal consort. He had recently found it, however, in taking over the organisation of what promised to be the greatest imaginable showcase of technical innovation and expertise to be found in the British Empire – the Great Exhibition – a giant industrial fair designed to encourage tourism and boost international trade. To counter an initially lukewarm response from the government, one of Albert's first actions was to drum up provincial support for the project by arranging a lavish dinner at the Mansion House, where he could gather all Britain's mayors under one roof and encourage their participation with a fabulous dinner and rousing speech. To his great delight Alexis was invited to supervise the event, which took place in the second week of October and was attended by the Archbishop of Canterbury and almost the entire political establishment, including Sir Robert Peel and Lords Russell and Stanley, but a sudden illness forced him to withdraw.

Alexis's health had actually been a matter of concern to his friends for some time. Now nearing forty, the decades spent toiling over toxic charcoal stoves, taking little sleep and few holidays were all taking their toll. For the first time in ten years Fanny Cerrito had decided not to spend the summer in London, but had toured Sweden with St-Léon, although their marriage was increasingly miserable. As he missed her company and had no other serious attachments, there had been no one to stop Alexis overworking and overdrinking. An accident in St James's Park just after Christmas in 1849 proved a further shock to his system. At around three in the afternoon on 29 December Alexis had been persuaded by a young companion to join several thousand other Londoners who had taken advantage of a spectacularly cold Christmas to skate and slide on the ice that had formed on the park's large ornamental lake. The authorities had tried to discourage the skaters by breaking up the thinnest patches of ice, but Soyer and his friend were among those who would not be deterred. He skated into the middle of the lake but, once opposite the Horse Guards Parade, hit a thin patch which promptly broke and pitched him into eight feet of freezing water. Weighed down by his clothes and in shock from the terrifying cold, he still had the presence of mind to shout to several men who had run over to help to keep right back or risk falling in themselves. Instead, and despite the fact that it was unlikely that he was a strong swimmer, he waited to be rescued by an iceman, who used a horizontal ladder to pull him clear of danger.

The iceman was employed by the Royal Humane Society, a charity which had been established seventy-five years earlier expressly to save lives in such circumstances. The Society's annual report describes how the 'renowned *chef-de-cuisine*' was carried to their purpose-built medical centre next to the Serpentine, where Mr McCann, a surgeon to the Society, 'immediately placed him in a hot bath, and, having been rubbed for some time, he was put to bed, where Mr McCann applied the restoratives recommended by the Society. After a lapse of a few hours, M. Soyer was able to be removed to his own residence in a cab.' Several papers reported the incident, which in turn led McCann to write to *The Times*, arguing with their description of the day's incidents as being 'nothing more serious than a few duckings'.

I beg to direct your attention to the fact, that, in addition to duckings, there were four persons whose lives were in the most imminent danger; and, had it not been for the means placed at my disposal by the Society, I do not hesitate to say that each of them would have lost his life: amongst the number was the well-known M. Soyer, of the Reform Club, who has directed me this morning to put his name down for ten guineas, thereby becoming a life-governor of the ROYAL HUMANE SOCIETY.

Alexis himself was in no doubt that McCann had saved his life, and he was extremely keen to express his gratitude. At a fundraising dinner for the Society held a few weeks later at the Freemason's Tavern, he gave a warm and witty speech of thanks, referring to the Society as 'like a second mother . . . [which] has been the means of bringing me . . . back to life again'. And as well as donating money, he set his mind to devising a more practical way for the icemen to rescue skaters who had fallen through the ice. Before long he had come up with a bizarre scheme which involved erecting a series of poles connected by pulleys along the length of the lake, with a rubber ball at the foot of each pole connected to a long rope. The idea was that the icemen would throw a rubber ball to distressed skaters, who would cling on to them while being dragged out by the rope. Delighted, Soyer duly submitted his invention to the Society, and wrote an account of it for the *Morning Post*, for once retreating behind the modest pseudonym of *Humanitas*. Needless to say, the Society, while offering thanks and approval, did not adopt the scheme.

Soyer was slower to recover from the skating accident than he should have been. There was a constant sharp pain in his side and, as he neared the age by which both his elder brothers had died, he began for the first time to become properly concerned about his health. After several weeks he finally consulted a doctor who recommended a programme of exercises to him, which Alexis took up with his customary enthusiasm. He had a gym set up in his office, and practised diligently. He stopped taking his late night snacks and began to eat regularly. Overall the effect, says Volant, 'was extraordinary, for, in less than three months, a development of the chest took place, his strength increased, and his general appearance was so improved, that he altered quickly'. It was as if the shattering near-death experience in St James's Park had finally made Alexis realise that he needed to behave responsibly and take better care of himself if he was to make the most of the days that remained to him. He also, for the first time, began to gain weight, and the slim figure of his youth was gradually replaced with the more traditional outline of the stout and cheerful chef.

10

'THE WORLD HIS CLUB,
HIS GUESTS ARE UNIVERSAL'

With his health restored, Alexis had become extremely keen – along with every other ambitious businessman in Britain – to cash in on the growing excitement that was now surrounding the plans for the Great Exhibition. Millions of visitors were expected to visit London for the four months of what was now being called the 'World's Fair', visitors who would all require transport, accommodation, entertainment and, most importantly, food, plenty of food – and was Alexis not the undisputed master of mass catering? He was already fielding numerous approaches from businessmen and restaurateurs anxious to secure his services for the duration of the Exhibition. Such was his popularity that the presence of Alexis Soyer in any kitchen, or associated with any catering enterprise in London at that time, would secure packed premises and enormous profits. Soyer, however, had had enough both of taking orders and of toiling for the profit of others, and now his fame and vanity dictated that any venture had to be entirely his own creation. Indeed, in March, when the Exhibition's building committee – led by such luminaries as Isambard Kingdom Brunel and Soyer's old friend Charles Barry – had called for innovative designs to be submitted for the Exhibition hall itself, Alexis had been one of nearly 250 hopefuls who entered the competition. His plans may have been rejected (in fact at that point they all were – the winning design was cobbled together two weeks after the closing date) but if anyone thought it was hubris for a mere cook to enter such a prestigious architectural competition, Soyer only had to answer that the eventual architect, Joseph Paxton, had started his career as the lowliest of garden boys.

It is unlikely that Alexis was surprised or particularly disappointed by the rejection of his Exhibition hall design. But his willingness to try shows how much his imagination had been fired by the whole scheme. Before long his fertile brain had produced another vision, only this time he stayed within his area of expertise and sketched out plans for a massive catering project, a culinary theme park designed to capitalise on the hordes of visitors to London that the Exhibition would produce. Soyer envisaged taking over a large site close to the Exhibition, where each night thousands of tired Exhibition-goers could congregate to eat, drink and relax in a cluster of exquisite, purpose-built bars and restaurants. Just as the Great Exhibition was to draw on exhibits from every corner of the globe, Soyer too would seek inspiration from the cuisines and cultures of the world, from Italy to China and North America, to provide an exotic theme for each venue.

It was a breathtakingly audacious and expensive scheme, and while he had saved a considerable amount of money during the last few years, he couldn't fund it on his own. He needed a backer who would not only bankroll the operation but, crucially, allow him to retain complete creative control. And during March, in the figure of a successful young Liverpool businessman called John Joseph Feeny, he found him. Limerick-born Feeny was an entrepreneur with a wide range of trade and manufacturing interests, from wine and biscuits to furniture and textiles. He was also the proprietor of a successful restaurant called the Merchants Dining Room and it was probably the success of this enterprise that encouraged him to become one of the many investors who approached Soyer about setting up an upmarket restaurant in the City. Alexis was not remotely interested in such a straightforward project, but he was, however, happy to avail himself of Feeny's considerable resources if Feeny would offer Soyer the capital he needed, plus a free rein in setting up the new enterprise, in exchange for a hands-off partnership. Feeny would, and so Alexis, for once keeping his ideas firmly under his hat, began drawing up his plans.

With the growing success of his business interests, for some time Soyer had been putting less and less of his energy into the Reform Club. And tolerant as his employers had been, there was a limit to how far they were prepared to put up with his extra-curricular activities. It was felt by a growing number within the committee that his commercial enterprises were now clashing with the interests of the club. It was one thing to have the kudos of the most famous *chef de cuisine* in the country looking after the appetites of your members, but it was quite another to have a showman in charge, whose public activities were sometimes highly embarrassing, and who dabbled, rather distastefully, in cheap goods. A number of Reformers had always resented the fact that their cook attracted more column inches in the press than the club itself, and felt that Soyer's continual exploitation of his privileged position there to flog his kickshaws rather undermined the Reform's dignity. The words cook and charlatan were sometimes being raised in the same sentence.

Alexis himself had grown weary of being, if not exactly a servant, then an employee, having to respond politely to an increasing number of petty or sniping comments from irritable members, and with the threat of disciplinary action never far away. For a long time he had been famous enough to make his way alone, without the borrowed glory of the club, and with money coming in from the books, the sauces, the Nectar and now the Magic Stove, he was financially independent enough to give up the security of his enormous salary and perks. And with Feeny's money on the table – as well as a number of other lucrative offers he was parrying – it was increasingly tempting. Even Soyer recognised that he could not launch his culinary theme park while still, nominally at least, running his day job. Yet the Reform had provided him with security for thirteen years, it had been the source of his fame and his second home, a steady, comfortable retreat through difficult times. In the end the decision was effectively made for him, when problems he was having with the committee reached crisis point.

Although the majority of Reformers were still dazzled by Alexis's artistry at formal banquets and impressed by the variety and quality of the dinners he provided every day, there had always been a grumbling undercurrent from those for whom he could do nothing right. The Coffee Room Complaints Book logged all such grievances, which ranged from 'beef tough, potatoes cold' and 'omelette bad and no oysters' to 'veal not good and badly dressed' and 'fish very indifferent'. In November 1842 a querulous Mr Queade complained that an underdone steak that he had sent back to the kitchen was returned overcooked. The committee were forced to assure him that 'the cook had been spoken to and cautioned to be more careful in the future'. Other members moaned about the cost. Even though club meals were well known to provide the best-value dinners in London, and Soyer made a particular effort to keep the prices low, the committee was regularly forced to placate disgruntled diners by quoting market prices and pointing out the very small margins taken by the club. When one signatory, an M. D. Gillow, complained about paying 4s. 6d. for a fowl that had cost the club four shillings, Soyer must have been reminded of poor Ude, bellowing in despair at the mean fool who had refused to pay the extra sixpence to have his fish dressed, believing it came from the sea with his exquisite sauce in its pocket.

But these mutterings – some no doubt justified – were part and parcel of running such a large catering organisation, and could easily be remedied. More difficult were the conflicts that arose from his loud and at times overbearing eccentricities, and his insistence on being involved in club matters outside the kitchen that were frankly none of his business. While humour and enthusiasm won over most members, others remained impervious to his charm, and some clearly despised him for his impertinence in 'getting above himself'. 'It was not without some difficulty,' concedes Volant, 'that he overcame, on many occasions, the opposition raised against his tenacity in upholding his privileges and his views for the Club. Whatever concerned that vast establishment was always most interesting to him, even if the matter did not directly relate to his department.'

This charge of 'getting above himself' would never be resolved, and over the years had led to a number of unpleasant run-ins between the chef and the management committee. In the summer of 1843 he had fallen foul of a member and future chairman of the committee, a Captain W. G. Beare, who ensured that Alexis was 'severely censured' for his insolence, in a move designed to underline his servant status. The minutes record that Soyer 'expressed his sorrow and made humble apology', a forced humiliation that would have rankled deeply. Yet the following March he was in trouble again, when exception was taken to a cheeky note he had written to a member, and the committee once more felt forced to 'consider the conduct of M. Soyer towards a certain member of the club'. This time the outcome was not recorded. These were minor skirmishes, though, compared to the far more serious charge brought against him a few weeks afterwards, that of financial dishonesty. Soyer, together with the butler and the kitchen clerk, was accused of having 'connived at the falsification of the butcher's account', presumably to skim off a profit for themselves. This was very grave. The butcher's bill was no trifle – after the wine, meat would have been the kitchen's most expensive outlay, running into many hundreds of pounds a year.

The accusation threatened not just Soyer's job at the club, but his public reputation and future career. All top chefs managed big budgets, leaving plenty of scope for sharp practice, and no employer would dream of taking on one with a tainted record. It did not help Alexis's case that he had always stood so heavily on his authority and, rather than delegate the detailed work, insisted on controlling all aspects of the kitchen finances. 'He was,' said Volant, 'jealous of any interference with his doings as *commander-in-chief*.' He supervised the ordering and negotiated with the suppliers, he would discuss the takings with the kitchen clerk and, after tallying up his expenses, would love to announce that by his economical management he had succeeded in feeding the club's servants for under five shillings a head for the week. As a result of his level of involvement, if there was any suggestion of corruption it was inevitable that he would be implicated in it. But while Soyer may have been a boaster and a peacock, he was certainly no petty thief. Apart from any other consideration, he hardly needed to clip pennies – as a single man with few overheads, his substantial salary combined with the fees raked in from his trainees earned him a very large annual income. And in 1844 he was already making money from his first private venture, the Reform Club kitchen lithograph. However, it is unlikely, in spite of his secretarial support, that he had kept completely accurate and comprehensive accounts of the kitchen bills, and it was this oversight that could make his situation very uncomfortable. If he was guilty of anything, it was of taking his eye off the ball.

It is not known how the charges were initially dealt with, but on 14 June 1844 a motion to sack Soyer was defeated by only seven votes to six. Instead, the committee decided 'that a further hearing of the charges against the cook be heard'. This happened the following day, and two days later it was followed by another, when seven witnesses were interviewed. At this point Alexis, furious and mortified, sent the committee a letter of resignation, but the investigation continued and on the fourth day, after seeing even more witnesses, Lord Marcus Hill, in an attempt to close the matter and bring Alexis back into the fold, moved that 'it appeared that M. Soyer has been guilty of no dishonesty whatever but of great irregularity, and the Committee resolve that he be called in, reprimanded, and informed that a repetition of such conduct will be followed by his immediate dismissal'. But the committee was still split – some members simply would not agree to let him off the hook so lightly. In the end a second motion was carried, by eight votes to seven, which stated that 'it is the opinion of this Committee that the charges preferred against M. Soyer have not been substantiated, but that in as much as he has been guilty of great irregularity his resignation is accepted'. If Alexis's resignation letter had been a bluff, it was one that was called. Three days later the butler and the clerk were officially reprimanded for having 'conjointly with the cook' connived at falsifying the butcher's account but, as 'it did not appear to have arisen from any fraudulent intention', they were not sacked.

So Alexis was out, despite nothing having been proved against him. But that would not be the end of it. In all likelihood it was Lord Marcus Hill who, working behind the scenes, managed to persuade enough members of the committee of the gross unfairness of the situation. Perhaps he pointed out the embarrassing consequences that could follow if *Punch*, the cook's great champion, ran a satirical story of how an ungrateful club had turned its back on its most loyal servant and creator of the finest kitchen in Europe. Whatever the backstage politics, on 28 June, a fortnight after his departure, the committee reconvened to consider a letter – again no doubt orchestrated by Hill – in which Alexis humbly requested his job back. This time, the vote swung in his favour, although only by nine to six, hardly a ringing endorsement. It was a chastened Soyer, therefore, who returned to his kitchens and his cosy office, and memories of the affair – including bitterness towards those colleagues who had testified against him – would stay with him for the rest of his time in Pall Mall.

Perhaps behind these accusations lay the suspicion, never fully relinquished by some members, that the exquisite little *petits soupers* that Alexis held, long after the kitchens had officially closed for the night, for those 'scientific, literary and artistic personages' that he had befriended through the club, were being furnished with the club's food and wine. After the débâcle over the butcher's bill, Alexis, while determined not to be forced into giving up the privilege of entertaining in his private office, was always on his guard to ensure that there could be no recurrence of such damaging allegations. 'Soyer, with his apparent levity, never lost sight . . . of what might be supposed a liberty taken with the Club,' said Volant. 'The expenses were always shown with the vouchers, so that, with the exception of the knives and forks belonging to the Club, used on those occasions, the Regenerator felt that he was perfectly independent; and, on every attack made against him, he generally refuted it with so much good sense, vigour, and wit, that the members of the Committee mostly enjoyed with him a good laugh.' Volant glosses over how deep the resentments really ran; he never mentions the dishonesty charges, and tries to ascribe most of Soyer's disciplinary appearances before the committee to interventions on behalf of other, less senior, servants who had got themselves into trouble. He does hint that Soyer remained on his guard and 'never allowed himself to be surprised' by awkward questions, which hardly indicated a relaxed environment. But he had learned how to keep his job safe, at least for the time being.

Over the next few years, however, as Alexis's successes outside the club mushroomed, members became less inclined to tolerate Coffee Room mistakes by their increasingly absent chef, and as the spring of 1850 progressed their dissatisfaction grew to outright revolt. In the minutes of the Annual General Meeting of 1850, which was held on 1 May, a motion was moved – and apparently carried – that the 'meeting begs to express to the Committee their dissatisfaction with the management of the Coffee Room and the attention of the cook to the comfort of the members'. It was a direct attack that could not be clearer. Soyer must stop treating his job as a sinecure – either his commercial activities must go, or his lucrative position at the club. Faced with what was effectively a vote of no confidence, within a few days of the AGM Soyer had resigned, and this time not even Marcus Hill could rescue the situation. *The Times* announced his departure on 13 May, and on 22 May the committee instructed the house subcommittee to find a new chef.

The resignation was dealt with diplomatically on both sides and Soyer was given the honourable get-out of using some proposed changes to the catering arrangements – which would increase his workload – as the reason for his resignation. In a dignified letter to the committee he stated that he was already finding his duties 'too laborious' and that any more responsibilities would render him unable to continue his job with credit to himself. According to Volant, the change he was referring to involved an amendment to the house rules which would allow Reformers to invite strangers to dine at the club every day, rather than twice a week. Soyer would naturally be opposed to such a move, as it would involve more work for the kitchen and turn the Coffee Room into a 'regular restaurant'. 'Not that he cared what they made of it,' he added, 'but the number of assistants in the kitchen must then be greatly increased, and . . . he thought that the same attention could not be bestowed, and the members served in the usual style.'

Here Volant is repeating the official line – but the facts do not support him. It is true that at the 1 May AGM it had been moved that a room (not the Coffee Room) should be made available to members for entertaining strangers to dinner, but a final decision on the matter was not taken for three weeks, by which time Soyer had gone. Even with this change, later records show that the number of non-members dining at the club accounted for only ten per cent of the meals served, so admitting strangers every day hardly caused a revolution in the kitchen. Whatever the exact thread of events, the upshot was that Soyer was going, this time for good, and with honour preserved on all sides. As chairman of the committee, the ever-loyal Marcus Hill wrote the official letter of acceptance. In it, he generously, if somewhat disingenuously, assured the chef of the club's regret at his departure.

. . . the Committee have unanimously desired me to assure you of the great reluctance with which they accept that resignation; and to express to you the high sense that they entertain of your very valuable past services, as well as of the zeal, ability, perfect integrity, and uniform respectability of conduct which you have devoted to the well-being of the Club, during a period of nearly thirteen years duration.

In response, Alexis sent Hill, whom he addressed as 'my dear protector', a personal and very emotional response in French, full of sincere thanks for his kindness, his wisdom and his unwavering friendship. He also confirmed – equally disingenuously – that he was leaving due to overwork. 'You, my lord, who know so well what is involved in running a unique establishment, please understand that these past thirteen years of hard work, of worry and continual responsibility such as is demanded by the club, these years could almost be counted double on the shoulders of a man who has carried such an extraordinary burden.' His white hairs, he said, on a head which had yet to see forty springs, bore witness to this. But, he quickly added, he *had* had a number of important and lucrative approaches – '*des offres très-advantageux et de haute importance*' – which he would like to discuss with Hill, as he would greatly value his advice. He finally asked Hill to pass on a 'thousand' thanks to the committee members for their charming letter and good wishes.

As soon as *The Times* announcement appeared, letters of regret began to flood in from friends and admirers who had toured the kitchens or eaten at the club. The smooth running of the kitchen was further hampered by the many members who dropped by, and the tradesmen and visitors who called in, for the last time, to confirm the shocking news and say their good-byes. The press was amazed by the resignation, which seemed to have come out of the blue. *Punch*, characteristically, responded with a ridiculous cartoon, showing Alexis assuming a dramatic pose against his *batterie de cuisine*, oversized beret on his head and one hand clapped to his weeping face, the other ceremoniously handing over a giant saucepan to a curtseying kitchenmaid. The caption read '*King Soyer resigning the Great Stewpan*'. Everyone began to speculate on what the great chef was going to do next, and to offer opinions on the merits and demerits of all the 'liberal offers' he had received. The proprietor of at least one 'immense hall' declared himself willing to lay 'any amount of money' at Soyer's feet if he would only transfer his talents to his business, but Soyer was never simply going to move from one employer's kitchen to another. Many assumed he would open his own restaurant in the city, but he had already concluded that as most of his potential clientele were likely to be clubmen, they were already well served by their clubs, and anyway, he wanted a change of direction, and to cook for all sorts of people, rich and poor, not just one type of wealthy male gourmet. Other enterprising opportunites that emerged at this time included the establishment of a cookery school – one of Alexis's long-held ambitions and already a proven way to make money – and the operation of a catering business for city banquets. But, as none of those who pressed Soyer for his services yet knew, the great chef was already committed to his next major project.

When the day of departure arrived, Alexis finally packed up his personal effects from the office he had designed, built and inhabited for so many years. He boxed up the gadgets and all the little work-in-progress inventions that he kept on a low table beside the fire. He took down Emma's paintings, which included *The English Ceres*, a portrait of a Kentish farm-worker harvesting corn, which she was said to have completed in just seventeen hours. Another one, *The Young Israelites*, depicting a couple of small boys selling lemons, had had special lights trained on it to show it to best advantage. He had to leave behind the table where his friends had eaten so many of his new creations, and Emma's satirical calling card, which she had scribbled on the wall so many years ago, and which he had preserved with a glass cover and frame. It would be nice to believe Sala, when he recalled in his memoirs that 'there was not the slightest ill-feeling between himself and the Committee when he left, and many members of the club, including Thackeray, Sir John East Hope, Mr Fox Maule (afterwards Lord Panmure), Mr Edward Ellice, and Lord Marcus Hill, remained his fast friends'. He did hang onto his friends, that was for sure, but the final parting, in spite of his desire to conquer fresh fields, could not have been quite as amicable as his final letters might suppose.

Certainly, the club had learned its lesson from Soyer's tenure. In future there were to be no such histrionics from the culinary department. Alexis's replacement, one M. Guerrier, was an undistinguished if competent chef, who earned a fraction of Soyer's wage. The *chef de cuisine*'s privilege of taking on improvers was also severely restricted. Alexis, for all his protestations of innocence when it came to taking liberties, had turned the kitchen into a glorified apprentice factory. His swarms of trainees may not have been on the payroll, but they all had to be fed, much to the annoyance of the committee, who regularly complained about the additional cost. Such was the rapid turnover of these improvers that when, in 1844, Soyer received a request from his old employer, Mrs Lloyd of Oswestry, to recommend a new chef, he was able to scribble back a reply to the effect that a young man had come in just the other evening who would suit, and that he would send him round to her Upper Brook Street residence directly.

So, stripped of its high salary and valuable perks the job could not attract a star chef, and the quality of the food gradually declined. The Reform Club never again reached the heights of culinary brilliance that it had enjoyed under Alexis Soyer, where the banquets were as famous for their bills of fare as for their celebrated guests. Guerrier did not stay long, and was replaced by Fidler, a former pupil of Soyer's who had extended his experience of mass catering by running the gigantic Crystal Palace kitchens once Paxton's giant glasshouse had been moved wholesale from Hyde Park to Sydenham. But Fidler did not shine any more brightly than Guerrier, and it was not until the appointment of Francatelli, in 1854, that the catering department began to revive.

With the club and all its associations behind him, it would have been with a profound sense of relief that Soyer found himself free, at last, to throw his energies into his own projects without being answerable to anyone. At forty, he had been a widower for eight years, but there was no sign of a serious new romance. His beloved Fanny Cerrito, for the time being at least, remained with her husband Arthur St-Léon in Paris, where the couple were a hugely successful double act, and if Soyer was ever lonely, he certainly was not idle. While quietly developing his plans for his Great Exhibition enterprise with Feeny, he took the time to add more material to the latest editions of his cook books, he took on some freelance catering contracts and spent a good part of the summer touring the country to promote the Magic Stove. A joky poem written by a friend, Lee Stevens, before his resignation, had suddenly become reality:

Soyer, no more to one small class confined
With Magic Stove now cooks for all mankind
Pall Mall but just sufficed for his rehearsal
The world his Club, his guests are universal

His first prestigious banquet commission as a freelance chef came just a few weeks after his departure from the club, and from an old friend, Benjamin Lumley, the brilliant manager of Her Majesty's Theatre, where Alexis had spent so much of his free time over the last thirteen years. Tall, dark, impressively bearded and exquisitely dressed, thirty-nine-year-old Lumley, whose fashion credentials had been boosted immeasurably after being painted by Count d'Orsay, was a Jewish solicitor who had acted professionally for the previous director of Her Majesty's. It had been Lumley's idea to sell leases to the boxes and stalls to pay for the restoration of the theatre. He had taken over creative control in 1842, and proved an inspired impresario. He knew Alexis principally through his association with Fanny – of whose talent as both a dancer and choreographer he was a huge admirer. Lumley had successfully fought off rival theatre managers to secure her services regularly through the 1840s, and he had arranged her famous *pas de deux* with Fanny Elssler at the queen's request, employing considerable tact to accommodate their clashing egos. He had also had to deal with Fanny's tantrums, her hard bargaining and her ghastly father – whom Alexis had also run foul of – so it was little wonder that the men found they had much in common. Like Soyer, Lumley was also media-savvy, often hyping up the rivalry between his *artistes* as a publicity stunt, and he was generous with tickets to anyone who might add glamour to the auditorium – Alexis had long ago given up paying to see anything.

Lumley was an equally generous host, and towards the end of each season would throw a lavish garden party, which he rather raffishly termed his *fête champêtre*. And in June 1850 Lumley asked Soyer to do the catering for his most important *fête champêtre* to date. Since the remodelled opera house in Covent Garden had opened three years earlier, the fortunes of Her Majesty's had been in decline. Most of Lumley's star performers had decamped to Covent Garden, and he had only managed to keep the theatre afloat by securing the services of the young Swedish phenomenon, Jenny Lind, 'the World's Sweetest Singer', whose extraordinary soprano voice guaranteed packed houses as 'Lind fever' swept through the country. But Lind had only stayed for a couple of seasons, and now Lumley found himself in trouble again. He pinned his hopes on a specially commissioned three-act opera called *La Tempesta*, a version of *The Tempest* written by two Parisian *artistes* at the height of their careers – the composer Fromental Halévy and librettist Eugène Scribe. The opera was very much in the French Romantic mould, with plenty of fantasy scenes involving dancing fairies and elf choruses, which Lumley was convinced London audiences would adore. The production represented his last chance to pull Her Majesty's out of its financial crisis, and he was prepared to throw everything at it to ensure its success.

Halévy and Scribe duly arrived in London on 18 May to rehearse a cast which drew together the very best performers Lumley could assemble, and *La Tempesta* opened on 8 June. To ramp up press interest in the opera and exploit the presence of his illustrious guests, Lumley suddenly decided to bring forward his annual party, and to make it the grandest, most extravagantly ostentatious *fête champêtre* to date. And of course no one but Soyer could pull off such an event. A week after the début, Lumley called on Alexis with a suggested venue – a marquee in the grounds of Chancellor House – and a date, 19 June, just four days away. Despite the short notice, it was to be the social event of the season, mingling the aristocratic patrons of the theatre with the stars of the opera, the drama and the ballet, and reported, of course, in all the newspapers.

Soyer immediately called on some of his most trusted helpers – a Mr Combes, 'an excellent stove cook' whom he had known since his time in Oswestry, and a Miss Frederick, a cook at the Russian Embassy. Like Sampayo, Lumley was willing to spend lavishly on the event and Soyer was given a free hand with the budget. Which was just as well, as the original projection of 500 guests quickly escalated – *Punch* estimated there were 800 diners, but Volant claimed there were nearly 2,000. Whatever the number, the 'scale of liberality' was certainly impressive, with the bill of fare covering several densely scripted pages. As usual, Soyer had created dishes for some of the star guests: *Escalopes de petites Solles à la Sontag* for pretty Henrietta Sontag, the Countess Rossi, who played Miranda, and *Filets de Rougets à la Halévy* and *Aiguillettes de petits Poussins à la Scribe* for the authors.

The star attraction though was a dessert, the most extravagant *pièce montée* he had attempted since the famous pyramidal confection of meringue, pineapple and gold leaf he had created for Ibrahim Pasha four years earlier. This time he produced a miniature ship, representing the storm-wrecked vessel bringing Ferdinand to Prospero's island – the central motif of *La Tempesta*. The *Croustade Shakespearienne, à la*

Halévy-Scribe, as he called it, was ingeniously contrived. The ship, crafted from *pain d'espagne*, foundered beside a reef of bon-bons, while gaudily coloured sugar characters swam about in a sea of spun sugar and transparent jelly. Spilled cargo, fashioned from grapes and apricots, floated around the prow, while inside the wreck you could make out two barrels carved from peaches. On top of the barrels a beautifully framed portrait of each of the guests of honour was just visible. The Frenchmen were suitably impressed by the novelty, wrote *The Globe*'s reporter, who then overheard a sycophantic exchange between Scribe's wife and Soyer, who, replying to Madame Scribe's acknowledgement of the honour given to her husband, declared, 'Honour, Madame! No honour could exceed his greatness; for if the shade of Molière were to rise from his tomb, it would be jealous of his talents.' The *Punch* correspondent (probably Thackeray) also quoted the chef, who, on being given just four days to prepare the feast, had apparently exclaimed, '*c'était impossible, mais c'est fait!*' In the end, *La Tempesta* was a critical and commercial success, and earned Lumley enough to keep his theatre going, if only for a few more seasons.

Immediately after the triumphant Halévy-Scribe banquet, Alexis began preparations for his first large-scale event outside London. The Royal Agricultural Society had awarded Soyer the contract to produce its Grand Dinner, the star attraction of an annual roving festival which that year was being held in Exeter. A week-long celebration of British farming, there were to be dozens of livestock competitions, companies from all over the country marketing the very latest tools and heavy equipment, public lectures in the elegant Athenaeum in Bedford Circus, and even an art exhibition of Turner's most popular rural scenes. The railways provided free transport for beasts and machinery, and most of the implements on display, from patented ploughs, turnip-cutters and steam threshing machines, were to reappear the following year at the Great Exhibition. It was a social as well as an agricultural event, with aristocrats and landowners mingling with the farm-workers – at one of the meetings the earl count alone consisted of m'Lords Spencer, Chichester, Falmouth, Leicester and Ilchester. Elaborate arches, woven from laurel and oak branches, were erected across the city streets bearing slogans such as 'Agriculture and Commerce', 'Peace and Prosperity' and 'Success to Agriculture', and as the festival wore on they accrued more crowns, flags and other loyal inscriptions.

The great banquet called for an entirely different approach from Soyer. A thousand hungry farmers were expecting a memorable spread – none of the exquisite little entrées and witty *gâteaux* that Soyer was famous for, but a substantial English feast reflecting the bountiful harvests that they had toiled for all year round. In the weeks prior to the event rumours had reached Alexis that the local Devon tradesmen had become anxious 'bordering on madness' that the upstart French cook would be bringing his own fancy supplies with him, thereby depriving them of a valuable retail opportunity. So Soyer took the sensible and imaginative precaution of travelling down to Exeter early and employing the town crier to announce that all those willing to supply the feast were invited to meet the chef at his hotel and agree terms. In fact it was more than a diplomatic move – Alexis needed all the help he could get to muster enough food for the gargantuan spread that he had planned.

As the week of the festival began, an excitable journalist reported in the *Illustrated London News* that 'the railway trains and other sources of conveyance are pouring in their thousands of visitors, and the city is becoming literally crammed'. The Exonians were determined to enjoy themselves, he added, as 'it appeared as though the whole population had turned out of doors; the numbers of fashionable and gaily-dressed ladies being not the least conspicuous.' The gala dinner – in fact a late lunch – was scheduled for Thursday, 18 July, the penultimate day of the fête, and the diners were to be housed in an enormous temporary pavilion in Queen Street, situated at the bottom of Northernhay. Soyer immediately spent a small fortune decorating the place. At one end of the marquee he erected a triumphal arch designed to eclipse all the street decorations in size and lavishness. It stood seventeen feet tall and twelve wide, was flanked by a pair of fully costumed beefeaters, draped with flags, and woven with dozens of symbols of British agriculture and produce, from spades, hoes and scythes to bushels of wheat and corn, baskets of fruits and vegetables, and stuffed animals – the heads of six horned bullocks, two stags and two pigs, a white swan and a cockerel, whole lambs and chickens, geese, ducks and rabbits. A plaque hanging from one rope of flowers carried the city's motto, *Semper Fidelis*, and under the arch a flower-strewn table bore a large and lavishly decorated boar's head. The *Bouquet de Gibier* that he had sent to Louis Philippe paled into insignificance beside this towering folly.

The bill of fare included – on top of a whole *Baron and Saddleback of Beef à la Magna Charta* – 33 dishes of ribs of beef, 35 dishes of roast lamb, 99 galantines of veal, 29 dishes of ham, 69 dishes of pressed beef, two rounds of beef *à la Garrick*, 264 dishes of chicken, 33 raised French pies *à la Soyer*, 198 dishes of mayonnaise salad, 264 fruit tarts and 198 dishes of hot potatoes. It also included 33 Exeter puddings, which Soyer had invented especially for the occasion. These were essentially an alcohol-steeped reworking of his boiled Plum Bolster, for which, in *The Modern Housewife*, he had applied the alternative name of 'Spotted Dick' for the first time in an English cook book. They were big, rich, doughy balls of suet and sugar, to which Alexis added rum and ratafias and then smothered with a sweet, shining blackcurrant and sherry sauce. To cook this quantity of food Soyer had to use the large Royal Subscription Room kitchen as a base and send teams of pastry-cooks and confectioners to borrowed kitchens all over the city, while relying on local workers to bring back the cooked dishes according to a rigid schedule.

But the *pièce de résistance* was a triumph of Soyer showmanship: in a prominent space in the city's Castle Yard he managed to roast to perfection an entire 535-pound ox by improvising a temporary gas stove. He instructed local workmen to build a low brick pit, without mortar, six foot six inches by three foot three inches, which he covered with a few sheets of iron for safety. Inside the pit half-inch-thick gas tubes were carefully wrapped around the ox. The tubes had been perforated with 216 holes, and when the gas was lit tiny jets were produced that 'frizzled and steamed' the animal to a turn in eight hours – and for a cost, Alexis noted a few years later, of less than five shillings for the gas. Soyer's calculations had to be precise – when the time came for the beast to be eaten, to have served the meat either raw or overcooked would have courted instant public humiliation. But to his relief his maths did not fail him and, as a local paper reported, 'the joint was withdrawn thoroughly cooked, the object of general approbation, and carried to the pavilion with flying colours, to the sound of a band of music'. The ox was ceremoniously borne through the pavilion to a table under the triumphal arch, where the decorated boar's head was whipped away to give it pride of place.

The astonished people of Exeter – many of whom had gathered outside the marquee to watch the proceedings – had never seen anything like it. Even a heavy burst of rain did not dampen the party mood. Inside, Soyer flew around the hall, charming the guests and ensuring that everyone was comfortably seated and furnished with everything on offer. Chaired by the president of the Royal Agricultural Society, the Duke of Devonshire, the dinner was declared a huge success. It was the first time the society had imposed their own cook on the event, and the Earl of Chichester later wrote that 'the splendid dinner provided would probably insure the employment of M. Soyer's talents on future occasions'. After the meal, more entertainments had been laid on, and of course Soyer grabbed the opportunity – and the captive audience – to give more demonstrations of the Magic Stove. He even changed into a dashing approximation of a French national dress, complete with a Normandy cap, and stood beside the stove, cracking jokes, while producing a stream of hot cutlets, chops and omelettes. 'Such a display of gaiety was never before witnessed!' wrote the *Trewman's Flying Post*.

He may have created an event that the diners would never forget, but Alexis had wildly over-provisioned. Although 1,200 diners had finally sat down to eat instead of 1,000, there was still an embarrassingly large amount of leftovers. Soyer suggested a second edition of the dinner, for 700 of the city's poor, with any extra costs being defrayed by public subscription. The idea was immediately adopted, and the charitable meal took place the following day. Deflecting attention from his purveying blunder, Alexis provided another exciting event for the townspeople to gossip about, and left his employers with the warm afterglow of charitable munificence. The committee weren't such fools as to bankroll this overspend, however, and the RAS council minutes record that on 19 July Soyer was paid £442 as per his contract – a huge sum, equating to around £34,000 in modern terms – but not enough to cover all that he had provided. However popular his adventures in Exeter had made him (the previously hostile tradesmen were no doubt thrilled to have doubled their trade receipts for the month), in the end the exercise was not a profitable one for Soyer. The supposed master of middle-class economy had once again shown a reckless disregard for budgetary concerns, and it was this tendency to get carried away that would in time prove disastrous.

After several days of being fêted by Devonshire society, Alexis left for London on 23 July. The night before his departure he wrote to the editor of the *Exeter Journal* to thank the local people for their help and many kindnesses during his stay, claiming that if he mentioned them all by name he would put the paper to 'the expense of a double supplement'. He added that once back in his London kitchen he would perfect the Exeter Pudding which had proved so popular (the *Illustrated London News* had declared that 'all the matrons of the ancient city were striving to obtain the recipe'), before sending the editor an accurate recipe for publication. To which the editor cheerfully appended the postscript: 'Why not send the pudding? We will cheerfully insert it in the proper quarter.'

Back in London, Alexis continued to juggle other projects while his Great Exhibition plans took shape. He spent time relaxing at Virginia Water, which looked glorious in the long summer evenings, and took the opportunity to visit Paris, where he saw old friends, including Fanny Cerrito. Although her relationship with St-Léon was deteriorating rapidly, both were at their artistic peak and their professional partnership was as strong as ever. They were currently enjoying a sell-out run at the *Opéra* in a new ballet, *Stella*, which Arthur had arranged and choreographed to highlight their individual strengths. While *Stella* had attracted some bad press for its derivative plot, the critics united in praise for Fanny's witty and vivacious portrayal of the heroine, and the agile virtuosity of her husband.

Whether or not the couple had ever been happy together, by 1850 the marriage was swiftly unravelling. Their personalities had never really complemented each other – where Fanny was warm and affectionate, St-Léon seemed to restrict his passion to dancing and playing the violin. He had been a somewhat passive lover from the start, and it is possible that he had no interest in Fanny sexually, or perhaps in any woman; he certainly seems to have had no other liaisons after their separation in 1851. The courtship had essentially been driven forward by Fanny's parents once they realised how lucrative the pairing could be. So perhaps it was not surprising when Fanny, a few years into their marriage, began to be linked to other men. She was young, beautiful, spirited and successful, and if she lacked male attention at home, she was not going to spurn it outside.

One of her most assiduous admirers had been the young Nepalese prime minister, Jung Bahadur. A few years earlier Jung Bahadur had famously overthrown his uncle and murdered all his enemies to secure his political position, and in 1850, with his power base assured, he decided to spend a year in Europe on a sort of post-coup sabbatical. Utterly captivated by Fanny, he presented the ballerina with two fabulously valuable diamond bracelets, while she in turn gave him a daguerreotype of herself. On another occasion she rather recklessly allowed herself to be seen in his official carriage, sitting beside him as he travelled to a formal engagement. While St-Léon may not have displayed any sexual jealousy, being seen so publicly with a man like Jung Bahadur could hardly have helped their domestic harmony. And her Nepalese suitor was just passing through anyway. In 1850 Fanny was thirty-three years old and, although as fit as ever, she was aware that she would not be able to dance so well for much longer. After five years together she and St-Léon had had no children, and the future, trapped in an arid marriage and with her career over, must have seemed very bleak.

The stress was clearly showing when a Hungarian diplomat, Count

Rudolf Apponyi, after watching her dance *Stella*, wrote in his diary that while the ballerina retained a ravishing figure, her face, though still pleasingly childlike, was 'very drawn'. In September 1850, as the strain in her marriage increased, she became prone to panic attacks – after one performance of *Stella*, during which her pallor had already caused her colleagues concern, she came off stage and immediately fainted in the wings. She and St-Léon would finally separate for good the following year, but in the meantime she was extremely relieved to have the comfort and support of her devoted Alexis in Paris during such a miserable time. If her relationship with Alexis had remained chaste in London while she held out for a good match, it is almost inconceivable that it remained unconsummated in Paris. Fanny's marriage was doomed, she had already been linked to other men, and while she insisted that their relationship remained a secret, there was no reason for them not to be together.

Partly to enable him to spend more time in Paris, Alexis became involved in another ambitious new scheme. It was suggested that he should spend a long weekend escorting a large party of English tourists around Paris in a sort of gastronomically themed package holiday, long before the age of the mini-break. He went as far as to launch a prospectus, which promised a dazzling if exhausting schedule which included, along with the usual sightseeing musts, a boat trip to St Cloud and a visit to the Sèvres porcelain factory. The food was to be a non-stop orgy of picnics, dinners and gala banquets which included: 'a *déjeuner à la fourchette*, promenade, and foot-race in the forest of Fontaine-bleau . . . A *fête champêtre* in the park of Rambouillet . . . A *fête dansante* at the Ranelagh in the Bois de Boulogne . . . A *fête Vénitienne* at Asnières . . . [and] a collation at Versailles'. Plus, of course, a meal in the grounds of St Germain where 'the dinner will be partly cooked on Soyer's *Liliputian Magic Stove* in the pavilion of Henry IV'. The fee per person was a hefty fifteen guineas – but it did include first-class carriage and ferry tickets, hotels, food, and entry to all the attractions.

It was an extremely novel concept – after all it was not until the following year that a sometime Baptist preacher called Thomas Cook took his first paying customers abroad. Cook, an evangelising teetotaller, had stumbled into the travel agency business a few years previously after arranging for 500 fellow temperance campaigners to travel by special train from Leicester to a meeting in Loughborough. Where Cook saw travel essentially as an educational tool, Soyer's only concern was to provide his paying guests with as much sensory gratification as they could take. Like so many of his enterprises, Soyer's holiday scheme would never get off the ground. In early August *The Globe* published an article suggesting that Soyer's French agent had been involved in some suspect deals with Parisian hoteliers for a large number of heavily discounted rooms. It was an accusation that led Soyer to distance himself from the whole scheme in an outburst of self-righteous indignation. In a furious letter to the editor he refuted any allegation of being involved in a 'monster speculation' and claimed that his 'magnificent prospectus' had only ever been intended for 'a select party of acquaintances, whom, at their own request, I . . . consented to lead and entertain in a manner hitherto never attempted, both as regards the gratification of sight-seeing in the capital of France . . . but also [to] give them a full opportunity of judging of what can be done in the way of living when led by a gastronomic caterer'. And then the matter was quietly shelved.

A few weeks later, the young artist and writer George Augustus Sala, out walking with one of his brothers, spotted Alexis shopping for lobsters in the Central Avenue of Hungerford market. Sala, who would soon be working for Soyer, watched as the chef ran his expert eye over the lobsters and, after assessing their weight, examining their claws, rapping their backs and poking their sides, negotiated a good price for them, as the fishmonger was clearly keen to keep on good terms with 'the foreign gentleman whose hat, coat, cravat and pantaloons were all so studiously awry'. To twenty-two-year-old Sala, Alexis, at forty, with his stout frame and closely cropped greying hair and moustache, appeared 'a little past middle age', and so eccentrically dressed that he could have been mistaken for the riding-master of a foreign circus.

He wore a kind of paletot of light Calmat cloth, with voluminous lapels and deep cuffs of lavender watered silk; very baggy trousers, with a lavender strip down the seams; very shiny boots, and quite as glossy a hat; his attire being completed by tightly-fitting gloves of the hue known in Paris as *beurre frais* – that is to say, light yellow . . . An extraordinary oddity was added to his appearance by the circumstance that every article of his attire, save I suppose, his gloves and boots, was cut on what dressmakers call a 'bias' or as he himself, when I came to know him well, used to designate as *à la zoug-zoug*. He must have been the terror of his tailor, his hatter, and the maker of his cravats and underlinen.

After a brief introduction Soyer invited the Salas to dine with him that night, and the brothers duly arrived at his latest lodgings, 'the upper part of a house in the dim regions of Soho'. It must have seemed a humble home for such a wealthy man, but in the 1850s the area was effectively a French ghetto, and Alexis, for all his social climbing, clearly felt a stronger need to be near his compatriots than in a smart part of town. After finally quitting his father-in-law's flat he had chosen a house that was surrounded by 'French *charcutiers*, French restaurants, hotels, barbers and hairdressers, newsvendors, circulating libraries and cigar-shops . . . while the floors over the French shops were tenanted by French tailors, milliners and dressmakers'.

Sala described Alexis's flat as having very small rooms which were plainly furnished, with the exception of one chamber which was hung with a number of Emma's 'very able and tasteful' oil paintings. Soyer had also, finally, created his ideal bachelor's kitchen, his sleek, modern 'Kitchen At Home' which Sala, recalling it even at a distance of many years, was able to describe with accuracy and admiration.

Soyer's apartments were not of much more commanding dimensions than would belong to a series of moderate-sized aviaries; but the eminently assimilative and inventive nature of the man had enabled him to set up in two or three little exiguous dens on the top floor, a miniature kitchen and larder and scullery, as complete in their way as the wonderful kitchen and annexes which he had arranged for the Reform Club. He had his roasting-range, his oven, his screen and plate-warmer; his bain-marie pan heated by water from the adjacent boiler, his 'hot-plate', his seasoning box and fish sauce-box; his refridgerator, and his knife-cleaning machine; his dressers and tables, and plate rack. The larder was as completely furnished as the kitchen; and on the floor beneath was his dining-room. I remember that, after we had consumed an admirable supper, which he had cooked with his own hands, with the assistance of a very small but obedient and handy Irish servant-girl, with shoes hopelessly down at heel, he brought forth that which seemed to be a kind of conjuring apparatus. It was his 'magic stove'. A chop or a steak was placed on a metal tripod . . . and by means of some ingenious blowpipe arrangement, a prolonged tongue of flame . . . was projected horizontally from the lamp into the tripod and under the frying-pan . . . where the flame assumed a circular shape, and cooked the meat to a nicety.

Later that autumn Alexis made several visits to the north of England, the first in order to tour with the Magic Stove and to cater for several important functions. At the beginning of September the Earl of Carlisle – no doubt on the recommendation of his sister, the Duchess of Sutherland – asked Soyer to travel to Castle Howard, one of the most magnificent mansions in England, to provide the dinner for a ball in honour of Queen Victoria and Prince Albert, who were staying for a few nights with their children, en route to a family holiday in Balmoral. The evening was a great success and Alexis, unfazed either by the grandeur of Vanbrugh's exquisite great hall or the illustrious company, had the temerity to bring out his Magic Stove to divert the guests after the formal part of the meal was over. Not even the presence of the monarch could come between him and a good marketing opportunity. As a slightly incredulous edition of *The Times* reported on 7 September:

> At the ball given on the evening of her Majesty's departure from Castle Howard, one of the greatest attractions was afforded by M. Soyer's cooking various dishes on the supper-table with his Lilliputian Magic Stove, surrounded by lords and ladies not a little surprised to see, for the first time, part of their supper *cooked in a ball-room*. The favourite dish amongst the ladies present was *les oeufs au miroir*, half-a-dozen of which seem to have been done every two minutes with the greatest ease and expedition.

His next visit to Yorkshire came the following month. Having missed the opportunity once before, he was finally to cook a banquet for Prince Albert. The occasion was the return dinner given by the British mayors, almost a year to the day since the queen's consort had entertained them so handsomely at the Mansion House to lobby their support for the Great Exhibition. It was an extremely important occasion. Although plans for the Exhibition were gathering pace, at this stage there was still plenty of political opposition to it; fanned by the press, loud objections were being voiced about its purpose, its estimated expense, and even its location in Hyde Park. Without strong support in the provinces, the prince's pet project could still have been derailed. The fact that Albert was travelling up to York specifically to attend the dinner told its own story – etiquette demanded that the people came to the royals, never vice-versa – but Albert was prepared to break with protocol to demonstrate his support for the Exhibition.

As for the host of the event, the Mayor of York was determined to put on the most sumptuous civic banquet in the city's history, and to show that, in hiring Soyer, Yorkshire could compete with London when it came to culinary sophistication. Each of the 238 guests paid four guineas a head, giving Soyer a staggering budget of nearly a thousand guineas. With it he first set the scene by transforming the Mansion House dining room into a dazzling banqueting hall. To do so he brought in Alfred Adams, who had created the triumphal arch at Exeter, to make a new, and even grander decoration, according to his design. Every possible effect was used to produce this monstrous artwork – portraits of Victoria and Albert, the arms of all the major English cities whose mayors were attending the feast, flags, laurels, classical figures representing Scotland and Wales, the Prince of Wales' feathers and wreaths of red and white roses representing the houses of York and Lancaster. And in the middle of it all was a giant statue of Britannia, surrounded by figures representing all the corners of the earth, each one laying before her examples of their industry. When the prince walked in, the statues were bathed in a flood of gaslight made even brighter by the use of carefully positioned reflectors.

The menu and the wine list were just as extravagant. The fifty dishes included the most expensive turtle soup; miroton of lobster with olives; ducklings with orange; pheasants with truffles; crevettes stewed in champagne; the famous grouse salad *à la Soyer*; delicate French raspberry jellies *à la Fontainebleau* and praline tarts with Montmorency cherries. The eighteen dignitaries seated at the royal table – which included the Archbishop of York and the prime minister, Lord John Russell – were provided with the rarest delicacies, which it was impossible to produce for the whole company. These included an extra type of turtle soup, a roasted peacock, white mullets *à l'Italienne* and galantines made from gosling meat. Soyer also slipped in some signature dishes for the guests of honour – including his Mutton Cutlets Reform and one of his joky sponge cakes shaped like a ham. But the *pièce de résistance* of the dinner, which would become a culinary legend, was a dish officially called *L'Extravagance Culinaire à l'Alderman*: a concoction of turtles, exotic game birds and truffles that quickly became known as the Hundred Guinea Dish. The reason for its extravagance was that the only fowl flesh Soyer used was the tenderest morsels – the two tiny, bite-sized oysters, or *noix*, that nestled either side of the spine of each bird. His inspiration came, perhaps, from the late Lord Alvanley, the extravagant gourmet lodger of Soyer's mentor Ude, whose favourite supper dish, *Suprême de Volaille*, had comprised the *noix* of twenty birds.

Due to the scale of the banquet, Soyer managed to amass enough oysters to furnish the entire dish. Had an epicure ordered it at any other time, Soyer calculated, it would set him back well over a hundred pounds – the equivalent of more than £8,000 today. In later editions of *The Gastronomic Regenerator* he even provided a breakdown of the bill:

		£	s.	d.
5	Turtles heads, part of fins and green fat	34	0	0
24	Capons, the small *noix* from each side of the middle of the back only used, being the most delicate parts of every bird	8	8	0
18	Turkeys, the same	8	12	0
18	Poulardes, the same	5	17	0
16	Fowls, the same	2	8	0
10	Grouse	2	5	0
20	Pheasants, *noix* only	3	0	0
45	Partridges, the same	3	7	0
6	Plovers, whole	0	9	0
40	Woodcocks, the same	8	0	0
3 doz.	Quails, whole	3	0	0
100	Snipes, *noix* only	5	0	0
3 doz.	Pigeons, *noix* only	0	14	0
6 doz.	Larks, stuffed	0	15	0
	Ortolans from Belgium	5	0	0
	The garniture, consisting of Cockscombs, Truffles, Mushrooms, Crawfish, Olives, American Asparagus, *Croustades*, Sweetbreads, *Quenelles de Volaille*, Green Mangoes, and a new Sauce	14	10	0
		105	5	0

The townspeople of York became caught up in the excitement of the banquet. A stream of interested onlookers passed by the Mansion House throughout the afternoon, watching the frantic comings and goings, and by late afternoon it thickened into a crowd, anxious to glimpse the arrival of the queen's husband and his entourage. Albert arrived, right on time, at six fifteen for the seven o'clock start, and on being led into the banqueting hall was immediately faced with Soyer's gaslit artwork. He was, according to one eye-witness, 'perfectly astonished at the brilliance and magnificent appearance of the place, and expressed his delight in terms of the greatest eulogium'. The dinner passed off without a hitch, and was followed by a stirring speech from Albert, which stressed that he had come not 'from the mansion of some neighbouring landed lord, but direct from the presence of the sovereign herself, prepared to express as from her own royal mouth the interest she feels in the trade and industry of her people'. It was a cleverly constructed, galvanising speech, and the audience, sated with fine wines and Soyer's fabulous dinner, roared their approval. The newspapers reported the event in the most glowing terms, and the evening was considered one of the pivotal moments in the lengthy campaign to get the public behind the Exhibition.

Back in London, Soyer's own secret plans to cash in on the Great Exhibition were also nearing completion. Two months later, on 30 December, he finally signed an expensive lease on Gore House in Kensington, an imposing three-storey mansion set in three acres of land – right across the road from Hyde Park and the site for the winning design which would become the Crystal Palace. In so doing, he locked himself into an enterprise that would consume him for the next two years, and bring him to the brink of ruin.

11

'ITS HALLS ONCE MORE GLITTER'

One of the many extraordinary aspects of the Great Exhibition was how quickly it came to fruition – from the first tentative discussions at Buckingham Palace in the summer of 1849, to its Grand Opening on 1 May 1851. The idea thrashed out at those Palace meetings, which were driven forward by the visionary civil servant, Henry Cole, soon to be chairman of the Royal Society of Arts, was a bold but simple one. Cole had recently been impressed with the latest Paris Exposition, and he had become keen to extend the RSA's own national exhibitions into something much bigger, and more befitting a capital city that was not just the hub of a nation, but of an empire. What he had in mind was a world-class trade fair, housed in its own, purpose-built arena. It would not just display the very latest technology from around the globe, but have a deeper, almost moral, significance. It would demonstrate that the progress of mankind depended on international co-operation, it would show how the economies of the different nations of the world were inter-related, and that the mission of the British Empire was 'to put herself at the head of the diffusion of civilisation'. It was a vision that captivated Prince Albert, who, as president of the RSA, immediately agreed to become the project's figurehead.

The practical difficulties began as soon as Albert and the members of the newly constituted Royal Commission looked for a suitable site for what had now been officially designated The Great Exhibition of the Works of Industry of All Nations. Battersea Fields, Regent's Park, Primrose Hill, the Isle of Dogs, Leicester Square and the courtyard of Somerset House were all rejected before a twenty-two-acre patch at the southern end of Hyde Park was finally settled upon. Many residents of

Kensington and Belgravia with homes near the park were horrified at what they believed would be an invasion of the commonest of working-class visitors, turning their genteel green space into what *The Times* dubbed 'a bivouac of all vagabonds'. The nuisance inflicted on the neighbourhood, continued the paper, would be indescribable: 'we can scarcely bring ourselves to believe that the advisers of the Prince cared to connect his name with such an outrage to the feelings and wishes of the inhabitants of the metropolis.' (A rather dramatic editorial U-turn, considering its enthusiastic support of Prince Albert's speech at the York banquet.) Residents raised a petition that was presented to Parliament, begging for the Exhibition to be diverted elsewhere. They were particularly furious when they learned that the price of entry to the Great Exhibition was to drop from a pound to just a shilling at the end of May – meaning that they would have to suffer hordes of the very poorest country bumpkins for an entire month, before 1 July brought the end of the London season and a welcome retreat to their country properties.

And the locals were not the only doubters. Some Londoners believed that the influx of the largest number of country folk ever to congregate in the capital – never mind all the foreign visitors – would lead to a shortage of food and other vital supplies, not to mention an increase in robberies and other types of crime. Some predicted riots and epidemics. The King of Hanover rudely called the project 'a rubbishy exhibition' and referred to Prince Albert as 'the great originator of this folly'. Although Parliament supported the project, the relevant bills did not pass through the Commons without much heated debate. Many MPs saw the show as little more than an unnecessary showcase for foreign paraphernalia, and a piece of tacit propaganda for the Free Trade movement. One of the most outspoken critics was Charles Sibthorp, MP for Lincoln, who declared in a Commons speech that the entire project was 'the greatest trash, the greatest fraud and the greatest imposition ever attempted to be palmed upon the people of this country'.

The hostility hardly lessened when the design of the building chosen to house the Great Exhibition was published. The commissioners rejected every single one of the 245 designs sent in to the official competition in favour of a giant greenhouse designed by an aristocrat's gardener! It was sheer madness, declared the Exhibition's detractors, who claimed that Joseph Paxton's fragile glass building – 'a cucumber frame between two chimneys', according to John Ruskin – could not possibly withstand any extremes of weather, or even the sheer weight of human traffic that it would be subjected to. In fact, Joseph Paxton had been experimenting with large-scale glass buildings for years on the Duke of Devonshire's estate, and had developed a unique 'ridge and furrow' roofing system that suited the needs of the commissioners perfectly. What Paxton proposed was a glass, wood and iron structure put together in modules based on a twenty-four-foot cube and reaching a maximum height of sixty-four feet, which would give the building three tiers. It could be pre-fabricated off site, then transported to Hyde Park and erected in a matter of months. By adding a barrel-vaulted transept at the front, Paxton was even able to enclose some ancient elm trees within the building, the prospective felling of which had inspired bitter arguments.

And so, against all fears and prejudice, Parliament, Prince Albert and the commissioners ploughed on. Gradually even the most vocal opposition began to give way to the general excitement of such a vast and unique undertaking. The successful building contractors, Messrs Fox & Henderson, moved onto the site in July 1850 and by January the breathtakingly elegant Crystal Palace was up and ready to be filled with all the marvels the world could produce. Its scale was overwhelming, the design and atmosphere owing more to a cathedral than a palace. The nave was almost 2,000 feet long, the Great Organ boasted 3,714 pipes and the main transept was larger than the dome of St Peter's in Rome. There were thirty miles of guttering and 200 miles of wooden sash bars – and all this enclosed by a staggering 1,500,000 square feet of glass.

Like everyone in London, through the second half of 1850 Soyer watched as the city was transformed by the coming of the Exhibition. The changes were not confined to the immediate vicinity of the Crystal Palace, where, just a stroll away from the club in Pall Mall, he could watch more than two thousand labourers erecting the mammoth glass structure. Marble Arch, Nash's grand entrance to Buckingham Palace, was moved wholesale to the north-east corner of Hyde Park. Charles Barry's newly designed Trafalgar Square, after years of delays, was finally finished. Slums were cleared as hotels and restaurants sprang up around the major railway terminals. Double-decker omnibuses, designed to ease congestion around the stations and transport the crowds around the city, appeared for the first time. Villages around the perimeter of Hyde Park, including Kensington to the west and Old Brompton to the south, were slowly swallowed into the city spread.

Never before had so many people been expected to converge on the capital over a single summer – the relative cheapness of third-class rail travel having put a trip to London within the grasp of millions of British citizens. And every Londoner wanted to take a slice of their spending money. Housewives prepared to offer bed and breakfast accommodation. Shops piled up souvenir stock in every cupboard and corner. Theatres, opera houses, lecture halls, galleries and pleasure gardens all geared up for the rush with extra facilities and special events, and a slew of new attractions sprang up within walking distance of the Exhibition. One of the most popular of these was Batty's Hippodrome, a huge equestrian circus constructed opposite the Broad Walk in Kensington Gardens, where up to 14,000 spectators could watch daily recreations of Roman chariot races and medieval jousts, performed to the anachronistic accompaniment of two brass bands. However great his celebrity, and however tempting his food and his prices, Soyer knew that his own attraction was going to have plenty of competition.

Meanwhile, the Great Exhibition's commissioners had turned their attention from the dazzling exterior of the Crystal Palace to the minutiae of the interior. As the committee intended to issue day tickets that would not allow visitors to leave and then re-enter the exhibition hall, it had to ensure that decent amenities were provided. Special retiring rooms were therefore equipped with 'monkey closets', an ingenious early version of the flushing toilet, designed by Brighton engineer George Jennings. Users were charged one penny to avail themselves of the new facilities, but for that money they were able to relieve themselves in peace and relative privacy. And as well over three-quarters of a million people did 'spend a penny' during the twenty-three weeks of the exhibition, Jennings's £1,790 net takings arguably made his novel convenience the most profitable invention in the building.

After dealing with the most basic requirements, refreshments were the next most important consideration. Any displays of over-exuberance caused by drink were particularly to be abhorred, and so it was proposed that alcohol should be banned. Eventually, it was agreed that one tea-room and two dining rooms would be set up, providing simple snacks but nothing cooked – sandwiches, sausage rolls, fruit and buns, and to drink, tea, coffee and cocoa, carbonated soft drinks such as lemonade, plus ginger and spruce beer in the dining rooms. Fresh filtered drinking water, in proper glasses, was also to be supplied, free of charge, by whoever won the catering franchise, although as the *News of the World* commented on 26 January, 'whoever can produce in London a glass of water fit to drink will contribute the rarest and most universally useful article in the whole Exhibition'.

The organisers were determined not to provide their customers with the sort of gastronomic experience they might wish to linger over; the aim was to produce a brisk throughput of visitors past the counters and back onto the Exhibition floor. At one point the ludicrous suggestion was made that food should only be consumed standing up. The newspapers – who commented extensively on every aspect of the Exhibition's progress – found the lack of choice on the proposed menu patronising and prescriptive. 'The scheme . . . allows nothing for the diversity of tastes among all the nations of the earth,' said the *News of the World*, 'but proceeds on the presumption that the whole world will be satisfied with tea and bread and butter. We recommend, before it is too late, that the regulations as to the refreshments should be modified in such a way as to provide for the admission of the food of all nations to the Great Exhibition.'

When tenders were invited for the supply of the refreshments, the commissioners had been surprised that no bid had been received from Soyer – surely the nation's leading expert on mass catering. The chef had even submitted a design for the building itself, so why on earth would he not want the lucrative catering contract? Feeling that perhaps Alexis could inject the necessary panache into their lacklustre arrangements, earlier in the month the committee had taken the highly unusual step of writing to him personally. 'If it is at all your intention to tender for the refreshments at the Exhibition, and you think it may be advisable to have *single* glasses of wine served, will you be kind enough to mention such wish in your tender?' ran the note, which, while ostensibly promising nothing, not only offered Soyer a thinly veiled invitation, but hinted that if he would only take over the catering, they might even allow him a limited (but highly profitable) sale of alcohol.

It was a huge compliment, but Soyer was now financially and legally committed to his own project, and for once even he knew that – however tempting – he could not do both. He wrote a regretful letter to the effect that 'as he had taken Gore House for a *restaurant* on a grand scale', he felt he could not do justice to both establishments, and therefore he must decline to tender. In the event the contract went to a little-known company called Messieurs Schweppe of Berners Street, who paid £5,500 for the privilege of providing the Exhibition visitors with meals and 'temperance beverages'. The food was frequently criticised as 'dry' and 'meagre', there were 'all kinds of fearful pastry and horrible creams', the sandwiches were small and the coffee cold, but it sold well enough to the captive audience. Nearly two million bottles of Schweppes soda and mineral waters were also sold, and, at sixpence a bottle, for an extremely healthy profit. That alone made the company's £5,500 tender the best investment in catering history, and turned Schweppes into the most famous maker of fizzy drinks in the UK for more than a century. Schweppes turned over a staggering £75,557 at the Exhibition, the equivalent today of nearly half a million pounds a week, and in the years that followed Alexis cannot have failed, at times, to have reflected on perhaps the greatest of the many miscalculations he had made in his life. Instead of Schweppes Soda, it could have been Soyer's Nectar.

Gore House was a compact but elegant Georgian mansion, its grand balconied entrance flanked by two bays which extended into three acres of mature and extremely beautiful grounds. This was a vast garden even for Kensington, which in 1850 was still considered, if not quite rustic, then something of a villagey outpost from the city proper. The symmetry of the three-storey house had been destroyed by the addition of a wing, but it remained a highly desirable residence: its attractive stucco façade was lined with sash windows overlooking Hyde Park, and privacy was ensured by a row of trees and a ten-foot wall fronting Kensington Road, which was broken by two imposing gateposts surmounted by large gas lanterns. A row of half a dozen small but elegant houses threaded along a lane to one side of the mansion, which had been named 'Kensington Gore' after the big house.

In its earliest decades Gore House had been the London home of at least one Field Marshal and one Admiral, Lord Rodney, who became a legend in the Caribbean after saving Jamaica from Spanish invaders. Later the great social reformer, William Wilberforce, spent his middle years there, moving in just months after his greatest victory, the passing of the bill that finally abolished the slave trade. But fourteen years earlier, its aura of quiet respectability had been radically enlivened by the arrival of the unconventional ménage of Marguerite, Lady Blessington, and her adopted son and lover, the tall and mesmerisingly handsome Alfred, Count d'Orsay.

Everyone in London society had known – and officially disapproved – of the beautiful, vivacious and extravagant Lady Blessington, whose own history dramatically outstripped anything she managed to drum up for the plots of the rather dull novels she wrote. Marguerite had spent the 1820s travelling on the continent with her husband, the fabulously wealthy bisexual landowner Charles Gardiner, Earl of Blessington, and the young Count d'Orsay, whom many assumed – perhaps correctly – to be the lover of both husband and wife. The besotted earl had failed to quash the rumours by insisting on a marriage between D'Orsay and his teenage daughter, Harriet, and Marguerite had not helped by inserting a four year no-sex clause into the marriage contract. When Blessington died in 1829, Marguerite returned to London with D'Orsay, who soon separated from his wife. For the sake of decency the count moved to lodgings around the corner from Marguerite's Mayfair home, but no one was fooled and the couple found themselves excluded from the top echelons of respectable society. Eventually, short of money as well as social acceptance, Marguerite decided to withdraw from the fashionable West End, and in 1836 took on Gore House, while D'Orsay – again with a pretence of propriety – moved into one of the properties on Kensington Gore.

A legendary shopper, Marguerite had soon spent thousands of pounds on repairs, alterations, new furniture and decorations, and in doing so she transformed Gore House into a magnificent residence. A veranda, hung with trailing vines and roses, was built along the entire length of the house, an army of gardeners turned the grounds into an elegant pleasure park and she even purchased some cows – perhaps she fancied herself, like Marie Antoinette, milking them into pretty porcelain pails. Inside, powdered and gorgeously liveried footmen tended to the needs of her guests, and the food served – influenced by their travels abroad and, no doubt, D'Orsay's friendship with Soyer – was always superb.

D'Orsay, who was as unrestrained as Marguerite, superintended the creation of an exquisité salon where the countess could, in an attempt to win over the intellectual élite of London society at least, host glittering literary soirées. Nominally a library, it was in fact two rooms knocked into one huge gallery, along which guests would slowly approach the hostess, theatrically seated at one end in a great armchair. Instead of the usual gloomy tones reserved for libraries, the bookshelves were bright white and the edges inlaid with mirrors, as were the door panels and handles. The room was filled with gold armchairs lined with delicate apple-green silk damask, and every detail contributed to the sense of comfort and luxuriousness.

And it worked. By the end of the decade Marguerite's cultured wit and D'Orsay's energetic networking had turned Gore House into a magnetic social arena as writers, philosophers and poets revelled in their generous hospitality. Dickens, Thackeray and Bulwer Lytton were regulars, while Walter Landor and Disraeli (now an established MP) used it as a glorified hotel. Thomas Carlyle and Douglas Jerrold came, the poets Robert Southey, Thomas Hood and William Wordsworth, and the painters Edwin Landseer and Daniel Maclise. International luminaries were attracted to Marguerite's soirées – D'Orsay persuaded the Americans Henry Longfellow and Nathaniel Willis to attend while visiting London, Hans Christian Andersen came, Liszt played the piano, and Chopin gave a private recital. Even Louis Napoleon, the future Emperor Napoleon III, regularly enjoyed the company at Gore House during his English exile. Now rarely out of the gossip columns, the Countess of Blessington's dinners and levées at Gore House undoubtedly constituted the most glittering salon in London – or at least on the fringes of it.

But the party could not go on indefinitely. The Blessington/D'Orsay household had run up enormous debts, which could not be hidden for long. Soon D'Orsay could only venture out on Sundays, when he could not be arrested for debt, and Gore House was turned into a mini fortress – visitors had to bring identification and were escorted to the front door by two huge guard dogs. Then, in March 1849, the Countess of Blessington's thirteen-year reign at Gore House came to an abrupt end. A writ was successfully served on her by a drapery store on Lower Regent Street, and Marguerite knew that as soon as word spread, all her creditors would be at the door. At three the next morning D'Orsay fled to Paris with a single portmanteau of clothes and the countess, after handing her house keys over to the liquidators, followed him a few weeks later.

By then, posters had started appearing in London advertising the sale of all the property of the Right Honourable the Countess of Blessington, who was, ran the euphemism, 'retiring to the continent'. The auction, scheduled for 10 May, was handled like a circus by Phillips of New Bond Street, who produced three-shilling catalogues which doubled as admission tickets. During the five viewing days it was estimated that nearly 20,000 people came to Gore House to view the priceless antiques, jewels and furniture accumulated by two of the greatest shopaholics of the age. Dickens and Thackeray both wrote about their sadness at the break-up of Gore House. Thackeray, in particular, who attended the auction, was appalled at the behaviour of the 'wretches . . . and . . . brutes' picking over the goods, and left in tears. Seven weeks after the auction Marguerite suffered a massive heart attack and died in D'Orsay's arms.

So splendid Gore House remained empty from April, when Marguerite and her reduced entourage had decamped to Paris, until the following December, when the new tenant, Alexis Soyer, signed the lease – for fifteen months initially, but with the option of extending it for a further twelve – and collected the keys. While Soyer had been on excellent terms with both Lady Blessington and D'Orsay – he had sent one of his monstrous *Bouquets de Gibier* over to Gore House just a few Christmases earlier, and in all probability had prepared banquets for the two cosmopolitan gourmets in residence – it was unlikely that he had ever been received as a guest at one of their salons. So while Alexis no doubt mourned the spectacular fall of the last tenants as much as their other friends, there must have been considerable satisfaction mixed with his feelings of regret as he became the legal lessee of the mansion. Born with no money or connections, he had achieved his place there through sheer talent and hard work – the servant was at last taking over the stately home. What was more gratifying to him was that within six months he would have attracted back all of the most glittering Gore House regulars – including Thackeray, Dickens and Disraeli – although the house (and the company) would be transformed beyond their wildest dreams.

For Soyer's vision was to create the most spectacular dining venue in Britain, if not the Empire, an attraction that would not simply run in tandem with the Great Exhibition but rival it. He had in mind a whole cluster of exotic eateries unprecedented in scale and luxuriousness – a culinary pleasure garden, in effect. And it would satisfy more than the appetite, it would be a feast for all the senses, encompassing art and sculpture, music, awe-inspiring special effects and all manner of mechanical innovations. And it would be absolutely vast. Soyer's vision involved feeding the five thousand – quite literally – on a daily basis. It would cater to all palates, and budgets too, excluding no one on the grounds of class and embracing anyone with a few shillings to spend and the imagination to attend. It would introduce ordinary people to flavours from parts of the globe they would never have the opportunity to visit. Just as the Great Exhibition was to encompass industry and innovation from around the world (or at least the Empire, which to many Victorians meant much the same thing), so Soyer's restaurant would also be a melting pot of cuisines from around the world, as the name he chose made plain: for Gore House was to house *Soyer's Universal Symposium of All Nations*.

As soon as he had signed the lease, Alexis began the wholesale transformation of Gore House into his Symposium. To help, he brought in Alfred Adams, the designer of his triumphant decorations at York, who oversaw the various carpenters, artists and set painters. And while he may once have admired the elegant appointments of the Countess of Blessington and Count d'Orsay, he certainly did not allow his deference to their taste to interfere with his plans for the future. Every last trace of the *ancien régime* was ripped out wholesale. He had just six months before the opening of the Exhibition to effect an enormous transformation. Every day mattered. Three firms of builders and some landscapers – all sworn to secrecy – were taken on to work simultaneously. Soon the house and grounds were packed with engineers, labourers, gardeners, craftsmen and decorators. Alexis had not been involved with a building site since the creation of the kitchens of the new Reform club house on Pall Mall, but that, for all his creative input, had been for the benefit of others. This time it was his own vision coming to life, and infinitely more exciting. One of the building firms he employed was Fox & Henderson, the contractor who was busily erecting the Great Exhibition just yards away on the fields of Hyde Park. They were commissioned to build a vast dining pavilion in Gore House's grounds to resemble a 'baronial hall', and – with a view to speed and efficiency – ended up using some of the spare steel panels designed to hold up Crystal Palace's roof.

To help supervise the transformation – and to paint a large mural – Alexis took on George Augustus Sala. Sala actually moved into Gore House for the duration of the works, along with Alexis, his new young business partner, Joseph Feeny, two country girls brought in as domestic servants, and a married couple, Samuel and Ann Adams, who arrived to give general assistance and brought along their four children. It must have made an unconventional household. Sala was only twenty-two years old and made most of his money painting scenery for the theatre and illustrating books. He was also developing as a talented satirical cartoonist in the mould of Cruikshank and Phiz, and had just finished his first publication, *The Great Exhibition Wot is to Be*, a twenty-foot-long panorama of a range of ridiculous exhibits that he prophesied might fill the Palace. (Alexis was in there, of course, among a series of clichéd representations of the French, standing in front of giant copies of his books above a mischievous caption which ran: French Cookery in the person of M. Soyer and his books. Air: 'Why, oh why did Soyer resign?') It was not until after the Great Exhibition that Dickens took Sala under his wing and began to publish his journalism in *Household Words*, which started Sala on the path to a long and profitable career as a writer and foreign correspondent. In 1851 Sala had been grateful to Soyer for the Symposium work, although in later years he became anxious to stress that he had never actually been on the payroll of a *cook*. He was taken on, he said, to act as Soyer's 'general adviser and keeper of his correspondence . . . accepting no regular salary, as did his regular *employés*; but taking from time to time a moderate honorarium from an always openhanded but sometimes necessitous artist'.

Sala's enormous oil and monochrome mural, in the form of an unravelling cartoon, was seventy feet long and ran up all three storeys of the house, the entire length of the grand staircase. It continued the style of *The Great Exhibition Wot is to Be* and showed a procession of caricatures of famous writers, politicians and – of course – celebrity chefs, sporting giant, grinning heads on tiny bodies and mounted on a vast array of exotic imaginary beasts, all pushing and shoving their way past each other in their haste to get to the Exhibition. Living people jostled with dead ones, as Mayhew, Jullien and Dickens were featured alongside Napoleon and Pitt the Younger, Fox and Brougham, Wellington, Cruikshank, Victor Hugo, Disraeli, and Mark Lemon, the editor of *Punch*. The mural ended on the top floor with a rather lame joke. The frontrunners knock on a door and are met by a polite gentleman who answers their enquiries with the words 'Exhibition! You've made a mistake, sir. The Exhibition is over the way. This is the Symposium; and we are so full that we can't take you in. You must go back again.' At the time, Sala, who took three months to complete the work, working eight hours a day perched on a ladder or standing on planks suspended by cords from the ceiling, considered it 'a highly comic panorama of the celebrities of the epoch', although in later years he would cringe at its remembered garishness. He particularly hated Soyer's insistence that he called it, in the little souvenir book the chef had commissioned him to write about the interior of the Symposium, 'The Grand Macédoine of All Nations, being a Demisemimimitragicomipanodiocosmopolyofanofun-niosymposiorama; or Suchagettingupstairstothegreatexhibition of 1851.' Calling Soyer 'nothing if not fantastic, and to a certain extent quackish', Sala later wrote: 'I groaned as I interpolated this hideous rubbish in my manuscript . . . I wrote, and eke I swore.' The mural wasn't so very untypical; indeed, it resembled the 'monster-mile panoramas' of the exhibits, statuary and textiles that would shortly be lining the nave of the Crystal Palace. Newspapers and magazines had already begun issuing long pull-out diagrams, and tourists would snap up the twenty-foot-long souvenir reels that were soon on general sale.

While Sala painted his mural and Feeny dealt with the day to day problems, Soyer embarked on a marathon three-month tour of the provinces with the Magic Stove, returning in late March to review progress and, no doubt, add a whole range of expensive extras. He quickly realised that his plans could not possibly be contained within the existing grounds. One of his first acts was to negotiate a sub-lease on an adjacent meadow from a neighbour, George Rummey, which provided him with the crucial extra acres for the modest sum of £35 per annum. Gore House's owner, a shrewd and successful lawyer called John Aldridge (no relation to the John Aldridge who wrote the report on Soyer's famine soups), was charging Soyer £100 rent, payable quarterly, but with a massive £500 premium payable up front – perhaps reflecting his assessment of the speculative nature of his flashy tenant's new venture. Aldridge also inserted a number of seemingly watertight legal restrictions into both leases, designed to protect not just the property but also the peace and sensibilities of the already nervous Kensingtonians.

Yet from the outset it appears that Soyer not only ignored them, but actively flouted them. The stipulation that he was not to 'cut or maim or injure any of the walls or make additions to erection upon or alteration whatsoever in the said messuage dwelling outbuildings and premises' seems laughable in the light of the wholesale remodelling that he was to inflict on the building. However, he did erect the seven-foot 'close boarded fence' that Aldridge insisted on to shield neighbours, although with the primary intention of keeping out prying eyes rather than out of respect for his lease. As for the rules on what could go on in the Symposium, Aldridge, who had clearly got the measure of his tenant, expressly forbade 'Balls or Concerts or any Fetes Fireworks or Exhibitions of any nature or kind whatsoever', and insisted that the business of the restaurant be conducted so as 'to cause as little annoyance as possible to the occupiers of the adjoining properties'. His caution was fully justified, if futile, and clearly shared by the licensing authorities, who delayed granting Soyer a music licence until May – and only gave in then because of the 'exceptional circumstances' of the Great Exhibition.

At the end of March, Soyer began his PR campaign, leaking tantalising hints and snippets of gossip to the press. The flow of information was carefully controlled – enough to fuel speculation and increase excitement, but never giving away exactly what was going on behind his fences. After all, he did have the blanket coverage of the Great Exhibition to compete with; he couldn't afford to drop off the public radar at the critical moment. On 25 March the *News of the World* reported that: 'Soyer is making Titanic exertions for the commencement of his cookery with which he will challenge comparison from any quarter of the globe'; the *Daily News* gave its readers the intriguing news that: 'In the evening, the grounds and mansion will be elegantly decorated with glow-worm lights, and at nine o'clock the clouds will be illuminated . . . for miles around by M. Soyer's mysterious flash of lightning' and Thackeray kept up his end with some gentle mockery in *Punch*:

Active arrangements are in progress for the opening, on a grand scale, of a grand Baked Potato Can of all nations, or Eel Pie and Kidney Pudding Symposium, under the immediate direction of BINKS, the renowned chef of cosmopolitan cookshoppery . . . Each department of this elegant moveable Symposium will be got up in a style appropriate to its particular object. The salt will occupy a space arranged as a salt mine; and the potatoes will appear in the celebrated jackets supplied by the masterly hand of nature.

When he wrote this Thackeray knew exactly what was going on at Gore House, having been shown round one Sunday afternoon by Sala. He certainly would not have had to read the lengthy *'catalogue raisonné, artistic, historic, topographic and picturesque of that unique and gigantic establishment'* that Soyer had had printed. *The Book of the Symposium, or, Soyer at Gore House* (entirely written by Sala) gave a full account and detailed illustrations of every corner of the gastronomic complex. The hand may have been Sala's but the self-aggrandisement and hyperbole were all Soyer's. It described Gore House as a phoenix 'arisen fresh and revivified; when its halls once more glitter with light and its chambers re-echo with the voices of the noble and the talented; when all its former glories are called into new and even more glorious life, by the enchanter's wand of Alexis Soyer.' It was a wand that would 'triumph over geographical limits, and laugh the restrictions of space to scorn' by welcoming visitors from all quarters of the globe, 'civilised or uncivilised'.

The transformation of Gore House was scarcely visible from the exterior – the only additions to the frontage being the words SOYER'S UNIVERSAL SYMPOSIUM picked out in large capital letters and a large round lantern, illuminated with the word SOYER, which swung from a tree. The sole hint of the garish interior were the two rampant lions installed above the outer gates, which supported palm trees filled with pineapples that lit up at night. Yet inside you truly entered another world. The first shock came in the courtyard, which had been filled with outlandish new statues placed in what Sala could only delicately describe as 'artistic juxtaposition'. The front doors were reached up a flight of stairs and, once through them, visitors found themselves in the formerly elegant entrance hall, the ceiling and walls of which were now painted vivid sky blue. Above visitors' heads a monstrous hand grasped a clutch of arrows, from which 'sinuous wreaths of bright, forked, snaky lightning' escaped, darting into the corners, 'rushing hither and thither, dazzling the eye, and astounding the spectator'. Above the next door the words *Soyer's Symposium* flashed like lightning darts. The effect, while horrifyingly vulgar to those used to the refined décor of Lady Blessington, would have made an immensely theatrical and exciting entry point to the complex. These lighting effects – which were put to great imaginative use all over the Symposium – were created by employing cleverly concealed magic lanterns, an early form of slide projector which could be used to create all sorts of impressive and sophisticated optical illusions. They were hugely popular in the 1850s and had long been a staple entertainment in pleasure gardens such as Vauxhall and Ranelagh, from which Soyer had drawn much of his inspiration.

Alongside the monster hand in the vestibule a fresco depicted a scene from *La Fille de L'Orage*, featuring Cerrito herself, the 'starry sylphide' who was, according to Sala, 'in the very act of riding on the whirlwind'. Most visitors would not have had the faintest idea to what this extraordinary image referred, but perhaps Alexis was attempting to win Fanny back with this typically overblown gesture. Moving into the main house, visitors would find themselves in the Hall of Architectural Wonders, an eclectic if eccentric tribute to Soyer's favourite landmarks around the world: 'scattered in picturesque confusion', a mixture of paintings and scale models including St Paul's, the Leaning Tower of Pisa, the Bridge of Sighs, the Mosque of St Sophia, the Sphinx, the Coliseum, the Eddystone Lighthouse and Pompey's Pillar. The hall had a fragrance as exotic as its contents, Volant recorded, as 'an immense quantity of the rarest and most fragrant flowering plants' were arranged on either side of the room.

Past the Hall of Architectural Wonders was one of the great showpieces of the house. Formerly Lady Blessington's expensive library and hub of her social life, the long gallery, now stripped of books and damask chairs, had been transformed into a mock Grecian temple, La Salle du Parnasse or The Blessington Temple of the Muses. (All the chambers were given at least two names.) The mirrored doors remained, but now there were also gold Ionic pillars, Grecian urns painted in the panelled recesses, pots of silver-painted wooden flowers, lots of flowing white drapery and a ceiling painted to resemble 'a genial summer sky'. Leading off from the Temple was a Transatlantic Ante-chamber decorated with stars and stripes, and in what was formerly Lady Blessington's dressing room, a 'triumphal arch of camellias and verdant foliage'.

Another large saloon, La Salle de Noces de Danaë, or more picturesquely, the Shower of Gems, featured hundreds of embossed gold and silver teardrops 'falling' down the walls from an exquisitely rendered green and gold latticework ceiling. The Moorish-style trompe l'oeil was apparently inspired by the Alhambra. Eight globes of silvered glass suspended from the ceiling created the shower effect – as they reflected light back onto the teardrops, it made them appear to sparkle and flash. The attention to detail, from the crystal door handles matching the crystal chandeliers, had spared no expense, and to complete the Oriental theme, waiters in Moorish robes were employed to mingle with the crowd. A hundred boys, the 'Symposium Pages', were employed to tend to the guests, Soyer having designed for them a range of outré costumes appropriate for each themed room, which were then made up by Nicoll's of Regent Street, one of the most fashionable couturiers in the West End. One set of French windows led onto the veranda, and the other onto a wide new Venetian bridge called The Doge's Terrace.

Beneath this terrace, reached via a wooden staircase, was an American-style bar called The Washington Refreshment Room, which was to all intents and purposes the first cocktail bar in London. It provided thirsty customers with such daring modern concoctions as 'flashes of lightning, tongue twisters, oesophagus burners, knockemdowns, squeez-emtights . . . brandy pawnees, shandygaffs, mint juleps, hailstorms, Soyer's nectar cobblers, brandy smash and *hoc genus omne*'. More than forty cocktails were on offer, and among the candidates for the job of barman, said Sala, was 'an eccentric American genius, who declared himself perfectly capable of compounding four at a time, swallowing a flash of lightning, smoking a cigar, singing *Yankee Doodle*, washing up the glasses, and performing the overture to the *Huguenots* on the banjo simultaneously'.

Soyer must have loved his comic potential, and later perhaps regretted overlooking him for a more conventional barman, a West Londoner called William York. The American bar proved such an immediate and lucrative hit that York was soon raking in £5 a week in tips from its grateful – and possibly sozzled – clientele. His good fortune was soon spotted by another Symposium worker, William Bishop, who offered Soyer's partner, Alexander Symons, who by then had been brought in to help manage the Symposium, £1 a week commission to take over the running of it. York quickly matched his offer, Bishop upped his to 30 shillings, and so it went on, until Bishop finally secured it for £2. 10s. A furious York then mounted a campaign of intimidation against Bishop, issuing death threats, trying to throw him in the Symposium fountain, and loitering outside his house with fierce-looking cronies. Eventually a terrified Bishop applied to the magistrates' court for

The flattering portrait of Fanny Cerrito painted by François Simonau in 1845. The commemorative medals and gold coronet beside her were trophies from a recent triumphant season in Rome.

Louis Jullien conducting one of his spectacular concerts at Covent Garden, which featured not just his own orchestra but four military bands.

Rare photographs of Fanny Cerrito dancing late in her career. Date unknown.

Lucile Grahn and Cerito's Sultane Sylphe à la Fille de l'Orage. (No 1315)
Garnish with a Silver Terpsichorean Attelette.

The ostentatious cake Soyer designed for Fanny: *Cerito's Sultane Sylphe à la Fille de l'Orage*, garnished with a silver terpsichorean *attelette*.

French Cookery in the person of M. Soyer and his Books. Air: Why, oh why did Soyer resign?

'French Cookery in the person of M. Soyer and his Books. Air: Why, oh why did Soyer resign?' Sala's mischievous cartoon of Alexis in his panorama *The Great Exhibition Wot is to Be.* Of course Sala would have been fully aware of the chain of events that led to Soyer leaving the Reform Club.

Soyer using his Magic Stove on a fallen capital of the Acropolis, *en route* to Constantinople at the start of his Crimean mission.

Scutari hospital in 1855, around the time of Soyer's arrival.

The Grand Opening of Soyer's newly improved kitchen at Scutari on Easter Monday, 1855, as depicted by *The Illustrated London News*. The event was almost derailed when Soyer suffered a temporary breakdown.

Soyer and Mary Seacole in the makeshift British Hotel. In her 1857 memoir Mrs Seacole wrote: 'There was always fun in the store when the good-natured Frenchman was there.'

Soyer demonstrating his field kitchen to Lord Rokeby and General Pélissier.

The original Soyer Stove.

Soldiers painting the scorched grass green outside 'Soyer's Villarette' in preparation for his farewell dinner party and concert on 27 May 1856.

Left Florence Nightingale, the 'Lady-in-Chief' of Scutari Hospital. While Nightingale was hated by many army and medical authorities, Soyer declared that he found her invariably 'amiable and gentle'; *Right* Florence Nightingale's carriage, which Soyer rescued from a heap of discarded carts and wagons and had shipped back to London on the steamship Argo as 'a precious relic for present and future generations'.

The Officers of the 48th Regiment of Foot, photographed in the Crimea by James Robertson. Soyer treated Robertson to a dinner of bouillabaisse in Marseilles after the war, and he in turn gave Alexis a signed copy of the photograph as a memento.

The Mission of Mercy: Florence Nightingale receiving the Wounded at Scutari, painted by Jerry Barrett in 1857. Soyer is on the extreme left, wearing a white ribbon around his hat. Charles and Selina Bracebridge are also pictured on either side of Florence Nightingale.

Soyer's last public appearance was at Wellington Barracks in London a week before his death, where he demonstrated his latest model kitchen for the army, designed in collaboration with Florence Nightingale.

Soyer's Phidomageireion or Modern Gas Cooking Apparatus, manufactured by Smith & Phillips. One of the earliest domestic gas cookers on the market, it was ahead of its time.

Soyer's Magic Stove, made by Gardner's, a firm of lamp makers.

The Tendon Separators, manufactured by Bramah and puffed in *The Gastronomic Regenerator*.

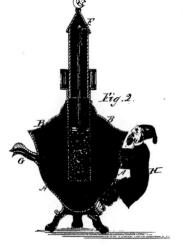

One of the more outlandish patent designs for Soyer's Scutari Teapot.

Soyer's large twelve-sided elm kitchen table, made for the Reform Club kitchens. 'I consider too large a table to be as bad as too large a kitchen, as much time is lost in the cleaning, and more in running about for articles required for use.'

protection and York was fined ten pounds, bound over to keep the peace for two months, and charged four shillings court costs.

The last chamber on the ground floor of Gore House transported visitors from Spain to a South American rain forest. La Forêt Péruvienne, or The Night of Stars, recreated a hazy moonlit forest scene, complete with real palm trees, a tropical breeze and, thanks to more special effects, a glowing moon and a carpet of twinkling stars overhead, 'the glow-worms of the heavens'. Guests then moved up the first flight of stairs, where they faced The Gallic Pavilion, a French-themed corridor decorated with flying cupids and draped tricolours carefully arranged to give the feeling of being in a tent. At night, when viewers stood at one end of the avenue, the narrowing perspective and the bright colours gave the impression of a 'zig-zag kaleidoscope, very curious . . . to behold'. Next to the French corridor was a Temple of Phoebus, lavishly draped with crimson and gold curtains, and after that one of the most spectacular features of the Symposium: The Grotte des Neiges Éternelles or The Rocaille des Lueurs Boréales, a recreation of a North Pole cavern, complete with impressive overhanging stalactites and a small Arctic fox (presumably stuffed) burrowing into a mound of snow. One wall displayed a painting of the Arctic coast lit up by the Aurora Borealis and artfully placed mirrors surrounded by dripping icicles served to make the apartment seem bigger. Bearing in mind that the Symposium was scheduled to run throughout the summer, the acquisition of so much valuable ice, which would have to be renewed every day, purely for a dramatic effect, was an extravagant investment in itself.

From the North Pole you moved on to an Italian palazzo, complete with murals of Calabrian landscapes, classical ruins and a luxuriant vine hung with bunches of wax grapes. Next came the Door of the Dungeon of Mystery, a gloomy portal of 'dark oak, studded with huge nails, and massive chains in hideous festoons'. Promising horrors but delivering little, the door simply opened onto Gore House's master bedroom, renamed Le Boudoir de la Vallière and redecorated with black and silver stripes (zig-zag, of course) with a Chinese puzzle on the ceiling. And so it went on with all the other public rooms of the house, which were given outlandish makeovers, filled with fresh flowers and appointed names like The Floral Retreat, or The Celestial Hall of Golden Lilies – a Chinese-themed, pagoda-style chamber with yellow walls, a gilt statue of Confucius and 'a characteristic hexagonal lantern'. Every room (with the exception of the main bedroom) was furnished with tables, chairs, plates and cutlery to enable wanderers to sustain themselves with champagne and light meals as they wandered around the house.

Outside, the grounds had been transformed into a cross between a park and a pleasure garden, which, throughout the life of the Symposium, furnished an arena for balloon ascents (although not, sadly, for the unfortunate George Gale), theatrical shows, juggling and acrobatic displays, musical performances and headline singers. There was a regular band of 'Ethiopian serenaders' and a firework display at the end of every evening. In perhaps Soyer's least tasteful decorative scheme (although the competition is fierce) the area in front of the Washington Refreshment Room was laid out as a giant shell, forty feet long and planted with rare flowers. Beside it were smaller shells, and some Cupid's hearts, all similarly planted, and some grassed pyramids which served as bases for a pair of statues of a shepherd and shepherdess. There was a large marble fountain, and in The Gipsey Dell you could consult Sibyl, the resident fortune-teller. Outside Sibyl's tent, instead of a Romany cauldron, there was a Magic Stove, with demonstrations of its remarkable versatility performed several times a day. (Magic Stoves, and indeed whole Magic Kitchens, were on sale at the Symposium at the usual retail prices.)

Meanwhile Rummey's meadow had become Le Pré d'Orsay and stuffed with bacchanalian vases and marble statues. It also hosted one of the more charming outdoor attractions – a small kiosk called The Impenetrable Grotto of Ondine or The Enchanted Cascade. Inside, visitors could gaze through a ceiling of crystal stalactites to see what looked like shoals of gold and silver foil fish swimming around. As Sala remarked:

This was certainly reversing the ordinary course of things, and with a vengeance too! Water and fish above our heads! – a miniature Thames Tunnel! . . . the entrance to Ondine's grotto is rendered almost impenetrable by the silvery spray from a cascade on the summit, which not only falls in misty moisture over the door, but surrounds the whole structure, enveloping this little palace of crystal and stalactites in a gauzy veil of pellucid spray. The interior of the grotto is impervious to moisture, but the problem to solve is the possibility of getting through the water without wetting oneself.

The answer, though, like everything within the Symposium, was ingenious. For fourpence you could hire an umbrella which would '*perhaps* carry the bearer scatheless through the silvery shower' and for sixpence 'an article is obtained, the efficacy of which can be warranted'. It was certainly worth attempting to reach the interior of the grotto, which promised more than just a vista of some pretty fish. For on top of the cave was a statuette of Hebe, the cupbearer of the gods, who held fast a goblet of nectar from which real liqueurs – *maraschinos, curaçaos* and *crèmes d'amour* – overflowed 'by some delightful process of Symposium legerdemain'. Whole glasses of these liqueurs could then be bought by those intrepid enough to have braved the showers from a pretty barmaid dressed as Ondine.

The gardens were not simply a source of add-on entertainment; the real business of the Symposium was reliant on this outdoor resource – it was all very well to sell a few elegant collations in the house, but Soyer's business plan relied on feeding five thousand people a day, and that could not possibly be done indoors. To do that he had to build dining halls big enough to accommodate hundreds of people at a time, and the answer was to create two enormous temporary structures, one in the garden and one in the meadow. The smaller of the two was the Fox & Henderson creation, which used recycled panels from the Crystal Palace. The Baronial Hall was, as the name suggested, painted to resemble a Gothic donjon, complete with crumbling stones and castellated battlements. As with all the other effects, however, the solidity of the Baronial Hall was an illusion; the medieval stone walls were actually made of stretched calico and the roof of glass – although thanks to the excellent system copied from Mr Paxton, it served to let in the light and make the interior bright and cheerful. A hundred feet long and fifty wide, it could comfortably seat five hundred diners in a horseshoe formation, and became a popular hire venue for private dinners and dances, especially as a musician's gallery, obscured behind some painted clouds, had been built above the chairman's dais. Inside, behind the statues, the vases, and the dozens of flags of all the nations Soyer hoped would be visiting, the walls were draped with crimson curtains and hung with a collection of 170 of Emma's oil paintings and drawings, extravagantly reframed, plus D'Orsay's famous crayon portraits of the habitués of the Gore House salons (borrowed from a Bond Street art gallery).

At the far end of the Pré d'Orsay stood the second, and far larger marquee, The Encampment of All Nations. At 400 feet long it could accommodate 1,500 people at a time – making it the largest public eating arena in London. Again ostentatiously furbished, the decorations included the monstrous trophy built by Alfred Adams for the York banquet that Prince Albert had admired so much. For the hundred-yard-long table Soyer required a special tablecloth, 307 feet long, eight feet wide and weighing a massive two hundredweight. Woven in Liverpool, it was said to be the longest in Britain, and cost more than fifty pounds (which was actually a good price, as it came – along with several pieces of bespoke furniture – from one of Feeny's small companies there). *Punch* even published a cartoon of the logistical difficulties of laundering the giant cloth, which showed a line of washerwomen bending over pails that stretched over the horizon. But while it may have garnered him some extra publicity, the tablecloth, like so many of his investments, turned out to be money wasted – it was stolen just five weeks after its arrival. Unlike the expensive service in the main house, or the private functions in the Baronial Hall, the Encampment of All Nations was designed to operate as a glorified canteen for those wanting dinner on a budget, or, as Sala tactfully explained it, 'for those who prefer the promiscuous refectation of a public banquet to the more select, yet less joyous society of a private room'.

To cater for the thousands of visitors Soyer expected on a daily basis, his Symposium kitchens had to dwarf even the culinary department at the Reform Club. In the end he created two – one indoors, which occupied the entire basement floor of the main house, and one outdoors, which could take care of many of the six hundred roasts a day that he anticipated serving. It was a huge enterprise, and the kitchen he created had to be a model of modern efficiency to cope with the expected turnover. In it, he courageously banished coal fires and roasting jacks entirely, in favour of lines of brick and metal gas ovens operated by a huge brigade of uniformed chefs operating in near silence. And it worked. 'The joints are done literally [sic] to a turn, though without turning, and are of a beautiful colour and delicious flavour,' wrote the admittedly partial Sala. In the outdoor kitchen – which principally supplied the Encampment of All Nations – Alexis put his experience at the Exeter festival to good use by roasting a whole ox by gas every day, which served not just to feed the masses but acted as an attraction in its own right. The Symposium's gas bill was astronomical – the daily ox roast, the huge gas ovens and the thousands of lights sprinkled through the house and gardens that came on at sunset each day (and all fitted by his old friends at Deane & Dray) led to so much fuel consumption that Alexis had a giant gas-meter erected in the grounds to amaze customers with the figures.

Three months before the opening of the Great Exhibition, the commissioners had announced – along with the award of the catering contract to Schweppe & Co. – the scale of charges that would apply for entry to the Crystal Palace. Season tickets were priced at three guineas for men and two for women, effectively limiting regular attendance to the well-heeled. In addition, entry on the opening day was to be restricted to season ticket-holders only, again keeping numbers down and *hoi polloi* out. On the second and third days, day tickets cost a hefty one pound, but dropped on the fourth day to a much more manageable five shillings. After the first month, the price fell to a shilling for those able to attend between Monday and Thursday, putting entry to the Exhibition pretty much within the reach of anyone with the will to visit.

The Crystal Palace's pricing strategy suited Alexis, who was relying on a steady stream of wealthy season ticket regulars to drink his expensive iced champagne in The Forêt Péruvienne, while the Encampment of All Nations would accommodate the shilling entry folk on one-off day trips from the provinces. He decided to issue his own season tickets, which he initially advertised in Soyer's Symposium Programme, an expensively produced document printed on satin paper with green scalloped edges. His season tickets, available from libraries and music shops, were priced at one guinea for a single person, one and a half for two, and three guineas for a family of five. A steep price when you considered how much more you would get for your Exhibition pass, but then Symposium season tickets did offer the holders unlimited access to 'all parts of this monstre and unique establishment'. Subscribers were also granted the special privilege of being permitted to view, between noon and two o'clock each afternoon, the Symposium kitchen itself, 'in which no less than 600 joints can be cooked with ease in the course of a day'. Single-entry tickets were priced at a modest shilling a head, whether or not visitors intended to eat, although after two o'clock the Symposium would close its doors to non-diners. Those staying for dinner had the price of their admission tickets knocked off their refreshment bills. And as the programme boasted, 'the charges . . . [would] not preclude persons of every station from partaking of the hospitality of the *Maison Soyer*'.

As the opening of the Great Exhibition drew near, it was noticeable that while the Crystal Palace was progressing more or less on schedule, Soyer's frequent changes and increasingly lavish additions to the Gore House plans meant that the Symposium was not. Having invested so many thousands of pounds in a project designed to match the Exhibition's limited lifespan, to delay the Symposium's opening was absolute folly, and would cost Soyer dearly. During the final fortnight, Sala, who was still finishing his mural, gave a series of private views to any celebrated visitors who could not wait until opening day to be shown around the property – including Benjamin Lumley, Disraeli, and, one Sunday morning, Thackeray. Sala showed Thackeray around the house before meeting Alexis in the grounds. 'I remember Soyer showing him a great tent in which half-crown dinners were to be served. "Zis," quoth the *chef*, "is ze Baronial Hall." "I should have thought," replied Thackeray, "that it was a *marquee*." There was not much in the joke, perhaps, but of course we all laughed.'

On Thursday, 1 May, the Great Exhibition opened, with all due ceremony and right on schedule. Queen Victoria later described it as the proudest and happiest day of her life – greater even than her coronation. 'I do feel proud,' her journal recorded, 'at the thought of what my beloved Albert's great mind has conceived.' At eleven o'clock the royal couple and their two eldest children left Buckingham Palace at the head of a procession of nine state carriages, waving at the densely packed crowds that filled Green Park and Hyde Park. Amid the dazzling state jewellery she wore around her neck the 106-carat Koh-i-Noor diamond, a recent gift from the Punjab, which after the ceremony became the Exhibition's most popular – and valuable – exhibit before being recut and incorporated into an imperial crown. After an early shower, rain gave way to bright sunshine, making the Palace's gigantic glass edifice appear to glitter, while a light breeze kept the flags of every nation rustling cheerfully. As the royal couple entered the nave, accompanied by ten-year-old Bertie, the Prince of Wales, wearing Highland dress and clutching Victoria's hand, and eleven-year-old Vicky, the Princess Royal, who wore a wreath of wild pink roses in her hair, the noise was suddenly overwhelming. Trumpets, organs, orchestras, a six-hundred-strong choir and even a military band playing the march from Handel's *Athalia* accompanied the royal couple's progress along the red carpet towards a canopied dais at the apex of the hall, where golden thrones awaited them. As they finally reached it, the music turned into loud cheering from the hundreds of fashionably dressed ticket-holders who were packed into seated galleries that had been rigged up for the day.

The queen, who had visited many times during its construction, was so enchanted with the finished Exhibition that she would visit more than forty times over the following months. On each visit she inspected several of the 13,000 displays, which together boasted 100,000 objects culled from around the world. Forty different countries were represented, with Britain and its Empire taking up one half of the building, and the rest of the world taking up the other. While industrial machinery and precision equipment fulfilled the serious, trade-boosting purpose of the show, there were plenty of aesthetic wonders to wow the domestic audience. These included exquisite displays of china, glass, cutlery, clocks and watches. Ceramics included French Sèvres and fine German porcelain, textiles encompassed Indian silks, Persian carpets, Spanish mantillas, Swiss embroideries and Aubusson tapestries. There were hourly demonstrations – of the electric telegraph, of an unpickable lock, and of machines that could produce fifty million medals a week, or print 10,000 pages an hour. The musical section included a collapsible piano, as well as a double-sided model for quartets. There was an 'alarm bed' that woke its occupants by tipping them upright, and another bed that turned into a life raft; a selection of papier-mâché furniture; a garden seat made of coal; a 'lighthouse' lamp; a knife with three hundred blades; a fountain flowing with eau-de-cologne; a stuffed frog carrying an umbrella; a chocolate-stirring machine, and, in the American section, busts of Queen Victoria carved from soap. (The economist Walter Bagehot commented that, 'It must be amusing to wash yourself with yourself.')

With just six months to show a return on his enormous start-up costs, Alexis should have had the Symposium running like clockwork by the date of the Grand Opening of the Great Exhibition. Yet the run-up to his own opening was marked by confusion, delays and sudden changes. Soyer first advertised the Symposium as due to open for public viewing on 28 April, with an admission price of half a crown, a date quickly changed to 1 May, and the entrance price reduced to a shilling a head. Initial plans for a 'splendid Collation' for several thousand people, set out in the Encampment of All Nations and timed to follow the queen's departure from the Crystal Palace, came to nothing. In the event meals only became available for the general public from 17 May, with the loss of more than a fortnight's potential trade, none of which augured well for the success of London's most audacious culinary enterprise. At least there were plenty of bookings for private dinners and other functions.

On 10 May the Symposium hosted its first important function, when the newly constituted Metropolitan Sanitary Association held a fund-raising dinner in the Baronial Hall. The Association, whose members included Thackeray and Dickens, had been formed in February to lobby for improvements in the sanitary conditions of the capital, which were reaching crisis point. The untreated sewage that filled the Thames made it a fetid swamp at the best of times, and the riverbanks reeked in hot weather. Soyer's common sense and practical mind, not to mention the influence of Thackeray over his thinking, made him an easy convert to the cause, and he was delighted to hold the function at Gore House. As with all matters connected with the Symposium, however, not everything ran smoothly. The date, originally fixed and advertised for 30 April, had to be changed to 10 May when it became clear that the venue would not be ready in time, and even then the event had to be switched from the main house to the Baronial Hall. The ticket price, originally set at a guinea a head for the dinner, with ladies admitted to the gallery for 7s. 6d. (to include refreshments), had to be hiked to twenty-five shillings.

Despite these early setbacks the function was well attended and convivial. The *Illustrated London News* commented on how the 'Chinese lanterns, suspended from the ceiling, diffused a mellow and pleasant light over the brilliant pageant below', and admired how the tables 'were decorated with a profusion of plate, rare exotics in vases, and silvered mirror globes which multiplied and reflected the brilliant scene'. A military band kept the atmosphere light as the diners tucked into *Turbot à la crème, Poussin à la Rachel* and *Pain d'orange framboise à la Carlisle* washed down with fine Bordeaux and champagne. In an affecting after-dinner speech the chairman, the Earl of Carlisle, described how, because of the sanitary conditions that were prevailing, diarrhoea, typhus, cholera and other 'epidemic and contagious diseases' in the city were causing more than 50,000 preventable deaths a year. Indeed London had just suffered one of the worst cholera epidemics in its history, and as the city rapidly multiplied in size, the need for cleaner water and a centralised drainage system had become imperative. The earl's speech was punctuated with plenty of 'hear hears' from the company, but it was Dickens who, rising to propose a toast to the Board of Health, gave the most celebrated speech. He spoke of contagion spreading through the infected atmosphere of the city (although in fact cholera was not an airborne disease); of how sickness was no respecter of class or wealth, and how all that people could be sure of was that 'the air from Gin Lane will be carried by an easterly wind into Mayfair . . . [and] that the furious pestilence raging in St Giles's no mortal list of lady patronesses can keep out of Almacks'.

The dinner was a big success, raising £300 in subscriptions and generating some important publicity for the Association. Most newspapers wrote favourably of both the banquet and the cause, with only the *Daily News* printing a sour political leader, damning both the 'foolish' Soyer and the Sanitary Association members as self-important meddlers seeking to impose expensive reforms on a city that could regulate itself perfectly well through its existing parishes.

The following Thursday Alexis himself chaired a press dinner for the British and international press, or 'A Grand Banquet for the *literati* of all nations' as he styled the gathering. More than three hundred reporters, editors, columnists and illustrators, who had gathered in London from Western Europe, Russia and the USA to cover the Great Exhibition, were invited to spend the afternoon wandering around the Symposium while the enticing smell of a sizzling baron of beef roasting in the Pré d'Orsay wafted through the grounds. At six o'clock promptly the joint was taken off the gas and, according to the *News of the World*'s enraptured journalist, 'borne in triumph by an army of cooks, preceded by a band of musicians playing "The roast beef of Old England", to the Baronial Hall'. The journalists then piled in for a sumptuous dinner which included red mullet and lobster, young lamb and new season's asparagus, soft fruit pastries and – as befitting any journalistic gathering – plenty of excellent wine. To accompany the feast the band played a range of national anthems and international tunes as befitting the cosmopolitan nature of the event, and after the removal of the cloth, Soyer gave the toasts: the queen, Prince Albert, the Prince of Wales, and the army and navy were all 'pledged in flowing bumpers' according to the *Daily News*.

Alexis then welcomed the journalists from around the world, and thanked them for their good wishes for the prosperity of the Symposium. After comparing himself to Caesar ('I have crossed the Rubicon, and unfurled the banner of gastronomy . . . to the world'), Alexis went on to unveil his future plans, which included the permanent establishment, within the grounds of Gore House, of 'a national school of scientific but economical domestic cookery'. The setting up of such a model cookery school, which would teach women from all classes not just to cook well but to run a household economically, was a great ambition of Soyer's – 'the dearest wish of my heart' – and one he had refined over many years. It would be 'a great social reform movement, the amelioration of the gastronomic art'.

After more cheers and toasts the guests reeled out of the Baronial Hall and back into the grounds, where they were entertained with a firework display and the ascent of a fire balloon, before the party broke up shortly before 11 p.m. Over the next few days, Alexis reaped the rewards of his expensive PR exercise with a host of warm reports about the evening's lavish hospitality. 'The dinner was first-rate, the wines unexceptionable, and the whole of the proceedings went off with the greatest *éclat*,' enthused the *Post*, while *The Sun* declared the evening to have been 'a combination of magnificent liberality and exquisite artistic taste'. The *Times* correspondent wrote that he had partaken of 'all the good things that the combination of art and nature can produce', but only *Punch*, in reporting Alexis's speech, dared to mention the best line of the evening. 'Why,' said Soyer, 'is this dinner the reverse of an *omelette soufflée*? Because,' followed the answer, 'an *omelette soufflée* is puffed to be eaten: now the dinner is eaten to be puffed . . .'

One journalist who had walked to the Symposium from his squalid lodgings in Soho, and whose views on the dinner never actually appeared in print, was Karl Marx. But his friend Friedrich Engels certainly noticed the inclusion of his name on the published guest list, and wrote a facetious letter to him about it a week later. 'I saw with pleasure in the papers that the *Neue Rheinische Zeitung* was represented by you in person also at Soyer's universal press symposium. I hope you enjoyed the *homards à la* Washington and the *champagne frappé*. But I am still in the dark about how M. Soyer found your address.'

In fact the *Neue Rheinische Zeitung* – as Marx and Engels knew perfectly well but Alexis probably did not – had been wound up two years earlier. But the great father of socialism, who was then so poor that Engels was having to subsidise the rent of his Soho lodgings, had clearly not been above indulging in a delicious freebie.

On 16 May the morning newspapers carried an announcement that the long-awaited 'Vatican of Gastronomy' was finally to open for refreshments the following day. Five shillings would buy you dinner in the Baronial Hall, although you could eat for just 2s. 6d. in the Encampment of All Nations. To eat in the more refined ambience of the main house would set you back at least 7s. 6d. – although the sky was the limit for those who went off *carte*. However, even these prices changed – with later handbills offering more than a shilling off dinners in the Baronial Hall and the mansion (where *tables d'hôte à la Français* were served at 5, 6, 7 and 8 p.m.). Hot fresh joints were promised in the Baronial Hall every quarter of an hour between 2 and 8 p.m. Sensible regulars with deep pockets simply gave Alexis the number of their party and left the planning to him – leading Soyer to have a Martial epigram painted above the door – *Dic quotus es, quanti cupias cenare, nec unum addideris verbum: cena parata tibi est.* (Say how many you are, and at what cost you wish to dine; Add not a word – your dinner is arranged.) In fact after further delays the Encampment of All Nations only opened on 31 May, when it was launched with a *Grand Table d'Hôte Banquet* to mark the queen's thirty-second birthday. A 140-stone ox was roasted in the Pré d'Orsay, the Band of the 2nd Life Guards was engaged to play popular airs, and in the evening a 'Pyrotechnic Display of Illumination of the most novel and brilliant description' was mounted. Meals, drinks and snacks were available from 10 a.m., with entry after 2 p.m. restricted to those with refreshment tickets.

For the first few weeks everything went smoothly, and the kitchens served on average a thousand covers a day. The choice of food and wine was unequalled in London, the Symposium pages looked after all comers, the daily ox roast proved a huge draw, and everyone loved the fireworks and hot air balloon rides – Sala was persuaded to go up once, although he was almost killed when it burst over Fulham church. Curiosity drew crowds, from agricultural and industrial workers, who took their chances with the buffet in the Encampment of All Nations, to the cream of political, artistic and aristocratic society, who enjoyed exquisite collations in the private rooms. The Duchess of Bedford threw a lunch party for the Duchesses of Inverness and Buckingham. Henry Cole, originator of the Great Exhibition, attended a private banquet given by the officers of engineers for the executive committee. Fanny Cerrito was one of the first through the gates to support her lover, along with Benjamin Lumley, the Duchess of Sutherland and the Duke of Wellington, who returned several times. Thackeray and Disraeli were regulars – the latter presented Soyer with a quotation on beauty from one of his novels, printed on white silk and edged with a gold fringe. He described the Symposium in a gossipy letter to Lady Londonderry:

> The most wonderful thing in the world is Soyer's Symposium, which he has made out of Gore House and its gardens – poor Lady Blessington's former abode. It is impossible to conceive anything more various and fantastical – dinner saloons of every kind of size and character – Turkish, ancient Greek, Louis-Quinze, roofs of Italian trellices with bunches of waxen grapes hanging over your head and longing to be plucked. One room presents a cavern near the north pole – its roof covered with icicles which drip upon the guests, but then it's only rose-water or eau-de-cologne – in the distance a beautiful scene where, I think, they must discover Sir John Franklin. In the gardens, amid a thousand other things as wild and gay, is a grotto, where a live Ondine is to preside, of matchless beauty, guarding a fountain with 100 jets each of which when touched by her fills your glass with maraschino, curacao or some kind of liqueur.

The large morocco leather visitors book was crammed with the names of the great, the good and the infamous. 'Jules Janin's name came close to the laborious *paraphe* of an eminent pugilist,' recalled Sala. 'Members of the American congress found themselves in juxtapositions with Frederick Douglass, and the dark gentleman who came as Ambassador from Hayti. I remember one Sunday seeing . . . a privy councillor, a Sardinian attaché the Marquis of Normanby, the late Mr Flexmore the clown, the editor of *Punch*, the Wizard of the North, all pressing to enter the whilom boudoir of the Blessington.' Alexis, dressed to the nines in a theatrical cape and his now classic beret, would hover around these distinguished guests, ensuring that they received the best service, the best provisions and a personal tour of the arrangements – just as they had done at the Reform Club – leaving Volant, Sala, Feeny and Warriner to look after the hundreds of regular guests.

Impressed by the sheer enormity and audacity of his vision, if any journalists were struck by the fantastically bad taste of much of the Symposium's décor, they loyally refrained from pointing it out. *The Times* described the transformation Soyer had wrought as 'a perfect metamorphosis', the *Manchester Guardian* declared that Soyer had created an even more 'brilliant domain' than that of the Countess of Blessington and the *Morning Herald* considered Alexis 'a man of great designs and lofty conceptions'. Only *Punch* poked some fun at its most vulgar excesses, and Thackeray, the author of much of the ridicule, the man who had shed tears at the Blessington auction, cannot fail to have been horrified by what his old friend Soyer had done to his elegant old haunt. Under the pseudonym of 'Gobemouche, Man of Letters, Man of Taste', Thackeray wrote several articles on Soyer and his Symposium. In the most famous, Gobemouche directs his cab driver to take him to the Palace of All Nations, only to find himself enchanted by the many rooms and halls he finds there, each decorated in the style of a different culture. In the park outside he admires a huge 'battlemented' hall with a transparent roof that he thinks must be the famous Crystal Palace.

'That is the Baronial Hall of All Nations', said a gentleman to me – a gentleman in a flowing robe and a singular cap, whom I had mistaken for a Chinese or an enchanter . . . I pause. I muse. I meditate. Where have I seen that face? Where noted that mien, that cap? Ah, I have it! – in the books devoted to gastronomic regeneration, on the flasks of sauce called relish. This is not the Crystal Palace I see – this is the rival wonder – yes, this is the Symposium of All Nations, and yonder man is ALEXIS SOYER!

Whether Thackeray also contributed the little poem, 'To M. Soyer, on his "Symposium"', is not known, but he would certainly have concurred with the sentiment.

> Soyer, the praise thy skill deserves
> Is perfectly immense,
> For nice discernment in the nerves
> Of gustatory sense;
>
> But now Gore House has been by thee
> So glaringly defaced,
> However good thy palate be
> We must dispute thy taste

Soyer's attention to detail had never kept pace with his ambitions, and despite the initial fanfare and impressive attendance, within a few weeks it quickly became apparent that the Symposium was heading into deep financial trouble. As he had put no brakes on his initial expenditure, there was little capital left to cover any shortfall in receipts. There simply were not enough people coming through the doors to make it pay. Soyer had banked on serving five to six thousand covers a day, a figure that was never realistic. Worse, he failed to appreciate that because day passes for the Great Exhibition did not allow for re-entry, unless visitors were prepared to pay twice, they were stuck inside the Crystal Palace all day, with only their packed lunches or a Schweppes sausage roll to eat. The lucrative lunch trade never materialised.

People began to mutter about slow service and the poor quality of the cheaper meals. Preoccupied with the most prestigious guests, Alexis effectively left the running of the rest of the catering department to managers who simply could not cope with such an enormous operation. Feeny was a businessman, Sala an artist, Volant a secretary and Warriner (who was running the Encampment) a chef – none had sufficient experience. People complained that the waiters were rude, the meals sometimes cold, and orders got confused. Many just felt it was all a bit of a let-down. As one tourist, W. S. Bell, complained in his diary: 'I was disappointed with the place. It did not come up to my expectations.' Soon, said Volant, letters complaining of 'bad management and indifferent dinner . . . were of common occurrence'. As it became clear to Abraham Hayward, author of the influential *Art of Dining*, Soyer may have been possessed of 'inventive genius and inexhaustible resource', but 'his execution is hardly on a par with his conception'.

By the second week in June, the business was rapidly unravelling. Soyer had recently, disastrously, appointed Volant as the Symposium's official manager. He now suggested that Volant should write a report outlining whatever steps were needed to restore quality control, improve profits and ensure the smooth running of the establishment. Volant, who had no real grasp of the business, attempted to impose some order on the daily chaos by insisting that they create a three-man board composed of the two directors, Soyer and Feeny, and himself as 'superintendent'. The three should meet, he said, first thing each morning to discuss the problems of the day ahead and to think up new ways of attracting more visitors, and suggested a three-way split of responsibilities – Feeny taking charge of all financial matters, Soyer of all the catering, and Volant himself resolving the problems on the floor.

But by now Feeny, who could not see any return at all for his huge investment, had had more than enough of the Symposium and everyone in it, and bailed out. In desperation, Alexis turned to Alexander Symons, his partner in A. Soyer & Co., with whom he had enjoyed so much success in the past with his two cook books and the Magic Stove. Symons agreed to come on board, but only if he took over as manager, and the amateurish Volant was demoted. Reluctantly, Alexis agreed.

With Feeny gone and a furious Volant back on clerical duties, the Symposium staggered on for three more months, still averaging a respectable one thousand visitors a day, but still losing money. Another crisis had arisen over staff and 'butlery' – the tables and chairs, glasses, plates, cutlery and other equipment which Soyer had hired in rather than bought. The badly conceived contract, which ran from 5 May for an inital six months, operated on a performance basis, with the Symposium paying the Bloomsbury-based supplier, John Simmonds, twenty shillings for every hundred customers who dined at 2s. 6d., thirty shillings for every hundred who dined at five shillings, fifty shillings for every hundred who dined at 7s. 6d., and so on up the scale. However, the figures had been worked out on the expectation of a far higher turnover, and Simmonds threatened to withdraw all his stock from the premises unless he was paid a flat rate minimum of £100 a week, which was, Symons told him, a 'preposterous' sum of money. Simmonds also provided twenty-two agency staff to work in the Encampment of All

Nations, whom Soyer and Symons could ill afford to lose, even though these cleaners and waiters were untrained and, according to Warriner, virtually uncontrollable. Relations with Simmonds, who was hostile and aggressive, had been difficult from the outset, and now he had the partners over a barrel. Symons parried for time as best he could, and when, in September, the first bill under the 'new arrangement' arrived, for a massive £680, he promised Simmonds a cheque in due course.

With only weeks to go before the Great Exhibition's close, and with it the end of the huge surge of visitors to the capital, something had to be done quickly to boost visitor numbers and inject some cash into the business. Alexis, still hopeful of keeping on Gore House after the Exhibition, was therefore delighted when a friend and fellow showman, the conductor Louis Jullien, suggested that the disastrous Encampment of All Nations should be replaced with a permanent music hall. A sort of year round winter garden, it would be somewhere people could not only dine but enjoy proper concerts and dances. Even better, Jullien offered to be fully involved in both the construction and the concert programmes. As he was currently the most famous musician in London, this was an opportunity not to be missed.

Soyer and Jullien had much in common beside their French background, their age (Louis was thirty-nine, Alexis forty-one), and their grandiose visions – matched only by their hopelessness with money. For one thing Jullien was every bit as much the peacock – he too sported gorgeous waistcoats and white kid gloves, and when performing wore lavishly frilled dress shirts with preposterously huge cuffs. He even had a special 'jewelled' baton for conducting Beethoven, which would be delivered to him on a silver platter at the appropriate moment. As a young man Louis had been compelled to leave Paris in a hurry (in his case to escape creditors), but once in England formed his own touring orchestra and soon achieved huge success. It was Jullien who introduced not just the polka, but the concept of large promenade concerts to London, which he ran in seasons at Drury Lane for nearly twenty years. These immensely popular shilling shows, which featured up to six orchestras and chorus lines of nearly a hundred singers, successfully blended light and classical music together, enabling Jullien to introduce serious music to a socially diverse audience for the first time. His techniques may have been flashy (one showpiece, 'The Firemen's Quadrille', used real firemen to put out a pretend fire), but, again like Alexis, he was passionate about extracting the maximum drama out of everything, and he sought out the finest musicians and singers for his concerts.

Unfortunately the magnificent scale of his productions regularly outstripped his resources, and he would fall bankrupt several times.

But in 1851 Jullien was at the peak of his career, and with him on board, Alexis immediately began planning his winter garden. One of his first tasks was to apply to the Middlesex magistrates court for an extension of his existing music licence, and there he finally came unstuck. The chairman of the magistrates was one Thomas Pownall, a Temperance Society stalwart more inclined to sympathise with the disgruntled Kensington residents, by now heartily sick of the noise and disruption caused by the Exhibition and its satellite attractions, than with an opportunist – and drinker – like Soyer. Pownall decided to see what sort of establishment the Symposium really was by carrying out an unannounced inspection. Unfortunately, the evening he chose could not have been worse from Soyer's point of view. According to Volant, the Symposium was particularly busy. On top of the usual four or five hundred diners and strollers, a large party of around two hundred 'country folk', escorted by the parson of their parish, having imbibed heartily in the Encampment of all Nations, had fanned out around the house and gardens, and were busily drinking in the various bars, dancing to the bands, and generally taking full advantage of the facilities while they could.

Pownall, horrified enough to find a 'cocktail bar' on the premises, was no doubt agreeably appalled, on meeting some of these drunken yokels, to have his worst fears confirmed. He deemed the Symposium 'a receptacle of the commonest description', and Soyer was told in no uncertain terms that he could not expect a licence 'after the orgies this magistrate had been a witness to'. Hearing this, Alexis was filled with a wave of self-righteous rage. As far as he was concerned, the meddling Pownall had ruined him. Not only were his plans for the money-making winter garden scuppered, but nothing could save the Symposium if his original licence was to be revoked. On 14 October, three days after the Exhibition's closure, Soyer locked the doors of the Symposium and posted a brief announcement on the gate for his creditors, advising that 'those who had claims were to apply at Messrs. Soyer and Co.'s office' at 5 Charing Cross Road, where they would be paid half of any outstanding amount, the rest to follow once the accounts had been finalised. Four days later, his temper unimproved, Soyer wrote a long letter to the newspapers, airing his grievances and declaring his intention to sue Thomas Pownall for defamation.

Faced with the full fury of Soyer and his supporters, Pownall did eventually withdraw his charges. But it was too late for the Symposium, whose ignominious closure finally brought the financial calamity to an end. When the receipts were tallied it transpired that during its five months of business the Symposium had taken an impressive £21,000 – but expenses came to a ruinous £28,000. According to Volant, Soyer 'never could understand how such a result could be'. He did, eventually, make good the entire £7,000 deficit, but at great personal cost – and with lasting repercussions.

The Great Exhibition, on the other hand, could only be described as an unqualified success. An average of 42,000 people a day had passed through the doors of the Crystal Palace, more than six million in all. All critics having long since been silenced, it was a 'complete and beautiful triumph' for Prince Albert, as Queen Victoria wrote with feeling – and justification – in her diary. The Exhibition had fuelled commercial and nationalistic pride and was also such an unexpected financial success that the profits paid for eighty-seven acres of land in South Kensington on which was built a complex of cultural, scientific and academic institutions as a lasting memorial to the great World's Fair and its leading light, Prince Albert. Ironically, Gore House and its grounds formed part of this 'Albertopolis', and the old mansion was finally pulled down to make way for a striking red-brick amphitheatre, the Royal Albert Hall, which would later specialise in those 'Prom' concerts pioneered by Louis Jullien.

12

'Vexation, disappointment and loss'

Fleeing from Gore House, from the press, his creditors, and London, Alexis embarked on a two-month tour of the provinces with the Magic Stove while accountants and solicitors sorted out the Symposium's financial chaos. He returned just before Christmas to face the music – but the enormity of the crisis far exceeded his estimates. Seven thousand pounds represented around seventy years' salary for a top *chef de cuisine* in an aristocratic household.

By the time Soyer returned to London a number of Symposium creditors had already started legal proceedings against both him and Symons, and at least one – the belligerent Simmonds – had already filed an affidavit in the Court of Bankruptcy. Alexis was, justifiably, terrified by the prospect of going bankrupt – which at the time still carried the real, if remote, threat of a prison term. Bankruptcy would not only bring about the complete and permanent collapse of his career and reputation, but the humiliation of another forced auction at Gore House – just two years after the horribly public dispersal of the Blessington household. He also felt considerable responsibility for dragging his loyal old friend and partner Alexander Symons down with him. Symons had only been persuaded to join the Symposium fiasco four months earlier, yet now he was facing utter ruin as well. But there was no way of keeping him out of trouble – until 1856, business investments assumed the unlimited liability of everyone in a company and, as the Symposium had been administered through A. Soyer & Co., Symons was as deeply involved as Alexis.

The Simmonds case first came to court on 28 November – presumably Alexis returned from his Magic Stove tour to attend – and was heard in the Court of Common Pleas. By now Simmonds's demands had escalated to £1,200 (the equivalent of nearly £100,000 in modern terms) for the hire of his goods, for the work done by his staff, and for damages. But such was the seriousness of the case and the sum involved that the sheriff ordered a jury to be convened, and the case was postponed until the New Year. The case was finally tried on 23 January, when the Symposium's dirty linen was well and truly aired in public – indeed with every detail gleefully reported in *The Times*. It proved to be rather a sensational case. First, Simmonds's barrister, a Mr Humfrey, detailed the 'low and ill-treatment of his [client's] goods, and . . . the incivilities he experienced from the servants about the establishment' which had forced him to threaten the termination of the contract on a number of occasions. In return Soyer's lawyers made 'equally numerous counter-complaints . . . of the insufficiency and badness of the things supplied'. This point was rather undermined, however, when Humfrey, no doubt with great comic timing, quoted at length Sala's pretentious prose in *The Book of the Symposium*, which praised Simmonds's furniture and fittings to the skies – referring to the 'handsomest knives and forks procurable' and 'the very cream of upholstery'. Hoist by his own petard, Alexis could hardly deny that the eulogy was his own.

However, all was not lost. Soyer's lawyers went over the crisis meeting of 5 July, when Simmonds, having failed to bully the partners into buying his goods, again threatened to remove them unless he was guaranteed £100 a week. He had later sent his deputy, a Mr Cawke, to confirm this threat, and under cross-examination Cawke claimed that it was at that meeting that Symons had finally caved in, saying to him, 'Oh, very well; if it is for a short time it will make no difference' – which as far as the plaintiff was concerned constituted a verbal agreement. However, Cawke admitted that after this meeting he continued to inspect the accounts each week, counting out the number and value of the dinners sold, and accepting small cheques on the same basis as previously. It was only when Simmonds sprang a large new bill on the partners – based on the supposed verbal agreement – and the partners failed to pay it, that everything began to unravel. As Soyer's lawyer began to sum up for the defendants, he was stopped in his tracks by the jury, and the foreman announced that they were of the unanimous opinion that no verbal agreement could be said to have existed – and a verdict was accordingly entered for the defendants. Soyer and Symons were awarded £192 and three shillings for their legal costs and court charges, and a hugely relieved Alexis was finally able to shed his most troublesome creditor.

The Simmonds case had only been one – if the largest – of Alexis's legal headaches. In June he had given two other suppliers, Thomas Savill and James Edwards, a bill of exchange (effectively a legal IOU) for £110, and when he failed to honour it they also started proceedings – eventually winning the case, plus interest and costs. And as there were plenty of others still knocking at the door, further radical measures had to be taken to avoid insolvency. It is difficult now to piece together exactly how Soyer raised the money, but from the few facts that exist it seems most likely that he used his most valuable assets – the Magic Stove, his book royalties and income from his stove licences and kitchen gadgets. It is possible that to compensate Symons for his losses and to extract him from A. Soyer & Co., he signed over some or all of his royalties from *The Gastronomic Regenerator* and *The Modern Housewife*, plus the separate little company, Soyer & Symons, also registered at 5 Charing Cross Road, that held the licences of his early stoves.

However, the bulk of the money certainly came from David Hart, the wealthy rum merchant whose Trinity Square foundry had manufactured some of Soyer's egg timers and other kitchen gadgets for A. Soyer & Co. On 22 November a humbled Soyer and Symons signed a deed of assignment, handing over all their interest and property in the Symposium to Hart, who promised to wind up the business and settle all existing claims and expenses. As security for the debt, it seems that Soyer also signed over the main interest in A. Soyer & Co., whose principal business was now the Magic Stove. The lease on Gore House did not expire until the following March, but Hart managed to negotiate an early release with John Aldridge and Soyer moved out to modest lodgings above a piano shop at 55 Great Russell Street. Hart's intervention at least removed the shadow of bankruptcy, but in return for bailing him out, Alexis was now hopelessly indebted to him. And so Alexis, whose vigorous personal endorsement of the Magic Stove was so critical to its continued success, was put in the invidious position of having to continue to promote it but with a much reduced return for his efforts. He was even forced to give up his little office in Charing Cross Road, and for the next few years he used 42 Trinity Square and 59 Fenchurch Street as his main business addresses. Both premises belonged to Hart, who no doubt planned to keep a close eye on his investment.

When the final Symposium bills were paid, Alexis had lost virtually everything. He had avoided bankruptcy but only at a very high price. He had lost not only his cherished culinary empire at Kensington, and the model school of domestic science that he had spent so many years planning, and which he had – in his eyes at least – been so close to establishing. But he had also lost his fortune and the business assets on which his current security had been based, and which he would find difficult, if not impossible, to rebuild, from his position and at his age. In just one year he had squandered everything. The abrupt closure of the Symposium had made him look at best foolish and, with Hart now milking his inventions, yet again he had to watch the fruits of his ingenuity going into someone else's pocket. In his bleakest moments he must have feared that he would never be free of his debt to Hart – the interest alone must have been frightening – and he was left with just £100 in the bank, his reduced share of the Magic Stove profits and the royalties from his Crosse & Blackwell sauces on which to live. Volant was putting matters very mildly indeed when he talked in his *Memoirs* of Soyer's 'disappointment'. Alexis was completely devastated, he sank into a deep depression and began drinking heavily, even by his generous standards.

Volant was correct that Soyer could not understand how it had all gone wrong, when he had achieved so much and the Symposium had been so popular. But without the safety net of the Reform Club his unbridled extravagance, his unwillingness to tackle the boring details, and his blinkered deference to the minority of titled customers at the expense of the majority of half-crown diners had proved costly. Even discounting these failings, the Symposium would have been in completely the wrong location for a large-scale restaurant once the Exhibition trade had gone, dependant as it was on hundreds of customers each day, drawn not from the aristocracy, but from the ordinary middle and lower classes. When, a generation later, such establishments did finally penetrate London, they naturally clustered in the West End and around the major railway stations. But, rather than facing the truth and accepting responsibility for such a monumental failure, perhaps it was only natural that Alexis preferred to blame Thomas Pownall's eleventh-hour intervention and pro-temperance prejudice for all his woes. Although his lawsuit against Pownall would come to nothing, he was still in fighting mood when he wrote a distressed letter to Lord Marcus Hill, four days after Christmas.

Since I last had the pleasure of seeing you at the Symposium, I have had to endure the most dreadful and unpleasant experiences, all because of the unjust remarks of Magistrate Pownall, which compelled me immediately to close Gore House, and on account of this my creditors have persecuted me in every possible way . . . Now at last, with perseverance and a great deal of philosophy, my affairs are almost paid up and in order. I now intend to make Monsieur the Magistrate give us proof of what he said about my establishment; your friend Lady Vernon and other close friends often came to see me there in the evening; I am certain they never saw any thing *immoral* . . . Even if I end up losing this case it is important for me to prove that Mr Pownall has committed an error and the greatest of injustices.

PS: Please accept a sample of my new *Pâté à la Symposium* and a bottle of my *Ambroisie*. Do not forget to slice the pâté.

At the same time Alexis anxiously wrote to other friends and patrons, to explain himself and the situation. His correspondents included another Reform Club mentor who wrote back with sympathy, some devastating I-told-you-so home truths and a sound piece of advice – which naturally Soyer ignored.

I am sorry to receive so bad an account of your speculation at Gore House . . . but to tell you the truth, I hardly expected much good [from that undertaking]. When you left the Reform Club and asked me for my advice, I recommended you . . . to take a house and to give therein, without any clap-trap, show or external demonstration, *the best dinners* that a man could get in London. Had you followed this advice you would have made your fortune, for your name stood as high as possible at the time; the world had faith in Soyer, and you might have commanded your own terms. As it was, you pursued a course the very opposite to the one prescribed, and the consequence has been the vexation, disappointment, and loss which you describe.

If you will set about repairing past mischief at once, keep yourself in your own hands, take a quiet place . . . people will still go to Soyer. But . . . I warn you, as you value your respectability . . . avoid anything that has the remotest resemblance to puff and charlatanism; you stand in need of neither, and may get on well without them.

Perhaps the most unexpected result of the Symposium débâcle was the reappearance in his life of Jean Lamain, the child he had abandoned in Paris twenty years earlier. Soyer had been walking through the grounds of Gore House one morning in the middle of the summer when a letter from Paris was handed to him. Although it was not a long letter, he was so busy giving orders and discussing the day ahead that it took him over an hour to read it. After a few minutes of agitated pacing, when the staff could see that 'the *governor* was not in his usual temper; in fact he was like a man beside himself', Alexis confided in Volant ('Read this, old boy'), and the two men went off to discuss the best course of action.

It seemed that news of Soyer's grand Symposium had reached even Paris, and it was not unreasonable that Jean, who now worked as a humble locksmith and mechanic after a poverty-stricken upbringing, should seek out this rich and celebrated father who so far had given him nothing. To judge by the elegant language and excellent grammar of the letter, Jean had paid a notary to compose it, and the translation Volant supplies is a humble, ingratiating document, in which Lamain excuses his 'boldness' in writing, which he said was driven by his great dream of meeting his father. Jean then gave a brief description of his birth in the Quai de l'École in June 1830; the death of his mother when he was seven, and the rest of his childhood, brought up first by a family friend and, when his business failed, by his uncle. He said he had quizzed his uncle about his natural father, but 'I could not get precise information from him, so that I was compelled for the time to give up the wish I felt to know the author of my birth.' But a few years later he asked again, and his uncle finally gave him Soyer's name.

'I then recollected having seen *your* name in the newspapers, as well as your address . . . I then thought of starting off for England; but on consideration, and in fear that my presence might displease you, I made up my mind to write and ask your permission to join you . . . something tells me that you are good – that you will kindly remember that you had a son, and that that son was separated from you without being known to him.' Besides, continued the letter, with perhaps a whiff of threat, 'My happiness may turn to bitterness if you refuse my request, and weigh heavily on my fate.' He signed the letter not with his Christian name Jean, but with his middle name, Alexis, Lamain.

Soyer did not refuse him, and in due course Jean was invited to join his father in London for a fortnight in July. The two greeted each other with mutual affection, and although his identity remained a secret to the wider world, young Alexis spent a happy few weeks in London before returning home to his uncle, 'his heart full of joy and gratefulness, to resume his business in Paris'.

For the next few years father and son corresponded irregularly, with Jean pressing to be formally acknowledged as Alexis's heir. Eventually, in 1853, Soyer went to Paris to sign the necessary legal papers to ensure Jean's right of inheritance, and when everything had been processed the son wrote to his father with the confirmation 'that in all future communications he could add, next to his Christian name of *Alexis*, the glorious one of *Soyer*'. Perhaps they met now and again after the papers were signed – it is possible that Alexis's many trips to Paris were undertaken to visit not just Fanny Cerrito but his new-found son. But in truth they had next to nothing in common, and it is more likely that Jean represented to Alexis a rather embarrassing reminder of a shameful episode in his early life. He certainly took care that his English acquaintance continued to know nothing about him, he did not name young Alexis in his will, and he seems to have shown little more inclination to paternal devotion than he had two decades previously.

By Alexis's standards, the period immediately following the Symposium was a quiet one. It afforded an opportunity to retrench and take stock. Yet even before the Simmonds case was resolved, Soyer had found his attention caught by a huge scandal about the disgraceful quality of the preserved meat being provided for the navy. Unable to help himself, he soon launched into the fray. In January 1852 *The Times* and the *Illustrated London News* ran a series of pieces on the large numbers of meat canisters which navy depots at Gosport and Portsmouth were having to condemn because of the putrid contents. It was reported that during one inspection alone, 2,707 cases of meat had been opened, only to find that 2,510 of them were contaminated and inedible. Canning was still in its relative infancy, and the Admiralty had added tinned meat to ordinary soldiers' rations only five years earlier, once the price had dropped to an acceptably cheap level.

Once the theme was picked up by the rest of the press, the government was forced to set up an inquiry. Eventually it transpired that almost all the condemned cans had been supplied by one contractor, a greedy entrepreneur called Stephen Goldner who had a factory in Moldavia, where meat and labour costs were much lower. Goldner – who had also supplied the tins for Sir John Franklin's disastrous Arctic expedition which were later suspected of giving the crew lead poisoning – cut corners by reducing cooking times, padding out the cans with bones and offal, and using inexperienced workers to solder on the lids. To the utter revulsion of the public, *The Times* revealed that Goldner's cans contained 'pieces of heart, roots of tongue, pieces of palate, coagulated blood, pieces of liver, ligaments of the throat, pieces of intestines – in short garbage and putridity in a horrible state', while the *Illustrated London News* pronounced that in others the animals had clearly died from disease.

The stench arising from the examination of such a mass of putridity was so great that it was impossible for the officials to carry out their duty without frequent and copious supplies of chloride of lime to the floor. Now and then a canister would emit such an odious stench as to cause all operations to be suspended for some minutes, and one was so overpowering that the examiners and their assistants had to beat a hasty retreat from the room.

Intrigued, Soyer persuaded the authorities to allow him to inspect some of the large cans himself. He examined seven, he wrote in a long and thoughtful letter to *The Times*, and in the first he too found the meat so stinking that 'the contents could not even be analyzed with safety'. Only three contained edible meat, and those had a considerably shorter shelf life than that claimed by the manufacturers. He then submitted a detailed and influential report to *The Lancet*, which contained much sensible advice about the quality of the meat selected and some sound guidance on canning – from the correct ratio of jelly and fat and the proper seasonings, to the importance of ensuring that, once the meat had been cooked in the canisters, each one was completely cold and airtight before being sealed and painted. He also declared that he considered the size of the cans far too large – each contained ten to twelve pounds of meat, which made it difficult to cook thoroughly, and he advised that in future cans should contain no more than six.

The inquiry eventually concluded, with Soyer, that while the abysmal quality of the meat was relevant, it was the size of the cans that was causing the main problem. However, the panel believed the canisters were too large to be made fully airtight, and it was this factor that had led to the deterioration of the meat. Alexis, on the other hand, while not getting the science quite right himself, had been nearer the truth: it was the impossibility of cooking the meat right through after it had been placed in such big canisters that allowed pockets of bacteria to destroy the contents. He even began experimenting with alternative refinements himself, canning his meat without the addition of any other liquids, but simply allowing it to set in its own jelly. The samples kept extremely well, and he bombarded the naval authorities, including Sir Charles Napier, with his cans, but made little immediate headway and soon dropped the project. The navy, despite its reluctance to give up any economies of scale, eventually bowed to the inevitable and from then on ordered smaller cans from supervised suppliers. Volant declared that Soyer had been 'instrumental in having the system altered altogether', which is certainly overstating the case, but his first intervention in the food of the armed forces was certainly a success, and he must have felt reassured that his professional views had been taken seriously, and that the failure of the Symposium had not, in fact, made him a public laughing stock. On a wider level, the scandal ensured that it was more than a decade before the general public was prepared to eat canned meat – however cheap it became.

For the rest of the year Alexis seemed to have little energy for work – unsurprisingly, given that Hart would be the chief beneficiary of any money he made. He retreated to his small Covent Garden flat, cramming it with Emma's paintings, hanging them not just on every inch of wall space but also from the door panels and cupboards – which were also jam-packed with her work. He even had one adapted as a firescreen. Visitors would invariably be subjected to lectures about the unique brilliance of the paintings and the artist, and whenever he saw a mark or a smudge on one, he would whip out a silk handkerchief and vigorously wipe it away. Instead of working, a chastened Alexis spent much of his time for the rest of the year reorganising the distribution of food from a large soup kitchen and hospice in Soho, the work proving, said one acquaintance sanctimoniously, that he was 'still anxious to benefit mankind, and bearing in mind the "never too late to mend" rule'.

Ham Yard was a grimy little enclave on the western side of Great Windmill Street, its name taken from the Ham & Windmill pub that had stood on the corner for more than a century. Beside the soup kitchen, there was a noisy blacksmith's forge, some cheap rooms for rent, and on either side of the yard, packed tightly together, empty wooden fruit and veg barrows, which were stored there by the owners while not being used in the Rupert Street extension of Berwick Street market. The soup kitchen had been established six years earlier by the social reformer Charles Cochrane and, while it fed many of the local destitute, it was not, he felt, being run efficiently enough. Cochrane asked Alexis to come in and recreate the system he had invented during the Irish famine, which he was delighted to do. 'He handsomely and most humanely offered his services *gratuitously*,' stressed Volant, and what was more, he arranged for Louis Jullien's band to come and cheer up the proceedings by practising their polkas and waltzes in the yard, while the paupers 'plied their willing knives and forks'. So successful was his work at Ham Yard that at Christmas Soyer pulled off his largest single feast to date – Christmas Dinner for 22,000 of London's poorest citizens. To raise the money he and Cochrane organised a Grand Ball in the fashionable Willis's Rooms, complete with gas cookery demonstrations – and Jullien's band providing the music. His old friends and patrons turned out in force, and the event raised enough to provide an extraordinary quantity of cooked food, to produce which represented a truly stunning feat of organisation. His bill of fare – as in the old days – was later published in full.

BILL OF FARE FOR THE POOR

Nine thousand pounds roast and baked meat
One hundred and seventy-eight beef pies*
Fifty hare pies
Sixty rabbit pies
Fifty pork and mutton pies
Twenty roast geese
Three thousand three hundred pounds of potatoes
Five thousand pints of porter
Five thousand pounds of plum-pudding
Fifty cakes
Six thousand half-quartern loaves
One cask of biscuits
Eighteen bushels of Spanish nuts
Eighteen bushels of chestnuts
Six boxes of oranges
Three thousand 2-oz packets of tea
Three thousand 3-oz packets of coffee
Five thousand half-pounds of sugar
One whole ox, roasted by gas – supplied by the Western Gas Company, under the gratuitous superintendence of Mr. Inspector Davies of that establishment.

*Each weighing from 10lb to 30lb; one of them, the 'monster' pie, weighing 60lb.

Buoyed by this triumph, Soyer later helped Cochrane set up another large-scale kitchen in Farringdon Street. But also that Christmas, just when Soyer was beginning to feel that the worst of the Symposium débâcle was behind him, came the worst aftershock of all. On 1 December he was again summoned to the Westminster Court of Common Pleas, but this time to answer an action, brought, unbelievably, by his old friend, drinking partner, confidant and secretary of so many years –

François Volant. The case rested on the matter of £54. 18s., a sum which Volant claimed was owed to him for work carried out while acting as 'clerk and manager' of the Symposium. While the claim was undoubtedly directed at the hated Symons, who had demoted and humiliated him, Alexis was mortified to be dragged through a court case yet again, and the fact that it was by Volant made it a devastating betrayal. Even worse, Volant claimed that Symons had deliberately falsified a receipt to cheat him of the money he was owed – adding fraud to the sordid mix. The case was tried in front of Lord Chief Justice Jervis – who had tried the Simmonds case twelve months earlier – and Symons and Volant slugged it out in the witness box, each calling on their own witnesses and branding the other a liar. In the end the jury found unanimously for Volant, and Judge Jervis ordered that the disputed receipt be impounded, in case the injured party should see fit to 'indict the defendant for perjury or for forgery, or for both'. Alexis, who had chosen not to show up, was found guilty by default, and the pair were ordered to pay Volant the full amount.

Two days later, Volant, perhaps in a fit of conscience, directed his lawyer, William Phelp, to send a letter to *The Times*, in which he attempted to 'acquit M. Soyer from any participation in, or even knowledge of, the alteration of the receipt in question', but it was too late for their friendship. Alexis never spoke to Volant again and shortly afterwards James Warren replaced Volant as Soyer's main secretary, helped by a friend of Alexis's called George Lomax. Six weeks after the verdict the case went to appeal. Soyer chose not to appear, but Symons did, and argued strongly that since the partners had handed over their interest in the Symposium, the responsibility for any debts now rested with David Hart. But the argument failed when Hart's solicitor refused to produce the deed of assignment and the judge decided that he could not be legally obliged to do so. The judgment for Volant stood – as well as the slur on Symons as a cheat and a liar – and the former clerk must have relished such a complete moral victory over a hated rival, even if it did come at the expense of his friendship with Soyer. Volant himself ended up in court for debt a short time later, but narrowly avoided bankruptcy.

As for the personal relationship between Soyer and Symons, the men had enjoyed a great deal of success together before the Symposium destroyed all that they had built up, and it seems that their friendship survived. In any case, the following year, on 4 September, Alexander Symons died. Joseph Feeny also died in 1854. Ruined by his involvement in the Symposium, he eventually went bankrupt after a brief, unsuccessful attempt to relocate his family to America, and died in Chester Lunatic Asylum of pulmonary tuberculosis – the 'white plague' that Alexis himself had dreaded for so many years. With his two former partners dead and his relationship with Volant ending in acrimony, the negative repercussions of the Symposium débâcle must have seemed unending.

By the beginning of 1853 the need to make some money was imperative, and Alexis began to attempt a commercial comeback. He would always be in demand for private catering, but he needed a new scheme, project or product – something that would do more than pay the daily bills. On 2 March he left a 'provisional specification' at the Patent Office for Soyer's Osmazome Food, his bottled meat essence. This invention, ran the spec, was a rich, highly concentrated meat stock which could be used as the basis for either a range of soups or a sauce. His unique method of preserving the Osmazome was to 'separate the fibrous part from the gravy, which is reduced by boiling, and afterwards deposited in bottles, or other receptacles, which are subjected to heat, and sealed, and in which it will keep till required'.

Nothing came of the Osmazome, and the application duly expired, but he was more successful with a new product for Crosse & Blackwell, Soyer's Aromatic Mustard, which had a spicy edge that was considered rather appetising. As usual, the company invested heavily in advertising, which described the new condiment as 'a most exquisite combination of the genuine Mustard seed with various aromatic substances: infinitely superior to all preparations of Mustard'. The public agreed and it quickly became a market leader, selling well for many years. However, Alexis's royalties from Crosse & Blackwell were not going to keep him in luxury, and he began to pin his hopes on a new book project that he had started some time earlier, and on which he was counting, not just to put him back on his feet financially, but to consolidate the reputation for respectable professionalism that his work on the navy canning scandal had begun to repair in the wake of the Symposium and its concomitant disasters.

In *The Gastronomic Regenerator* he had mentioned in passing that 'some correct historian' could do well by writing a complete history of cookery. Now he decided to produce one himself – only without putting in any of the arduous scholarly research necessary for such an undertaking. Just as he had once acquired the Magic Stove from the shadowy Lemolt, it seems he now 'bought' the manuscript of just such a work from a London-based French teacher and unsuccessful writer called Adolphe Duhart-Fauvet, whom he had probably met through Henry Campkin, a great friend of Duhart-Fauvet's and the librarian of the Reform Club. Duhart-Fauvet's *magnum opus*, delivered to Soyer in French, was a dull affair, with a somewhat tiresome obsession with Roman methods of grinding corn and seasoning meat. But it certainly fitted Alexis's criteria of covering roughly the right ground, being stuffed with hundreds and hundreds of impressive literary allusions – and coming from a nobody, it was easy to palm off as his own.

Alexis duly spent the summer preparing what he hoped would be his latest bestseller. He had the manuscript translated into English and shoehorned in some illustrations that Volant had prepared before the court case which destroyed their friendship. He then grandly entitled the work *The Pantropheon, or History of Food and its Preparation, from the Earliest Ages of the World*, and even had the gall to assert on the title page that 'The Author reserves his right of Translating this Work'. Avoiding his usual overblown prefaces and dedications, he inserted a cheeky frontispiece designed by Alfred Adams, which comprised a reproduction of Emma's now long-outdated portrait of him surrounded by an ornate border of classical books, fish, game, utensils, and a naked chef-cherub wearing Soyer's trademark beret perched on top. He also added a completely incongruous final chapter called 'Modern Banquets', which concluded that out of the dozen or so most important banquets of the century (including the coronations of Napoleon, George IV, Charles X and Victoria) the humble author had produced the most significant ones. At the close of the book, he reprinted (once again) his 'Culinary Dialogue' with Lord Marcus Hill and a letter containing an unequivocal claim of authorship. He recalled that in *The Gastronomic Regenerator*, 'I observed that if any author were to write a work on the History of Food and Cookery, it would not only be very interesting, but also an extremely useful production. No one, however, having entertained my suggestion, I determined to undertake the task, and, after several years of deep study and perseverance, have completed this voluminous work.'

Published by Simpkin, Marshall & Co., *The Pantropheon* appeared in early September, priced one guinea, with an American edition swiftly following. Copies were sent to the usual newspaper and magazine editors a few days before publication, with a note from the author humbly requesting that the volume should 'find a corner in your private library'. He even had the chutzpah to send one to Louis Napoleon, for which he received a polite thank you note from the emperor's secretary. In the

Memoirs, Volant, who knew perfectly well that Soyer had not written a word of the main text, managed to declare with a straight face that 'the researches necessary for this work are almost incredible'. And the press agreed. 'M. Soyer now appears before the world as the great historian of the aliment of man,' declared the the *Morning Post*. *The Pantropheon* was 'a book of luxurious reading abounding in classic anecdote and olden gossip' according to the *Illustrated London News*, while the *United Service Gazette* called it 'a most elegant, instructive, and interesting book . . . Soyer has dived deeply into the mines of classic lore, and brought up all the wealth the poets and historians had accumulated . . . a copious index helps us to the most sparkling gems and choicest minerals; it [completes] Soyer's contributions to gastronomic literature, rendering him one of the greatest benefactors of the age.'

But not even friends in the press could save *The Pantropheon* from its own mediocrity, and it did not sell well. According to some angry margin notes made by Duhart-Fauvet in his own copy, it did not help that the work had been execrably translated, or that the 'Modern Banquets' chapter had turned his book from a work of scholarship into a kitchen manual. Duhart-Fauvet claimed in one of these notes that he had sold his manuscript to Soyer for £130. 10s., with the contract guaranteeing another £200 from the profits – but that the contract certainly never stated that Soyer's would be the *only* name to appear on the work. It is highly unlikely that Soyer had £130 – around £10,000 today – to give him, and whether poor, naive Duhart-Fauvet got any money for his efforts is unclear. On 3 September, when he signed his copy with a loving dedication to his wife Pauline, it does not sound as though Alexis had even paid him his delivery fee – even though he had had the manuscript in his possession for long enough to get it translated, illustrated and printed. Adolphe probably ended up with very little for his trouble – his labour of love serving only to give a small boost to Alexis Soyer's literary reputation.

Alexis's social life was gradually reviving along with his spirits. He visited friends around the country, travelling as far as Yorkshire and Devon. He remained a committed freemason, and in August 1853 was installed as a Sovereign Prince Rose Croix – a position of impressive seniority. He regularly visited Virginia Water, where he had befriended the owners of the Wheatsheaf, a Mr and Mrs Jennings, and began to treat the hotel as a second home, inviting guests from London and holding well-lubricated, often riotous dinner parties, in advance of which he would commandeer part of the kitchen. On his regular trips to Paris he might see Jean Lamain, and often saw Fanny, who had new lodgings in the ninth district. The house was in a quiet street, the Rue de la Tour d'Auvergne, between the *Opéra* and Montmartre, and no. 37 had been occupied by the great Victor Hugo himself until two years earlier, when he had been forced to go underground in the aftermath of Louis Napoleon's *coup d'état*. Unfortunately Alexis's romantic ambitions with Fanny had become derailed yet again. Despite their renewed intimacy during the breakdown of her marriage, the devotion had been rather one-sided. Old habits died hard, and yet again Fanny was resisting Alexis's warmth and faithfulness in the pursuit of richer, better-connected suitors.

At thirty-six Fanny was still beautiful, and her career, which she knew could not last many more years, flourished. She had recently become involved with a hugely wealthy, aristocratic, married Spanish nobleman who laboured under the multiple moniker of Don Manuel Antonio de Acuna y de Witte La Cueva y Benavides, Marques de Bedmar y de Escaluna. In his early youth Bedmar, as he was better known, had been the favourite squire of Spain's impetuous young Queen Isabella, who had a string of lovers after being forced into a teenage marriage with her homosexual cousin. Before long Bedmar's affair with Cerrito became common knowledge, his wife was reported to have slapped the ballerina in public – and in due course Fanny became pregnant. On 6 October she gave birth to a little girl, Matilde, at the house in Rue de la Tour d'Auvergne. It has been speculated that the child was Alexis's, but that Fanny preferred to pin paternity on a moneyed and doting nobleman, even a married one, rather than on a not-always-sober cook with a poor record of fatherhood. It is certainly true that Alexis was in Paris at the time of the conception, and it did take Fanny a long time to declare that Bedmar was the father. If this theory is true it was a shrewd way to protect her daughter, for Bedmar doted on Matilde for the rest of his life and, in the absence of a legitimate heir, left her a fortune in his will.

Whatever the truth about Matilde, there was no question of Bedmar leaving his wife. Fanny returned to work shortly after the baby's birth, and the whole episode simply added to Alexis's growing frustration. With no domestic anchor in his own life he was drinking far too heavily and could became unpredictable and difficult. On occasion his work was affected. Young Garnet Wolseley, the future army Commander-in-Chief, who engaged Soyer on occasion for dinner parties, later recalled it as 'an expensive arrangement . . . for whilst so employed [he] used to drink copious draughts of Champagne'. But friends bore the brunt of his misbehaviour. One of them, a fellow chef called Cossard, bailed him out on a pleasure trip to Boulogne in the summer of 1853, when it transpired that Alexis had arrived without a passport. Cossard rushed around the town drumming up acquaintances to vouch for Soyer, and eventually got him released from the custom house. But that night he again 'partook of too much Champagne' and, after staggering up to his room, decided to have a quick smoke before bed. He made a spill to light it with out of a scrap of paper he found on the floor – and in so doing burned poor Cossard's own passport to a crisp.

Alexis spent most of the summer and autumn of 1854 at Virginia Water, hosting his own miniature *fête champêtre* for a few dozen friends by the side of the lake, otherwise living relatively quietly, his life punctuated by regular visits to Fanny and Matilde in Paris. It was at Virginia Water that he hit on the formula for his next book, this time to be a genuine product of his own talent, and for an entirely new audience – the poor. As he wrote in the preface, with *The Gastronomic Regenerator* he had instructed 'the higher class of epicures', in *The Modern Housewife* he had educated 'the easy middle class', and now, *Soyer's Shilling Cookery for the People* would school 'the million' – the industrious, honest, labouring classes – on how best to eat well on a restricted budget. His preface set out his plan:

> While actively employed . . . in a mission to Ireland, in the year of the famine, 1847, it struck me that my services would be more useful to the million than confining them, as I had hitherto done, to the wealthy few. I set to work, but soon found out my error, that I was merely acquainted with the manners and ways of living of the above two classes of society . . . Perceiving that it would be impossible to cure a disease without first arriving at its cause and origin, I found that the only course . . . was to visit personally the abodes, and learn the manners of those to whom I was about to address myself. Whilst semi-buried in my fashionable culinary sanctorum at the Reform Club, surrounded by the *élite* of society . . . I could not gain . . . the slightest knowledge of Cottage life. Determined to carry out my . . . project, I cheerfully bade adieu to my wealthy employers . . . and like a joyful pilgrim . . . set forth on my journey, visiting on my route every kind of philanthropic and other useful institution, but more especially the domains of that industrial class, the backbone of every free country – the People.

The *Shilling Cookery* is a surprisingly thoughtful piece of work. While Alexis certainly did not trawl the nation on a comprehensive survey of working-class eating habits, it does represent a distillation of his many years' charitable work, and of his concern to promote good domestic management and avoid wastage ('certain [as] I am that huge mountains might be erected with the food daily and hourly wasted, even at the doors of the poor'). It was a classic Soyer paradox: while it could be argued that the Symposium was a monument to excessive consumption and wastage of all kinds, he also passionately believed in promoting the values of thrift and resourcefulness. Following the formula of *The Modern Housewife*, Hortense and Eloise made a comeback, with a newly impoverished Hortense dispensing advice from the vantage point of her reduced circumstances.

Soyer's projected readership covered a range of income brackets within the working class – from the families of fully employed labourers, existing on a few shillings a week, to skilled artisans earning a pound or more, to reasonably well educated tradesmen and clerks, with an income of perhaps two or three pounds a week. However, it was realistic for him to assume that for all readers, living conditions would be cramped, money tight and cooking skills minimal. With this book he was not aiming to help the very poorest people (for whom a shilling's outlay for a cookery book would be unthinkable) – for them subsistence rested largely on bread and milk, plus, when funds allowed, ready-cooked food from street vendors and pie shops, or a small joint roasted, for a fee, in the local baker's oven. Only those with enough coal for a consistent fire, a few utensils and some idea of how to cook – perhaps from a stint in domestic service – ventured into the realms of home cookery. And so Soyer could take for granted a decent fire, a few tools (a gridiron, a frying pan, a saucepan and a few dishes) and access to basic raw food (the cheapest cuts of meat, the cheapest fish, such as herrings and sprats, flour, cabbage, potatoes and milk).

Within these restrictions, Soyer came up with some excellent recipes. He relied heavily on simple English classics – bubble and squeak, toad in the hole, jugged hare, fish pie, bread and butter pudding, calves' foot jelly and Welsh 'rabbit' (rarebit). He provides possibly the very first English recipe for potato crisps ('almost shavings' of potato fried in hot oil) and excellent advice on basic kitchen skills – such as how to boil eggs, chop onions, mash potatoes, toast bread, make jam and brew coffee. He, or rather Hortense, gives sound tips on avoiding greasy meat (fry it in ready-heated fat rather than from cold), on how to choose the freshest produce, and on how to turn to good use the cheapest and most neglected of ingredients – cow heels, pigs' ears, scrag of mutton, rabbits, ox livers, tongues and tripe, turnips, nettles and dock leaves. At all times he remained aware of the very limited resources of his readers, and encouraged and cajoled them into using their money wisely. The prose, too, is far less flowery than in his previous books, and the selection of miscellaneous essays included an article on why he felt the government should reduce tax on imported *vin ordinaire*.

He also added an appendix of engravings of his most popular gadgets. Although his obligations to David Hart were not yet paid off, Alexis had somehow managed to extract the designs for his kitchen appliances from A. Soyer & Co. – and Hart's foundry – and re-licence them to Deane & Dray, the ironmongers who had produced his Cottager's Stove nearly a decade earlier. He was therefore able to announce in the *Shilling Cookery* that his Alarum, a mechanical oven-timer, his Vegetable Drainer, a perforated steamer complete with a 'crusher' to press out the water, and his Improved Baking Dish, which included a mesh tray to separate the meat from the potatoes, were all being manufactured 'in large quantities by Messrs. Deane and Dray' of King William Street. He even had a new invention to add to their list, designed for the working-class kitchen and registered in September 1854 to coincide with publication. Soyer's Baking Stewing Pan was essentially the first sealed pressure cooker, which slashed cooking times, tenderised even the toughest meat, cut down on wastage through evaporation, and kept in the cooking smells – a particularly valuable feature for single rooms and tiny cottages. It could be hung over the fire, balanced on a hob or placed in an oven, and Alexis even, with great novelty, fitted a padlock to the top. The purpose of this was 'to prevent any person raising the lid while cooking, as by so doing the best part of the flavour would immediately escape'. However, as Volant pointed out, the real purpose of the padlock was probably to defeat the 'purloining propensities of the baker', should the owner of the Baking Stewing Pan ever be unwise enough to send it to the bakery oven, as the said baker may well possess 'an inquisitive spirit or pilfering fingers'.

When the manuscript was ready, Soyer carried it across town to the Farringdon Street office of the entrepreneurial publisher George Routledge, who during the past five years had made a fortune selling huge quantities of shilling books. A rapidly expanding urban population, sharply improving literacy rates, and, with the arrival of the railways, a new 'commuter' class, had combined to create a massive market for affordable literature, and George Routledge had been one of the first to tap into it. In the early days the *Routledge Railway Library* relied on cheap editions and reprints of popular fiction (often unauthorised), which could be produced with minimal capital outlay. But soon he was printing original material, and in 1852 he hit the jackpot with Harriet Beecher Stowe's abolitionist novel, *Uncle Tom's Cabin*, which sold two million copies in the first five years alone, and quickly became the bestselling novel of the nineteenth century – its sales second only to the Bible. On the back of this success Routledge had opened a New York office in Beekman Street, Manhattan's fashionable publishing district, and was now in a position to invest heavily in new works.

Most importantly for Alexis, unlike his old publishers, Simpkin & Marshall, Routledge actually paid writers for the right to publish their works (although with a reduced royalty system), rather than expecting the initial production costs to come from the author's pocket. For Soyer, this modern contract system was a godsend. No capital was needed, therefore no partner had to be found – and for once he could keep all the royalties. A deal was struck in which Soyer promised not to attach his name to any other cookery book costing a shilling or less, and he was paid £50 for the first 10,000 copies, with royalties kicking in for future editions. He was also allowed to make money by selling advertising space at the front and back of the volume, a task he entrusted to his new secretary, James Warren. Cronies duly rallied round and the early editions were crowded with their ads: Nicoll's, the couturiers, who had fitted out the Symposium pages, and Gardner's Lamps, the company that made the Magic Stove, both took out a full page; Smith & Phillips took four, while Deane & Dray and Crosse & Blackwell both had double-page spreads. Some of Alexis's favourite drinking haunts were prevailed upon to advertise and Radley's in Bridge Street clubbed together with the Sablonière and the Provence Hotel in Leicester Square for a page. Even Symons took half a page to advertise a newly patented egg-cooking machine.

Soyer's Shilling Cookery for the People, Embracing an Entirely New System of Plain Cookery and Domestic Economy was published to instant acclaim. The first print run sold out within two days. A further 50,000 went in the first six weeks, up to 110,000 within four months. It continued to sell in huge numbers for the rest of Alexis's life. In 1867, sales tipped a quarter of a million copies. Alexis updated the text periodically. He ditched a passage in which Hortense describes a visit to the rebuilt Crystal Palace in Sydenham, and added new recipes – for cheap puddings, goose stuffing, various ways of preparing sprats, and a whole section on Christmas. For the 110,000th copy he included a new preface, and a new picture of himself, taken by the fashionable West End photographer and microscopist, Jabez Hogg. Comparing Emma's old portrait and the new photograph it is clear why Routledge thought it best to update his image from youthful rake to authoritative chef. The same strong features are there, but the youthful locks have been replaced by short grey hair, the curly sideburns by a neat moustache, and the slim chest has disappeared under a portly frame encased in a splendid waist-coat and velvet-lapelled coat. Only the jaunty beret of the younger man remains. In the spirit of the times, Soyer also added a number of references to the war in the Crimea, including, after the victory at Alma on 20 September, a recipe for Alma Allied Pudding. In his enthusiasm for this patriotic dessert he rather forgot the financial restraints of his readers. 'The first I made I ornamented with a sugar drum fixed on the top, the three allied flags passed through, forming a trophy, surrounding it with brandy balls; a gill of French brandy round it, set on fire, and serve.'

Continuing the war theme, he included his ideas for a portable army kitchen, based on the horse-drawn soup kitchens he had used in Ireland to take food to rural parishes. He had taken the trouble, he said, to visit the military bases at Chobham, and at Satory, near Paris, and seeing, 'by the ordinary manner in which the provisions for the different messes were cooked . . . that a large amount of nutriment of the food was lost, it occurred to me that, if a moveable kitchen could be made to travel with the army, it would be exceedingly useful, whilst on the march, or when encamped'. Soyer's Kitchen for the Army was essentially a barrow-sized bain-marie, six feet by three feet, with sheet metal sides and an oven fitted over a central steam boiler. Using fuel and water picked up en route, Alexis's ingeniously contrived kitchen could, he claimed, provide a well-cooked, hot meal for a thousand men within two hours – and all while on the move. A few months later Soyer also added a collection of recipes suitable for the field kitchen, *Soyer's Camp Receipts for the Army in the East*, which were also published in *The Times*. The dishes, which included pea soup, stewed beef, and floury dumplings, contained the same virtues as those in the *Shilling Cookery* – simplicity, flexibility, economy, and an assumption that the cook has little or no cooking experience.

The success of the *Shilling Cookery* seemed to put Soyer back on track, restoring not just his bank balance but his confidence. He finally had another bestseller on his hands. While the royalties would never make him rich, at least he did not have to share them and he also had exclusive rights to his royalties from Crosse & Blackwell, as well as those from

Deane & Dray. The relief must have been immense, with the end of his debt to Hart in sight. Shortly afterwards, he was approached by the French organisers of the next Paris Exhibition, which was to take place from May to November of the following year. Napoleon III had been hugely impressed by Prince Albert's success with the Crystal Palace, and was determined that the next Paris Exhibition would rival its scale and magnificence and act as a showcase for his new empire. Possibly it was also the emperor who, remembering Gore House during the Blessington era and the flood of gifts Soyer still regularly sent him, felt that Alexis would be just the man to organise the catering. It seems that the French wanted him to recreate something along the lines of the Symposium – news of its ignominious closure had clearly not spread far. Soyer accepted gladly – here was an opportunity not just to redeem the English disaster, but to learn from Schweppes' success at the Crystal Palace and make another fortune. But, as so often happened in Alexis's career, other events would intervene. And in this instance, the following summer found him not at the hub of the Parisian *bon ton*, but in the filthy, blood-soaked hospitals of the Crimea.

13

'Pro bono publico'

As the leaves turned gold in the woods around Virginia Water, the British army had become mired in its first foreign campaign for a generation. The causes of the Crimean war were complex and multi-layered but, as with most nineteenth-century conflicts, at its heart were the conflicting expansionist ambitions of rival empires, and the desire of each to secure strategic military and trading routes. In this case, it was the weakness of the vast, crumbling Ottoman Empire, which stretched from the Adriatic to the Persian Gulf, that had encouraged Russian eyes to look longingly at some of their neighbour's prized possessions. These included Constantinople, the gateway to the Mediterranean, and Jerusalem in the Holy Land. In June 1853 a Russian army invaded Moldavia and Wallachia, principalities then under Turkish protection, and by October the two countries were officially at war. Britain and France, while not geographically connected, soon became involved – not least because any Russian expansion into the Middle East was a potential threat to their own territories in Africa and India. France was anxious to renew its military prestige through an alliance with Britain, and Napoleon III shared the view of the British public, boldly expressed by Prince Albert, that 'The Emperor of Russia is a tyrant and the enemy of all liberty on the Continent'. After a winter of further Russian aggression, France finally joined the fray on 26 March, and the next day England followed suit.

It was not until the autumn that any British or French soldiers actually set foot on Russian soil. On 14 September, after a nightmarish journey across Europe – which included a three-month delay at the Bulgarian Black Sea port of Varna, where insanitary conditions had led to a devastating outbreak of cholera at the cost of 10,000 lives – a combined British, French and Turkish force landed on the Crimean peninsula, with the intention of capturing and disabling the crucial Russian naval base of Sebastopol. Within a week the allies had engaged with the enemy beside the River Alma, pitting 62,000 men against just 36,000 Russian troops. Even on enemy territory, depleted by dysentery, and fought by troops who had never seen active service before, the sheer force of numbers ensured a resounding victory for the allied generals, Lord Raglan, leading the British army, and Marshal Saint-Arnaud, commanding the French.

It was not a triumph of military discipline or tactics. On the contrary, the battle of Alma served to highlight the inefficiency of an unmodernised army that had lost its way in forty years of peace – an army in which inexperienced aristocrats could 'purchase' regiments, which they then dressed and drilled like a troop of toy soldiers. Alma had shown there to be disastrously little control at brigade or divisional level, or coordination between infantry and artillery. There had not even been an agreed battle drill, the conduct of each regiment depending on the whim of their commanding officer. Some regiments had formed lines and advanced methodically, others had simply rushed the enemy as quickly as they could. However, might had won the day, and Raglan urged Saint-Arnaud to capitalise on the gain by chasing the retreating Russians into Sebastopol and taking the city. Yet Saint-Arnaud dithered, preferring to march around it and attack from the south. This delay was to give the Russians time to recover from the battle and put their superb city defences into proper order. It was to prove a catastrophic mistake, and condemned the allied troops to two hungry, bitter winters on the siege lines around Sebastopol. An enormous British camp was established on the heights above the city, seven miles from the army's supply base at the small village and harbour of Balaclava.

Success at Alma had come at a high price – two thousand British lives – but the botched handling of the survivors would cost many hundreds more. Where the French were equipped with ambulance wagons, crates of medical supplies and comforts, the English had next to nothing. Most of what they had brought was left behind in Varna; the incompetence of the antiquated supply departments in London had ensured that there were not enough transport ships to take both the troops and their baggage onwards to the Crimea, and so the equipment had simply been abandoned – even such basic essentials as horses, carts, tents and bedding, cooking and hospital equipment. The absence of any transport meant that many of the injured could not be carried from where they had fallen to the ships lined up in the harbour at Balaclava, ready to take them across the Black Sea. More than a quarter of those who did make it to the ships then died before they set sail – for while the voyage itself was short, delays of up to a fortnight before leaving Balaclava were not unknown, while the men simply rotted on the decks unaided. The vessels were filthy and disorganised. Some sailed without any doctors or medical supplies at all, only a few soldiers' wives to tend to hundreds of sick and severely injured men. The decks were covered in vomit and excrement, the food crawled with flies and beetles, maggots infested every wound and lice swarmed over everyone.

Once the men arrived in Constaninople, they were taken to the General Hospital in Scutari, a thinly populated district on the Asian side of the Bosporus, which at the start of the war had been considered large enough to accommodate all British casualties. But the General was now too full of cholera patients to accommodate the wounded from Alma, and so the men were simply laid out along the long corridors of the semi-derelict Selimiye Kislasi barracks a hundred yards away. The crumbling barracks had been built to house five thousand Turkish soldiers at the end of the previous century, and only recently donated to the British for use in their Russian mission (the French had already secured much better premises in Pera, on the European side). At first the hundreds of rooms and miles of corridors that wound around a huge central quadrangle must have seemed a good enough repository for the extra wounded British troops – before it was discovered that they swarmed with disease-ridden rats and were built above brimming sewers. One side of this enormous building had been gutted in a fire, and the central courtyard was full of rubbish. The new Barrack Hospital was not just squalid but, initially, completely bare. There were no beds, no chairs, no blankets, towels or dressings. There were no plates or cups, so at first the men could not even be provided with food or clean water. They were simply dropped in long rows on the broken tiles of the corridor floors, still wearing the blood-soaked clothes in which they had been picked off the battlefield.

The British public began to learn of these horrors from the pages of *The Times*. Over the centuries the British army had suffered such privations before, but little had been known about it in the world beyond the theatre of war. Now there were newspapermen, uncensored 'Special Correspondents', to send back detailed reports of the suffering of the men at Scutari and in the British camp. To begin with Thomas Chenery,

The Times's man in Constantinople, and William Howard Russell, its dedicated war reporter, sent their reports back to London by sea, and so even battle accounts took up to a fortnight to reach the presses, but within six months they were filing their despatches via the new electric telegraph, and their eye-witness accounts reached every London street corner within forty-eight hours.

The first outcry followed two reports by Thomas Chenery, published on 12 and 13 October, that highlighted the conditions at this new Barrack Hospital. It was with feelings of surprise and anger, wrote Chenery, that the public would learn that no sufficient medical preparations had been made for the proper care of the wounded. Not only were there not enough surgeons, he wrote, but there were no clean clothes, no clean sheets, 'not even linen to make bandages'. Perhaps most worryingly, there were no nurses, who could tend to the men and carry out the doctors' instructions between visits. 'Here the French are greatly our superiors,' he added, in a statement guaranteed to stir up jingoistic ire. 'Their medical arrangements are extremely good, their surgeons more numerous, and they have also the help of the Sisters of Charity, who have accompanied the expedition in incredible numbers. These devoted women are excellent nurses.' The public certainly *were* surprised and angered by Chenery's reports, and demanded to know, as he did, 'Why could not this clearly foreseen event have been supplied?' As more and more anguished reports came out about the soaring death rates in the Scutari hospitals as the medical system buckled under the strain, popular support for the war vanished, to be replaced by blind rage at the government for sending the army so ill-equipped to its destruction.

For those back in the Crimea, life was no better. As the autumn drew on, the men's smart summer uniforms became threadbare, there were few blankets or greatcoats to protect them from the biting Russian weather and their forty-year-old tents 'let the rain through like a sieve'. Food was a constant problem. The harvest of local fruit and vegetables had long since been devoured, scurvy reappeared, and the men were back to a virtually unbroken diet of biscuits and salt meat – which was often in short measure and could not be cooked anyway for lack of firewood. The entire area had been picked clean of every flammable tree, branch, stick and root. So there was no question of the men roasting the green coffee beans that the commissariat department had somehow expected them to transform into a palatable drink, or of boiling the handful of rice and dried peas that appeared occasionally. The men, now freezing, began to starve. The purveyors in Balaclava had set up a few storerooms in a derelict house near the harbour, but would watch fresh supplies rot before releasing them without the necessary paperwork. Famously, a shipload of cabbages were dumped in the harbour, a consignment of scurvy-beating lime juice was withheld from the troops for two months, and warm blankets remained in store while the men slept uncovered on the sodden ground – just because the paperwork was not in order. The area around Balaclava, which was constantly overcrowded with ships, had become a sea of putrid mud and congestion, and the refuse in the stinking harbour water now included the roughly amputated limbs of battle survivors. Unsurprisingly, diarrhoea and cholera began to spread again. After the battle of Balaclava, with the pointless sacrifice of the Light Brigade and the Russian capture of the Woronzoff Road, the army's only safe route to the harbour was severed, making the supply situation desperate. Then, most cruelly, in November a hurricane ripped away almost all the ragged tents and destroyed every ship in Balaclava harbour – including the eagerly awaited *Prince*, a large vessel which had just arrived, laden with food and warm clothing.

Following Chenery's appeal for the British patients to be supplied with nurses, Florence Nightingale was recruited by the beleaguered government to provide exactly that. On 5 November she had arrived at the Barrack Hospital with a hand-picked corps of thirty-eight nurses. In spite of enormous hostility from the hospital authorities, Nightingale soon made headway. With supplies she had bought en route at Marseilles, she set up an extra-diet kitchen dedicated to special foods for the most severely sick and malnourished survivors of Balaclava, and as hundreds more wounded men poured in after the ferocious battle of Inkerman, the nurses began frantically stuffing sacks to serve as makeshift beds. Using a large fund she had brought with her, much of it raised by readers of *The Times*, she bypassed the purveyor's department and started to buy essential provisions and equipment on the open market – food, scrubbing brushes, clothes and sheets, plates and cutlery, operating tables and screens, towels and soap. In December she employed workers to repair and clean the damaged wing of the hospital, which could then accommodate another thousand men.

By early January 1855, there were more men in hospital in Scutari than there were left in the camp before Sebastopol, and still the numbers kept rising, causing Nightingale to write despairingly that it had become a 'calamity unparalleled in the history of calamity'. Alarmingly, as the numbers of sick rose, so did the death rate – in spite of the cleaner wards and improved rations, men were dying faster than ever. An epidemic of 'famine fever', similar to cholera, broke out, which started to kill not just the patients but a number of the doctors, until many became fearful of walking the wards. Back home, people talked and wrote of nothing but the shocking treatment being meted out to Britain's military heroes. They simply could not believe that thousands of gallant young Englishmen were perishing from hunger and neglect because of the meanness and incompetence of the government, and their angry bewilderment soon turned into furious demands for cabinet heads to roll.

Thoroughly humiliated, the prime minister, Lord Aberdeen, was forced to resign at the end of the month, and his ministry collapsed with 'such a whack', according to the chancellor, William Gladstone, 'that they could hear their heads thump as they struck the ground'. Lord Palmerston immediately took the helm, and one of his first actions was to appoint Lord Panmure as his secretary-at-war. Within weeks, Panmure had sent out a proper Sanitary Commission to investigate the conditions in the hospitals and camps. The commissioners arrived at the Barrack Hospital in early March, and their discoveries were horrifying. Despite Nightingale's efforts, the death rate was soaring, due to the airborne diseases rising from the choked up cesspits on which the hospital was built. The entire water supply had been contaminated by rotting animals, and the building itself stood 'in a sea of decaying filth; the very walls, constructed of porous plaster, were soaked in it. Every breeze, every puff of air, blew poisonous gas through the pipes of numerous open privies into the corridors and wards where the sick were lying.' The energetic commissioners quickly got down to work – every able-bodied man pitched in to help; a massive operation began to dig out the sewers, limewash the walls, clear away the debris and flush out the rats. And it was while this important work was in progress that Alexis Soyer arrived in Scutari.

On 16 January 1855, at the height of the miserable midwinter of hunger and disease that had followed the battles of Balaclava and Inkerman, *The Times* printed a letter from a soldier at the camp before Sebastopol, which asked M. Soyer to provide some simple recipes that the common soldier could prepare for himself – bearing in mind the paucity of his rations, his ignorance of cookery and his woeful lack of fuel. What he wanted, he said, was 'a receipt or two of how to concoct into a palatable shape the eternal ration of pork and biscuit which is issued to us'. Soyer immediately began experimenting with the official rations, and the result was a series of recipes, *Soyer's Camp Receipts for the Army in the East*, published six days later and eventually incorporated into the *Shilling Cookery*. In fact some copies of the *Shilling Cookery* were already circulating among the men in the Crimea, who were finding it extremely useful. A Captain Richards wrote to his aunt from Camp Sebastopol, 'I remember there is one thing you may send me, but it must be sent by post, as if it is sent by hand it would be too long in coming, viz, Soyer's Shilling cookery book, which would assist me much in my compounds.' One paper reported that even *The Modern Housewife* was being used as a war manual – as 'officers being compelled to cook for themselves, have with the aid of Soyer's Housewife and their servants, attained a degree of culinary skill which would astonish their friends at home'.

A few days before Richards wrote to his aunt, Soyer had been leaving a performance of a popular pantomime at Drury Lane when he was persuaded to join some friends for a late supper at the Albion in Little Russell Street. He had an errand to run first, and when he arrived, shortly after midnight, a harassed waiter mistakenly showed him into the wrong private room. As he waited for his friends – who were already eating elsewhere – he picked up a copy of *The Times* and read Russell's latest shocking account of the privations being suffered by the troops. He read the report through twice, and by the end of the second reading, he said later, 'a few minutes' reflection on my part enabled me to collect my ideas, and established in my mind a certain assurance that I could, if allowed by Government, render service in the cooking of the food, the administration of the same, as well as the distribution of the provisions. These were matters in which . . . some change was much needed.' Accordingly, he called for a pen and paper, and wrote his own contribution to the next edition of the paper.

THE HOSPITAL KITCHENS AT SCUTARI

To the Editor of *The Times*

SIR, – After carefully perusing the letter of your correspondent, dated Scutari, in your impression of Wednesday last, I perceive that, although the kitchen under the superintendence of Miss Nightingale affords so much relief, the system of management at the large one in the Barrack Hospital is far from being perfect. I propose offering my services gratuitously, and proceeding direct to Scutari, if the Government will honour me with their confidence, and grant me the full power of acting according to my knowledge and experience in such matters.

I have the honour to remain, Sir,
Your obedient servant,
A. SOYER
Feb. 2, 1855

Alexis's offer was not quite as spontaneous as his letter made it sound. Volant says he had already discussed the pros and cons of travelling to the East with some friends over drinks at the Provence – albeit 'under the rose' (on the sly). However the notion came to him, he was serious about it, and at that point believed that he could travel to Constantinople, effect a complete overhaul of the army's hospital catering within two or three months, and still have ample time to return to London and complete the arrangements for his great culinary extravaganza at the Paris Exhibition. The following morning he kept an arrangement to travel to Virginia Water for a long weekend, possibly with Fanny, where he found that his letter was causing consternation among his Surrey friends. Jennings, the landlord of the Wheatsheaf, no doubt loath to see his best customer risk his life by travelling to a scene of unrelieved death and disease, pointed to the daily fatalities list and told him that it was a 'hundred to one' that he would ever return. To this Alexis replied, in a rare moment of religious reflection, that 'My firm belief is, that no fruit falls from the tree to the ground until it is perfectly ripe; and I also believe that we are never gathered from this frivolous world till we are really wanted in the other.' In spite of such an apparent disregard for his personal safety, it did require considerable courage to go to Scutari, especially after the latest, particularly virulent cholera epidemic at the Barrack Hospital, and only the most dedicated volunteers chose to. Thackeray had recently declined the offer to travel east as special correspondent for the *Illustrated London News*, and Soyer soon found that few were willing to accompany him on his own little expedition.

He returned from Virginia Water to find a summons to a meeting with the Duchess of Sutherland. At Stafford House he was met by a gathering of influential Liberals, including the Duke of Argyll, a member of the ministerial council, who was en route to a meeting at Downing Street but stayed long enough for Soyer to outline his plans for the Scutari kitchens, should the government back him. Soyer proposed that immediately on arrival he and his staff – a small team of carefully recruited assistant chefs – would take over the catering for just a few hundred patients, gradually increasing the number until they had responsibility for the entire hospital. Then, once his 'model' system had been successfully established in Scutari, and a new group of men trained to take over from his own chefs, it could be repeated at all the other British hospitals in the East. He promised that he would not interfere with the hospital authorities or introduce any special diets that had not been approved by the chief medical officer.

For his task to succeed, he would need the government to give him absolute authority in some areas. These included access to any provisions already in the hospitals, and the right to request the purveyor's department to purchase immediately whatever else he needed. He also claimed the right 'to condemn inferior provisions, and to substitute better'. Unabashed by the criticism heaped upon him by his detractors over the Irish soup kitchens, who had claimed that by sticking to stingy government budgets his famine soups had been too watery to keep a cat alive, he promised to exercise the greatest economy by using only 'the same quantity of provisions as at present allowed by Government, or even less'. He felt confident of delivering such savings, as from his enquiries he had learned that 'too much is given of one thing, and not enough of another. Having, therefore, the power to vary the ingredients and quantity . . . will greatly assist me in my undertaking.'

In reality Alexis was not nearly as confident as his assertive presentation implied, but his first job was to persuade the authorities to send him and if he achieved that, he wrote, he was certain that he could work out the details later, that 'the active part would easily develop itself to my free and experienced mind'. Lord Argyll, suitably impressed, promised to use what influence he could with Lord Panmure, who already knew Soyer well from his Reform Club days. As the former Fox Maule, MP, Panmure had written admiringly of 'the great Soyer' following the banquet for Ibrahim Pasha; he had subscribed generously to *The Gastronomic Regenerator* and chaired the Humane Society fundraiser at which Alexis had spoken so affectingly of his rescue from the icy waters of Hyde Park lake. Argyll kept his word, and with his recommendation backed up by the Duchess of Sutherland, Alexis found himself at the War Office within the week. He arrived well prepared for Panmure, having spent the intervening days putting the finishing touches to his new hospital diets, based on existing army rations, and refining his plan of action. He devised further dishes for the soldiers in camp to prepare for themselves and used himself as a guinea pig, one day eating nothing but a bowl of simple, thick peasemeal porridge and a single biscuit, before declaring that it had sated his appetite adequately. 'I do not mean that such fare would do for a continuance, but when nothing else could be obtained, it certainly would be a great comfort for the troops to get a hot meal, made in a few minutes, and without trouble.'

Panmure, just weeks into the job, was delighted to have such a welcome public relations coup dropping into his lap, and agreed to all Soyer's requests. The arrival of Florence Nightingale the previous November may have proved unpopular with the medics, but had been a huge morale booster for the men, and also for the public back home. Panmure proved willing not only to sanction Soyer's plans for the Scutari kitchens, but suggested a further journey across the Black Sea to the Crimea itself, where instead of just sending recipes, he could actually teach the men in the British camp how to make the best of their rations in person. It was even agreed that Soyer would commission a new army stove, built to his design and specifications, to replace both the soldiers' tin kettles and the few iron stoves that were used by officers. The twelve-pint camp kettles were proving particularly inadequate – far too small for the eight men they were meant to serve, the sheet iron they were stamped from was not nearly strong enough for purpose, and unrealistically large bonfires were needed to cook anything in them. As for the heavy old charcoal stoves, inefficiency was compounded by danger – the thin tin linings had worn out, leaving the food to come into contact with dangerous metal alloys. And when used inside huts, users risked carbon monoxide poisoning. Three officers died in one such disaster. To replace these 'poison manufactories', as *The Times* dubbed them, Soyer came up with what would become his most famous invention and his greatest contribution to the war effort: a portable coal- and wood-burning stove that could be made in a variety of sizes and used either indoors – in hospitals, tents and huts – or outdoors, in the field, in the trenches, and even while on the move.

Like all of Alexis's best ideas, its genius lay in its simplicity. The stove essentially consisted of a large, heavy-lidded cylindrical drum with a small furnace fitted into the bottom. A large cooking pot slotted into the top, while an external flue extracted the smoke and steam. The benefits over previous cooking methods were enormous, by far the most valuable being the saving it allowed on fuel. Instead of having to make a huge fire merely to boil a kettle, the internal burner of a Soyer Stove required just a fraction of the amount of wood, thereby solving at a stroke the biggest logistical problem of the entire war. In an army which turned out to be almost bereft of transport, this single achievement was enough to make Soyer a military hero. The stoves themselves, when empty, could hold enough wood for two days, and if the men carried just one stick each, that would be sufficient for several more. Soyer estimated that each stove would consume around twelve to fifteen pounds of fuel, and allowing twenty stoves to a regiment, that meant 300 pounds of fuel per thousand men – less than ten per cent of its current consumption.

There were many further advantages. The decent metal used meant that no tinning was required to protect the food from contamination. The simplicity of the apparatus meant that even with heavy use, they could last years without needing repairs. They were strong, but lightweight and easy to carry – one mule saddled up with two stoves provided enough capacity for a company of a hundred men. A simple regulator enabled the cook to have some control over the heat, so that not every dish had to be boiled to death. The efficiency of the extraction flues meant that when used in camp or in the trenches, there were no flames or smoke to attract enemy attention. They were easy to keep clean, and could be fitted with an apparatus for baking, roasting and steaming. When used indoors there was no risk of carbon monoxide poisoning, there was no need for a chimney or brick hearth, and they could be moved around 'as easily . . . as any piece of furniture in the room'. Alexis estimated that one large stove could service up to sixty men, not just by feeding that number but by keeping their hut permanently warm in winter (while in summer it could simply be moved outdoors). They could also be made in virtually any size, according to use.

Within a few days Alexis's friends at Smith & Phillips had made up a working model of the stove from his drawings – 'one inch to the foot' – and Soyer returned to the War Office for Panmure's approval, which was immediately granted. It was agreed that they would be manufactured as quickly as possible, with ten large ones following Soyer out to Scutari for use in the hospital kitchens, and a further four hundred smaller ones sent directly to Balaclava for use in the camp. It was further agreed that Soyer should take just a few assistant cooks, as he planned to train ordinary soldiers to do the cooking in due course. To help with this training, he would arrange for each recipe to be whittled down into a few lines of simple instructions, then printed, framed and hung up in the hospital kitchens, clearly enough for any literate soldier to follow them. As for money, while he was determined to take no salary, Alexis told Panmure that he would accept the reimbursement of his expenses for staff, accommodation and travel – especially if his mission was now to include a further journey to the Crimea.

Leaving the War Office, Alexis immediately took his prototype stove to Isambard Brunel, having been given the engineer's address by

Panmure's secretary. His timing was, by lucky chance, impeccable. Brunel, at the height of his fame and influence, had just been formally requested to design a thousand-bed hospital to be erected at Renkioi on the Dardanelles, south of Scutari. Within six days he would present to the War Office his detailed designs for a timber-framed series of pavilions made from prefabricated sections that could be transported to Constantinople on five ships and then erected at great speed.

Brunel had benefited from Florence Nightingale's observations on the necessity for good lighting, ventilation and hygiene, and his 'model' hospital was the first to employ a fresh-water supply system, proper drainage and early forms of air conditioning. There were even wash basins and water closets, complete with toilet paper (and instructions on how to use it). Recognising in Soyer a fellow innovator, Brunel was impressed with the field stove and immediately adopted it for the Renkioi hospital kitchens. It had been a bold undertaking – to design a building for an unseen site, but it worked superbly and Brunel's state-of-the-art facilities helped bring the death rate from infections down to just three per cent, where in Scutari it peaked, shockingly, at more than forty. Brunel was to make a small fortune from his hospital – he was not only well paid by the government, but controlled all the contracts to build it. Later that year he was awarded the Légion d'honneur at the Paris Exhibition for the design. Soyer, on the other hand, made nothing from his stoves, which could certainly be said to have conferred a greater overall benefit. He put his name and label on them, but refused to register or patent the design, declaring that he gave the stove to the nation – '*pro bono publico*' – and would hate to be seen to be making money out of a national crisis. He may have expressed it pompously but the gesture was sincere, and by making it he truly did sacrifice a goldmine.

Alexis passed the following days in a rush of preparation – settling bills, packing up personal effects and supplies (including two cases of the *Shilling Cookery*), procuring a passport from the French Embassy and saying his good-byes. He had recently moved to roomier lodgings in Bloomsbury Street, which he shared with a couple of servants and two cats. The apartment was packed up and his precious collection of Emma's paintings deposited at the Crosse & Blackwell headquarters, where Edmund promised to keep them safely for his return. He kept back just one, *The Young Bavarians*, which travelled everywhere with him, and would later provide a sense of comfort and civilisation in even the most squalid lodgings. He collected up letters of introduction to the various medical and military authorities from friends and patrons, including Lord Panmure, the Duke of Cambridge, who had recently returned from Scutari, and the Duchess of Sutherland, who wrote warmly on his behalf to Florence Nightingale.

He was less successful in recruiting staff. He desperately needed a secretary: Volant was obviously out of the picture; Sala resisted the inducement of what he himself acknowledged to be 'very handsome terms'; and now his friend George Lomax, having first accepted, dropped out at the eleventh hour, having been frightened out of the trip by stories of the certain death that would inevitably result from such an expedition. Two of the chefs that Soyer had employed 'at high wages' also dropped out, leaving him with just four cooks, headed by Louis Jullien's nephew. Eventually Alexis persuaded another friend, a mixed-race man called Thomas Garfield, to accompany him as personal assistant in return for being 'well paid, and all expenses defrayed'. This turned out to be a lucky appointment. Garfield became a valuable and loyal helper and caused quite a stir among the soldiers at the front, who were invariably amazed to see a dazzlingly dressed and voluble cook trotting through the war zone, accompanied by his white-clad 'mulatto secretary'.

Finally, just a month after writing his impulsive letter to *The Times*, Soyer and his team left London Bridge on the evening train to Folkestone, with a noisy, affectionate send-off from a crowd of twenty friends. And the echo of their cheers, wrote Soyer later in his memoir of the journey, *A Culinary Campaign*, 'still vibrates in my heart'.

After what must have seemed like a very short night at the Pavilion Hotel in Folkestone, the Boulogne steamer set off at 7.30 the next morning, navigating its way across the Channel through heavy rain and thick fog. Soyer almost missed the boat, for he had risen before dawn only to find that he had mislaid all his money and letters of introduction. In a panic he despatched Thomas back to London to search for the documents, before finding them again wedged inside the frame of his bed. He telegraphed ahead of Thomas instructing him to return immediately, and the message reached him at Tonbridge, where it was loudly relayed down the platform as 'Stop a gentleman of colour – it's all right!' Garfield quickly changed trains back to Folkestone, and arrived just in time to join Soyer on the packet.

After some socialising in Boulogne, where the valet of Napoleon III (another old friend) told him how pleased the emperor had been to hear of his Scutari mission, Alexis took the overnight train to Paris. There he met Brunel again and was shown around the city's military hospitals, including the imposing seventeenth-century Hôpital du Val de Grâce, where he diligently took notes on all the ingredients and special diets. He made a few hurried visits, possibly to Fanny and Jean Lamain (who was now calling himself Alexis Soyer), and within twenty-four hours his team was moving south again, first to Lyons and then to Avignon. From there it was just a short journey to the port of Marseilles, the French rendezvous point for all passenger and supply voyages across the Mediterranean to Constantinople. As their ship was due to sail the next day, Soyer lost no time in finding the army warehouses and general stores to research provisions for transportation to Scutari. He was horrified by the poor quality and high prices of what he found, declaring that 'with such a stock of provisions any Government might keep its army in a state of perfect *starvation*'.

In the end he did not sail the next day, but was delayed for a further forty-eight hours as his first-class cabins had been allocated to a group of French nurses en route to a hospital in Smyrna, and he did not relish having to sleep on deck (after all, his generosity had a limit). He was also tempted by the promise of a more luxurious new ship, stopovers in Messina and Athens, and the company of some well-connected French and English officers. It seems his eagerness to bring succour to the ravenous troops was flexible enough to accommodate a little sightseeing. He resigned himself to the delay by spending the following day enjoying the most famous of Marseillaise dishes – the half-soup, half-stew, fish and saffron delicacy known as *bouillabaisse*. For the most authentic version, he went to the exclusive Hôtel de la Réserve, which was picturesquely sited on the rocky promontory high above the ancient port with views across the harbour to the lighthouse. The patron plied his small gathering with local oysters while preparing the great dish, and Soyer, naturally, took down the recipe in great detail, later producing both an original version, and an amended one, *Bouillabaisse à l'Anglaise*, which took into account the most commonly available fish in England, and the English distaste for anything too garlicky.

Next day, with instructions to be on board by 6.30 p.m. at the latest, it was finally time to leave. As the small party and their baggage were deposited at the eastern quay of the harbour the gruesome reality of what lay ahead finally came home to Alexis. The entire landing area between the Institution Sanitaire and the low stone customs houses was now lined with allied casualties just arrived from Scutari. Greyfaced men, many with limbs missing, lay quietly on hundreds of grimy stretchers and matted straw bales. Shocked by what he saw, Alexis's holiday mood immediately turned to a reflective one.

It was indeed a spectacle calculated to pain the soul of the greatest philosopher. The quays around the harbour were thickly lined with sick and wounded. There were about seven or eight hundred, who had just been landed from two French steamers, one from Constantinople, the other from the Crimea . . . Their appearance, I regret to say, was more than indescribable. All the afflictions so common to the fate of war seemed to have met and fallen at once upon those brave fellows, who, a few months previous, were the pride of their country. Many of them . . . had not enjoyed a chance of facing the enemy; while those who were wounded looked joyful compared with those who were the victims of epidemics – typhus fever, diarrhoea, dysentery, cholera, or frostbite. I conversed with several; not one complained, but merely regretted the friends who had died on the passage and those sick left behind . . . M. Giraldo, who had superintended the disembarkation, informed me that such scenes were of daily occurrence.

Once on board the plush new *Simois*, Soyer's spirits revived. They were told that four-hundred troops had not arrived in time for the departure, prompting one female passenger to declare, 'Oh, thank God for that! I cannot bear soldiers!' They caught the expected tide in spite of increasingly heavy rain and 'furious' waves, but in sixteen hours only managed to travel as far as the Corsican coast, where the captain decided to pull into the Bay of Ajaccio and wait for calmer weather. Soyer used the delay to lead an afternoon excursion to the birthplace of Napoleon I, now a museum, and met Signora Grossetti, the Bonaparte family's housekeeper for more than thirty years. The eighty-three-year-old servant happily showed his party around the main rooms of the house before Alexis asked to see the kitchen, a request the signora claimed she had never had before. A rusty key was found, and Soyer enthusiastically poked around the ruined stoves, ovens, hearths and jacks. Leaning on a dilapidated charcoal stove, he described the scene in an excitable piece for *The Times* (which never arrived – Garfield posted the relevant copy without a stamp) and took away a cracked red tile and an old meat-hook as souvenirs for his kitchen in Scutari. Finally taking his leave of Signora Grossetti, he kissed her on both cheeks *à la Français*, a favour which, to the entertainment of the English contingent, she enthusiastically returned.

The next morning brought clear skies and a fresh breeze, and the

Simois rapidly reached Sicily, which prompted another lengthy travelogue to the *Illustrated London News*, this time rhapsodising about the beauties of Messina and the mighty Mount Etna, where 'lilies, roses, and violets perfume the air; whilst peas, beans, artichokes, and asparagus are gathered at the foot of the mountain'. From Sicily it was two days sailing eastwards to Greece and the Athenian port of Piraeus. The *Simois* anchored at Piraeus for four hours, giving Soyer and an adventurous little group of generals, colonels and captains just enough time for an al fresco *petit déjeuner à la fourchette* on the Acropolis. Furnished with Sicilian and Greek wines, it was cooked with great panache on a Magic Stove, which the great chef had balanced, with a suitably dramatic flourish, on a fallen capital of the Parthenon.

The final leg of the voyage, across the Aegean and through the Dardanelles into the sometimes stormy Sea of Marmara, passed without incident. The last evening on board was spent playing cards and draughts, listening to the French *sous-officiers* from the second-class cabins singing comic songs and choruses. The *Simois* reached the mouth of the Bosporus at nine the following morning, and nosed its way through the crowd of steamboats and frigates, Turkish barques and small, brightly painted caiques that lined the riverbanks. Alexis was bitterly disappointed that heavy rain and fog obscured much of the famous panoramic view of Constantinople, with its cypress-covered slopes, Oriental wooden kiosks, exotic domed mosques and high, elegant minarets. Once again though, his touristic excitement fled when he caught his first glimpse of the tall towers and vast stone edifice of the Barrack Hospital looming over the city. Looking up at the grim building as the ship passed by the Scutari boat landing stage, Soyer's nerve momentarily gave way.

My mind was quite overpowered when I learnt that the monster building before us was the Scutari Hospital – a town in itself – and I reflected that it was full of sick and wounded; that each patient would require from three to four articles of diet daily, making a total of several thousand per diem to be provided in some shape or other; and that I had undertaken to reform and introduce a better organization in the cooking department, where all was confusion, in so strange a country. I must confess that, for an hour or so, I was quite at a loss to think how I should commence operations. I did not know one official there. I had not the least idea how I should be received; and, after all, I might probably catch the fever, or some other complaint at the time raging within its walls.

A little further downstream he saw another large hospital, the red-brick General, housing a further five or six hundred soldiers, and his courage soon returned as he remembered his plan of action and grew anxious to resume work. As soon as the *Simois* docked, he sent his small staff to Pera, the Christian quarter, to secure rooms at the palatial Hôtel des Ambassadeurs, while he stayed on board and interviewed an English-speaking dragoman to be their guide and interpreter. The sun had come out and the dragoman was now able to point out the most attractive landmarks to an enchanted Alexis, before two watermen – known as *caidjees* – helped them into a small caique and rowed them to land. They were deposited at the Tophane steps, the main passenger landing stage on the European shore, but as Soyer finally touched down on 'the land of the Moslem', his romantic visions instantly evaporated.

The culture shock was immediate and deeply unpleasant. He was horrified by Tophane itself, which for a major arrival point was 'nothing but a heap of rotten planks'. Far worse was to come. The *caidjees* lining up for customers to take to the opposite shore stood among 'heaps of manure and the carcase of a dead horse . . . [while] a number of ill-looking, half-famished dogs were feeding upon that heap of corruption'. Dead rats littered the streets. The stench was abominable, and as the dragoman led him towards the hilltop district of Pera, little improved.

> We passed through a number of dirty narrow streets, full of a black liquid mud, very ill paved . . . amidst which numerous leperous and villainous-looking dogs were snarling and fighting. Donkeys loaded with tiles, stones and long logs of wood filled up the filthy road; besides gangs of powerful and noisy Turkish hamals or porteres, carrying enormous loads upon long poles. The enchanting mirage of the panoramic Constantinople vanished rapidly from before my dis-enchanted eyes; this ephemeral Paradise of Mahomet changing at once into an almost insupportable purgatory. I could not imagine how such a mass of ruins and of miserable wooden houses could, from so short a distance, take such a brilliant aspect or create such ravishing sensations, as the first view of Constantinople had raised in my mind from the deck of the *Simois*.

His spirits revived when he reached his hotel room in the more civilised surroundings of Pera, which was home to all the foreign embassies as well as the grand European hotels. His hotel was on the highest point of the hill, and the view of the city from the safety of the terrace once again took on an exciting exoticism. The following morning he toiled further uphill to the British Embassy, a majestic and very English grey stone palace which reminded Alexis of the Reform Club – unsurprisingly, since it was designed by Charles Barry. Here he had a brief audience with the British ambassador to Turkey, Lord Stratford de Redcliffe, whose personal grandiosity and aggressive anti-Russian diplomacy had helped tip the government into war. The ambassador (whom Florence Nightingale considered 'bad-tempered, heartless, pompous and lazy') wished Alexis's mission well but offered little practical help, and it was left to his well-meaning wife, Eliza, to make Soyer welcome. Lady Stratford discussed his plans and then introduced him to the Embassy's chef, an Italian, Roco Vido. With Vido's help she had been sending out 'comforts' each day for the English patients – strengthening compounds such as beef-tea and mutton broth, arrowroot and calves' foot jelly – which were taken by caique to the hospitals in Scutari, plus a cluster of new ones situated in Koulali, a few miles further along the Bosporus. It was a well-intentioned effort but about as useful, given the scale of the victualling problems, as sending out a single uniform to clothe an army – and the effect was anyway ruined the following year when Lady Stratford sent the government a bill for the food totalling £8,200 which the authorities felt obliged to pay. Nightingale would have nothing to do with Lady Stratford, whom she saw as a pointless socialite, but in his less judgemental way Soyer praised her efforts, and pointed out (not entirely accurately) that when the dilapidated Selimiye Kislasi barracks had first been taken over as a British military hospital, it had been 'entirely destitute of beds, sheets, blankets, chairs, tables, cooking utensils or food of any description . . . the whole of which were supplied by Lady Stratford'.

His next audience was with Lord William Paulet, who, like Nightingale, had taken up quarters inside the Barrack Hospital. Paulet – who had attended the opening of Soyer's model soup kitchen in Dublin eight years earlier – had been appointed Commander of the British Forces on the Bosporus, at Gallipoli, and the Dardanelles in November, but still found time to greet Alexis warmly and promise to find a house for him and his party in Scutari, to save him the rough, twice-daily caique ride across the Bosporus to Pera. In bad weather this journey could take more than an hour of fighting against the fast-running currents, which invariably left the passengers both frightened and soaked through. Although accommodation was now scarce in Scutari, in due course a rat-infested, tumbledown wooden kiosk was fitted up for him near the great Turkish cemetery in the newly named Cambridge Street – and swiftly named 'Soyer House'.

Wisely, Alexis made it his first task to greet and humbly solicit the help of all the chief medics and hospital bureaucrats whose help or intransigence would mean the success or failure of his mission. These included Dr Alexander Cumming, the chief medical officer, and the purveyors – Mr Milton, the purveyor-in-chief, and his deputy, a Mr Tucker, who by good fortune turned out to be 'an old London friend . . . of ten years' standing'. Alexis's wide-ranging personal contacts would stand him in good stead – he already knew many officers from the Reform Club; Florence Nightingale's influential companions, Charles and Selina Brace-bridge, turned out to be friends of his old patron, the Warwickshire baronet, Sir George Chetwynd, and it soon emerged that even the storekeeper, a very useful ally called Mr Bailey, was an old acquaintance. Although Nightingale later wrote that Soyer had been 'coolly received' by the authorities, all of these men at least listened to his ideas and offered assistance, even if in practice some were more helpful than others.

Unlike Nightingale, who had already alienated many potential allies with her brusque manner, her wide-ranging (and therefore deeply resented) authority, and her top-level War Office contacts, which made many believe that she was really a spy, Soyer at least had the advantages of great personal charm, a transparent sincerity of purpose, and a limited field of operation that offered little threat to the status quo. And it did not hurt that he was a man in such an exclusively male sphere; that his brilliant clothes added a much-needed dash of colour to an environment of otherwise unrelieved drabness; that he had boundless energy, was quick to laugh and had a keen sense of humour. Throughout his time in the East he got on well with even the most bullish doctors, and this easy persuasiveness made his goals significantly easier to achieve. Unfortunately the army authorities would prove less amenable to his charms than the medical ones. Stubbornly resistant to change, they saw Soyer much as they did Nightingale, as an interfering government stooge, and so, like her, at times he found it almost impossible to cut through the red tape and get 'a plank, or even a nail' fixed in any of the hospitals.

In March 1855 there were six British hospitals established in and around Scutari (it would eventually rise to thirteen) and, after making his introductions, Alexis set to work acquainting himself with them all. At the Barrack Hospital, like every other visitor, he was almost overcome by the stench and squalor suffered by the sick and dying men who filled every groaning ward and corridor. 'I must say that, in spite of the *sang froid* and energy I possess, the sight of such calamities made a most extraordinary impression upon me, and produced an effect which lasted for several days afterwards,' he wrote. Next, accompanied as always by Garfield, he rode out to the three small hospitals at Hyder Pacha along the Bosporus, and then back to Scutari and the large General Hospital. He also visited the new Koulali hospital with Lady Stratford. Situated on the river front past Therapia, a wealthy suburb five miles north of the city, it was considered cooler and less cramped in the summer months. He examined all their kitchens, their supplies, and their different methods of cooking and distributing the men's rations. While the quality of food and the system of distribution in these hospitals was also fairly grim, Alexis realised that they could be remedied reasonably easily by the installation of makeshift wooden kitchens and civilian cooks. His main challenge lay back in the Barrack Hospital.

It was on his return there that he finally met Florence Nightingale, when he was ushered to her austere quarters at the top of a corner tower. On her arrival four months earlier Nightingale had been allocated a tiny, damp, bedless closet to sleep in (a deliberate snub by the authorities), but by now she had managed to secure for herself the best accommodation in the hospital – a small bedchamber directly above a reception room, which looked out over the spot where the three great waters of Constantinople met – the Bosporus, the Golden Horn and the mouth of the Black Sea – giving her not just a wonderful view, but a window onto the comings and goings of the city. Nightingale obviously knew of Soyer's reputation – her beloved aunt, Julia Smith, had attended one of his charitable soup-making classes back in the forties. She greeted him cordially enough, taking his parcels and letters of introduction and enquiring politely after his journey before remarking, after reading the Duchess of Sutherland's letter, that she was sure the chef would 'render great service in the kitchen department'. If she found his excitable manner and costume as laughable as many of her circle would do, she appreciated his common sense and inventiveness, and while over the next fourteen months she would make the odd private complaint about him in letters home, her outward courtesy never failed her – despite the fact that he was the only man in Turkey who insisted on calling her '*Mademoiselle*'.

Florence took Alexis on a tour of the hospital's kitchens, listening carefully to his comments on the smoky and chaotic chambers they found, and noting later that 'Soyer was almost as shocked by the state of the great coppers where the cooking was done as the Sanitary

Commissioners had been by the state of the latrines'. Alexis then went off to inspect the storerooms and see the cooks in action, while Nightingale promised to join him on a tour of the wards the following day, to observe how the cooked rations were distributed. It did not take Soyer long to identify the problems – but where to begin? The sheer scale of the chaos made any attempt at reform daunting. The main kitchen, a massive, high-ceilinged chamber, was now filthy and full of rats, the only equipment left behind by the Turkish army being a few badly smoking open braziers and thirteen enormous copper cauldrons. As the coppers were screwed into marble bases none of them had ever been cleaned adequately, and five were completely unusable, having lost their tin linings. With these inadequate tools the cooks had to supply more than four miles of beds – up to four thousand patients – daily, with three meals a day plus tea and coffee.

Far worse than the equipment was the convoluted catering system which had somehow evolved, with none of the cooks or orderlies having any notion of how to run a busy kitchen. On his first visit just before a meal time, Alexis was astonished by the racket and lack of discipline.

Such a noise I never heard before . . . The market at old Billingsgate, during the first morning sale, was nothing compared to this military row. Each man had two tin cans for the soup. They kept running about and knocking against each other, in a most admirable disorder. Such confusion, thought I, is enough to kill a dozen patients daily. As a natural consequence, several must go without anything; as, owing to the confusion, some of the orderly waiters get more and others less than their allowance. Any attempt to alter this at the time, would have been as wise as endeavouring to stop the current of the Bosphorous.

Ordinary soldiers served as cooks in rotation, but they had been given no training, and the hellishly hot and smoky conditions in the kitchens – exacerbated by the indiscriminate burning of whole trees, leaves and all, to keep the copper furnaces fired up and the water boiling fiercely – meant that the job was despised and the men escaped to external duties as quickly as they possibly could, frequently within a week. Their role was supplemented by a team of elderly orderlies, roughly one to a dozen men. One of the orderlies' most important morning tasks was to queue up and collect the meat rations for their patients (generally mutton was given to convalescents) from the storeman who weighed and issued it for the entire hospital, a process so slow and laborious that the weak and undernourished patients were lucky to get their midday meal by teatime. Once the orderlies had got their joints of meat, they skewered them onto thick wooden paddles, then bound them up tightly, and plunged them into the coppers of fast boiling water. To identify their joints later, they would attach to the paddles some individual mark of ownership – a string of buttons, a red rag, a pair of surgical scissors, or even, in one case, some ancient underwear.

> The discovery of this brilliant idea was greeted with shouts of laughter from Miss Nightingale, the doctors, and myself. It consisted in tying a pair of old snuffers to the lot . . . All this rubbish was daily boiled with the meat . . . On telling the man with the snuffers that it was a very dirty trick to put such things in the soup, the reply was – 'How can it be dirty, sir? sure they have been boiling this last month.'

Once the paddles had been fished out of the water again, each orderly took his precious bundle to his own bed and roughly divided up the meat – or, as it often was, inedible bone and gristle – which the poor patients finally received on a tin plate with some potatoes. With no cutlery available, they were left to tear it apart as best they could. Yet it was still only the lucky ones who found that their meat was cooked through – the agonisingly slow issuing system meant that some joints were boiled to ribbons, while others remained virtually raw in the middle. In any case the system of binding up the meat so tightly meant that while the outside edges of the joints swelled in the water, the heat could not properly penetrate to the centre. While various hospital authorities were busy assuring the new government that everything was now running like clockwork, no wonder Nightingale had already written to Sidney Herbert, the former minister-at-war, that 'the waste in the wards was enormous because the men were really unable to eat diets so badly cooked'. Charles Bracebridge later told an inquiry that to his mind many 'had been lost from want of nourishment', as the patients had not been able to digest the terrible food they were given.

Alexis found that the men were at least getting the correct weight of rations, but that most of the provisions were of an abysmal quality. A man on full diet was officially allowed a minimum of one pound each of meat, bread and potatoes, plus two pints of tea and half a pint of porter, with the portions diminishing pro rata for half and quarter diets. Regular soldiers were able to supplement these basics by buying themselves extra food, but in hospital this was impossible, and so soup was also provided.

Mainly liquid 'spoon' diets were meant to be for those too weak to ingest anything as tough as meat, and consisted of just bread and tea, plus whatever nourishing extras, such as beef-tea or arrowroot, could be rustled up for them. In practice, doctors often put relatively fit men on spoon diets, on the basis that at least they would get some nourishment from a bowl of broth, as opposed to none at all from the inedible meat.

All other basics, such as vegetables, coffee and condiments, were purely discretionary, and it was immediately obvious to Soyer that the hospital purveyors were being cheated by local traders. The meat was appalling, the poultry elderly, the 'fresh' vegetables half rotten. Only the bread was praiseworthy. Worst of all was the terrible charcoal, 'which smoked terribly . . . was nothing but dust . . . [and] interfered materially with the expedition of the cooking, which is a subject of vital importance in an hospital, where punctuality is as essential as quality'. Although the soldier-cooks burned whatever wood they could find, charcoal was still the basic fuel, and without decent supplies it was impossible to create a properly functioning kitchen.

Since her arrival in November Nightingale and a few forward-looking doctors had set up some extra-diet kitchens, providing pails of arrowroot and wine and beef essences for the men on spoon diets, and initially some of the nurses and orderlies had prepared little extras for a few of the patients on the wards with portable stoves that Nightingale had sourced in Marseilles, but provisions were in very poor supply and in any case it could only help a tiny fraction of the men. Doctor Cumming, who had appeared so affable to Soyer, in fact proved less than helpful – he had already banned any cooking on the wards, and now flatly refused one of Soyer's most pressing requests, the small but important matter of the meat being supplied to the orderlies already boned, to ensure that each man received a properly stewed portion, free of bone and gristle. Soyer had also told him that the bones could be used to make excellent soup. Yet Cumming had decreed, in a perfect example of the blinkered, bureaucracy-obsessed dogmatism that was destroying the army, that it would need 'a new regulation of the Service' to bone the meat. 'Amid all the confusion and distress of Scutari Hospital, military discipline was never lost sight of, and an infringement of one of its smallest observances was worse than letting twenty men die of neglect,' wrote one nurse bitterly. It was equally clear to Nightingale and Soyer that, if the men were to have any hope of being adequately nourished back to health, the entire catering system needed breaking down and reconstructing.

Once he had decided on how best to achieve lasting change, Soyer threw himself into action with his usual focus and efficiency, ignoring the red tape, the grumblings of his cooks, the privations of his noisy, rat-infested house and the debilitating bouts of diarrhoea that, like everyone else in Constantinople, he regularly suffered. Much could be done immediately, with no outlay beyond a little practical culinary sense and some time spent with the cooks and orderlies. He demonstrated to the orderlies how to tie up their joints loosely, so that the meat had a chance of cooking right through. He taught the cooks not to throw out the cooking water, as they had done previously, because it made superb stock. He then taught them how to transform it into decent soup by the addition of seasoning, flour and brown sugar, and showed them that if they skimmed the fat off this broth, it made an excellent dripping to go on their bread – far fresher and tastier than the rank butter that was bought in from the market at fifteen piastres a pound – and it was free! As the men had only one tin bowl each, they were used to eating their meat first, followed by their pint of watery soup, but Soyer pointed out that if the orderlies poured the soup *over* the meat, it could be consumed hot while the meat was kept warm.

Gradually, larger progress was made. The boilers were cleaned and retinned. By appealing to the chief engineer, he managed to get a charcoal stove and an oven built, a storeroom and larder partitioned off, and chopping blocks and dressers made. Hygienic, numbered metal skewers replaced the wooden stakes. He introduced a system of weights and scales to help the cooks manage quantities better. He showed them how to use the wood and charcoal more efficiently, so that the furnaces burned at a more moderate rate and did not need to be extinguished with buckets of water. This alone had the triple benefit of saving precious fuel, reducing the heat, smoke and steam in the kitchen, and stopping all the food from tasting burnt.

Supervised by Jullien and his little team of chefs, the soldier-cooks learned how to stew meat and cook the basic dishes and soups well – aided by Soyer's clear instructions, which had by now been reduced to basic principles, framed, and pinned on the walls. Before long, Soyer wrote proudly, 'my new regiment began to manoeuvre admirably under my command'. He then started to introduce the new extra-diet dishes and drinks that he had devised before his arrival – chicken, mutton and veal broths, lemonade, barley and rice waters, panadas, sago jelly and digestible puddings made of bread, rice, vermicelli, macaroni and sago. He even set up a makeshift testing and demonstration kitchen in the corner of one of the stairwells, where examples of the latest nourishing dishes were exhibited. Eventually the preparation of almost all the extra-diet dishes, plus the staff meals, moved into the smoothly running main kitchen, under the supervision of two civilian cooks assisted by just six soldiers instead of twelve, and the inefficient extra-diet kitchens were closed down. By bringing virtually all the catering under one roof, the number of soldier-cooks necessary dropped by twenty, and the consumption of fuel plummeted. It became possible to send hot food all over the hospital from the main kitchen in double-cased trolleys filled with boiling water – a solution suggested by Nightingale. Indeed, so efficient was the reformed kitchen that by the time Soyer left it could have fed far more patients than the hospital was able to accommodate.

Within a month, provisions had also improved – 'the old fowls got unexpectedly younger, and the fuel was better.' Alexis had even managed to produce, for the first time, a decent cup of that most English of essentials, tea. Previously, the cooks had tied up tea leaves in a cloth and then tossed the bundle into a copper of boiling water which had just been emptied of soup. Inevitably the brew tasted of old soup and little else, as the bundle shrank in the water and few of the leaves were able to diffuse. Soyer improvised by placing a coffee filter into a two-gallon kettle, putting twenty rations of tea leaves into the filter and filling the kettle with boiling water. It worked perfectly, and 'to my astonishment made about one-fourth more tea, perfectly clear and without the least sediment'. Four kettles were enough to furnish the entire hospital, although Soyer ordered additional, smaller versions for each ward, so that the nurses could make the men tea during the night. So successful were these kettles that they inspired Soyer to turn his makeshift creation into a proper appliance, although he claimed that it was 'more a happy thought than an invention'. In due course his Scutari Teapot was launched on the public. There were two versions, a large functional one with a straight cylindrical body and a fantastical lid, which was a tiny model of the Galata Tower topped by a crescent moon and star, and a smaller, even more fanciful version, with the same lid, a more curvaceous body and a joky handle shaped like a Turkish man, complete with fez, clinging to the side. Soyer was so pleased with the second design that he registered it back in London, describing himself on the paperwork as Alexis Soyer of Scutari. It was, unsurprisingly, the more practical version that took off. Nightingale ordered one for her own personal use and the design enjoyed considerable popularity.

Alexis knew that all his work would come to nothing if the old system of rotating the soldier-cooks every few days or weeks remained un-changed. Even with his energetic teaching and written instructions, and even with a permanent sergeant now overseeing the cooks, he knew that the skills would not be passed down the line for long. Therefore he proposed to Lord William Paulet what would eventually become a simple, disciplined catering corps. Before leaving Scutari he set out the blueprint for his new system, which would not just be used in hospitals, but adapted in the camp at the front line. Paulet immediately approved it. It stated that:

> For every important hospital, a professed man-cook shall be engaged, with a civilian assistant, instead of military . . . [but] to be under military rules and regulations . . . That all military men now engaged cooking in the hospitals and barrack kitchens shall be immediately instructed in the art of camp cooking. As they are already acquainted with the plain mode of cooking, it will only require a few lessons from Monsieur Soyer . . . to become thoroughly conversant with this branch of culinary operations . . . Monsieur Soyer feels that if present in the camp for a few weeks he will be enabled to carry out this important object, at the same time introducing wholesome and nutritious food made out of the usual allowances of provisions supplied to the army, so soon as his field or bivouac stove shall be adopted by the Crimean authorities.

By now Alexis was so pleased with the general progress that not even the privations of Constantinople at war were going to stop him having a party. He decided to hold a 'Grand Opening' of the newly improved kitchen, and persuaded Paulet to summon the most senior army officers, while Dr Cumming agreed to invite the medical heads of all the hospitals, including the French and Turkish ones. The plan was to lay out two versions of every dish served in the hospital, from chicken broth to beef soup to sago and port, and then make the guests decide which was prepared under the old regime, and which under the new. The date was fixed for Easter Monday, just six days away, when Alexis had an attack of nerves. He recognised that if anything went wrong after such a fanfare he would be a laughing stock, and his hard-won reputation in tatters again. He was, he felt, 'risking the labour of twenty years against an uncertainty'.

The event very nearly was derailed – as on the Friday morning, after inspecting several kitchens, Alexis was suddenly taken ill. 'I seemed to have forgotten everything, and experienced at the same time a sensation of brain fever. Although I was quite conscious of what I had to do, I was entirely incapable of doing it, or of ordering anything or directing anyone.' It was not, thankfully, the dreaded Crimean fever, but some sort of temporary breakdown, caused by overwork and, according to the doctor, who prescribed rest and a soothing medicine, 'the effect produced by the immense number of sick and wounded I was in the habit of seeing daily and the numerous dead bodies passing before the windows to be buried'. The diarrhoea that he had suffered since his arrival could not have helped. He had lost a great deal of weight rapidly, and was getting little sleep. The rest cure worked. By Sunday night he felt fully recovered, and at lunchtime on Monday more than a hundred distinguished guests crowded into the Scutari kitchen.

Those who did not know Alexis already were curious to meet this celebrated chef who had now taken to dressing entirely in white, except for a huge floppy blue cap edged in gold, and equally eager to taste his famous food. Everyone duly inspected, tasted, marvelled and praised, and Soyer was once again in his element. Although bad weather had meant that Lady Stratford and some of the French and Turkish contingent had been unable to cross the Bosporus, the event was a huge success, and at the end of the party, as was his lifelong habit, Alexis solicited written 'testimonials' of his good work from the most eminent guests. Paulet's praise summed up the general approbation: 'It is with great pleasure that I state I have carefully viewed and tasted the new diets introduced by Monsieur Soyer in the hospitals this day; and had I not seen and tasted them, I could not have believed that such amelioration could have been produced from the same materials as allowed by Government.'

Soyer, who was still issuing a stream of letters to the London press, immediately sent back a copy of Paulet's letter, with an account of the Grand Opening, which duly appeared, fully illustrated, in the *Illustrated London News*, reading for all the world like a society gathering of London's *beau monde*. Even Queen Victoria heard of his success when Lady Stratford, one of her regular correspondents, wrote that 'M. Soyer has done much good in the kitchens. He is a most ridiculous man, but quite perfect in his way.' A less patronising fan was Lady Alicia Blackwood, a philanthropic doctor's wife who had set up a laundry in the basement of the Barrack Hospital to give employment to the destitute wives of dead soldiers. She enjoyed the stir Soyer's arrival had made and recalled him affectionately in her memoirs.

[Soyer's] good-natured and cheerful countenance was quite refreshing, and his presence was hailed with much welcome as a very useful adjunct to a very needful department. His peculiar appearance also enlivened the monotony of our everyday routine. M. Soyer's dress corresponded with the bent of his mind, which was in all things devoted to his profession . . . His thoughts seemed concentrated on his own hobby, it was paramount, the beginning, continuation, and ending of everything with him . . . the arrival of M. Soyer was a cheering and cheerful addition, for we all, more or less, benefited by his coming, and we thankfully record it when we revert to those times.

After the Grand Opening it remained for Soyer to transfer the same, or similar, system of management to the other hospitals, while badgering the engineers to repair the kitchens and the purveyor-in-chief into sourcing better equipment. Towards the end of April, he felt it was time to follow Panmure's instruction to move on to the Crimea and tackle the terrible standard of cookery among the soldiers in the British camp. Aware that by doing so he would have to abandon any hope of getting home in time to execute his plans for the Paris Exhibition, he finally resigned himself to writing off a second potential fortune in as many months.

As it happened, Florence Nightingale and the Bracebridges were also planning to leave for the front. Having just supervised the arrival of a consignment of two hundred soldiers from Balaclava, who were success-fully bathed, clothed in hospital gowns, put into clean beds and given hot, well-cooked food – Nightingale was finally able to write to Sidney Herbert that the hospital had achieved 'the first really satisfactory recep-tion of the sick'. She was now able to think of travelling further east. Soyer gratefully accepted an invitation to join her party, and the date for their sailing was set for 2 May 1855. He had hoped to take with him the four hundred field stoves destined for the peninsula, but they had still not arrived, so he anxiously arranged for them to follow after him, along with the ten stoves originally earmarked for Scutari. (Since the Turkish coppers had been so successfully cleaned and retinned, he felt the stoves would be better employed in the Crimea.)

Satisfied that everything in the hospitals was now running smoothly under the guidance of two of his own cooks, and promising to 'run down from the Crimea now and then' to check on progress, on the day of sailing Alexis made his farewells and proceeded to the harbour with the faithful Garfield, the other two cooks, Emma's cumbersome painting, letters of introduction to the commander-in-chief, Lord Raglan, and his precious bundle of testimonials praising his work in Scutari. 'Monsieur Soyer,' read one, 'Miss Nightingale's name and your own will be for ever associated in the archives of this memorable war.' It was from General Vivian, and the one of which Alexis was most proud. He could not have known that, within a single generation, his name would have been largely effaced from the record.

14

'Captain Cook'

Just as his mislaid documents had almost cost him the cross-Channel packet from Folkestone two months earlier, Soyer's fast-moving caique only just managed to catch up with the large troop ship, the *Robert Lowe*, as she steamed out of Tophane. Although scheduled to leave at noon, the captain had decided to leave early to avoid the risk of losing his slot in the overcrowded harbour at Balaclava, but his revised timetable had failed to reach Soyer, and Florence Nightingale and the Bracebridges had almost given him up before his booming laugh was followed by his ample frame on deck. Soyer had gone native and adopted a sort of Oriental travelling costume involving a red and white gauze turban and a long hooded cloak, which must have contrasted sharply with Nightingale's simple, functional outfit. Yet as the ship slowly moved towards the Black Sea, the pair chatted easily about the exotic views passing before them, and of the problems still unresolved in the hospitals they were leaving behind.

The weather was fine, the waters calm, and the journey progressed smoothly as the passengers enjoyed the fresh air on deck. Soyer relished having the 'amiable and gentle' Nightingale for a captive audience and showed every sign of being mildly infatuated with her. He grasped every opportunity to chat about matters other than business and shower her with embarrassing compliments. He admired her charming conversation and wit, and declared her vastly attractive in spite of her plain dress code – a simple grey or black dress worn with a white cap and rough apron. He claimed he thoroughly approved of this 'religiously simple and unsophisticated' appearance – although anything short of garish splendour *à la Cerrito* would have seemed religiously simple to Soyer.

Florence lectured him on what to expect in Balaclava, even though this was a first visit for both of them, and told him that it would be even more difficult to get anything done there than in Scutari, 'the distance from supplies being so much greater'. The fine weather kept up until the *Robert Lowe* – nicknamed the *Robert Slow* by an impatient Nightingale – approached the Russian coast, and Charles Bracebridge, Nightingale and Soyer stood on deck watching the impressive cliffs and mountainscapes through their telescopes. Once in the bay of Balaclava, a long and deep natural gorge, they admired the ruined Genoese tower, built on a rocky crag two hundred feet above them. Nightingale pointed out the Sanatorium on the heights next to it, and on lower ground the row of huts which made up the General Hospital. At the end of the bay, the ship entered the calm waters of the harbour, slowly threading its way through dozens of other steamers, men-of-war, troop ships and supply vessels to its pre-arranged mooring opposite the commandant's house. The small harbour was even busier than usual, as word had spread of Nightingale's arrival and 'the decks of all the large vessels at anchor were crowded with curious spectators, in expectation of seeing that lady, of whose devotion to the sick and wounded they had heard so much'. They would be disappointed of a glimpse of the heroine of Scutari that day, however, as the party decided it was by then too late to venture on shore. Accommodation, in any case, was so scarce on land that 'it was impossible to procure either a house, hut or even a tent', and the new arrivals were grateful to accept the captain's offer to sleep on board until he returned to Constantinople.

The next morning the most important of Nightingale's visitors could no longer be put off, and she held a kind of 'floating drawing-room', receiving many of the head doctors, inspectors, sanitary commissioners and commissary staff in her cabin, while Bracebridge ran errands and Soyer, having already despatched four of his soldier-cooks to the Sanatorium, waited to accompany her on a tour of the hospitals. The next few days passed in a blur of inspections and introductions. Florence was accompanied by Bracebridge and her twelve-year-old page, Robert Robertson, and Soyer by Thomas Garfield or one of his servants. Most hospitals they found to be in a depressing state of dirt and confusion. Nightingale would concentrate on the wards and Soyer on the kitchens – generally roofless, ill-equipped mud huts burning up vast quantities of fuel. He would rush around taking notes and sketching out plans for simple but efficient new wooden structures. They travelled through both the French and English camps, which stretched for miles around the besieged city of Sebastopol, and in the latter stopped at several regimental hospitals and cookhouses. Alexis was childishly excited by the vastness and bustle of the military camps, from the 'myriads of white tents, [which] appeared like large beds of mushrooms growing at random', to 'the sound of trumpets, the beating of drums, the roar of cannon from Sebastopol . . . whilst military manoeuvres, and sentries placed in every direction, gave a most martial aspect to the landscape, backed by the bold and rugged range of mountains by which Balaclava is surrounded'.

While most of the regimental hospitals they visited were badly managed, a notable exception was one run by a Dr Blake, who later wrote to his wife about the extraordinary visit of this 'most incongruous party'.

I was walking up and down the camp when we saw a lady and three gentlemen ride up to the hospital and an orderly came to say Miss Nightingale sent her compliments to know if I had any objection to her going over my Hospital. Of course, I had none so I joined the party which consisted of Dr Sutherland (one of the Sanitary Commission), Soyer, and a *half-caste!!!* Miss Nightingale is a most pleasing person . . . she was delighted with all she saw . . . Soyer was in raptures with my kitchen, built by Sergeant Desmore (the Hospital Sergeant) and whilst Miss Nightingale and I were discussing matters of Hospital detail, Soyer rushed up and carried her off to see the establishment and his *delight* at the grate made of Turkoman gun barrels was beyond everything.

Soyer was in high spirits. His experiences at Scutari, and the conviction that his camp stoves, when they eventually arrived, would transform not just how every British soldier ate in the future, but solve the age-old logistics problem of ferrying around fuel, had given him every confidence of great success in the Crimea. He was delighted to be considered an important part of Miss Nightingale's congenial party – while still retaining his own area of competence and acting on his own authority from the secretary-at-war. Despite his large clutch of testimonials and letters of introduction, his friendship with Nightingale certainly did not hurt when it came to gaining easy access to some of the most influential players, and he studiously avoided the political battles in which she quickly became embroiled. He had missed the worst of the horrors and privations of the previous winter, and was now enchanted by the balmy weather, the early summer wild flowers and the 'transcendentally beautiful and refreshing' coastal views.

Morale among the soldiers had improved radically with the better weather and the easing of the supply crisis – as plenty of clothes, food and tents finally got through their conditions improved beyond all recognition – and although the camp was still in 'the infancy of luxury', dinner parties were in vogue once again among the officers, among whom there proved to be as many old friends as in Scutari. Even on short walks, said Soyer, 'it was a constant nodding of heads and shaking of hands'. As the servant of no one but the government, and with the social boundaries that in London would have stopped him mixing on equal terms with colonels and generals in abeyance, he anticipated a convivial time ahead. Like many philanthropically minded Victorians, Alexis could see no moral dilemma in reconciling his charitable work with a little social climbing. And sure enough, within a few weeks he was spending 'about an hour' each morning writing apologies to the invitations he – regretfully – could not shoehorn into his social calendar.

Not that he mixed exclusively with soldiers and medics. He quickly became an habitué of the makeshift British Hotel, a combined restaurant, bar, café, shop and clinic run by the talented and formidable Creole nurse, Mary Seacole, the mixed-race healer from Jamaica. The pair were delighted with each other, the reputation of each having preceded their first meeting, and soon Soyer was calling the 'good and benevolent' Seacole *la mère noire*, while she dubbed Soyer 'the great high priest of the mysteries of cookery'.

To reach the Crimea Seacole had had to show even more courage and enterprise than Soyer. She had initially tried to join Nightingale's group of nurses, and had travelled all the way from Kingston, Jamaica, to London to apply in person. But in spite of glowing references from high-ranking British officers who had experienced her care while stationed in the Caribbean, her spotless character, and her acknowledged expertise in the treatment of cholera, diarrhoea and dysentery, she was repeatedly and rudely rejected – a direct result, she was forced to conclude, of her 'yellow' skin. There's little doubt that Seacole was fully justified in claiming to be a victim of racism. She was turned away from Nightingale's team on the basis of there being no vacancies, and yet when the first party set sail, they were still two nurses short of the full complement. Nightingale never softened in her antipathy towards Seacole. When Seacole stopped at the Barrack Hospital en route to the front and requested a bed for the night, Nightingale pointedly ensured that she had to doss down with the washerwomen. In later years Nightingale would claim that the British Hotel had been little better than a 'bad house' – that is, a brothel.

In the face of all opposition Seacole had persevered, travelling to the Crimea under her own steam to set up a business offering the soldiers a very personal blend of home comforts: effective home-made remedies, decent home-made food, a few imported luxuries and plenty of beer, sherry and champagne, the tariff varying according to the rank and means of her clients. Seacole made no bones about charging outrageous prices, particularly for alcohol, to anyone with money to spare, in order to subsidise the cost of the healing potions and remedies that she administered for free to those without any money. She had arrived in February, and with the help of a business partner, Thomas Day, quickly built the collection of iron sheds and wooden storerooms that became the British Hotel on Spring Hill, strategically placed near the English camp and the new railway, one mile from the British headquarters and two from Balaclava. Their eccentric appearance stemmed from the fact that many of the materials used in their construction were so much flotsam and jetsam that had recently been floating in Balaclava harbour. By mid-May, when Soyer first visited, the hotel was doing a very brisk trade, having become not just a favourite canteen and watering-hole, but also the hospital of choice for many of the men, who found that Mary's simple cinnamon waters and pomegranate juices did more to alleviate their symptoms than anything the doctors had to offer.

The two sociable Crimean celebrities shared more than an expanding girth and a colourful wardrobe. (Seacole's favourite outfit was a bright yellow dress teamed with a red-trimmed blue bonnet.) Each was dedicated to the art of living well, yet excelled at making the most of the paltriest of resources. Both were energetic, exuberant and incessant self-promoters. Seacole even shared Soyer's compulsion to collect references from anyone prepared to put pen to paper, indicating an underlying insecurity, a deep need to build up positive reinforcements against a rainy day. They also shared a touching and sometimes mystifying loyalty to England, a country that did not always return the compliment, and an unshakeable belief that their talents made them as valuable a part of the war effort as Russell, Nightingale, or any of the other civilian volunteers.

A friendship was quickly established. Alexis, when not with Nightingale, was delighted to find a comfortable and convivial oasis, well stocked with champagne, so close to hand, and he clearly admired Mrs Seacole's tenacity and business acumen. He did, however, share the casual prejudices, both racial and gender, of his age, constantly joking about Seacole's dark or 'dusky' skin and calling her a jovial old woman – although at fifty she was only five years older than him. He lectured her on how to put her business on a good financial footing, and cautioned her against using her outhouses to offer accommodation for visitors, who either slept on ships in the harbour, or, if they were military men, under canvas in the camps. Instead, he told her: 'Lay in a good stock of hams, wines, spirits, ale and porter, sauces, pickles, and a few preserves and dry vegetables – in short, anything which will not spoil by keeping . . . [and] you will no doubt make money, as you are so well known to all the army.' It was good advice, and kindly meant, but immensely patronising to a woman who had already established a flourishing enterprise in the face of the most extraordinarily difficult conditions.

In time, as the trickle of goods into the Crimea became a flood, thanks to the public outcry in the UK, Mother Seacole was able to supply far more than the scanty provisions Soyer suggested – she was also proud to sell 'linen and hosiery, saddlery, caps, boots and shoes . . . meat and soups of every variety in tins . . . salmon, lobsters, and oysters, also in tins, which last beaten up into fritters, with onions, butter, eggs, pepper, and salt, were very good; game, wild fowl, vegetables, also preserved, eggs, sardines, curry powder, cigars, tobacco, snuff, cigarette papers, tea, coffee, tooth powder, and redcurrant jelly'. It was almost inconceivable that just a few months earlier the army had been at the point of starvation. To provide a taste of home for the men, Seacole dropped her Jamaican cuisine for hot stodgy British favourites that went down well whatever the weather, and became a dab hand at Irish stews and meat pies, Welsh rarebit and rice puddings, pastries, tarts and sponge cakes. Seacole's achievement at the British Hotel was quite astonishing, and yet it is ironic that Soyer's own – entirely justifiable – sensitivity to being condescended to by his betters did not stop him from instinctively patronising her. In the long ladder of Victorian social hierarchies, some-how the black 'doctress' still came in several rungs lower than the white labourer's son from Meaux.

For her part, Seacole was delighted to have, as a very open-handed customer, the famous chef of whose relish and sauces she had sold 'many and many a score', and after the war she would praise him warmly in her popular memoir, *Wonderful Adventures of Mrs Seacole in Many Lands*.

[Soyer] was often at Spring Hill, with the most smiling of faces and in the most gorgeous of irregular uniforms, and never failed to praise my soups and dainties. I always flattered myself that I was his match, and with our West Indian dishes could of course beat him hollow, and more than once I challenged him to a trial of skill; but the gallant

Frenchman only shrugged his shoulders, and disclaimed my challenge with many flourishes of his jewelled hands, declaring that Madame proposed a contest where victory would cost him his reputation for gallantry, and be more disastrous than defeat . . . Then he would laugh and declare that, when our campaigns were over, we would render rivalry impossible, by combining to open the first restaurant in Europe. There was always fun in the store when the good-natured Frenchman was there.

Most of those early days were dedicated to accompanying Miss Nightingale's entourage around the various hospitals, however, and at the end of one such excursion the party determined to 'take a peep' at Sebastopol for themselves. They rode up to the Woronzoff Road to watch the shelling of the city through telescopes in a stone redoubt. On a whim, and against the advice of the sentry, they decided to venture a little closer, and made it to a three-mortar battery in a trench half a mile further on. There, against the sound of constant firing in the background, Soyer insisted on setting up a dramatic visual tableau – the Angel of Mercy seated on a warlike cannon, which he later recalled in *A Culinary Campaign*.

> I begged Miss Nightingale, as a favour, to give me her hand, which she did. I then requested her to ascend the stone rampart next the wooden gun carriage, and lastly, to sit upon the centre mortar, to which requests she very gracefully and kindly acceded. I then boldly exclaimed, 'Gentlemen, behold this amiable lady sitting fearlessly upon that terrible instrument of war! behold the heroic daughter of England – the soldier's friend!' All present shouted, 'Bravo! bravo! hurrah! hurrah! Long live the daughter of England!'

It was an innocent enough speech, although Russell – who was not there – later wrote a more comical, if less respectful, version of it in a bitchy private letter to his employer, *The Times*' editor, John Delane. 'Soyer dragged her [Nightingale] into a battery . . .' he wrote, 'and put her on the stern of a gun with the elegant expression meant to be neat and well-turned – "Voilà! The Child of Peace had her breech on the breech of the Son of War!"'

At the first opportunity Soyer proudly demonstrated the scale model of his field stove to Lord Raglan, the British commander-in-chief, who gave him a warm welcome and reminisced fondly over his Reform Club days. Raglan had also known Ude, having been a friend of the late Lord Alvanley, the quarrelsome chef's eccentric lodger, which gave Alexis the chance to rehearse his well-polished anecdotes about Ude's notorious birthday parties. Raglan asked Alexis to improve the kitchen at headquarters, and agreed that when the long-awaited consignment of field stoves finally arrived, Soyer could begin the process of introducing them into each regiment. Soon, workmen were detailed to construct the first of his new hospital kitchens, at the Sanatorium on the Genoese Heights, although – with by now depressing predictability – the operation soon ground to a halt, a lack of adequate men and materials being cited, as usual, as the cause. In the end a desperate Alexis resorted to locking the chief engineer, one Captain King, into his office for ten minutes while he forced him to go over his plans and promise to supply the appropriate resources.

In the midst of all this activity, on 12 May – her thirty-fifth birthday – Florence Nightingale was suddenly struck down with such a severe bout of Crimean fever that few expected her to live. She was immediately moved to the Castle Hospital, a new, relatively well-run hospital on the heights, and Soyer, like the rest of her party, was shocked and subdued. The news, he said, 'seemed to paralyse all our energies. Indeed for a few days no business of consequence was transacted.' But work had to go on, and soon he resumed his visits alone. Indeed, Nightingale's illness may indirectly have helped his mission, as her absence enabled him to establish constructive relationships with some of her most powerful enemies: men who were unwilling to assist one of Nightingale's men, but who did help him out with manpower and materials once he had managed to explain his work – and his independence – to them. These included the vindictive Dr John Hall, chief medical officer of the British Expeditionary Force, a strict disciplinarian who had, the previous October, when conditions at the Barrack Hospital in Scutari had been at their filthiest and most destitute, assured his paymasters back in London that all was 'on a very creditable footing and that nothing is lacking'. Dr Hall famously disapproved of the use of chloroform for operations, even amputations, considering any pain relief as pampering. He once wrote that 'the smart use of the knife is a powerful stimulant and it is much better to hear a man bawl lustily than to see him sink silently into the grave'.

Nightingale despised Hall as a liar and a sadist, and Hall in turn wielded his authority to belittle and undermine Nightingale, reversing her commands and persecuting anyone who dared to support her. Yet

Alexis, alone in her circle, developed a good rapport with Hall. They went on many hospital visits together, they corresponded amicably, and Hall even used his influence to expedite the hospital kitchen refurbishments. His tendency to play the buffoon possibly played to Soyer's advantage in building friendships with the more jealous, resentful officials like Hall – men who recognised his expertise and usefulness but could never seriously consider as a threat a man who came out with a stream of bad songs and worse puns, and who dressed so ludicrously that he was becoming something of a camp mascot – or a '*chien du régiment*' as he called himself.

An early fiasco with a succession of borrowed horses had rather unfortunately cemented his reputation as a fool to many. It began when he borrowed a doctor's horse for a quick trip to headquarters, which was only three miles from Balaclava, but had got waylaid at the British Hotel by some cronies who saw him trotting past and shouted after him to join them. After a few drinks Alexis left the bar only to find that the Zouave to whom he had entrusted his horse had handed it over to a complete stranger. Mary Seacole's business partner, Thomas Day, immediately lent him his own pony and told him to rush over to the Post Office at headquarters, where he could make enquiries and leave a description of the missing animal. But at headquarters Alexis bumped into Russell, who laughed at his ineptness and persuaded him to stay for dinner with some friends, which turned into yet another bacchanalian feast – the fairly awful meal compensated for with copious amounts of wine. As the party drank and smoked their chibouques Russell's lengthy anecdotes gave way to jokes and songs, the last becoming so noisy that it attracted complaints from all the surrounding tents – until the complainants were invited to bring their own drink and join the party, which broke up after midnight. Soyer slept in an empty hut 'wrapped up in a horse-cloth, with a pair of top-boots for a pillow' and emerged the next morning, hung over and dishevelled, to find an angry Thomas Day reclaiming his mount.

Soyer continued the search for his original horse with a pony from Lord Raglan's stable, but got side-tracked yet again, this time by a brief amnesty that had been declared to give each side a chance to bury their dead. He could not resist the opportunity to scramble through the French trenches and into Sebastopol itself to watch the proceedings from a Russian perspective, only to retreat at the end of the truce to find the pony missing. In fact, the man he had left guarding it had simply been ordered to move further behind the front line for safety, but by the time Alexis finally returned to Balaclava, three days after leaving for what was meant to be a brief trip to headquarters, rumour had spread that the idiotic Soyer had managed to borrow and lose three horses in as many days – not to mention himself. The joke was completed when Raglan's horse was confiscated by a policeman, who declared that it had been 'stolen from Monsieur Soyer' and refused to believe that Garfield – who was then riding it – was his secretary. 'My mishap afforded much amusement; and the standing jest in camp for some time was "Who lost the four horses?"' Which was all very droll, but when combined with his ridiculous costumes and boisterous behaviour, it did little to enhance his claims to a seriousness of purpose.

Nightingale's sufferings were intense as she lay in bed believing, in her delirium, that her hospital room was full of people screaming for supplies, and that an engine throbbed in her head. In the end the fever did not kill her, but after it passed she was so severely weakened that for some time she was unable even to lift a spoon to her mouth or speak above a whisper, and it was obvious that she needed time and space to recuperate. The doctors naturally urged her to return to London, but she was not to be got rid of so easily, and consented only to a brief convalescence in Constantinople. Lord Stratford was compelled to offer her accommodation at the palatial British Embassy. Although she was still too ill to receive visitors, Alexis had visited the Sanatorium every day to prepare some delicacies for the invalid, and within a fortnight Florence was deemed just about well enough to travel.

The timing of her journey suited Alexis perfectly. Jullien, his head chef in Scutari, was ill and threatening to resign, which would have severely compromised the entire Turkish operation, and Alexis was anxious to return for a while and smooth things over. He also wanted to get his hands on the first batch of a dozen full-scale stoves, which had finally arrived in the East but been mistakenly disembarked at Scutari instead of Balaclava. Having waited so long, he was determined to track them down and not let them out of his sight again. Lord Ward, the future Earl of Dudley, had recently arrived in his magnificent yacht, the *London*, and graciously lent it to Nightingale and her entourage for the crossing back to Constantinople. The party left Balaclava on 8 June, a little over a month after their arrival. Having lodged in a couple of rat-infested troop ships since the *Robert Lowe*'s departure, Soyer relished the luxuriousness of the *London*, and was only sorry that seasickness stopped him taking full advantage of the superb catering – although on the last morning he did manage a breakfast of some devilled fowl and an *omelette aux fine herbes*.

In Scutari, Soyer was elated to find that his reforms were still in place and operating like clockwork – a situation that would be commented on in Parliament a few weeks later, when Peel informed the Commons that 'the services of that accomplished artist [M. SOYER] had been effectively applied to the improvement of the military kitchens'. A Sergeant Thompson, who had been appointed as the permanent supervisor of the soldier-cooks, handled the men well, and the food – based on his simplified recipes – remained a huge improvement on what he had originally found. The problem remained, however, that as soon as a new batch of cooks had been adequately trained, they were removed to other duties, making it a hard slog for Thompson and his civilian chefs to keep on repeating the process. Meeting up with Paulet, Soyer renewed the pressure for the establishment of a proper medical corps. While it would be many months before that was achieved, Paulet did, however, assign to him a permanent brigade of a dozen soldier-cooks, whom he trained to use the dozen field stoves that had arrived, until they were fully competent to instruct the soldiers in each regiment back in the Crimea.

Soyer stayed in Scutari for more than a month, ironing out his staffing and supply problems. With Jullien gone he had to roll up his sleeves and take over the cooking at the Barrack Hospital until two 'tolerably good cooks' were found to replace him. He went back to Soyer House, his spacious, if run-down, wooden kiosk in Cambridge Street, which required some major rat-removal measures to become habitable again. At least the better weather had made the draughts more tolerable, if not the incessant hammering from the Turkish carriage-builders below, and ripe cherries and mulberries could be plucked from branches right outside his window. It was lucky that Soyer House had nine rooms, as his entourage was growing. As well as twelve soldier-cooks, Alexis would be returning to the Crimea with his ever-faithful secretary, Garfield, a Mr Mesnil, 'my major domo', a Sardinian servant and an Armenian groom for his four new horses. Also in his party was Peter Morrison, a timorous travelling gentleman who had latched on to Soyer on his last voyage to Balaclava, and François Bornet, a former Zouave who had been wounded at Inkerman. Soyer had employed Bornet to act as 'my aide-de-camp, écuyer, master of the horse, and shield, in case of blows'. Bornet and the twelve soldier-cooks, said Soyer proudly, 'composed the brigade of Captain Cook – a title I had assumed in the camp'. In fact Bornet was quite clearly a quarrelsome drunk and more trouble than he was worth, but Soyer, who could be a hopeless judge of character, was delighted with him and kitted him out in a special uniform to complement his own dazzling new quasi-military rig-out, which *The Times* lost no time in satirising in a mock-dialogue between 'John Bull' and an innocent onlooker.

'I beg your pardon, but who is that foreign officer in a white bournous and attended by a brilliant staff of generals – him with the blue and silver stripe down his trousers I mean, and gold braid on his waistcoat, and a red and white cap? It must be Pélissier?'

'That! why, that's Monsieur Soyer, *chef de nos batteries de cuisine*; and if you go and ask him, you'll find he'll talk to you for several hours about the way your meat is wasted. And so I wish you good morning, sir.'

Alexis and his now sizeable staff returned to the Crimea for the second phase of his culinary campaign. He arrived on the *Ottawa*, loaded with a dozen stoves, enthusiasm for the great task ahead, and a pile of letters and messages from Florence Nightingale, in advance of her own anticipated return a few weeks later. In fact much had changed in the short time he had been away, making it a melancholy return. Raglan was dead – the old man finally worn out by anxiety and diarrhoea – and so were a shockingly large number of other friends, while many useful contacts in senior positions had been replaced with newcomers from London. His entire network of connections would have to be rebuilt. 'It was like beginning my mission afresh,' he said, 'making it not only very painful as far as feelings went, but also difficult.' Yet the new officers generally turned out to be as sympathetic to his mission as their predecessors, and happy to let him continue his various schemes of improvement.

For example, before his departure Soyer had been unimpressed with the army's supply of dried vegetables, which, while expensive, were so overprocessed that they had lost any goodness or flavour. In addition, each vegetable was supplied separately in large cases, giving the men little variety, and as dry rations were issued every third day, the lack of understanding about how to rehydrate the food usually meant that the amateur cooks would toss their entire half-weekly supply into the canteen pan on the first night. Soyer therefore designed an ingenious 'vegetable cake', which mixed together a variety of finely chopped, ready seasoned vegetables, which were then dried in clearly marked sections, like a chocolate bar. Each cake comprised ten break-off sections of ten rations each, and could therefore serve a hundred men – perfect for use with one of his field stoves. He gave a lot of thought to the ideal texture of the mix, which he decided should be 'coarse julienne', and worked out that each hundredweight of fresh vegetables should consist of twenty pounds of carrots, turnips and cabbage, fifteen of onions, ten of parsnips and leeks, and five of celery. Added to this would be a pound of seasoning, which broke down as four ounces each of pepper, thyme and savory, two of bay leaf and one of cloves. Soyer had just convinced the commissary-general to order samples of these vegetable cakes from a specialist firm in Paris – in fact the company, Chollet, was based in Meaux-en-Brie, and so there was possibly a personal connection to it – when he left for Scutari. But on his return he was delighted to find that the new commissary-general, Sir George Maclean, had not only taken delivery of the precious samples, but already issued some to the troops, and was pleased to tell the chef that they were 'highly approved of'.

His other new invention was a rusk, or 'bread-biscuit' as he called it, made of three parts wheat flour and one part peasemeal, which was 'somewhat like common bread, but baked in flat cakes about twelve times the size of an ordinary biscuit; it would keep for months, and then eat well, though rather dry; it would soak well in tea, coffee, or soup, and be very palatable . . . and was reported upon by the medical gentlemen as being very nutritious and wholesome.' Essentially a softer version of the hard tack that for centuries had been issued to soldiers and sailors, what Soyer had come up with was, in theory, an invaluable breakthrough – as spongy, bleeding gums, a result of the ubiquitous scurvy (a problem as historic as the biscuits), made it impossible for many men to chew through the rock-hard biscuits unless they were first soaked for hours or smashed with a bayonet handle. Although the men were now getting decent bread in the Crimea, thanks to a new floating bakery called the *Abundance*, Soyer was well aware of the long-term potential of his softer bread-biscuits for the army, and he had date-stamped samples made up which he then used to lobby anyone important who crossed his path, in the hope that they would recommend their adoption to the War Office.

His targets included the Duke of Newcastle, who had visited the Barrack Hospital kitchens on a brief trip to Scutari and found Alexis, who was covering for Jullien, in the middle of making up hundreds of mock rice puddings. Soyer persuaded the duke to sample some three-month-old bread-biscuit which had been soaked in mutton broth for five minutes 'until it had the appearance of a piece of fresh bread'. Suitably impressed, Newcastle later wrote to Alexis that 'your philanthropic labours in this country deserve the thanks of every Englishman, and for one I am grateful for what I have seen of your good work at Scutari'. Soyer also managed to coax General Sir James Simpson, who had replaced Raglan as commander-in-chief, to sample the bread-biscuit at their first meeting. Simpson, who had bad teeth, was initially reluctant, but after taking a bite even he admitted it was softer and 'much more palatable than the common biscuit'. However, Soyer's bread-biscuit never got off the ground, possibly because his tests had not proved that it could be kept for as long as hard tack, which lasted years, or possibly because his energies were too widely dispersed for him to promote it vigorously enough. Perhaps, had he lived longer, the army would, in time, have adopted the Soyer biscuit along with the Soyer stove.

Simpson, rather surprisingly as he was known not to favour 'spoiling' the men, proved as amenable as Raglan, and immediately agreed to provide Soyer with tents and equipment for his staff, and to attend a Grand Opening of the first field kitchen, in which Soyer proposed to make a public trial of his field stoves before all the great and good of the army, before they were gradually introduced 'for the benefit of the army at large'. Such a demonstration was hardly necessary, but as usual Soyer could not resist putting on a show. Simpson suggested the Guards' camp in the First Division area as a suitable location to stage the event, and appointed Lieutenant Colonel Francis Seymour, commander of the Scots Fusilier Guards and formerly Prince Albert's aide-de-camp, as the military co-ordinator.

Seymour, an old Reform Club regular, clearly shared Soyer's sense of occasion and 27 August was selected as the most appropriate date, as Lord Stratford, attended by all the military top brass, was scheduled to be awarding several Orders of the Bath that morning, and would be able to move seamlessly from the formal ceremony to the lighter atmosphere of the Grand Opening. Soyer then selected a suitable spot to erect his field kitchen – in the central avenue between the Coldstreams and the Scots Fusiliers, and arranged for his stoves to be sent over the next morning by way of the new railway line from Balaclava. By the time Alexis himself arrived back in camp, he found to his delight that the stoves had not only been unloaded and unpacked, but that the Highland Brigade were already using them to cook their dinners.

Though I had given special orders that no one should meddle with them until I arrived, it gave me great pleasure to find that the men were using them to the best advantage and without instruction . . . Although I had not given them my receipts, they found they could cook their rations with more ease, and hoped they should soon have them for everyday use, instead of the small tin camp-kettles, and their open-air system of cooking.

Soon, several hundred invitations had been despatched to all the heads of the military and medical authorities, tents and marquees were pitched and decorated with evergreen garlands and bunting, the soldier-cooks perfectly drilled, and the large Soyer stoves arranged in a semi-circle around some tables and benches that a team of carpenters had knocked up especially for the occasion. The tables were dressed with white cloths and the soldiers' rough plates, mugs and cutlery, and the area enclosed within ropes attached to suitably laureled posts, to create the illusion of a proper outdoor dining room. On top of a large quantity of ration stock, Soyer had negotiated with the purveyor-in-chief and the butcher to have some extra fresh meat – in the form of the precious ox heads and feet that were usually thrown out. He also bought – presumably at his own expense – a quantity of ice, wines and champagne from one of his new cronies, a general dealer who had based himself in Kadikoi named Frederick Crockford (who had no connection to the famous club of the same name). He even organised some music, from the band of the Coldstream Guards – to provide a suitably martial accompaniment.

There were the usual hiccups. A day before the opening the carpenters ran off before the furniture was finished, having stolen all they could carry from the tents. Then Seymour was struck by a splinter of a shell in the back of the neck. Although the injury did not prove, as first feared, to be fatal, it meant that a number of personal invitations he was due to deliver were never sent out. However, the day dawned bright and sunny, and with the busy preparations for Lord Stratford's inspection there was an excitable, even festive mood permeating the camp. Soyer and his men spent the morning in a whirl of activity, transforming humble army rations into food fit for a 'great martial banquet *al fresco*'. The bill of fare consisted of 'plain boiled salt beef; ditto, with dumplings; plain boiled salt pork; ditto, with peas-pudding; stewed salt pork and beef, with rice; French pot-au-feu; stewed fresh beef, with potatoes; mutton, ditto, with haricot beans; ox-cheek and ox-feet soups; Scotch mutton-broth; common curry, made with fresh and salt beef'.

At three o'clock the first of several hundred of British, French and Sardinian guests began to wander in, and at four sharp the official reception began with the arrival of the allied commanders, General Simpson and Marshal Pélissier, and their respective staff, 'in a gorgeous cavalcade'. The band struck up the military 'Leaving for Syria', by then virtually the French national anthem, as a compliment to Pélissier, and Soyer, in his lavish hat and silver striped trousers looking almost as splendid as the generals in their full dress uniforms, moved into his element, first showing off the stoves by lifting off the lids with a flourish and demonstrating that even with the contents boiling away fiercely, no fire or steam was visible to attract enemy attention. He explained that the stoves being used were far bigger than the proper campaign ones that were on order, having been designed for hospital use, but the principles were the same. The generals then tried and highly approved of his various soups and *pot-au-feu* and, just to push the point home further, Alexis then led the generals over to the dirty old regimental kitchen, with its old-fashioned, built-in stone hearths and wasteful, smoking furnaces. 'Your excellency must agree with me that this day has been remarkably well spent,' Lieutenant General Henry Barnard joked with Pélissier, 'we devoted the morning to the *cordon rouge*, and the afternoon to the *cordon bleu.*'

The generals left at seven, but the remaining guests continued eating and drinking until nine, when the band closed the proceedings with 'God Save the Queen'. Although the press of people – Soyer estimated, perhaps optimistically, that between eight hundred and a thousand 'persons of distinction' had visited the makeshift banqueting hall during the day – had sometimes strained the resources even of his huge stoves, everyone had been fed, and the day was an undoubted triumph. 'He certainly made very nice ragouts and soups . . .' another friend, Captain Frederick Dallas of the 46th Foot, wrote home, 'but I fear it will be a very long time before we can do it for ourselves.' However, acknowledged Dallas, 'his dishes had the additional advantage of being washed down with iced Champagne'. Perhaps Soyer had deviated from his military rule of basic principles and utter simplicity to impress the generals, but three weeks later the *Illustrated London News* printed a detailed picture of the event, drawn by their war artist Robert Landells and captioned 'Opening of Soyer's Field Kitchen Before Sebastopol', which showed the chef, looking very dashing alongside the two generals, and was accompanied by the sort of report and guest list that made it sound like a London society event.

For the next few days, Soyer continued to bask in such elevated company. Lord Rokeby, Commander of the First Division, requested his recipe for *pot-au-feu*. Sir Edmund Lyons, Commander of the British Fleet, told him that having sorted out the soldiers so well, he should not neglect the sailors. He was invited to attend a meeting of the generals to discuss whether it would be possible to fulfil a directive of Lord Panmure's that every man in the trenches should be supplied with a basin of hot soup at night, in exchange for a reduction in his rum ration. The order from the War Office included the instruction that 'His lordship believing Monsieur Soyer to be still in the Crimea, requests the Board to inquire of him if such would be practicable'. Of course it would be possible, said Alexis, as soon as the four hundred new field stoves – the order for which had been agreed after the successful grand opening but, to his frustration, still not telegraphed to London – were up and running.

Less than a fortnight later, after bravely holding out against the allied forces for nearly a year, Sebastopol finally fell. The final bombardment had begun on 18 August, the day after the massacre at the Tchernaya River, and over the next few weeks the strength and ability of the Russians to keep on repairing their fortifications slowly ebbed away. The final assault took place on 8 September, with the French and British capturing the principal defences, first the Malakoff Tower and then eventually the Redan. Nearly 23,000 lives were lost on that one blood-soaked day, and when the last Russians evacuated the city via a hastily built pontoon bridge, they left little behind them but rubble and ruins. In the wake of the carnage Soyer helped out in the General Hospital, relieving the cooks who had been up all night, before rushing back to his camp kitchen to prepare huge quantities of lemonade, arrowroot, beef-tea, rice puddings and other easily digestible dishes for the wounded, which a dozen men then carried back to the hospitals. He later returned to the hospital, where he witnessed so many amputations that during the afternoon 'several buckets' were filled with the limbs.

By eight in the evening, when he had done all he could at the hospital, Alexis trudged back to the camp. 'The painful scenes I had witnessed weighed heavily upon the heart and mind, and a little relaxation became necessary.' This took the form of a dinner invitation from a few friends, but the meal was interrupted by the news that Sebastopol was in flames – the retreating Russians had set fire to their own city. Not one to miss out on an historic sight, Soyer and Mr Mesnil, his major domo, rushed through the darkness to view the flames and continuing explosions from the top of Cathcart's Hill, armed with a sword and a revolver. They stayed to watch the conflagration until two in the morning, when Soyer marked the occasion by penning a flowery description of the 'sublime and terrific' scene for the benefit of the press and public back home. The next morning, with Bornet in tow, he finally entered the city. Their first port of call was the Redan to view the devastation, but having been refused admission, the men sneaked round the back and clambered in another way. They then made for the Russian barracks, where the single-minded Soyer made straight for the kitchens and bakery. There they sampled the cabbage soup ('extremely bad and entirely deprived of nutritious qualities') and the black bread – until Soyer suddenly clutched his stomach and tried to look pitiful, telling Bornet that he was sure the food had been poisoned. The Zouave turned pale, 'putting his fingers in his throat in order to throw off the dreadful meal' – until Soyer laughed and called him a coward. Giggling like a couple of truanting kids, they carried off a number of 'culinary trophies', including a ladle, an iron fork and some black bread.

A week after his triumphant rush into Sebastopol, Alexis succumbed to an attack of the dreaded Crimean fever which had brought Florence Nightingale so close to death, and the after-effects of which she would not shake off for another twenty-five years. At first he thought his symptoms were simply the result of overtiredness, and went to bed without bothering to call a doctor, although his tent was hardly conducive to rest – after days of rain the canvas was wet through and the floor covered in mud. Soon though, it was apparent that he could 'neither lie, sit, nor stand, without great suffering' and a Dr Linton made the awful diagnosis. To begin with he seemed to rally well, and a few days later he was on his feet again, anxiously visiting the regimental hospitals where his cooks were now busy teaching the soldiers the basics of camp cookery. But the exertion brought on a second attack, far worse than the first, and the loyal Mr Mesnil was warned that this time it could prove fatal.

Alexis lay in bed for three weeks, bobbing in and out of consciousness and submitting, in all likelihood, to the same remedies and treatments that Nightingale had just endured, which included the placing of hot suction cups on his back to draw the inflammation from his lungs. The disease popularly referred to as Crimean fever was actually a form of brucellosis, a bacterial disease caught from livestock, which was usually transmitted from tainted meat or unpasteurised milk. It was also called remittent fever, because sufferers, like Nightingale and Soyer, would often appear to recover for a few hours during the day, only to relapse again in the evening. Symptoms included delusions, nervous irrit-ability, flushing, anaemia, insomnia, headaches, tremors, indigestion, palpitations, general debility and breathlessness. Once over the initial illness, sufferers appeared to age sharply, required a long period of convalescence, and were almost always left with rheumatism or sciatica. More cruelly still, as the parasite took months or even years to work its way through the body, patients could continue to suffer serious complications. Brucellosis could even have a serious impact on the sufferer's personality, and even previously sunny and optimistic people often became depressed, frustrated, irritable and emotionally unstable.

At the beginning of October, as Soyer lay in bed, Florence Nightingale, herself still white-faced and emaciated, had returned to the fray, weak but determined to carry on as before. During her stay in hospital she had learned that nothing was progressing in her absence – her enemies were still causing difficulties for her nurses, and some additional extra-diet kitchens she had asked Soyer to build had not even been started. On 19 October she wrote bitchily to her Aunt Mai: 'I hear Soyer is called humbug, because he leaves work half-done and goes to something else, while that goes to ruin, which is true.' It was not her first complaint about Soyer, but this accusation was deeply unfair, as Soyer was as subject to the frustrations of bureaucratic officialdom as she was. But at that point Nightingale, miserable, sick and frustrated at every turn, was in no mood to be generous. As soon as the crisis had passed and Soyer was back on his feet, 'so altered that scarcely anybody could recognise me', he dragged himself on a hospital tour with her, and the relationship, at least outwardly, remained cordial.

However, Alexis's doctor insisted that he too needed a period of convalescence in Constantinople, and a severely debilitated Soyer needed little persuasion to leave the increasingly harsh weather on the peninsula as the winter drew on. A few days before leaving, he managed to climb one of the steepest hills in the camp in order to say good-bye to a friend but, losing his bearings, found himself in the wrong tent. As he was clearly out of breath, the officer he had barged in on cordially offered him a seat and a sherry, and the men began to chat. In spite of his unique costume, the officer did not recognise the renowned chef, and writing up the encounter in a letter to the *Illustrated London News* some time later, described his unexpected guest as a 'tall, stout, rather handsome-looking man, aged about fifty years. He wore a drab-coloured "wide-awake" wrapped round with a red scarf, and a white blouse, heavily braided about the sleeves. His hair had been black, now rapidly changing into grey; and his whiskers, moustache, and beard (the latter primly cut), were of the same "Oxford mixture".' A few minutes later a Maltese servant appeared with dinner – undercooked beef and rock-hard potatoes – but when Alexis raised his eyebrows and began to offer some advice, the officer took umbrage, and declared that he usually supervised the servant, and could cook as well 'as any fellow in the Crimea, perhaps excepting Soyer; and some people say that he is a great humbug'. Nevertheless, Soyer quickly sliced the meat and potatoes, added onions and seasonings, and within a few minutes produced a dinner 'fit for Sardanapalus'.

'So you would not call Soyer a humbug to make this?'

'Soyer!' I said in disdain – 'Soyer never made or invented a dish half as good in his life! Talk about French slops in comparison with prime English beef and onions!'

. . . 'One more glass of sherry,' said the stranger, 'and then I go. I am very glad to have made your acquaintance, and I hope you will come and see me when you come down to Balaclava. I shall be on board the ship *Edward* in the bay . . . Come on board and ask for me.'

'With very great pleasure – and your name?'

'Oh! my name – *Soyer*,' said he; and he sat down and laughed until the tears stood in his eyes.

Soon afterwards Soyer left for Scutari, where he just managed to see his staff and visit his old contacts – who were all horrified by his haggard appearance – before his health collapsed again. The weather was now so wet and miserable that the noise, rats and draughts of Soyer House became unbearable, and as a servant had stolen all his furniture anyway, he crossed the river to Pera and took up lodgings in a decent hotel, planning to return to London as soon as he was sufficiently recovered. But his sufferings were soon heightened by such a severe attack of dysentery that it took another three months before he was well enough to travel anywhere. During those long weeks of sickness he learned that the next consignment of his stoves – fifty of the campaign size – were about to leave for the East, and although the war was virtually over, he decided that instead of going home he would make one last trip to the front, to ensure that the stoves were properly distributed and the soldier-cooks adequately trained to use them in their future postings. The doctors were not impressed with his decision – Dr Sutherland, the famous sanitary commissioner, tried to persuade him to recuperate in Malta, but Soyer told him he was determined to return to Russia. 'In that case,' said the doctor, 'don't forget to take your tombstone with you.'

In the end Soyer stayed in Constantinople until the end of the following March, having enjoyed a very sociable Christmas season, which included an invitation to a lavish fancy dress ball at the British Embassy where he drank so much that he was ill for days afterwards. He was also in Pera to celebrate the armistice, which was finally signed on 29 February at the Paris Peace Conference. With the hostilities at an end, at least he would be safe from enemy action in the Crimea, if not from sickness. He had been waiting to join the ship carrying the stoves, the *Cape of Good Hope*, when it stopped at Constantinople en route for the Crimea. In the end, to his intense frustration, the ship steamed right through the Bosporus and on to Balaclava without stopping, and he had to follow on a few days later in the *Ottawa*. He was able to take with him his civilian cooks as, to his delight, a military staff corps had finally been established in the hospitals, which was able to run his new catering system to his complete satisfaction.

He arrived back in Balaclava shortly after Florence Nightingale, and made her extra-diet kitchens – the subject of her spiteful comment to Aunt Mai – his first priority, ensuring that they were up and running within a week. He also made a point of meeting yet another new commander-in-chief, General Codrington, who had taken over as commander after the resignation of the much-criticised Simpson. Codrington was happy to allow Soyer to continue his training programme, on the basis that he would use only the stoves that had already arrived – there was no point shipping out more from England, when the troops would soon be going home, and so it was agreed that the remainder would be distributed among the regiments stationed at Aldershot barracks and elsewhere, and in British army camps abroad. Quite why, when four hundred stoves had been ordered by the War Office as long ago as October, the first batch had consisted of only forty or fifty units, is unclear – even a smallish company like Smith & Phillips should have been able to turn them out more quickly than that. However, with the stoves had come the son of one of the firm's partners and Soyer's closest friends, Charles Phillips junior. Phillips had travelled out to ensure the smooth implementation of the stoves, although Soyer stressed as a point of pride that he 'had nothing to do professionally as regards the repairing of the stoves'. Phillips proved, however, to be a courageous and resourceful companion, with a good sense of humour and an excellent singing voice, and happily followed Alexis around on his 'camp cruises' from regiment to regiment.

Soyer had quickly worked out an efficient *modus operandi*, whereby one stove was delivered to each of the regiments, and then moved about from company to company. A number of men from each company, including the colonel, were then given a lecture by Soyer himself on all aspects of using the stoves and preparing his simplified recipes for fifty men at a time, which were handed out on officially printed cards – the idea being that these men would not only disseminate the information to the rest of their company, but be able to pass it on wherever they were stationed. He also liaised with the divisional commissariat and regimental quartermasters to reform the distribution of the food – ensuring that rations were issued daily instead of every three days to stop the cycle of wastage followed by shortage, and so that preserved meats could be soaked properly prior to cooking, to ensure that all the salt was extracted. With more than forty regiments still in the camp this was not only a massive undertaking, but one that had to be seen through as quickly as possible, as the embarkation plan to get the troops home would be completed within two or three months, and Soyer was determined to have his system fully embedded in the army's routine before the soldiers were dispersed. He was on his horse between six and seven every morning, and rarely finished before nightfall, 'which, for a bad cavalier, was a great exertion, especially after so severe an illness'.

He was not too busy, however, to pick up his social life. With the signing of the peace treaty he happily made the most of the 'giving-parties mania' that had given the camp the appearance of a 'monster banqueting-hall'. Invitations flooded in from General this and Lord that, from captains, majors and colonels, 'to each and all of whom I cannot but feel grateful – not alone for their liberal welcome, but also for the honour of having been admitted to their friendship'. Real life must have felt suspended as he finally found himself on terms of genuine friendship with these eminent men. It was a situation that would never come again, and he relished every minute of it. He was quickly taken to the heart of the Fourth Division, in the middle of whose camp on Cathcart's Hill a large wooden hut had been built for him, which swiftly became known as Soyer's Villarette. Frederick Dallas, now ADC to the divisional commander, wrote home on 16 April that 'Alexis Soyer is living with our Division and is great fun. He dined with us last night. He is a most pleasant amusing man, and great friends with my Chief, with the power of whose stomach he is greatly struck. He has known and met such a variety of people, and tells his anecdotes so well, that he is capital company.'

Anxious to repay such glamorous hospitality, Alexis was no slouch at giving parties himself, 'which was of course expected from me, the Gastronomic Regenerator', and the first of several bank-breaking *petits diners* and *déjeuners à la fourchette* was attended by Lord William Paulet and no less than three generals, three colonels, two majors (including Dallas) and a number of captains. He took pains to decorate the table and fill his hut with wax candles, and provided an extraordinarily full and inventive bill of fare, which included turbot, lamb and chicken dishes, a *filet de boeuf piqué mariné, sauce poivrade*, a mayonnaise *à la Russe*, garnished with caviar, plum puddings, lemon ices and a magnificent dessert, which he called *La bombe glacé à la Sebastopol*. It was a great success, and 'I shall probably never again have the honour of entertaining such a distinguished circle under similar circumstances,' he acknowledged afterwards. He was also called upon to assist with a large number of official banquets, including a grand luncheon in honour of the defeated Russian commander, General Alexander Lüders, which was to accompany a review of the entire allied armies. With less than a day's notice, Soyer managed to assemble a concoction as ludicrously opulent as the hundred guinea dish at Exeter – a sort of vast pickled *fruits de mer* – which was so large it could not be contained in the biggest dish available and he had to improvise with the lid of a field stove, which was then carried to the table by two soldiers. Lavishly titled the *Macédoine Lüdersienne à l'Alexandre II*, the list of ingredients showed what an extraordinary range of delicacies could now be rustled up in the post-war Crimea.

SOYER'S CULINARY EMBLEM OF PEACE
The Macédoine Lüdersienne à l'Alexandre II

This monster dish was composed of –
12 boxes of preserved lobsters
2 cases of preserved lampreys
2 cases of preserved sardines
2 bottles of preserved anchovies
1 case of preserved caviar
1 case of preserved sturgeon
1 case of preserved tunny
2 cases of preserved oysters
1 pound of fresh prawns
4 pounds turbot clouté
12 Russian pickled cucumbers
4 bottles pickled olives

1 bottle mixed pickles
1 bottle Indian ditto
1 bottle pickled French beans
2 bottles pickled mushrooms
Half bottle pickled mangoes
2 bottles of pickled French truffles
2 cases of preserved peas
2 cases of preserved mixed vegetables
4 dozen cabbage lettuces
100 eggs
2 bottles of preserved cockscombs

Each eminent diner, he was delighted to report, tucked into his novel *Lüdersienne* twice – and when Marshal Pélissier jokingly chided him for not having stoned the olives, he retorted that, 'It is all very well for you to take the Malakhoff in a few minutes, but it took me four hours to make that dish.'

But the highlight of this social round was his own grand dinner party and concert, held on 27 May as a fond farewell to the departing Fourth Division, when no trouble or expense was spared in his determination to make it one of the most memorable nights of the post-war festivities. As usual, Soyer paid as much attention to the décor as the cooking, and in the run-up to the party his hut was strewn inside and out with so many evergreens and wild flowers shipped in from surrounding valleys that the area looked like a bizarrely fertile oasis on the otherwise vegetation-free plateau around Cathcart's Hill. Flags and paper lanterns were embedded in the foliage, and the newly laid turf, which had immediately shrivelled in the sun, was returned to its original glory with the aid of a pot of opal green paint borrowed from the army theatre. Outside, the hut was lit by hired round glass lamps fuelled with ration fat, which hung across the doorway and along the roof, while the inside was filled with wax candles and a makeshift chandelier, specially made by Charles Phillips.

At the appointed hour fifty invited guests managed to squeeze into the villarette, to the sound of the band of the Rifles, who played glees, polkas and quadrilles, until the musical highlight of the evening – a concert by the Crimean Madrigal Club. Afterwards came the supper, accompanied by the endless 'pop pop of the confined corks'. Among the surprise offerings was a dish called *Soyer's Tally-ho Pie, or the Contrast of War and Peace*. When the crust was removed a pet fox cub leapt out 'and commenced to play about the room', although, as one eye-witness later wrote for the *Weekly Dispatch*, 'what the contrast was one could not so well see; perhaps there were enigmatical bellicose devices on the pastry'. Towards midnight, the speeches were led by Lord Rokeby, the unofficial chairman, who, according the *The Times*, 'proposed M. Soyer's health, and passed a high eulogium on the services he had rendered to the army by his exertions to promote good cooking and the use of palatable food'. Soyer naturally returned the thanks 'with propriety and feeling', and the festivities almost came to a dramatic end when a paper lantern caught fire and the flames quickly spread across the roof – but a young officer hoisted himself up to the beams and managed to extinguish it. The band resumed, and Alexis produced his special punch – *Crimean Cup à la Marmora* – a lethal blend of iced champagne, cognac, Jamaica rum, maraschino, orgeat syrup, soda water, sugar and lemons.

At two o'clock Lord Rokeby and the generals left, leaving Soyer to launch into his comic song repertoire, to the amusement of a sizeable crowd which had now gathered outside, and the last guests eventually staggered home at 5 a.m. *The Times*, no doubt basing its intelligence on Soyer's own report of the evening, declared the event 'a triumph of culinary art over Crimean resources', before listing the impressive list of distinguished guests. Two days later Frederick Dallas wrote: 'We had a wonderful Soirée a few nights ago at old Soyer's . . . as you may imagine, Soyer is a most popular man and gets on with everybody.' He was, however, less impressed with Russell, who sang some amusing songs, but nevertheless remained a 'vulgar Irishman'.

Alexis was to stay on in the Crimea until the bitter end, making sure that his precious stoves were kept moving to the right destinations – and were kept out of the clutches of the 'marauding Tartars' who were busily looting the rapidly emptying camps – and drilling as many soldiers as possible in the Soyer system, so that his commonsense methods would have a life in the army that extended well beyond the limits of the current campaign. Ever the tourist, he managed to fit in some sightseeing – he revisited the ruins of Sebastopol with Charles Phillips, where a live shell went off just yards from his horse, and joined a pleasure cruise to Yalta, which also nearly ended in disaster when a big wave pushed away his small boat just as he was trying to board the steamer and left him dangling by a rope in the middle of Balaclava harbour. A more successful expedition was a week's visit to Odessa in the middle of June with a few friends, including Crockford and Russell. He stayed at the plush Europa Hotel, and visited a military hospital and an orphanage before writing a long report to *The Times* about the food served in each establishment, and on the huge amount of crayfish and caviar consumed by the Russian population.

Returning from Odessa, Soyer learned that his staff and possessions had been moved into a ward in the now empty General Hospital, the authorities having decided that the deserted camp was too dangerous to stay in. Russell was less lucky – he found that although his house had been pulled down, like many other buildings, to stop them falling into Russian hands, nothing else had been provided for him. 'What do you think?' he wrote in a plaintive note to 'My dear Monsieur Soyer'. 'I am now a houseless, homeless wanderer: they have pulled down my house, so it is really time for me to evacuate the Crimea. The shell of the house only stands; and as I am not a lobster or an oyster, that will scarcely give me shelter . . .'

Although they often dined together – being excellent singers and raconteurs they were in great demand at social gatherings – Russell's attitude to Soyer, like many others, was a double-edged one. In spite of outward displays of bonhomie, Russell was often privately contemptuous of Soyer, who was not, he felt, a gentleman. Shortly after his arrival Russell had written to Delane at *The Times*, 'Soyer is here eating whatever he can get and obstinately deaf to all hints that he ought to come in time to cook the dinner.' Russell was clearly unwilling to recognise Soyer's wider function in the Crimea, instead deliberately relegating him to the role of greedy, lazy servant. It did not help that Soyer fancied himself as a bit of a journalist, sending Delane a stream of pompous letters and rambling eye-witness accounts which Russell's boss was delighted to publish. When, in one of his later despatches, Russell slipped in a catty comment that it was a shame the field stoves could neither bake or roast, Soyer, stung, shot back a letter to the effect that they could – he had thought of a way of adding an oven and a steamer, which would give the men more variety when in barracks, but it had not been appropriate to have such accessories in the Crimea, where the priority had been to teach the men to boil and stew simple dishes.

Soyer's final trial was in front of Codrington and the last remaining grandees, when he ably demonstrated that two newly trained soldier-cooks from the 56th Foot could cook a palatable meal for the entire regiment of six hundred men on their own, from ration stock only, using a dozen stoves and very little fuel. His system worked perfectly, and he came away, as usual, with a clutch of positive testimonials. The generals were particularly impressed with the statistics Soyer had compiled for the saving of fuel if the entire army cooked exclusively with his stoves. Soyer had worked out that a regiment of eight companies would make a huge daily saving of 3,600 pounds of wood, 'independent of the economy of transport, mules, labour etc'. That meant that in an army of 40,000 men, the government would save the cost of a stupendous 32,850 tons of wood a year. Within a few days the Fourth Division had left, and soon afterwards all that remained of the army were two Scottish regiments at Kamara, the Land Transport Corps, and part of the 56th Regiment at headquarters, which was serving as Codrington's bodyguard. Balaclava was dismal, and the empty, ghostly camp depressing and increasingly dangerous. Soyer himself was only waiting for the Land Transport and General Hospitals to close, so that his field stoves could be packed up and returned to England, for 'not only was I responsible for them, but I had to give my official report to Sir William Codrington, and close the mission entrusted to me by the British Government'.

Florence Nightingale had already gone, and although Mary Seacole, who had stayed through thick and thin for a year and a half, still remained, selling a few provisions to the last soldiers in Balaclava, the British Hotel had been pulled down. Seacole also had mixed feelings about the end of the war. She was glad to hear of peace, but she also knew that it meant financial disaster, as her capital had been sunk into supplies that were now virtually unsaleable, and in the end she had even taken a hammer and smashed up her caskets of wine to save them falling into Russian hands. More importantly, she sensed, like Soyer, that this was the end of her finest work. Both were leaving the Crimea for an uncertain future, and perhaps that explained why both, though claiming to be desperate to leave, in fact hung on to the very end.

Soyer finally left the Crimea for Constantinople on 10 July, on the steamship *Argo*, along with his souvenirs and trophies, which included a Russian officer's tent looted by Bornet from Sebastopol, a wounded horse called Inkerman, bought from Dr Hall's French manservant, and Florence Nightingale's carriage, which, after a long search, he had found among a pile of discarded carts, wagons and harnesses that were about to be auctioned to the locals. He bought it as 'a precious relic for present and future generations', and during the Black Sea crossing Robert Landells sketched it for an August edition of the *Illustrated London News*.

The day before sailing, Soyer embarked on one last 'solitary pilgrimage' around Balaclava and the ruined buildings, stables, huts and sheds that still littered the countryside – the burned out detritus of a departed army. He mounted his horse at six in the morning, armed with sandwiches, a bottle of brandy-and-water and a loaded revolver, and spent the next fifteen hours in a melancholy ramble around the deserted camp. He visited the hospitals, the trenches, the cavalry stables and the former British headquarters, now all empty, and the valleys and plains where the great battles had been played out. He passed a total of thirty-seven separate cemeteries, saw the ruins of Mary Seacole's hotel, and stood for the last time on the top of Cathcart's Hill, staring at the ruins of Sebastopol. Soyer's Villarette, 'though dilapidated, still remained', as did Florence Nightingale's hut near the Sanatorium, where he found some sticks of furniture, 'no end of waste paper' and the wooden stool on which she used to sit – and of course took that as a trophy too.

His last day was fine but windy, and at noon, along with Mary Seacole and a small group of spectators, he watched the official handover of Balaclava back to the Russians. But by the time they were ready to board the *Argo* the weather had changed to violent rain, and travelling from his quarters in the General Hospital to the ship, Soyer did not pass a soul. 'Nobody was out,' he wrote, as he described his approach to the harbour for the very last time, 'but myself, my horse, and my umbrella.'

15

'He has no successor'

In her autobiography Mary Seacole wrote that she did not return to England by the most direct route, 'but took the opportunity of seeing more of men and manners in yet other lands'. Alexis was equally disinclined to rush home. So when the *Argo* left the Bosporus for Southampton, Soyer was not on board, having, he said, made up his mind to take six months' holiday, 'and travel wherever my fancy might lead me'. In fact it would be nearer ten months before he reached London, and he had quite specific plans of what to do with his time. This included further research into Turkish cuisine, which he admired hugely, and planned to publish in a large international cookbook. He had even thought of a title for it – *The Culinary Wonders of all Nations* – and roughly mapped out the contents, which would include some of his English recipes, plus material gathered in Russia and the other countries he hoped to visit on his meandering route home – Greece, Malta, Italy and Germany. The rest of the book he would, he thought, pad out with a few borrowed recipes from the rest of Europe, America and Asia. He also intended to spent several months in Paris, where he could write up his memoirs of the war in peace – no easy job as he had lost the notes, or 'daily tablet' that he had assiduously kept for the past two years. While in the capital he also planned a sentimental visit to Meaux, probably for the first time since he had taken Emma to visit his mother, although by 1856 all his family had either died or moved away. Most importantly, knowing that she would be in Paris that spring, having finished her final tour, he hoped to woo Fanny once again. And with her dancing days all but over and Bedmar still with his wife, he was optimistic of success.

Soyer spent the rest of July, the whole of August and much of

September at the Hôtel d'Angleterre in Constantinople. Shortly after his arrival the Scutari hospitals had finally closed, and he had been able to gather a last batch of testimonials from the medical authorities, including a treasured one from Florence Nightingale. He had written to her on 26 July, a long flowery letter of thanks for the 'constant interest' she had shown in his culinary mission in the East and to express – yet again – his unquenchable admiration for her.

> Fourteen months have passed since I first had the honour of being introduced to you; I did not dream, when I left Albion's shores thinking only that I might help out for a few weeks at the Scutari hospital . . . that together we would view the end of this gigantic drama, which buried not just Europe but almost the entire world . . . In the midst of incessant fatigue and terrible illness, God led your virgin banner through great danger to a noble conclusion, for which your Fatherland will never cease to thank you and in spite of your small-minded – very small-minded – enemies . . .

The following day he wrote again, enclosing the translation of a Russian Orthodox service Nightingale wanted engraved on a memorial she was planning to raise at Balaclava, but this time he ended his letter with a grovelling postscript. 'A few words from you expressing your candid opinion of the humble services I have been able to render to the Hospitals would infinitely oblige your very humble servant.' And of course Nightingale did oblige, with a reply that spoke of Soyer's 'very essential usefulness' as he 'restored order where all was unavoidable confusion . . . [and] took the soldiers' rations and patients' diets as they were, and converted them into wholesome and agreeable food'. As for his stoves, 'I have tried [them] in the Crimean hospitals where I have been employed, and found them answer every purpose of economy and efficiency.' It was almost tragic that Soyer, even at the end of the war, felt such a compulsive need to keep soliciting these puffs. He had proved his value over and over again, his ingenuity and his public spirit had made him one of the most famous men in England; there was absolutely no need for him to keep accruing more and more of these stilted references. He may have resented being treated like a servant by Russell and others, but it was hardly surprising when he seemed unable to stop behaving like one.

With the hospitals closed, Soyer was entirely free to socialise and take in the sights he had been too busy to see before. He hired a dragoman and, although his health was still fragile, rushed around town visiting all the mosques, bazaars and palaces that they could cram in. He began his investigation into Turkish cuisine, and regaled readers of *The Times* with his discoveries of these strange new foods – oyster pilaff, stewed aubergines, stuffed dolmas and 'the monster and delicious kebab'. Although the rest of his staff had been despatched back to London along with Charles Phillips (whose next child would be christened Alexis Soyer Phillips), he was accompanied on these tours by his latest acquisition – a destitute Russian orphan of about twelve years of age called Daniel Chimachenka, a stowaway on the *Argo* who, on being discovered, had pleaded to be taken into service after being ill-treated in his home village. Soyer took pity on him, had him cleaned and dressed in a new livery *à la Russe*, and kept him as a valet. It is not known what happened to Daniel, but Soyer promised to take him back to London, where he said he would educate him, 'and hope he will turn out a good man of business and useful to society'.

Just before leaving Constantinople he gained, through Lord Stratford, a brief audience with the Sultan in the magnificent new marble palace of Dolma Batchi, and presented him with a complete set of his books and various stoves. He also revisited Scutari Hospital, now reverted to a Turkish barracks and housing four thousand of the Imperial Guard, and noted that while few changes had been made in the vast kitchen, where the cooks were preparing an excellent pilaff, the floor was rather dirty. From Constantinople he travelled through Greece to Malta, and from there through Italy to Germany. He finished this section of his culinary 'grand tour' in Strasbourg, and from there travelled to Marseilles, where he arrived at the beginning of February. At some point he had hooked up with the Pera-based photographer James Robertson, who had taken over coverage of the war from Roger Fenton the previous year, and in Marseilles Soyer took Robertson to the Hôtel de la Réserve for another feast of excellent *bouillabaisse*. From Marseilles he retraced his steps to Lyons, and then on to Paris, which he had last seen on his journey out more than two years earlier, and his long hoped-for reunion with Fanny.

Now approaching forty, Cerrito had not relinquished her career lightly. In fact at the end of 1855, when Alexis had been laid up in Constantinople with Crimean fever and dysentery, Fanny had also been busy in the East, at the Bolshoi Theatre in St Petersburg, showcasing a new ballet called *Armida*, as even the war had not stopped the movement of theatre and ballet troupes between the countries. But nowadays the receptions were a little cooler and the critics tempered their praise with reservations about her age and stamina. 'She is indeed an exceptional dancer,' said the correspondent of the St Petersburg newspaper, the *Severnaya Pchela*, before comparing her to Taglioni and Elssler. 'Neither of the first two dancers were in their early youth when they arrived here, and the same may be said of Cerrito, although she has retained more of her beauty and freshness than they.' Nevertheless she persevered. The following summer she appeared in *Eva* at the Lyceum in London – Covent Garden's temporary home since its theatre had burned down that March – and in the autumn returned to Russia, to dance at the coronation celebrations of Alexander II in Moscow. In October she appeared in *La Fille de Marbre* – a retitled version of *Alma*, a role she had created fourteen years earlier when 'Cerrito-mania' was at its height. At the end of the ballet a trapdoor failed to open and some scenery and ropes fell on top of her, throwing her to the ground and setting her costume alight. Fortunately, help was close enough to extinguish the flames before she was burned, but her shoulder was badly bruised and the incident left her deeply shocked. She managed to complete her Russian engagements and left Moscow for home at the end of February – just as Alexis was arriving in Paris to greet her.

It seems that Fanny and Alexis lived comfortably together with three-year-old Matilde in Paris for the next three months. Alexis did visit Meaux, but there were too few reminders of his childhood to keep him there for long. Instead he spent his days working on the manuscript that would become his final book, *A Culinary Campaign*. He had an audience with Napoleon III at the Château des Tuileries, and again demonstrated his model field stove. The emperor was impressed enough to ask him to send a full-size version from England, 'to serve as a model for his army', and commissioned him to inspect and submit a report on the network of Parisian soup kitchens, which were subsidised by the French government.

Most importantly, more than a dozen years after their first meeting, he finally persuaded Fanny to marry him. There are no surviving documents to prove where or when the union took place, only a briefest mention of their names in a local Paris newspaper, but it seems the couple went through a sort of private marriage ceremony or blessing, along the lines of an English Fleet wedding, where money was taken and vows exchanged, with few questions asked. Afterwards, their relationship continued – as it had done before – in the strictest secrecy. Even if any residual doubts Fanny may have entertained about marrying a cook, albeit a famous one (and after all, her father was still alive), had subsided, she was still legally married to St-Léon, although she had not seen him for years. The scandal that would be courted should it be known that this famous couple had formed a bigamous alliance was absolutely unthinkable. Neither was Fanny prepared to risk a breach with Bedmar, who firmly believed that Matilde was his daughter, provided for her handsomely, and was still, at that time, seeking a legal route to legitimise her. On the certificate the couple gave their address as a hotel on the Rue de l'Arc de Triomphe – Fanny's house had been occupied by her brother during her travels, and anyway she could hardly take her new husband there.

Extraordinarily, the couple did manage to keep this change in their circumstances a secret, and when Alexis finally returned to England in the first week of May 1857, Fanny discreetly followed on a day later. She had a professional reason for travelling to London – her farewell performance was to be held that week at the Lyceum, where she played the title role of *La Brésilienne* in a new ballet. She did dance once more – a minuet in the opera *Don Giovanni* on 18 June, but no fuss was made over this last appearance, and she finally retired from the stage without any fanfare, in future dividing her time between Alexis and Matilde, and London and Paris.

In contrast to Fanny's low-key retirement, Soyer came home to a warm reception from his old friends. Dinners were given for him, and he was regularly greeted in the street by appreciative veterans. At the end of June he submitted his accounts to the War Office, which had agreed to pay his expenses. These had mounted up – payments to his private secretary alone had cost £20 a month, the cooks' salaries had come to £150, and the 'Outfit, Hotel Expenses, Travelling Expenses for himself and staff' had come in at a whopping £309. 8s. 6d. These and his other outgoings were eventually rubber-stamped by the various financial departments, although one civil servant understandably queried the hire of a 'Confidential Agent' (£2. 10s. per week) as 'rather a questionable item'. It would have been churlish to contest such sums in the light of Alexis's contribution to the war effort, however, and the nature of this confidential agent was not raised with him. On the contrary, Lord Panmure approved a suggestion that Soyer should be paid, in addition to his expenses, at the rate of 27 shillings a day (£500 a year) for the period of his service, plus 'a gratuity of six months pay on termination of his Mission'. Although Soyer had set out declaring that he would take no salary for his services, the length and arduousness of the work had clearly changed his mind. Panmure's generous formula amounted to quite a windfall – £500 represented the salary of a colonel – but to Soyer it meant far more than cash; it represented the gratitude of the establishment, and confirmation that he would never be thought of as an employee again, but as a respected member of society and an acknowledged expert in his field.

Perhaps to reflect his new status, Alexis rented a house in Kensington Square, and began looking for a house to buy. Eventually he settled on one in Marlborough Road, St John's Wood, the quiet, leafy suburb he had grown to love during his many visits to the Bakers, and whose well-run household had provided the inspiration for Hortense in *The Modern Housewife*. At forty-seven it was a reflection of his increasing age and respectability – not to mention his new, if unconventional, family ties – that he now preferred a solid, expensive suburban villa to a raffish rented apartment in the centre of town. It was also a restful environment, for his health had not recovered from the Crimean fever as well as he had hoped. He did seek medical advice – in fact he took to consulting several doctors a day, and 'many were the occasions that certain hours were fixed for their seeing him, so that they should be prevented from coming into contact; and the nostrums of the outgoing doctor would be put out of sight, so as not to offend the eyes of the incomer'. Yet ultimately he ignored all of them – particularly the regular injunction to rest. He was still weak and losing weight, and a liver complaint brought on by the brucellosis, and no doubt aggravated by a lifetime of heavy drinking, also made the doctors urge him to give up alcohol – a recommendation that he also ignored.

Instead, he arranged a party for a group of friends at his beloved Virginia Water. However, that day his horse appeared unusually restless, and he was advised to dismount and take the train. Feeling up to the ride, and unwilling to make any concessions to his health, Soyer insisted on riding, but got no further than Holland Park when the horse bolted, and instead of his being thrown clear, one of his feet got caught in the stirrups and he was dragged halfway down Kensington Road before somebody managed to stop the horse and rescue him. Miraculously, no bones had been broken, but the shock to his fragile constitution was profound. He even insisted on continuing to Virginia Water in a hansom cab, so as not to disappoint his friends, and arrived at the Wheatsheaf shaken and bruised, with his clothes in shreds. It took weeks to get over the accident, and just as he was recovering he received another shock – his niece Augusta, Philippe's eldest daughter, had died in childbirth at the age of just twenty-three. Deeply distressed, Soyer arranged for her to be buried near to Emma in Kensal Green cemetery.

In spite of all setbacks, he continued to work. Putting his knowledge of

Eastern cookery to good use, he created his final and most exotic new product, Soyer's Sultana's Sauce. It was, he wrote to John Delane at *The Times*, a concoction of 'various Turkish herbs and condiments' and he enclosed a sample. Produced by Crosse & Blackwell, the sauce was packaged in an elegant long bottle with the decoratively frilled label bearing the now decidedly out of date portrait painted by Emma all those years ago. As with his other industrial sauces, the Sultana's Sauce promised to fulfil a multiplicity of functions – 'a small quantity will suffice to give a most exquisite relish to . . . Meat, Hashes, Stews, Chops, Steaks, Fish, Soups, Poultry, and above all, Salads', ran the first advertisement. Again, the press approved. 'Savoury, Piquant and Spicy, worthy the genius of Soyer,' was the view from *The Observer*, while *The Lancet* decided that the relish 'affords considerable aid in cases of slow and weak digestion'. The sauce also sold well in America.

Most of Alexis's efforts, however, went into the completion of his Eastern memoir, and in the autumn of 1857 *A Culinary Campaign, being Historical Reminiscences of the late War, with the Plain Art of cookery for Military and Civil Institutions, the Army, Navy, Public, etc*, was finally published by Routledge in England and America. The reception was generally positive. All the reviewers respected Soyer's immense contribution to the war effort, but some found his long-winded anecdotes, incessant name-dropping and self-congratulatory tone difficult to take. 'M Soyer magnifies his office,' said the *North American Review* bluntly. 'Yet this very inordinate vanity . . . this singular simplicity of egotism, makes the Crimean cook-book vastly amusing . . . The anecdotes are flat, and the attempts at wit are appalling; yet, somehow or other, we get from the volume a better picture of the gay and convivial life of the camp, than we find even in the brilliant sketches of Russell.' Even *The Times*, having detailed his mission in such detail over the past two years, poked fun at the way 'Alexis the Succulent' was, if nothing else, 'a consistent personage, except where, possibly from his wanting a little medicine, he forgets for a moment that he is the centre of creation'. Although *A Culinary Campaign* received more coverage than most of the Crimean memoirs that were flooding the market, the public appetite for such books was quickly sated and sales were disappointing.

Early in 1858 – as if to cement his new status as a distinguished authority – Alexis was invited by the council of the United Service Institution in Whitehall to give a public lecture on the subject of military and naval cookery. It took place on 18 March with Lord Rokeby in the chair, and the hall was packed with high-ranking officers, including

General Codrington. Soyer turned out to be a brilliant speaker, expounding wittily and at length on his Crimean experiences, then describing his new design for a 'travelling cooking carriage' for an army on the march (a variation on the travelling soup kitchen he had designed during the Irish famine), before finishing, as a parting gesture, by producing some soup and omelettes from a field stove for the consumption of the grateful audience. 'This being the first occasion on which M. Soyer has appeared as a lecturer before the public we cannot but congratulate him . . .' wrote a reporter from *The Times*. 'We understand that M. Soyer regards this only as a preliminary lecture, and contemplates extending to the public at large, by the same means, the benefit of his experience in the highly useful and interesting branch of art to the study of which he has devoted 40 years of his life.' Unfortunately, with only five months to live, Alexis was never able to repeat this success.

Those months, in spite of his failing health, were among the busiest of his life. He was appointed to the committee to decide on the final specification for a military cooking wagon, and was delighted, if not exactly surprised, to see his design formally adopted and sent to the army's carriage department at Woolwich for development. He was also approached by the Emigration Commission to devise a better system of cookery for those travelling abroad on government-assisted passages. Anyone undertaking a lengthy voyage to seek a new life abroad was, almost by definition, going to be dependent on the daily salt meat rations, which were similar to those issued in the army. Soyer produced a small pamphlet of new recipes and recommendations, which included the suggestion that food should be prepared in messes of eight people, each group being issued with a Scutari kettle and a baking-stewing pan.

He was also invited to formalise his diets for military hospitals, and with the help of his old friend George Warriner, who was now running his own hotel in Wakefield, he produced a comprehensive booklet, *Instructions to Military Hospital Cooks, in the Preparation of Diets for Sick Soldiers*, which by 1860 had became standard issue. His last public project found him collaborating with Florence Nightingale once again. In October 1857 Nightingale had been appointed to the Barracks and Hospitals Sub-Commission, charged with improving the accommodation and diet of the ordinary soldier. After recommending the immediate adoption of Soyer stoves in every regiment, Nightingale invited Soyer to help devise a system for training military and hospital cooks, to create a comprehensive series of army recipes, and to draw up a new 'model' kitchen, to be installed at the Wellington Barracks in Birdcage Walk, the home of the

Coldstream Guards, and later at the naval headquarters at Chatham. Soyer was thrilled to be asked for his practical expertise, but with his health deteriorating further – by now he was spitting blood on a daily basis – he found himself deferring to Nightingale's increasingly bossy interventions. The captain overseeing the Birdcage Walk kitchen was a Douglas Galton, and Nightingale wrote to him impatiently.

> Dr Sutherland desired I would further the kitchen plan for the Wellington Barracks, for which, it appears, you are waiting. So I sent up to Soyer, who is ill, for it, found it was done, sent it (with temporary directions) to Smith and Phillips in Skinner Street, and expect it back today at Soyer's. Soyer wishes it to be looked at here first . . . and appoints Monday. I do not know his reason for not going at once to the place where it is to be put up. But I think that if you could find any hour between one and four on Monday, it would be as well to do as he wishes. Soyer gives up about the men dining in the kitchen, and admits that it is undesirable.

It is probably thanks to Nightingale that the model kitchen was completed before Soyer became too ill to see his plans come to fruition. He did, however, manage to attend the official opening on the morning of 28 July and demonstrate his new stove, which could, reported the *Illustrated London News*, 'roast, bake, broil, fry, boil and stew', and was equally capable of cooking 'a dinner either for one man or a battalion'. The *Morning Chronicle* described the stove as 'three or four unpretending looking cylinders', but from it, the master chef was able to produce a stream of superbly tasty dishes from ordinary rations – pea soup, salt pork with cabbage, stewed beef and dumplings, roast mutton and potatoes, fried liver and bacon, rice pudding. The authorities were suitably impressed. The drawing that accompanied the piece in the *Illustrated London News* shows a robust-looking man in the prime of life, but in fact it was to be Soyer's last public appearance.

His health was now failing fast, although he refused to rest, 'but ran on in a mad career of gaiety'. In his weakened state he had never fully recovered from the fall from his horse, he was still spitting blood and losing weight, and it seems that he had episodes of furious rage followed by manic, almost frenzied energy. During these episodes one friend described how he would rush around the kitchen, shouting at the servants for their carelessness, 'then he would dive into stew-pans and kettles; and drink that which he should not have drunk, namely, wine;

and then would he go to bed and feel so much exhausted, and the next morning complain of so much weakness, that the doctor was sent for, and the usual remedies applied; and so was Soyer patched up, and thus matters went on until his death.' One explanation for these periods of mental distraction could certainly be explained away by drunkenness – and Alexis was certainly still drinking far too much. But Soyer had been a heavy drinker since his teens, and it had never before made him vicious to his servants or behave in such an uncharacteristic way. His behaviour could also be seen as consistent with the Crimean fever, or brucellosis, with its headaches and nervous irritability, and which – as we now know – could change the very personality of the sufferer from that of a genial optimist to a delusional depressive.

On Monday 2 August, Soyer visited the rebuilt Crystal Palace at Sydenham, to see a fine arts exhibition featuring some of Emma's paintings that he had provided on loan for the event. He booked himself a room at the Paxton Hotel in Norwood for a few nights, which was owned by a friend and within easy walking distance to the Palace. The outing tired him, but he seemed to rally the following morning, and invited some friends down to join him for dinner the next day. However, as the evening progressed his condition declined sharply; instead of spitting blood he began to vomit a black discharge.

At eight o'clock it was decided that he should be rushed home, to his own bed and his own doctor. Loyal, stable Charles Pierce, the former Chirk Castle steward who had been his closest friend for twenty years, struggled to get him back to St John's Wood in a cab, where a few hours later he sank into a coma. He lingered on for another two days, attended by Pierce and his old friend Charles Phillips, his secretary James Warren, and his housekeeper Sophia Cooke. Where Fanny was throughout this final crisis is not known – perhaps she was in Paris, or perhaps discretion kept her out of the few accounts of Soyer's last hours. He died without regaining consciousness at 9.42 p.m. on the evening of 5 August 1858, and the doctor officially recorded the cause of death as melaena (a stomach ulcer) and serious apoplexy (a stroke). He was forty-eight years old.

Despite the presence and assistance of his closest friends during his last illness, things seem to have fallen apart after his death, and his affairs were strangely neglected. It fell to a maid, Sarah Sales, to report the death five days later. As she was illiterate the certificate is signed with a cross. Sales clearly had not known much about her late employer or his work, for she wrongly had his age entered as fifty, and for his occupation hazarded the noncommittal phrase, 'formerly a cook'. In material terms, Alexis left virtually nothing behind. After a lifetime of fortunes won and fortunes squandered, his goods and property were valued at less than £1,500. His will left a number of Emma's paintings to the National Gallery, and a few to Edmund Crosse and Thomas Blackwell; a small legacy to his housekeeper, Sophia Cooke; and a few other minor bequests. Neither Fanny nor Jean were mentioned, but in any event it seems that none of his wishes was respected. Four months after his death David Hart succeeded in annexing the will, on the basis that Alexis still owed him more than his net worth. His executors, Edmund Crosse and Sophia Cooke, failed to challenge the process, and Hart was awarded all of Soyer's possessions, from his precious paintings to his personal papers, which thereafter vanished into thin air as completely as if their owner had never existed.

The funeral, held the following Wednesday at Kensal Green cemetery, was equally botched. There was a decent enough crowd, but half of the expected mourners were missing due to a last-minute change from an afternoon to a morning service. Many of Alexis's extended family were either not aware of the date or failed to make it – Simonau attended, and Newton Jones, Emma's brother, but only Philippe's son, Alexis, was there to represent the Soyers. It seems Jean Lamain was not even informed of his father's death. Otherwise the crowd was made up of old friends, the two Charles Phillips, Charles Pierce, George Warriner and Lomax. Volant turned up, as did the artist Henry George Hine, who had only recently finished illustrating *A Culinary Campaign*. A number of fellow chefs put in an appearance, including Rocco Vido from the British Embassy in Constantinople, and former suppliers, like the grocer Lewis Solomon of Covent Garden, with whom Soyer had traded for decades. But there were none of the lords, generals and colonels with whom he had rubbed shoulders in the Crimea, in fact there were no senior officers or doctors at all – there was no one present to remember or commemorate his wartime achievements. Neither was there any representative from the Reform Club, from his Irish mission, or from any of his soup kitchen committees. Russell was in India covering the siege of Lucknow, and the reporter sent by *The Times* managed to arrive too late for the ceremony.

Fanny was nowhere to be seen. Only the eagle-eyed correspondent of the *Morning Chronicle* even hinted at her existence in a closing paragraph.

The parties having retired from the grave, an attendant descended and placed at the head of the coffin two large bouquets of very beautiful flowers, gathered, it was said, from certain favourite vases on which the eye of poor Soyer had been wont to rest affectionately in the home his absence will now render desolate. The tender hand of woman could alone provide an offering at once so delicate and graceful. The presence of his widow was thus manifest in this last attention, if she were not seen . . .

It is possible that it was Fanny, acting in the shadows, who ensured that the funeral remained as low-key as it did, as the best way of safeguarding the anonymity that sly insinuations, such as that in the *Chronicle*, could easily have blown. Such a revelation would have been disastrous for her, not least because it would have raised the question of what business a second wife had in burying her husband with his first. It would certainly account for the outraged comment in the hastily published *Memoirs of Soyer*, which were cobbled together by Volant and James Warren, with help from George Lomax, that, 'the relatives of poor Soyer were never consulted, and that the only nephew who could follow his dear uncle to the grave, as chief representative of the family, had merely received a general invitation to the cemetery . . .'

At least the journalists that did make it through the muddled arrangements to the hasty service gave the flamboyant chef who had been for so long a staple of their columns a decent send-off, and a variety of overblown obituaries detailing his professional achievements appeared the following week. Florence Nightingale was rather more prosaic in her sentiments, and seemed more irritated by the inconvenience than saddened by the loss. 'Soyer's death is a great disaster,' she wrote to Galton. 'Others have studied cookery for the purpose of gormandizing, some for shew, but none but he for the purpose of cooking large quantities of food in the most nutritious and economic manner, for great numbers of men. He has no successor.'

It was left to George Augustus Sala to write about Alexis the man, the 'kindly, erratic, frivolous, warm-hearted' man, who may have been a *poseur*, but whose vanities were harmless. Who was 'no vulgar charlatan . . . [but] full of inventive ingenuity'.

He was as kind a hearted Christian as you might find, an admirable cook, an inventive genius, a brave, devoted, self-denying man, who served his adopted country better in the Crimea than many a starred and titled CB. He had no call to be a quack; there was no earthly reason why he should inundate the newspapers with puffs, and wear impossible trousers, or cloth-of-gold waistcoats, cut diagonally. The man had a vast natural capacity . . . yet he quacked so continually, that many people set him down as a mere shallow pretender, and some even doubted whether he could cook at all. He was, nevertheless, a master of his difficult art . . . I have taken of succulent dainties cooked in their daintiest manner by the cunning hands of the illustrious *chef*: and I tell you he could cook, when he chose, like St Zita.

'He was but a Cook,' Sala added in another piece, perpetuating that unthinking condescension that Soyer had despised so much, 'but he was my dear and good friend. He was an original. [He] did a vast amount of good in his generation; and even those who laughed at him, loved him for his simple childlike ways and generous candour. Peace be to his ashes, for he was the worthiest of souls.'

EPILOGUE

Although none of the military top brass attended Soyer's funeral, the British army did not quite forget the voluble friend who had finally brought them palatable food in their hour of greatest need. For more than a hundred years the Soyer stove saw service wherever the British army (and latterly the Royal Navy and the RAF) was to be found, from Egypt to Kenya and Malaya. Wherever wood was in short supply the soldiers successfully adapted the stoves to local conditions, burning peat, gas, and even, memorably, dried camel dung. They remained standard kit through both World Wars until the Falklands conflict in 1982, when, on 25 May, an Exocet missile hit the massive supply vessel *Atlantic Conveyor*. The ship went down with not just a vital consignment of Chinook helicopters, but the bulk of the army's stock of Soyer stoves.

The stoves have also had a distinguished role in civil defence. In the early 1940s the Queen's Messenger Service established the 'Flying Food Column', a detachment of five lorries loaded with Soyer stoves and provisions which hurtled around the country taking sweet tea and hot meals to the shocked citizens of recently bombed cities. The original dustbin-sized stoves eventually spread through the commonwealth as far as Canada and Australia, where 'Soyer Boilers' are still stored in significant numbers by local authorities and disaster agencies as part of their emergency planning protocols.

More significantly, it was Soyer's passion for training that remained at the centre of army thinking. Within a few decades, schools for the training of regimental cooks had been established at Aldershot, Reading, and other military bases. And the guiding principles, inherited from Soyer, remain today – to invest resources, not in expensively processed foods or sophisticated equipment, but in highly trained chefs – which is why the British army still feeds so successfully in the field. Alexis himself is remembered each November at the Annual Dinner for Army Food Service Officers, an eight-course Reform Club-style extravaganza held in the officers' mess at Aldershot. At the end of the dinner, glasses are raised to the memory of the great man, and an extract is read from *A Culinary Campaign*. A silver model of a Soyer stove is currently being made, which is to become the trophy awarded to the Officer Caterer of the Year.

Within twelve months of Alexis's death, a twenty-two-year-old journalist, Isabella Beeton, had started to pinch significant amounts of *The Modern Housewife* for the first instalments of what would become the *Book of Household Management*, the manual that would have the greatest impact on middle-class eating habits for another century. (Ironically, Mrs Beeton also stole material from *The Pantropheon*, for the same reason Soyer had – to give herself a little borrowed intellectual lustre.) Although British cookery had been suffused with French influences since William the Conqueror stormed across Hastings beach, long periods of English antipathy towards anything Gallic meant that by the 1860s Mrs Beeton was in a position to make a scaled down version of *haute cuisine* fashionable all over again. And who better to turn to than Alexis Soyer? Out of all the professional chefs who had produced cookery books, it was Soyer who had most successfully managed to think himself out of the commercial kitchen and into the restricted budgets, *batteries de cuisine* and skills sets of the domestic environment.

Beyond the reach even of Mrs Beeton, Soyer's ideas and recipes have trickled through the twentieth century by way of food writers from Elizabeth David to Jane Grigson. And of course the Reform Club still keeps Soyer's memory alive with the inclusion of his signature dish, *Lamb Cutlets Reform*, on its daily menu – where it has remained since 1846. It is cooked exactly as Soyer instructed, although the chilli and tarragon elements of the complex sauce have been toned down for modern palates. Periodically, the club has produced some of Soyer's more lavish creations, including the *Dindonneau à la Nelson* and *La Crème d'Egypte à l'Ibrahim Pasha*, although with some dishes taking up to eighteen days to prepare, such experiments are understandably rare.

So could Alexis Soyer claim to be the original 'celebrity chef'? There had been plenty of famous chefs before him. Some had written famous books. But none had interacted as cleverly with the media, or understood the value of publicity, on anything like the same scale as Soyer. It was Soyer who penetrated the collective consciousness so successfully, and created for himself such a powerful public image, that he was able to reach (albeit not always successfully) towards the most dazzlingly ambitious commercial and philanthropic goals. Which of our modern celebrity chefs, with their prime-time shows and books-of-the-series and heavily branded products, ever approaches the audacity of the Symposium, the vision of the Irish project, or the courage of the Crimean mission? If any of these chefs are tempted to think of themselves as pioneers, then they are mistaken. Because one man had already achieved it all. And he did so with a level of ingenuity, far-sightedness and sheer panache that remains unrivalled to this day.

ACKNOWLEDGEMENTS

Although I have noticed that an agent rarely comes at the top of a list of acknowledgements, in this instance I must first of all thank Barbara Levy for her invaluable and unstinting support for what at times felt like a dauntingly ambitious project. I am deeply indebted to Sir Martin Gilbert for organising our overland trip to the Crimea in Soyer's footsteps. As well as planning every detail, Sir Martin accompanied us as far as Istanbul and enlivened every train mile with his astonishingly detailed knowledge of European history. Max Arthur saw the journey through to Sebastopol – even braving the Black Sea crossing on a scary cargo ship of unimaginable vintage. To Max I owe countless thanks – for his company, and for providing me with an endless supply of books, advice, contacts, jokes and encouragement.

On the journey we met many people who helped us generously. I must thank Onur Ozyesuk for escorting us around the former Scutari Hospital in Istanbul and Sergey Rylov for showing – and rowing – us around Balaclava. In Sebastopol, Ludmila Golikova, head researcher at The Museum of Heroic Defence and Liberation of Sebastopol, was particularly helpful, while Eugene Glibin and Constantine Fill ensured that every day in the Ukraine went smoothly.

In England, thanks must go to Simon Blundell, curator of the Reform Club archives, and Henry Vivian-Neal, chief guiding supervisor of Kensal Green Cemetery. Col Paul Budd of the Defence Food Services School, Lt Col (Rtd) Tony Monk of the Army Catering Corps Association and John Stelling of the Military Vehicle Museum gave me excellent information on the Soyer stove. I am grateful to Andrew Millard for information on Crosse & Blackwell, David Rose and Pete May for showing me their Soyer's Nectar bottles, and to Michelle Berriedale-Johnson and Brian Steele for allowing me to browse through their wonderful libraries of culinary history. Thanks are also due to William Griffiths for inviting me into Aston Hall. After years of studying Alexis Soyer, Frank Clement-Lorford shared much information and many helpful insights with me.

In France, Jean-Louis Duffet of the Meaux-en-Brie Historical Society gave generous assistance. For help with my very faulty French I am grateful to members of the Society of Dix-Neuviemistes, including Laure Doumens, Marlo Johnston and Priscilla Ferguson. I would also like to thank my dear friend Debra Oxhorn for researching the pictures of Fanny Cerrito in the Cia Fornaroli collection in the New York Public Library so diligently.

I owe thanks to the staff of the following libraries, museums and record offices: the National Portrait Gallery, the Wellcome Library for the History and Understanding of Medicine, Essex Record Office, the Family Records Office, Guildhall Library, the British Library, the London Library, the National Army Museum, the Public Record Office, the National Library of Wales, *Punch* Library, Colindale Newspaper Library, Oswestry Library (local studies section), the Law Society Library, the New York Public Library, the Paris Archives, the Balaclava Museum, The Museum of Heroic Defence and Liberation of Sevastopol.

At Weidenfeld & Nicolson I must thank my editor Francine Brody for her unfailing charm and graciousness in the face of many missed deadlines. For additional comments on the manuscript I am grateful to Catherine Blyth, Vicky Thomas, and the incomparable Matthew Littleford. Many friends and colleagues have been immensely encouraging during the progress of the book, and with apologies to those left out, I would particularly like to thank: Lee Henderson-Williams, Ali Phelan, Deborah Brown, Deborah Moggach, Sue Norris, Jon Sayers, Kathryn Hughes, Midge Gillies, Isabel McIver, Rachael Desgouttes, Emma Justice, Jane Cunningham, Jacquie Richardson, Cath Christof, Joseph and Joanna Spooner.

I would like to thank my mother-in-law, Pauline, for traipsing to north London on so many baby-sitting missions when Samuel was tiny, enabling me to work. And most importantly I must thank my husband, Jeremy, who through most of our marriage has had to put up with the loud intrusion of Alexis Soyer into our daily lives. He has done so without a word of complaint, with great humour, and far more practical and moral support than I had any right to expect.

London
January 2006

NOTE

After a century of neglect, plans are now being formed to restore the Soyer memorial in Kensal Green Cemetery. The appeal has already raised much of the £20,000 needed, although there is still some way to go. Should any reader wish to contribute, cheques should be made payable to the Reform Club, with 'Soyer Appeal' written on the back, and then sent to Nicolas Mellersh, The Reform Club, 104 Pall Mall, London, SW1Y 5EW. All contributions will be acknowledged.

SELECTED BIBLIOGRAPHY

Acton, Eliza, *Modern Cookery for Private Families*, London, 1845
Ackroyd, Peter, *London: The Biography*, London, 2000
Altick, Richard D., *Punch: The Lively Youth of a British Institution, 1841–1851*, Ohio, 1997
Anon., *Hints on Etiquette*, London, 1834
Bentley, Nicolas (ed.), *Russell's Despatches from the Crimea*, London, 1966
Berriedale-Johnson, Michelle, *The Victorian Cookbook*, London, 1989
Best, Geoffrey, *Mid-Victorian Britain 1851–75*, London, 1971
Booth, Michael R., *Theatre in the Victorian Age*, Cambridge, 1991
Brillat-Savarin, Jean-Anthelme, *La Physiologie du goût*, Paris, 1825 [Translated into *The Philosopher in the Kitchen* by Anne Drayton, London, 1988]
Carême, Antonin, *Le Maître d'hôtel Français*, Paris, 1822
Carême, Antonin, *L'Art de la Cuisine Française au XIX Siècle*, Paris, 1833–47
Chesney, Kellow, *Crimean War Reader*, London, 1960
Colquhoun, Kate, *A Thing in Disguise: The Visionary Life of Joseph Paxton*, London, 2004
Cook, Sir Edward, *The Life of Florence Nightingale*, London, 1914
Currah, Ann (ed.), *Chef to Queen Victoria: The Recipes of Charles Elme Francatelli*, London, 1973
David, Elizabeth, *An Omelette and a Glass of Wine*, London, 1986
Davies, Jennifer, *The Victorian Kitchen*, London, 1989
Davy, Christopher, *Architectural Precedents*, London, 1842
Dickens, Charles, *Oliver Twist*, London, 1837–39
Dickens, Charles, 'The Water-Drops'; short story: *Household Words*, London, 1850–59
Dickens, Charles, *Little Dorrit*, London, 1855–57
Ehrman, Edwina; Forsyth, Hazel; Peltz, Lucy; Ross, Cathy R., *London Eats Out: 500 Years of Capital Dining*, London, 1999
Fagan, Louis, *The Reform Club: Its Founders and Architect*, London, 1887
Foulkes, Nick, *Last of the Dandies: The Fashionable Life of Count D'Orsay*, London, 2003

Francatelli, Charles Elme, *The Modern Cook*, London, 1846

Gallagher, Thomas, *Paddy's Lament: Ireland 1846–1847, Prelude to Hatred*, New York, 1982

Goldie, Sue, *A Calendar of the Letters of Florence Nightingale*, Oxford, 1983

Goldie, Sue (ed.), *Florence Nightingale: Letters from the Crimea, 1854–1856*, Manchester, 1997

Gray, Peter, *The Irish Famine*, London, 1995

Grigson, Jane, *English Food*, London, 1974

Guest, Ivor, *Fanny Cerrito: The Life of a Romantic Ballerina*, London, 1956

Hayward, Abraham, *The Art of Dining*, London, 1852

Hibbert, Christopher, *The Destruction of Lord Raglan*, London, 1961

Hibbert, Christopher, *Queen Victoria: A Personal History*, London, 2000

Hill Hassell, Arthur, *Food and its Adulterations*, London, 1855

Hughes, Kathryn, *The Short Life and Long Times of Mrs Beeton*, London, 2005

Kelly, Ian, *Cooking for Kings: The Life of Antonin Carême*, London, 2003

Kerr, Paul (ed.), *The Crimean War*, London, 1997

Langley, Andrew, *The Selected Soyer*, London, 1987

Leapman, Michael, *The World for a Shilling: How the Great Exhibition Shaped a Nation*, London, 2001

Leslie, R. F., *The Age of Transformation: 1789–1871*, London, 1964

McKirdy, Michael, 'Who Wrote Soyer's Pantropheon?' article: *Petit Propos Culinaire*, 29, 1988

Madden, R. R., *The Life and Correspondence of the Countess of Blessington*, London, 1855

Mawson, Michael Hargreave (ed.), *Eyewitness in the Crimea: the Crimean War Letters of Lt Col George Frederick Dallas, 1854–1856*, London, 2001

Monsarrat, Ann, *An Uneasy Victorian: Thackeray the Man 1811–1863*, London, 1980

Morris, Helen, *Portrait of a Chef*, Cambridge, 1938

O'Malley, I. B., *Florence Nightingale 1820–1856: A study of her life down to the end of the Crimean War*, London, 1931

O'Rourke, John, *The History of the Great Irish Famine of 1847*, Dublin, 1875

Picard, Liza, *Victorian London: The Life of a City*, London, 2005

Porter, Roy, *London: A Social History*, London, 1994

Price, Roger, *A Social History of Nineteenth-Century France*, London, 1987

Quayle, Eric, *Old Cookery Books*, New York, 1978

Ray, Elizabeth, *Alexis Soyer: Cook Extraordinary*, Lewes, 1991

Rossi Wilcox, Susan, *Dinner for Dickens: The Culinary History of Mrs Charles Dickens' Menu Books*, London, 2005

Royle, Trevor, *Crimea: The Great Crimean War 1854–1856*, London, 1999

Sala, G. A., *The Book of the Symposium, or Soyer at Gore House*, London, 1851

Sala, G. A., *Twice Round the Clock; or, the Hours of the Day and Night in London*, London, 1859

Sala, G. A., *Things I Have Seen and People I Have Known*, London, 1894

Sala, G. A., *The Thorough Good Cook. A Series of Chats on the Culinary Art and Nine Hundred Recipes*, London, 1895

Sala, G. A., *The Life and Adventures of George Augustus Sala*, London, 1896

Salaman, Redcliffe N., *The History and Social Influence of the Potato*, Cambridge, 1949

Seacole, Mary, *Wonderful Adventures of Mrs Seacole in Many Lands*, London, 1857

Shephard, Sue, *Pickled, Potted and Canned: How the Preservation of Food Changed Civilisation*, London, 2000

Simmons, Godfrey; Pearce, Keith; Fry, Helen (eds), *The Lost Jews of Cornwall: From the Middle Ages to the Nineteenth Century*, Bristol, 2000

Slater, Michael (ed.), *Dickens' Journalism: Sketches by Boz And Other Early Papers*, London, 1994

Small, Hugh, *Florence Nightingale: Avenging Angel*, London, 1998

Soyer, Alexis, *The Gastronomic Regenerator*, London, 1846

Soyer, Alexis, *Soyer's Charitable Cookery, or The Poor Man's Regenerator*, London, 1848

Soyer, Alexis, *The Modern Housewife or Menagère*, London, 1849

Soyer, Alexis, *The Pantropheon*, London, 1853

Soyer, Alexis, *A Shilling Cookery for the People*, London, 1854

Soyer, Alexis, *A Culinary Campaign*, London, 1857

Soyer, Nicolas, *Soyer's Paper-Bag Cookery*, London, 1911

Spang, Rebecca L., *The Invention of the Restaurant: Paris and Modern Gastronomic Culture*, Massachusetts, 2000

Sweet, Matthew, *Inventing the Victorians*, London, 2001

Taylor, D. J., *Thackeray*, London, 1999

Tegetmeier, W. B., *A Manual of Domestic Economy*, London, 1862

Thackeray, William Makepeace, *Vanity Fair*, London, 1847–48

Thackeray, William Makepeace, *The History of Pendennis*, London, 1849

Thackeray, William Makepeace, *The Book of Snobs and Sketches and Travels in London*, reprinted London, 1904

Thackeray, William Makepeace, *Roundabout Papers*, reprinted London, 1946

Ude, Louis Eustache, *The French Cook*, London, 1827

Vaughan, Adrian, *Isambard Kingdom Brunel: Engineering Knight-Errant*, London, 1992

Visser, Margaret, *The Rituals of Dinner: The Origins, Evolution, Eccentricities and Meaning of Table Manners*, Toronto, 1991

Volant, F. and J. R. Warren, *Memoirs of Alexis Soyer*, reprinted Sussex, 1985

Warner, Philip, *The Crimean War: A Reappraisal*, Herts, 2001

Warner, Philip (ed.), *Letters Home from the Crimea*, London, 1977

West, Sir Algernon, *Recollections 1832–1886*, London, 1899

Willan, Anne, *Great Cooks and their Recipes*, London, 1995

Wilson, C. Anne, *Food and Drink in Britain*, London, 1973

Wood, Anthony, *Europe 1815–1945*, London, 1964

Woodbridge, George, *The Reform Club, 1836–1978: A History from the Club's Records*, New York and Toronto, 1978

Woodham-Smith, Cecil, *Florence Nightingale, 1820–1910*, reprinted London, 1952

Woodham-Smith, Cecil, *The Reason Why*, London, 1958

Woodham-Smith, Cecil, *The Great Hunger: Ireland 1845–1849*, London, 1962

Young, George Malcolm, *Early Victorian England: 1830–1865*, London, 1934

INDEX

Aberdeen, George Hamilton Gordon, 4th Earl of, 258
Abundance (floating bakery), 294
Acton, Eliza: *Modern Cookery in All Its Branches*, 89–91, 172
Adams, Alfred, 197, 208, 217, 244
Adams, Samuel and Ann, 209
Ailsa, Archibald Kennedy, 1st Marquess of, 28–30, 65, 85
Ainsworth, William Harrison, 104
Ainsworth's Magazine, 104
Alarum (timing device), 138, 249
Albemarle, William Charles Keppel, 4th Earl of, 32
Albert, Prince Consort: sees Cerrito dance *Ondine*, 68; Francatelli cooks for, 91; supports Great Exhibition (1851), 173, 196, 200–2, 220, 231, 252; stays at Castle Howard, 196; York banquet (1850), 196–9, 201, 217; and Crimean War, 253
Albion dining rooms, Little Russell Street, London, 23, 259
Albion Hotel, Pall Mall, London, 37
Aldershot: AS commemorated in, 324
Aldridge, John (owner of Gore House), 211, 234
Aldridge, John (report writer), 130–2
Alexander II, Tsar of Russia, 313
Alma, Battle of (1854), 254
Alvanley, William Arden, 2nd Baron, 58, 197, 289
American Whig Review, 170
Ancot, Jean, 53
Andersen, Hans Christian, 207
Apponyi, Count Rudolf, 193
Argo (ship), 308–10

Argyll, George Douglas, 8th Duke of, 260–1
army field kitchens (and stoves), 251, 262–3, 288–9, 295–8, 301–3, 306–13, 323
Arney's Patent Jelly and Blancmange Powders, 104
Aston Hall, Shropshire, 24–6, 28
Atlantic Conveyor, MV (supply ship), 323
Austin, Captain (Arctic explorer), 164

Bagehot, Walter, 221
Bailey (storekeeper in Scutari), 271
Bailey's (poulterers), 143
Baker, Mr & Mrs (of St John's Wood), 166–7, 171
Balaclava, Crimea: AS travels to, 3, 282–4; British base in, 254–7; AS leaves, 291; AS revisits, 308; handed back to Russians, 309
ballooning, 165
Bank Charter Act (1844), 145
banquets: for Ibrahim Pasha at Reform (1846), 69–75, 140; Dublin gala lunch (1847), 108–10, 123, 129; for Osbourne Sampayo (1946), 140–3; Lumley's for Halévy and Scribe (1850), 186–8; Royal Agricultural Society (Exeter 1850), 188–91; Prince Albert's (York 1850), 196–9, 201
Baring, Thomas, 115
Barnard, Lieut.–General Henry, 297
Barry, Alfred, 41–2
Barry, Sir Charles: designs Reform Club, 39–44, 48; membership of Reform, 56; serves on Great Exhibition buildings

committee, 176; designs Trafalgar Square, 202; designs British Embassy in Constantinople, 270
Basevi, George, 39
Bass, Michael Thomas, 173
Bath Herald (newspaper), 170
Batty's Hippodrome, London, 203
Bazalgette, Sir Joseph, 23
Beare, Captain W.G., 179
Beaufort, Henry Somerset, 7th Duke of, 79
Beauvilliers, Antoine, 13, 94
Bedford, Anna Maria, Duchess of, 225
Bedmar y de Escaluna, Don Manuel Antonio de Acuna y de Witte La Cueva y Benavides, Marques de, 246, 310, 314
Beeton, Isabella: *Book of Household Management*, 324
Bell, W.S., 227
Bell's Life in London, 23
Bessborough, John William Ponsonby, 4th Earl of, 109, 124, 127, 129, 172
Biddulph, Thomas Myddleton, 25
Bishop, William, 214
Blackwell, Thomas: uses AS's image on labels, 3; collaborates with AS, 153; background, 154; gives evidence on adulteration of food, 157; AS leaves Emma paintings to in will, 320; *see also* Crosse & Blackwell
Blackwood, Lady Alicia, 279
Blackwood's Magazine, 103, 106
Blake, Dr, 284
Blake, Joseph, 19
Blake, Louisa *see* Hill, Louisa
Blessington, Charles Gardiner, 1st Earl of, 205

Blessington, Marguerite, Countess of, 107, 123, 205–7
Bloomsbury Street, London, 264
Blore, Edward, 39
Bonaparte, Louis, King of Holland, 79
Bornet, François, 292, 299, 308
Borthwick, Peter, 82
Boulogne, 247
Bouquet de Gibier ('Sporting Nosegay'), 107, 127
Bourdin, Ernest, 149
Boyd, Elizabeth, 100–1
Brabazon, William, Baron (*later* 11th Earl of Meath), 108
Bracebridge, Charles, 271, 274, 280, 282–3
Bracebridge, Selina, 271, 280, 282
Bramah, Prestage & Ball, Piccadilly, 100, 102, 118, 121, 135
Brick Lane, Spitalfields, 117
Brillat–Savarin, Jean Anthelme, 10, 13, 89, 136
Bristol Mirror (newspaper), 170
British Hotel, Spring Hill, Balaclava, 285–7, 308
Brompton Road Consumption Hospital, London, 117
Brontë, Charlotte ('Currer Bell'): *Jane Eyre*, 151
Brontë, Emily ('Ellis Bell'): *Wuthering Heights*, 151
Brooklyn Daily Freeman (newspaper), 170
Brooks's club, St James's Street, 37–8
Brougham, Henry Peter, Baron, 105
Brown & Co. (Dublin), 133
Brown, Rev. Joseph, 120–1
brucellosis *see* Crimean fever
Brunel, Isambard Kingdom, 56, 176, 263–4, 266
Buckingham Palace: kitchens, 91
Builder, The (journal), 47

Calvin, John, 10
Cambridge, Prince Adolphus Frederick, Duke of: employs Philippe Soyer as chef, 15–16, 19, 55; AS works in kitchen, 16, 19; sends condolences to AS on Emma's death, 65; AS dedicates *The Gastronomic Regenerator* to, 93; at Dublin Esplanade gala luncheon, 108; commends AS's fruit drink, 160
Cambridge, Prince George William Frederick Charles,

Duke of: and AS's visit to Crimea, 265
Camp Kitchen *see* Soyer's Magic Stove
Campkin, Henry, 244
Cape of Good Hope (ship), 302
Capitole, La (magazine), 65, 104
Captain White's Curry Paste and Powders, 104
carbonated drinks, 158–9
Cardigan, James Thomas Brudenell, 7th Earl of, 79
Carême, Marie Antonin, 15, 46, 73, 89–91, 97–8, 106, 149
Carlisle, George William Frederick Howard, 7th Earl of, 196, 222
Carlyle, Thomas, 170, 206
Carrera Water Manufactory, 159, 161
Carroll, Lewis, 94
Castle Howard, Yorkshire, 196
Cawke (Simmonds's deputy), 233
Cerrito, Fanny: appearance, 67, 76–7, 144; dancing, 67–8, 78, 192–3, 312–14; AS's relations with, 68, 75, 77–8, 82–3, 87, 185, 192–3, 238, 246–7, 260, 266, 310, 312–13; fame and success, 75–6, 86–7; marriage to St–Léon, 75, 79–81, 87, 144; rivalry with Taglioni, 78–9; admirers, 79; background and career, 81–2; AS writes comic ballet for, 83–4; Simonau paints portrait, 83; AS creates new dish for, 84; accompanies AS to inauguration of Emma's memorial, 85–6; tours Sweden, 173; deteriorating marriage relations, 174, 185, 192–3; Lumley employs, 186; liaisons, 192; health concerns, 193; separates from St–Léon, 193; depicted on Gore House fresco, 213; at Universal Symposium, 225; daughter born (Matilde), 246; private marriage ceremony with AS, 313–14; retires from stage, 314; and AS's final illness, 319; and AS's funeral, 320–1; unmentioned in AS's will, 320
Cerrito, Marianna (Fanny's mother), 80–1, 86
Cerrito, Matilde (Fanny's daughter), 246–7, 313–14
Cerrito, Raffaele (Fanny's father), 76, 80–2, 87, 186
Charlemont, Francis William Caulfeild, 2nd Earl of, 108
Charles X, King of France, 6–7, 9

Chenery, Thomas, 255–7
Chetwynd, Sir George, 173, 271
Chimachenka, Daniel, 312
Chirk Castle, Shropshire, 25–6
Chiswick: Horticultural Society's gardens, 70
cholera, 153; London epidemics, 222; in Scutari hospital, 260
Chopin, Frédéric, 207
Clayton, Messrs William & Co., 153–4
Cleopatra's Needle, Thames Embankment, 171
Cochrane, Charles, 240–1
Codd, Charles, 159, 161–2
Codd, John, 162
Codrington, General Sir William John, 302, 307–8, 317
Cole, (Sir) Henry, 200, 225
Coleridge, Samuel Taylor, 170
Combes (stove cook), 187
Comte (head chef of Baroness Rothschild), 150
Constantinople, 268–9, 311–12
Cook, Thomas, 193
Cooke, Sophia, 319–20
cookery books, 89–90
Cooper, James (stone bottle maker), 104
Coppelia (ballet), 80
Cork Examiner, 124
Corn Laws, 113, 115
Cornhill (magazine), 96
Corsica, 267
Cossard (chef), 246–7
Cottager's Stove, 135–6, 249
Courrier de l'Europe, 50
Court Journal, 82
Covent Garden theatre, 186
Coventry House Club, London, 91
Crimean fever (brucellosis), 299–300
Crimean War (1854–6): outbreak, 253–4; conditions, 254–8, 284–5; AS reorganises field kitchens, 275–80, 292; ends, 302, 308
Crockford, Frederick, 296, 306
Crockford's club, London, 18–19, 57, 91
Crosse & Blackwell (pickle manufactory): uses AS's image on labels, 1, 156–7; AS's agreements with, 153–8, 243; AS's royalties from, 235, 243, 251; advertises in AS's *Shilling Cookery*, 250; markets Soyer's Sultana's Sauce, 316
Crosse, Edmund: collaborates with AS, 153; background, 154; as AS's

executor, 158, 320; looks after Emma's paintings during AS's absence in Crimea, 158, 264; AS leaves Emma paintings to in will, 320

Crystal Palace: houses Great Exhibition, 201–2; relocated in Sydenham, 250, 319

Cumming, Dr Alexander, 271, 275, 278

Daily News, 222

Dallas, Captain Frederick, 297, 303, 306

David, Elizabeth, 324

Day, Thomas, 286, 290

Deane & Dray, London Bridge, 136, 218, 249–50, 252

Delane, John Thadeus, 57, 288, 307, 316

Desmore, Sergeant, 284

Devonshire, William George Spencer Cavendish, 6th Duke of, 190

Dickens, Catherine, 101, 138; *What Shall We Have for Dinner?* (by 'Lady Maria Clutterbuck'), 171–2

Dickens, Charles: social status, 12; on Sadler's Wells audiences, 23; satirises officialdom, 115; supervises Catherine's finances, 172; at Gore House, 206–8; employs Sala on *Household Words*, 209; membership of Metropolitan Sanitary Association, 221–2; *Dombey and Son*, 151; *Hard Times*, 94; 'The Water–Drops', 172

Dickinson, William, 18

Disraeli, Benjamin (Earl of Beaconsfield): dines at Universal Symposium, 22; on Victoria's coronation, 36; membership of Westminster Club, 38; baptised, 139; praises AS's sauces, 154; at Gore House, 206, 208, 220

Donoughmore, John Hely–Huchinson, 3rd Earl, and Barbara, Countess of, 108

Dotesio (proprietor of Royal Hotel, Slough), 150

Douglass, Frederick, 226

Dublin: gala luncheon (1847), 108–10, 123, 129; AS in, 126–7, 132; AS's Model Kitchen in, 129, 132–3; nutritional value of soups in, 130–1

Dublin Evening Herald, 110, 129

Dublin Evening Packet, 129

Dubourg's, London (restaurant), 147

Duff, General Sir Alexander, 98

Duhart–Fauvet, Adolphe, 244–5

Duncannon, John George Brabazon, Viscount, 108

Dysart, Louisa, Countess of, 38

Edward, Prince of Wales (Bertie), 220

Edwards, James (supplier), 234

Ellice, Edward, 37–9, 184

Elssler, Fanny, 78, 186

Engels, Friedrich, 153, 224

Ernest I, Duke of Saxe–Coburg, 63, 104

Esterhazy, Prince Paul, 32, 79

Evans's Late Supper Rooms, Covent Garden, 147

Exeter, 188–91

Exeter Journal, 191

Fagan, Louis, 29, 37, 43, 69, 73

Fayot, Frédéric, 149

Feeny, John Joseph, 177, 185, 209–10, 218, 226–8; bankruptcy and death, 242–3

Fenchurch Street, London, 234

Fenton, Roger, 312

Fidler (chef), 185

field kitchens *see* army field kitchens

fish: AS's recipes for, 168

'Flying Food Column', 323

food additives: harmful effects, 157

Fox & Henderson (contractors), 202, 209, 217

Fox, Charles James, 37

Francatelli, Charles Elme: appointed chef at Reform Club, 185; *The Modern Cook*, 90–1, 99, 104–5

France: in Crimean War, 253–6; *see also* Meaux–en–Brie; Paris

Franklin, Sir John, 164, 238

Gale, George Burcher, 165, 216

Galton, Captain Douglas, 318

Gardner's (lamp manufactory), 162, 164, 250

Garfield, Thomas, 265, 267, 280, 283, 291, 292

gas: development as fuel, 45–6, 137–8

Gas, Light & Coke Company, 46

Gastronomique Innovation (annual), 150

Gautier, Théophile, 76–7

George IV, King of Great Britain: death, 16

George V, King of Hanover, 160, 201

Gérard of Paris (dealer), 65

Gillow, M.D., 178

Gladstone, William Ewart, 258

Globe, The (newspaper), 33–4, 75, 106, 160, 164, 188, 194

Goldner, Stephen, 238

Gore House, Kensington: AS leases, 199, 204–5, 207, 211; Lady Blessington occupies, 205–7; AS redesigns, 208–9, 211–12, 219, 226–7; demolished to make way for Royal Albert Hall, 231; *see also* Soyer's Universal Symposium of All Nations

Gouffe, Alphonse, 148–9

Grande Taverne de Londres, Paris, 13

Great Exhibition (1851): Prince Albert patronises, 173, 191, 196, 200–2, 231, 252; AS submits design for building, 176–7; catering, 176, 185, 203–4; exhibits and displays, 188, 220–1; AS's plans for eating places, 191; site, 200–1; speed of achievement, 200; Paxton designs building ('Crystal Palace'), 201–2; facilities, 203; entry prices, 219; opens, 220; closes, 230; success, 231, 252; *see also* Crystal Palace

Great Russell Street, London, 234

Grendon Hall, Atherstone, Warwickshire, 173

Greville, Charles, 31

Grey, Charles, 2nd Earl, 56, 62

Grigson, Jane, 324

Grisi, Carlotta, 82

Grissell & Peto (contractors), 40

Grossetti, Signora (Bonapartes' housekeeper), 267

Grove (butcher of Charing Cross), 101

Grove's (fishmonger of Bond Street), 143

Guadalquivir, The, SS, 100

Guerrier (chef), 185

Gwydyr House, Whitehall, 33, 36, 40, 42–3

Hale, Sarah, 172

Halévy, Fromental and Eugène Scribe: *La Tempesta* (opera), 187–8

Hall, Dr John, 289–90, 308

Hall, Thomas, 106

Ham Yard, Soho, 240

Hart, David: relations with AS,

138–40; settles AS's claims and expenses, 234–5, 249; profits from AS's enterprises, 240; and Volant's case against AS and Symons, 242; AS pays off debt to, 252; annexes AS's will, 320

Hart, Jacob James, 139

Hart, Lemon (*born* Asher Laemle ben Eleazar), 139

Hart, Mary, 139

Hayward, Abraham, 228

Hedges and Butler (Regent Street caterers), 35, 143

Henries, Louise, 11

Her Majesty's Theatre, Haymarket, 186, 186–7

Herbert, Sidney, 274

Hill, Louisa (*née* Blake), 19

Hill, Lord Marcus: wedding, 19; as chairman of Reform Club, 44; 'Culinary Dialogue' with AS, 103, 244; as patron of AS at Reform, 103; and AS's resignation and reinstatement at Reform, 180–1; and AS's final departure from Reform, 183–4; letter from AS on Pownall, 235–6

Hine, Henry George, 320

Hogg, Jabez, 251

Hood, Thomas, 206

Hope, Sir John East, 184

Household Words (magazine), 172, 209

Howley, William, Archbishop of Canterbury, 35

Huguenots: in Spitalfields, 117, 120, 134

Hume, Joseph, 62

Humfrey (Simmonds's barrister), 233

Hundred Guinea Dish (*L'Extravagance Culinaire à l'Alderman*), 197

Hutin, John, 150

Hyde Park: as site of Great Exhibition, 200–2

Ibrahim Pasha, Viceroy of Egypt, 69–71, 73–5, 79, 140, 261

Illustrated London News: on Ibrahim Pasha banquet, 71, 75; on Irish potato famine, 114; on Royal Agricultural Society Exeter festival, 189; on AS's Universal Symposium, 222; on supply of contaminated meat to navy, 238; reviews AS's *The Pantropheon*, 245; Thackeray declines offer to report on

Crimea, 260; AS sends reports to, 268; reports AS's activities in Crimea, 279, 297, 300, 308, 318

Inkerman, Battle of (1854), 257–8

Inkerman (horse), 308

Isabella, Queen of Spain, 246

Janin, Jules, 226

Jaquet, Monsieur (of Johnson's Tavern), 125, 128

Jay's (fishmongers), 143

Jeffs (of Burlington Arcade): publishes AS's *Délassements Culinaires*, 88

Jennings, George (engineer), 203

Jennings, Mr & Mrs (of the Wheatsheaf, Virginia Water), 245, 260

Jerrold, Douglas, 56, 85, 104, 206

Jervis, Sir John (Lord Chief Justice), 242

Jews: in business, 139–40

John Bull (journal), 155

Johnstone, Christian Isobel, 172

Jolly (singer), 74

Jones, Elizabeth (Emma's mother) *see* Simonau, Elizabeth

Jones, (Elizabeth) Emma (AS's wife): funeral and memorial stone, 1–2, 64–6, 85; marriage to AS, 18, 54; AS meets for portrait, 26–8; paintings, 45, 55; pregnancy, 51, 60, 63; art training and practice, 52–3; birth, background and upbringing, 52–3; wit, 53–4; paints AS's mother in France, 55; home life, 59; death in childbirth, 63; Duke of Saxe Coburg praises paintings, 63; self-portrait and tribute in AS's *Gastronomic Regenerator*, 103–4; AS holds exhibition of paintings, 122–3; paints AS eating truffles, 142; paintings left with Crosse & Blackwell, 158, 264; AS hangs paintings in home, 240; AS bequeaths paintings in will, 319–20; *Buy–A–Broom Girl and Boy*, 103; *The English Ceres*, 184; *The Farmer's Wife*, 55; *La Jeune Fermière*, 59; *The Juvenile Anglers*, 56; *The Organ Boys*, 63; *The Young Bavarians*, 264; *The Young Israelites*, 65, 184

Jones, Newton (Emma's brother), 52–3, 320

Jones, Richard (Emma's father), 52

Jullien, Louis, 229–31, 240–1

Jullien (Louis' nephew; head chef in Scutari), 276, 291–2, 294

July Ordinances (France 1830), 6–8

Jung Bahadur, 192

Kalos Geusis, 153–4

Kensal Green Cemetery, London: Emma's funeral and memorial stone, 1, 64, 85; Augusta Soyer buried in, 315; AS's funeral in, 320

Kensington Square, London, 315

King, Captain (Royal Engineers), 289

Knesbeck, Baron de, 104

Kourakine, Prince Alexander, 97

Lamain, Adelaide: son by AS, 14, 16; AS abandons, 27; death, 54, 237

Lamain, Jean Alexis (AS's son by Adelaide Lamain): birth, 14, 16; adopted, 54; writes to and meets AS, 236–7; AS legally acknowledges, 237; AS visits in Paris, 246, 266; unmentioned in AS's will, 320

Lancet, The (journal), 128, 130, 160, 239, 316

Landells, Robert, 297, 308

Landor, Walter Savage, 206

Landseer, Sir Edwin, 107, 206

Leicester Square, London: AS shares flat with Simonau, 83, 100

Leman Street, London, 117

Lemolt, Chevalier, 162, 243

Lemon Hart rum, 139

Leopold I, King of the Belgians, 63

Lewis (teacher), 66

Lind, Jenny, 93, 186

Linton, Dr, 299

Liszt, Franz, 207

Literary Gazette, 104

Literary Mirror, The, 169

Lloyd, William and Louisa, 24–6, 185

Lomax, George, 242, 265, 320–1

London: French chefs in, 15, 18; expansion and population growth, 21; theatres and entertainment, 22–3; sanitary conditions, 221–2

London (yacht), 291

London Gourmet (journal), 48

Londonderry, Frances Anne, Marchioness of, 225

Longfellow, Henry Wadsworth, 207

Longman, Thomas (publisher), 90

Louis XVIII, King of France, 6
Louis Napoleon *see* Napoleon III,
  Emperor of the French
Louis–Philippe, King of the
  French, 9
Lüders, General Alexander
  Nikolaievich, 304
Lyons, Admiral Sir Edmund (*later*
  Baron), 297

McCann (surgeon), 174–5
Maclean, Sir George, 294
Maclise, Daniel, 206
Macready, William Charles, 22
Mahoney, James, 114
Maison Douix, Paris (restaurant),
  14
Malleville, Vicomtesse de, 50
Maltby, Edward, Bishop of
  Durham, 35
Manchester Examiner (newspaper),
  170
Manchester Guardian, 226
Marble Arch, London, 202
Marlborough Road, St John's
  Wood, London, 315
Marseilles, 266, 312
Marsh, Sir Henry, 130
Marx, Karl, 153, 224
Maule, Fox *see* Panmure, 2nd
  Baron
Mayhew, Henry, 91, 160
Meath, John Chambre Brabazon,
  10th Earl of, 108
Meaux–en–Brie, France, 10–12, 54,
  122, 310, 313
Mehemet Ali, Viceroy of Egypt,
  69, 73
Melbourne, William Lamb, 2nd
  Viscount, 49, 107
Mendelssohn, Felix, 31–2
Merchants Dining Room,
  London, 177
Mesnil (AS's major domo in
  Crimea), 292, 298
Metropolitan Sanitary Association,
  221–2
middle classes: AS writes cookery
  and household management
  book for, 166–7
Milnes, Richard Monckton (*later*
  1st Baron Houghton), 85
Milton (chief purveyor in Scutari),
  271
Model Soup Kitchen, 129, 132–3,
  166
Molesworth, Sir William, 38
Morel's (caterers), 143
Moret, Philippe, 150
Morning Avertiser, 105, 118, 155

Morning Chronicle, 2, 35, 65, 94,
  101, 155, 318, 320–1
Morning Herald, 77, 106, 226
Morning Post, 67, 73, 76, 86, 105,
  155, 163, 169, 175, 224, 245
Morrison, Peter, 292
Murillo, Bartolomé Esteban, 65
Murray, Lady Augusta, 17

Napier, Rear Admiral Sir Charles,
  70, 73–4, 239
Napoleon III, Emperor of the
  French (*earlier* Louis
  Napoleon): at Lady
  Blessington's, 207; AS sends
  copy of *The Pantropheon* to,
  244; *coup d'état* (1852), 246;
  plans Paris Exhibition, 252; and
  Crimean War, 253; and AS's
  visit to Crimea, 265; AS meets,
  313
Nash, John, 202
National, Le (newspaper), 9
navy *see* Royal Navy
Neue Rheinische Zeitung, 224
Nevill, Lady Dorothy, 82
Newcastle, Henry Pelham, 5th
  Duke of, 294
Newland's (butchers), 143
News of the World (newspaper),
  204, 211, 223
Nicholas I, Tsar of Russia, 68
Nicoll's of Regent Street
  (couturier), 214, 250
Nicolson, Renton, 57
Nightingale, Florence: on AS's
  death, 3, 321; in Crimean War,
  257–9, 262, 264; on Stratford de
  Redcliffe, 270; on AS's arrival in
  Scutari, 271; AS meets, 272–3;
  sets up extra–diet kitchens, 275,
  300, 302; suggests hot–water
  trolleys for serving food, 277;
  visits to front in Crimea, 280,
  282–4, 288, 293; antipathy to
  Mary Seacole, 285; conflicts
  with John Hall, 289; contracts
  Crimean fever, 289, 291,
  299–300; complains of AS, 300;
  AS rescues carriage, 308; leaves
  Crimea, 308; testimonial for AS,
  311; serves on Barracks and
  Hospitals Sub–Commission,
  317–18
Norfolk News, 170
North American Review, 316
Nubar (interpreter), 74–5

Observer, The (newspaper), 156, 316
O'Connell, Daniel, 37

Odessa, 306–7
Ombre, Iram de l', 102
Orsay, Alfred, Count d':
  encourages Emma's sketching,
  27; as arbiter of fashion, 77, 152;
  AS sends *Bouquet de Gibier* to,
  107; paints Lumley, 186; liaison
  with Countess of Blessington,
  205–7; debts, 207; flees to Paris,
  207
Osmazome, 136, 243
Ottawa (ship), 293, 302
Ottoman Empire: in Crimean
  War, 253

Pall Mall: clubs, 36–7; gas lighting,
  46
Palmerston, Henry John Temple,
  3rd Viscount, 70, 74, 115, 139
Panmure, Fox Maule, 2nd Baron
  (*later* 11th Earl of Dalhousie): on
  Reform Club food, 140;
  friendship with AS, 184; and
  Crimean War, 258, 261–3, 265,
  280, 298; approves payment
  to AS for services in Crimea,
  314
Paris: anti–July Ordinances riot
  (1830), 8–9; restaurants, 13; AS
  revisits, 192–3, 238, 245–7, 312;
  AS proposes gastronomic tour,
  193–4; International Exhibition
  planned, 252, 260, 280; AS stays
  in on way to Crimea, 266; Peace
  Conference (1856), 302
Parliament, Houses of (Palace of
  Westminster): rebuilt by Barry,
  40–2
Patrie, La (newspaper), 165
Paulet, Field Marshal Lord
  William, 108, 270, 278, 292,
  304
Paxton, Sir Joseph, 56, 70, 176, 185,
  201–2, 217
Peel Sir Robert, 75, 105, 113, 115,
  173, 292
Pélissier, Marshal Aimable
  Jean–Jacques, 296–7, 305
Pera, Turkey, 269, 301
Perrot, Jules, 67–8
Phelp, William, 242
Phidomageireion (gas–cooker),
  47–8, 137–8
Philippe (French conjurer), 144–6
Phillips (auctioneers), New Bond
  Street, 207
Phillips, Charles: relations with
  AS, 137–8; at AS's funeral, 320
Phillips, Charles, junior: in
  Crimea, 138, 302, 306, 312; with

dying AS, 319; at AS's funeral, 320
Piccalilli, 155
Pierce, Charles: at Emma's funeral, 2; friendship with AS, 26, 148; with AS during final illness, 319; at AS's funeral, 320; *The Household Manager*, 26
Polignac, Jules Armand, Prince de, 6–9, 14–15
potato blight (*Phytophthora infestans*), 113–14
Pownall, Thomas, 230, 235–6
pressure cooker, 249
Prince (ship), 257
Prince of Wales' Bazaar, 122
Protestant Churchman (US newspaper), 170
Protestantism: in Meaux, 10; *see also* Huguenots
Provence Hotel, Leicester Square, 23, 147, 250
Public Health Act (1848), 156
Pugin, Augustus Welby Northmore, 41
Punch (magazine): on AS's sensitivity, 62; Thackeray contributes to, 65, 124, 148; AS sends *The Gastronomic Regenerator* to, 104; on AS's efforts in Ireland, 124, 128; spoof on Cambridge chair for study of eating, 151; quip on Disraeli, 155; and AS's departure from Reform Club, 181, 183; on Lumley's banquet, 187–8; on AS at Gore House, 211–12; on AS's speech at Universal Symposium, 224; mocks design of Gore House, 226
Puyenbroeck, Pierre, 85

Quaker Central Relief Committee, Dublin, 116
Quakers: in London, 134
Qualiotti (Italian cook), 155
Queade (Reform Club member), 178
Queensberry, John Douglas, 6th Marquess of, 58

Radley's, Bridge Street (bar), 250
Raglan, Fitzroy James Henry Somerset, Baron, 254, 281, 288–9, 295; death, 293
railways: investments in, 144–5
Raleigh, Sir Walter, 112
Reform Bill (1832), 22, 28
Reform Club, London: banquets, 3, 69–75, 140–3, 186–8; AS

appointed *chef de cuisine*, 18–19, 30, 39; Hill's chairmanship, 19; established and developed, 29, 37–40, 42; and Victoria's coronation, 33–5; kitchens, 41–51; gas-fired ovens, 45–6, 137; membership, 56; AS's activities at, 59–60, 140, 146; Emma's pictures at, 59, 65; AS publishes print of kitchen department, 61, 180; cost of supper, 62; gives banquet for Ibrahim Pasha, 69–75; perpetuates AS's *Lamb Cutlet Reform*, 98–9, 324; and AS's publicity, 107; AS's entertaining in, 146–7; differences with AS, 177–9, 182; AS's resignation and reinstatement (1844), 180–1; AS finally resigns from (1850), 182–4; non-members dine in, 182–3; appoints successor to AS, 185; not represented at AS's funeral, 320
Renkioi, Dardanelles: Brunel designs hospital for, 264
Rennie, George, Jr, 56
revolutions of 1848, 153
Revue des Deux Mondes, La, 65, 104
Richards, Captain, 259
Rignon, Georg (restaurateur), 7, 12–13
Robert Lowe (ship), 282–3, 291
Robertson, James, 312
Robertson, Robert, 283
Roden, Robert Jocelyn, 3rd Earl of, 108
Rogers, William, 85
Rokeby, Colonel Henry Robinson–Montagu, 6th Baron, 297, 306, 316
Rosenberg, Charles, 81
Rossini, Gioacchino, 53
Rothschild, Lionel de, 115, 139
Rotivan, Auguste, 30, 38
Routh, Sir Randolph, 124
Routledge, George, 249–51, 316
Royal Academy, London, 53, 56
Royal Agricultural Society, 133; 1850 banquet, 188–90
Royal Albert Hall, London, 231
Royal Dublin Society, 130
Royal Humane Society, 174–5
Royal Navy: contaminated meat supplies, 238–9
Royal Society of Arts, 200
Russell, (Sir) William Howard, 256, 259, 288, 290, 306–7, 320
Russia: in Crimean War, 253–4, 257, 298; Cerrito dances in, 313

Sablonière Hotel, Leicester Square, 250
Sadler's Wells theatre, 23
Saint–Arnaud, Marshal Armand Jacques Leroy de, 254
St–Léon, Arthur, 75, 79–81, 84, 86–7, 173–4, 185, 192–3, 313
St–Léon, Léon–Michael, 79
St George's Church, Hanover Square, London, 17–19, 30
St Margaret's House, Twickenham, 28–9, 66
St Matthias Church, Spitalfields, 120–1
Sala, George Augustus: on AS's character, 4; membership of Reform Club, 57; attends memorial service for Emma, 85; on AS's home kitchen, 100, 195; on food at Dubourg's, 147; on Thackeray's regard for AS, 152; AS confides Relish recipe to, 155; on AS's leaving Reform Club, 184; encounters AS in London, 194–5; paints Gore House mural, 209–10, 219–20; shows Thackeray round Gore House, 212, 220; on prospective barman at Gore House, 214; on Gore House catering, 218; gives private views of Gore House, 220; receives guests at Universal Symposium, 226–7; declines to accompany AS to Crimea, 265; obituary of AS, 321–2; *Book of the Symposium*, 212, 233
Sales, Sarah, 319
Sampayo, Osbourne, 140–3
Sandys, Arthur Hill, 2nd Baron, 19
Satirist (magazine), 79
Savill, Thomas (supplier), 234
Schweppe & Co., Messrs (caterers), 158, 204–5, 219
Scotsman, The (newspaper), 170
Scott, Walter (Reform Club secretary), 33–4
Scribe, Mme Eugène, 188
Scutari: AS travels to, 3, 258, 268–72; hospitals, 255–8, 268–9, 271–2; AS's proposals for hospital kitchens, 259–62; death rate, 264; conditions of kitchens and catering, 273–5; AS reorganises and improves catering, 275–8, 292; AS returns to from Balaclava, 291–2; hospitals close, 311
Scutari Teapot, 277
Seacole, Mary, 285–7, 308–10;

Wonderful Adventures of Mrs Seacole in Many Lands, 287
Sebastopol, 254, 259, 283, 288, 290, 298–9, 306, 309
Sefton, William Philip Molyneux, 2nd Earl of, 18, 57
Seymour, Lieut.–Colonel Francis, 295–6
Shee, Sir Martin Archer, 56, 103
Shelley, Harriet (*née* Westbrook), 17
Shelley, Percy Bysshe, 17
Sibthorpe, Charles, 201
Simmonds, John (supplier), 228–9, 232–3, 238
Simois (ship), 267–9
Simonau, Elizabeth (*earlier* Jones; *née* Newton; Emma's mother), 52, 54
Simonau, François (Emma's stepfather): and AS's courting of Emma, 26–8, 30; Emma studies under, 52; marries Emma's mother, 52; lives with AS and Emma, 55; travels with Emma, 55; and Emma's death, 63–6; meets and paints Fanny Cerrito, 83; shares Leicester Square flat with AS, 83, 100–1; portrait of Emma on memorial, 85; AS leaves flat for own lodgings, 166; attends AS's funeral, 320; *Monsieur J. Ancot* (painting), 53
Simonau, Gustave, 27
Simonau, Pierre, 26–7, 64
Simpkin & Marshall (publishers), 169, 244, 250
Simpson, General Sir James, 295–6, 302
Skibbereen, Co. Cork, 114, 132
Slough: Royal Hotel, 150
Smirke, Sydney and Robert, 39
Smith & Phillips (gas engineers), 137–8, 154, 250, 263, 302
Smith, Julia, 272
Smith, Mai (Florence Nightingale's aunt), 300, 302
Solomon, Lewis, 320
Soult, Marshal Nicolas Jean–de–Dieu, 32
soup kitchens, 117, 121–7, 130, 132, 166, 240; *see also* Model Soup Kitchen
Southey, Robert, 206
Soyer, A. & Co.: established, 61; offices, 135; enterprises, 138; and Magic Stove, 162
Soyer, Alexis Benoist: and memorial for Emma, 1, 85; funeral and obituaries, 2–3,

319–22; achievements, 3–4, 324–5; appearance, dress and manner, 4, 27, 77, 144, 147, 175, 194, 251, 272, 279–80, 282, 290, 293, 300; supervises kitchen for Polignac banquet, 5–8; trains at Rignon's restaurant, 7, 12–14; escapes rioters, 8, 15; singing voice, 8, 10, 12, 14, 24, 148; reputation in Paris, 9–10; birth, 10–11; excels as performer, 10, 14; social status, 11–12, 41–2, 152, 307, 311; attends Protestant seminary, 12; incomplete education, 12; enjoyment of entertainment and life's pleasures, 13–14, 22, 66–7, 147–8; career as chef in Paris, 14; son born, 14–15; moves to England, 15–16; writes doggerel verse, 15, 56, 101; appointed *chef de cuisine* at Reform Club, 18–19, 30, 39; marriage to Emma Jones, 18, 65; early employment in London, 19–20; awareness of poverty, 22; appreciation of simple English food, 23; drinking, 23, 235, 246–7, 302, 315, 319; preference for simple life, 23, 116; post at Aston Hall, Shropshire, 24–6; first meets and falls for Emma, 26–8; flattery and sycophancy, 26, 93, 311; portrait, 26–7; returns to London from Shropshire, 28; freemasonry, 29, 147, 245; provides Reform's coronation lunch, 34–5; and planning of Reform Club kitchens, 41–51; installs and employs gas–fired cookers, 45–7; fear of tuberculosis, 55; marriage relations, 56; social circle and friendships, 56–7, 144, 151; activities at Reform Club, 59–61; business interests and enterprises, 61–2, 135–6, 138, 153, 161–2, 177; earnings and financial position, 61, 106, 144, 180; temperament, 62, 71; told of Emma's death, 63–4; travels with Duke of Saxe Coburg, 63; employs secretary, 66; sojourn at St Margaret's House, 66; attachment to Fanny Cerrito, 68, 75, 77–8, 82–3, 86–7, 185, 192–3, 238, 246–7, 310, 312–13; and staff trouble at Ibrahim Pasha banquet, 71; kitchen equipment inventions, 72–3;

99–100, 101–2, 135–8, 162–3, 249, 262–3; and Fanny Cerrito's marriage, 75; shares Leicester Square flat with Simonau, 83, 100; depicted in Thackeray's *Pendennis*, 84; books reviewed, 88, 104–6, 169; writings, 88–9, 92, 117, 166, 168–9, 243, 249–50, 310, 313; appoints kitchenmaid, 92; recipe book, 92–9, 102–3; signature dishes, 98–9; on method of carving, 101; endorses products, 104; Dublin soup kitchen (1850), 108–11, 124–5; concern for nutrition of working classes, 116–19, 121–3, 134, 247–8; simple tastes, 116, 147; develops soup kitchens, 117–18, 120–2; recipes for famine soups, 118–20, 124–31; charitable fund–raising, 122–3; criticised for nutritional inadequacy of famine soups, 125, 128–30, 132; visits Dublin, 126–34; generosity, 144; investments in railways, 144–5; and Philippe's defection, 145–6; entertaining in Reform Club, 146–7; organises gathering of top chefs, 150; collaboration and agreements with Crosse & Blackwell, 153–8; markets sauces, 153–7; fruit drinks, 158–62; tours with and demonstrates Magic Stove, 164–5, 185, 195, 232; health concerns, 173–5, 315, 317–18; skating accident, 174–5; puts on weight, 175; submits design for Great Exhibition hall, 176–7; differences with Reform Club, 177–9, 182; plans culinary theme park with Feeny, 177–8; resignation and reinstatement at Reform Club post, 180–1; finally resigns from Reform Club post (1850), 182–4; as freelance chef, 186; desserts (*pièces montées*), 187–8; proposes Paris gourmet tour, 193–4; Soho home and kitchen, 195; Great Exhibition plans for eating places, 199, 203–4, 208; leases and redesigns Gore House, Kensington, 199, 204–5, 207–8, 211–17, 219, 226–7; and opening of Universal Symposium, 223; receives important guests at Universal Symposium, 226; Thackeray satirises, 227; court cases against, 232–4; financial near–bankruptcy, 234–5; moves to Great Russell Street, 234; son Jean Lamain writes to and meets, 236–7; legally acknowledges son Jean Lamain, 237; investigates polluted meat supplies to navy, 238–9; organises Christmas dinner for London poor, 240–1; supervises Soho soup kitchen, 240; Volant brings legal action against, 241–3; develops army stove, 251, 262–4, 323; financial recovery with success of *Shilling Cookery*, 251; and plans for Paris Exhibition, 252, 260; provides recipes for Crimean soldiers, 258–61; visit to Crimean War, 260–1, 265–71; moves to Bloomsbury Street, 264; reorganises Scutari kitchens and catering, 275–8, 292; holds Grand Opening of Scutari kitchens, 278–80; illness in Scutari, 278–9; visits to front in Crimea, 280–4, 288–91, 293–4, 301; friendship with Mary Seacole, 285–8; mishap with horses, 290–1; prepares vegetable cakes and bread–biscuits in Crimea, 293–5; demonstrates field kitchen in Crimea, 295–7; and fall of Sebastopol, 298–9; contracts Crimean fever (brucellosis), 299–301; unidentified by officer in Crimea, 300–1; and delivery of field stoves to army in Crimea, 302–3, 306–7; social activities with army in Crimea, 303–6; leaves Crimea, 308–9; travels after leaving Crimea, 310–12; collects references, 311; private marriage ceremony with Fanny Cerrito, 313–14; payments for services in Crimea, 314; returns to London (1857), 314; buys house in St John's Wood, 315; riding accident, 315, 318; lectures on military and naval cookery, 316–17; public services, 317–18; manic episodes, 318–19; death, 319; will, 320; military legacy, 323–4; *La Crème de la Grande Bretagne*, 88, 149; *A Culinary Campaign*, 265, 288, 313, 316, 320, 324; *Culinary Wonders of All Nations* (proposed), 310; *Délassements Culinaires*, 84, 88;

Dialogue Culinaire, 103; *La Fille de l'Orage* (comic ballet), 83–4, 88; *The Gastronomic Regenerator*, 92–9, 101–7, 122, 127, 140, 143, 148, 153, 156, 166, 198, 243–4, 247, 261; *Instructions to Military Hospital Cooks*, 317; *The Modern Housewife or Ménagère*, 166–71, 173, 247–8, 259; *The Pantropheon*, 244–5, 324; *The Poor Man's Regenerator* (*Soyer's Charitable Cookery*), 127–8, 133, 166, 171; *Le Rêve d'un Gourmet*, 88; *Shilling Cookery for the People*, 117, 247–9, 251, 259, 264

Soyer, Alexis (Philippe's son), 320
Soyer, Augusta (Philippe's daughter): death, 315
Soyer, Elizabeth (*née* Williams; Philippe's wife), 55
Soyer, Emery Roch (AS's father): in Meaux, 11; and AS's childhood, 12; death, 54
Soyer, Louis (AS's brother): birth, 11; with AS in London, 55; death from tuberculosis, 55
Soyer, Marie (*née* Chamberlan; AS's mother): in Meaux, 11–12; remarriage (to Pierre Traver), 54; Emma visits and paints in France, 55, 122
Soyer, Philippe (AS's brother): birth, 11; works as chef, 12; in England, 15–16, 19; at AS's wedding, 17; death, 54–5
Soyer's Aromatic Mustard, 243
Soyer's Baking Stewing Pan, 136, 249
Soyer's Camp Receipts for the Army in the East, 251, 258
Soyer's Celebrated Roaster, 137
Soyer's Deluxe Kitchen Range, 135–6
Soyer's Diamond Sauce, 153–4
Soyer's Egg Cookery Apparatus, 138
Soyer's Improved Baking Dish, 136, 249
Soyer's Magic Stove, 162–5, 185, 191, 195–6, 216, 232, 234
Soyer's Modern Housewife's Kitchen Apparatus, 163
Soyer's Nectar, 159–62
Soyer's Osmazome Food, 136, 243
Soyer's Phidomageireion, 137–8
Soyer's Philanthropic Gallery, 122
Soyer's Relish, 156–8
Soyer's Sauces, 153–5
Soyer's Sultana's Sauce, 158, 316
Soyer's Universal Symposium of

All Nations: designed for Gore House, 208, 211–13; gardens, 216–17; cooking and catering, 217–18; kitchens, 218; functions at, 221–3; opening delayed, 221–2, 224–5; prices, 224; financial failure, 227–32, 234; closes, 230–1, 235, 252; music licence refused, 230; legal action against, 232–3; *see also* Gore House, Kensington
Spectator, The (journal), 48, 61, 88, 169
Spitalfields, London, 117, 120–1, 123, 134
Stafford House, London, 20–2
Stanley, Edward Henry, Lord (*later* 15th Earl of Derby), 173
Stella (ballet), 192–3
Stevens, Lee, 185
Stowe, Harret Beecher: *Uncle Tom's Cabin*, 250
Stratford de Redcliffe, Eliza Charlotte, Viscountess, 270, 279
Stratford de Redcliffe, Stratford Canning, 1st Viscount, 270, 291, 295–6, 312
Sultana's Sauce *see* Soyer's Sultana's Sauce
Sun, The (newspaper), 106, 155, 160, 224
Sutherland, Dr (of Crimea Sanitary Commission), 284, 301, 318
Sutherland, Harriet, Duchess of: Queen Victoria visits, 21; accompanies Queen Victoria to Abbey for coronation, 32; regard for AS, 88, 123; philanthropy, 123; recommends AS to brother Earl of Carlisle, 196; and AS's travel to Crimean War, 260–1, 265, 272
Symons, Alexander: as AS's business partner, 106, 163, 169; as manager of Universal Symposium, 228; sued over Symposium liabilities, 232–4; death, 242; and Volant's action against AS, 242; advertises in AS's *Shilling Cookery*, 250
Symposium *see* Soyer's Universal Symposium

Taglioni, Marie, 78–9, 82
Talbot, William Henry Fox, 21
Tarring, John: *The Kitchen Department at the Reform Club* (lithograph), 61

Tegetmeier, W.B.: *Manual of Domestic Economy*, 91
Temps, Le (newspaper), 9
Tendon Separator (gadget), 101, 118
Thackeray, Isabella, 152
Thackeray, William Makepeace: at Reform Club, 57, 62, 92; contributes to *Punch*, 65, 124, 148, 151; journalism, 65; and AS's comic ballet *La Fille de l'Orage*, 84; promotes AS's relief trip to Ireland, 124; patronises Evans's, 147; regard for AS, 151–2; spoof letter on establishing chair of eating at Cambridge, 151; appearance, 152; friendship with AS, 184; on Lumley's banquet, 188; at Gore House, 206–8, 211–12, 220; membership of Metropolitan Sanitary Association, 221–2; dines at Universal Symosium, 225; writes on AS's Symposium, 226–7; declines offer to travel to Crimean War, 260; *Pendennis*, 84, 92; *Vanity Fair*, 151–2
Theatrical Inquisitor (magazine), 54
Thompson, Sergeant, 292
Tighe, Very Rev. Dean, 110
Times, The: on Emma's death, 65; on Arthur St–Léon's dancing, 80; reviews AS's *Délassements Culinaires*, 88; reviews AS's book with Francatelli's, 104–5; AS writes to on soup kitchens and recipes, 118, 121, 1267; on AS's catalogue of Emma's paintings, 122; Jaquet challenges AS's soup recipe in, 125; prints AS's statement on poor relief foods, 133–4; on banquet for Sampayo, 141, 143; reviews AS's *The Modern Housewife*, 169; McCann writes to on skating accidents, 174; reports AS's departure from Reform Club, 183; on AS's demonstrating Magic Stove at Castle Howard, 196; on Hyde Park as site of Great Exhibition, 201; on transformation of Gore House, 226; reports court case against Symposium, 233; on scandal of meat supplies to navy, 238–9; letter from Volant on case against AS, 242; prints *Soyer's Camp Receipts for the Army in the East*, 251; reports conditions

in Crimea, 255–6; letter from Crimean soldier requesting recipes from AS, 258; AS's letter on hospital kitchens at Scutari, 259; mocks AS's dress in Crimea, 293; on AS's entertaining in Crimea, 306; AS describes Turkish foods in, 312; on AS's solipsism, 316; reports AS's lecture at United Service Institution, 317; and AS's funeral, 320
Titchfield, William John Cavendish–Bentinck–Scott, Marquess of, 124
Tonge (of Dublin), 127
Tophane, Turkey, 269, 282
Tortoni's Anana (beverage), 159
Townshends (poulterers), 143
Travellers' Club, Pall Mall, 39–40
Travet, Pierre, 54–5
Trevelyan, Charles, 124
Trewman's Flying Post, 191
Trinity Square, London, 234
truffles, 142
Tucker (deputy purveyor in Scutari), 271
Turkey *see* Ottoman Empire
turtle soup, 94–5
Tussaud, Marie, 50

Ude, Louis Eustache: as chef in London, 15, 18–19, 91; at AS's wedding, 18; character and reputation, 57; friendship with AS, 57–8; fined for serving grouse out of season, 58; lifestyle, 58–9; refuses to sell back Emma painting, 59, 103; death, 106; Raglan knows, 289; *The French Cook*, 18
United Service Gazette, 245
United Service Institution, 316
United States of America: AS's *The Modern Housewife* published in, 170–1
Universal Symposium *see* Soyer's Universal Symposium

Varna, Bulgaria, 253–4
Vaughan, Sarah (maid), 55
Vegetable Drainer, 249
vegetables: AS recommends in recipes, 168
Verdi, Giuseppe, 79, 93
Vernet, Horace, 74
Versailles Sauce, 153
Vestris, Madame Eliza, 22
Victoria, Queen: visits Harriet Sutherland, 21; coronation

(1838), 31–6; sees Cerrito dance *Ondine*, 68; welcomes Ibrahim Pasha to London, 69; Francatelli works for, 91; dislikes turtle soup, 94; contributes to Irish famine relief, 116; stays at Castle Howard, 196; and opening of Great Exhibition, 220; on success of Great Exhibition, 231; learns of AS's success at Scutari, 279
Victoria, Princess Royal (*later* Empress of Germany), 220
Vido, Roco, 270, 320
Virginia Water, Surrey, 149, 191, 245, 247, 253, 260, 315
Vivian, General Sir Robert John Hussey, 281
Volant, François: on official non–recognition of AS, 2; on AS's childhood, 12; on AS's portrait, 27; and AS's Reform Club catering, 34; shows Reform Club kitchens to visitors, 49; on AS's entertaining at Reform Club, 60, 146; and Emma's death, 63–4; secretarial work for AS, 66, 140, 145; on AS's *La Fille de l'Orage*, 84; on Emma's memorial, 85; on Elizabeth Boyd's visit to AS's flat, 100; on Douglas Jerrold, 104; on AS in Dublin, 126; on AS's return from Dublin, 132; on banquet for Sampayo, 141; on AS's gullibility, 144; on AS's singing, 148; accompanies AS to Windsor, 149; on AS's sauces, 153; on AS's fruit drinks, 159; and Soyer's Magic Stove, 162–3; on death of Mrs Baker, 171; on AS's health recovery, 175; and AS's status at Reform Club, 179–82; on Lumley's banquet, 187; at Universal Symposium, 226–8, 230; on failure of Symposium, 231; on AS's financial losses, 235; on Soyer's role in navy meat supply scandal, 239; on AS's work for Soho soup kitchen, 240; brings legal action against AS, 241–3; provides illustrations for AS's *Pantropheon*, 244–5; on AS's Baking Stew Pan, 249; and AS's visit to Crimea, 260, 265; attends AS's funeral, 320; *Memoirs of Soyer*, 12, 14, 27, 145, 235, 245

Walrow, Charlotte, 18
Ward, William Humble Ward, 10th Baron (*later* Earl of Dudley), 291
Warren, James: on official non–recognition of AS, 2; replaces Volant as AS's secretary, 242, 250; with dying AS, 319; collaborates with Volant on *Memoirs of Soyer*, 321
Warriner, George, 126, 131–2, 134, 165, 226–7, 317, 320
Waterford, Henry de la Poer Beresford, 2nd Marquess of, 19–20
Watts, William, 66
Weber, Carl Maria von, 53

Weekly Despatch, 306
Wellington, Arthur Wellesley, 1st Duke of: attends St George's Hanover Square wedding, 18–19; on Queen Victoria, 32; Queen Victoria confesses dislike of turtle soup to, 94; AS's career compared to, 106; at Universal Symposium, 225
Wellington Barracks, Birdcage Walk, London, 317–18
West & Wyatt (catering company), 154
Westminster Club, 37–8
Westminster, Palace of *see* Parliament, Houses of
Westmorland, Jane, Countess of (*née* Saunders), 82

Wheatstone, Charles, 21
White, Robert, 127
White's Chocolate House (*later* Club), 37
Wilberforce, William, 205
Willis's Rooms, London, 241
Wolseley, Garnet Joseph (*later* Field Marshal Viscount), 246
Wyatt, William, 154
Wynne, Sir Watkin Williams, 25

Yalta, 306
York: Prince Albert's banquet (1850), 196–9, 201
York, Prince Frederick Augustus, Duke of, 20